SUSE LINUX

USER GUIDE

9. Edition 2004

Please direct suggestions and comments to `documentation@suse.de`.

Authors: Jörg Bartsch, Gernot Hillier, Marcel Hilzinger, Johannes Meixner, Matthias Nagorny, Siegfried Olschner, Marcus Schäfer, Jens Daniel Schmidt, Arvin Schnell, Christian Schuszter, Adrian Schröter Rebecca Walter
Translators: Daniel Pisano, Tino Tanner
Editors: Jörg Arndt, Antje Faber, Karl Eichwalder, Berthold Gunreben, Roland Haidl, Jana Jaeger, Edith Parzefall, Inés Pozo, Thomas Rölz, Thomas Schraitle
Layout: Manuela Piotrowski, Thomas Schraitle
Setting: DocBook-XML und LaTeX

This book has been printed on 100 % chlorine-free bleached paper.

Contents

VI Excursions 375

Welcome

Congratulations for selecting SUSE LINUX. A few clicks are all that is needed to prepare the installation, which takes fifteen to twenty minutes. After configuring the users and their passwords and selecting the screen resolution, your SUSE LINUX system is ready for use. If you are familiar with earlier versions of SUSE LINUX, you will notice how much the configuration with the system assistant YaST has been expanded and simplified.

The simple quick installation is explained first. If you have special wishes in connection with the programs to install, the partitioning of your hard disk, or other features, read the chapter about the custom installation. YaST additionally facilitates the configuration and administration of your hardware, Internet access, and system — without repeated reboots.

Get to know the graphical desktop environments KDE and GNOME and learn how to adapt them to your personal preferences. The following sections introduce some very useful and interesting programs from the large range of available applications, including office programs such as OpenOffice.org, web browsers, file managers, scanning tools, and image editing tools.

Additionally find information about the SUSE help system and the available information sources containing further documentation. Also included are a list of frequently asked questions about SUSE LINUX and a glossary of the most important terms from the world of computers and Linux.

Changes in the User Guide

The documentation of the previous version (SUSE LINUX 9.0) has been modified as follows:

- The instructions for the installation and configuration with YaST have been updated.
- Due to new features, the following chapters have undergone substantial editing:
  - ▷ The KDE desktop: everything about KDE.
- The following chapters are new in this edition:
  - ▷ A section about Kopete, an instant messenger application, has been added.
  - ▷ A section explains the configuration of SPAMassassin in KMail.
  - ▷ The section about gqcam shows how to create picture series with webcams.

Typographical Conventions

The following typographical conventions are used in this book:

- `/etc/passwd`: files or directories
- ⟨*placeholder*⟩: replace the character string ⟨*placeholder*⟩ (including the angle brackets) with the actual value
- `PATH`: an environment variable
- `ls`: commands
- `user`: users
- (Alt): a key to press
- 'File': menu items, buttons

Acknowledgements

With a lot of personal commitment, the Linux developers continue to promote the development of Linux. We would like to express our sincere gratitude for their efforts. Without them, this distribution would not exist. Additional thanks go to Frank Zappa and Pawar. Special thanks, of course, to LINUS TORVALDS.

Have a lot of fun!

Your SUSE Team

Part I

Installation

Quick Installation

In the best case, a few clicks are sufficient to install SUSE LINUX on your computer. If no Linux system was installed on your computer previously, your hard disk is partitioned, an installed Windows system is resized, a software selection is installed, and your hardware is configured automatically. If you do not like the suggestions of the system assistant YaST (Yet another Setup Tool) or have special requirements for your system, change the individual installation suggestions manually as described in Chapter 2 on page 11.

1.1 Step One: The Start Screen

Turn on your computer and all connected hardware components and immediately insert CD 1 or the DVD in the respective drive. In the start screen, select an installation mode or boot an installed operating system. Following the successful installation, the CD only needs to be inserted in the drive occasionally to install additional software. As the CD can be forgotten in the drive, the option to boot the installed system is preselected. For installation, use the arrow keys to select 'Installation'.

Note

If your computer does not boot from CD 1 or the DVD, read Section 2.2 on page 13.

Note

1.2 Step Two: Accept Suggestions

After the system is booted from CD or DVD, the SUSE system assistant YaST is started. First, select the language for your system. The language setting is automatically adopted for the keyboard layout. Then YaST checks your system. If you already installed a SUSE LINUX version on your computer, the next dialog asks whether to install SUSE LINUX from scratch or perform an update of your previous system.

If Linux was not installed on your computer previously or if you select 'New installation', YaST checks all your hardware and list the result in the suggestion dialog, shown in Figure 1.1 on page 8. This dialog also displays the partitioning suggestion (possibly resizing) and the selected installation type. If installing Linux for the first time, accept these suggestions, which are usually suitable.

The following messages and suggestions are displayed after the system check:

Mode 'New installation' is the default value here.

Keyboard The keyboard layout defaults to the selected language. This can easily be changed.

Mouse The detected mouse type is listed here.

Partitioning Suggests a suitable partitioning. If Windows 9x or ME (FAT32 file system) exists on the hard disk, the resizing rate is indicated.

Software A default system with office applications is preset.

Booting Determines where SUSE LINUX installs the boot manager. The Master Boot Record (MBR) of the first hard disk is the default setting.

Time Zone Depending on the selected language settings, the time zone of the respective country is selected. Check this setting as many languages are used in several countries.

Language Shows the language setting.

Modify the YaST suggestions at any time by clicking the respective heading. The dialogs displayed enable detailed settings. The exact procedure is described in Chapter 2 on page 11. After the changes, you are returned to the overview and can proceed with the installation using the modified values by clicking 'Accept'.

Caution

If the hardware was detected correctly, you do not need to change anything. Do not change the boot loader, partitioning, or hardware settings unless you know what you are doing.

Caution

1.3 Step Three: Installation

Before the installation begins, YaST asks in a green window whether to install with the current settings. Confirm the request with 'Yes' to start the installation. Depending on the performance of your computer, installation of your system with a large selection of application packages takes approximately fifteen minutes.

1.4 Configuration

Following the installation, make some important settings before starting using SUSE LINUX (see Section 2.6 on page 34 for detailed instructions).

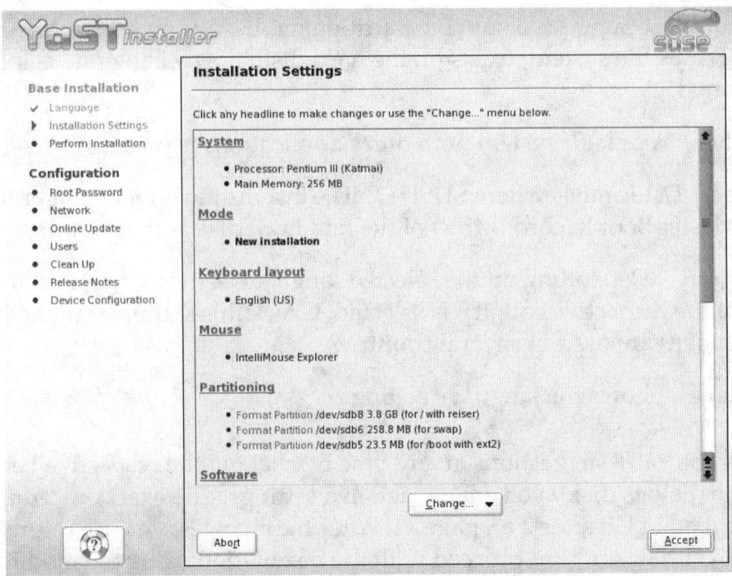

Figure 1.1: Suggestion Screen

First, set a password for the system administrator (user ☞*root*).This special user is always configured by YaST and is needed for system maintenance tasks.

Caution

Remember the root password because you can only modify the system or install programs using the `root` identity.

Caution

If a network card or other communication hardware (such as a modem or ISDN card) is found during the installation, these can now be configured and a connection can be established with the Internet or a local network (LAN). This enables use of various services during the remaining part of the procedure.

For example, if you configure an Internet connection, can perform an online update immediately. In this way, include the latest updates for your system.

If you establish a connection with a local network, you can configure a name service such as NIS. YaST assumes that you will not manage any local users on your system.

This is usually the case with commercial workstations, whose users are administered centrally (e.g., on a department server). If you do not configure a name service, set up local users intended for normal operations on the system.

An additional overview displays the detected screen, graphics card, and other hardware components (printer, sound card, etc.). If necessary, change settings, such as the suggested screen resolution or the color depth. Refer to Section 2.7 on page 42. Some of the dialogs for the configuration of the additional hardware are able to search for connected devices. However, these settings do not need to be made at this stage. You can also skip this step and do it later. After the completion of this last step, your newly installed system is booted and you can start using it.

Have a lot of fun with SUSE LINUX!

Custom Installation

The previous chapter covered the quick installation procedure. This chapter provides detailed information about the settings you can modify by starting the relevant module from the suggestion window. This gives complete control over the installation.

2.1 Starting Your System from the CD-ROM

Insert the first SUSE LINUX CD or the DVD into the drive. Then reboot the computer to start the installation program from the medium in the drive.

2.1.1 Possible Problems when Starting from the CD/DVD

If you experience problems booting from CD 1, one of the following items is probably the cause. Resolve the problem as described.

- The CD-ROM drive is not able to read the boot image on the first CD. In this case, use CD 2 to boot the system. CD 2 contains a conventional 2.88 MB boot image, which can be read even by older drives.
- The boot sequence in the BIOS (Basic Input Output System) is incorrect. The BIOS is a software for activating the basic functions of a computer. Motherboard vendors provide a BIOS that is adapted to the hardware. Information about changing the BIOS settings is provided in the documentation of your motherboard and in the following paragraphs.

  Normally, the BIOS setup can only be accessed at a specific time — when the machine is booting. During this initialization phase, the machine performs a number of diagnostic hardware tests. One of them is a memory check, recognizable from the memory counter. When the counter appears, look for a line, usually below the counter or somewhere at the bottom, mentioning the key to press to access the BIOS setup. Usually the key to press is (Del), (F1), or (Esc). Press this key until the BIOS setup screen appears.

  To change the boot sequence in an AWARD BIOS, look for the 'BIOS FEATURES SETUP' entry. Other manufacturers may have a different name for this, such as 'ADVANCED CMOS SETUP'. When you have found the entry, select it and confirm with (Enter).

  In the screen that opens, look for a subentry called 'BOOT SEQUENCE'. The boot sequence is often set to something like `C,A` or `A,C`. In the former case, the machine first searches the hard disk (C) then the floppy drive (A) to find a bootable medium. Change the settings by pressing (Page up) or (Page down) until the sequence is `A,CDROM,C`.

Leave the BIOS setup screen by pressing Esc. To save the changes, select 'SAVE & EXIT SETUP' or press F10. To confirm that your settings should be saved, press Y.

If you have a SCSI CD-ROM drive, you need to change the setup of the SCSI BIOS. In the case of an Adaptec host adapter, for instance, open the setup by pressing Ctrl + A. After that, select 'Disk Utilities', which displays the connected hardware components. Make a note of the SCSI ID for your CD-ROM drive. Exit the menu with Esc then open 'Configure Adapter Settings'. Under 'Additional Options', select 'Boot Device Options' and press Enter. Enter the ID of the CD-ROM drive and press Enter again. Then press Esc twice to return to the start screen of the SCSI BIOS. Exit this screen and confirm with 'Yes' to boot again.

- Your CD-ROM drive may not be supported because it is an older model.

2.2 The Boot Screen

'Boot from Hard Disk' boots the already installed system. This item is selected by default because the CD is often forgotten in the drive. Select 'Installation' with the arrow keys. This will load YaST and start the installation.

The boot screen provides several options for starting from the CD. The options and the actions triggered by them are:

- **Boot from Hard Disk**: Boots the system installed on the hard disk (the system normally booted when the machine is started). This option is preselected.
- **Installation**: The normal installation mode. All modern hardware functions are enabled.
- **Installation — ACPI Disabled**: If the normal installation fails, this may be due to lacking ACPI (Advanced Configuration and Power Interface) support of the system hardware. In this case, use this option to perform the installation without ACPI support.
- **Installation — Safe Settings**: The DMA mode (for CD-ROM drives) and any critical power management functions are disabled. Experts can also use the command line to enter or change kernel parameters.

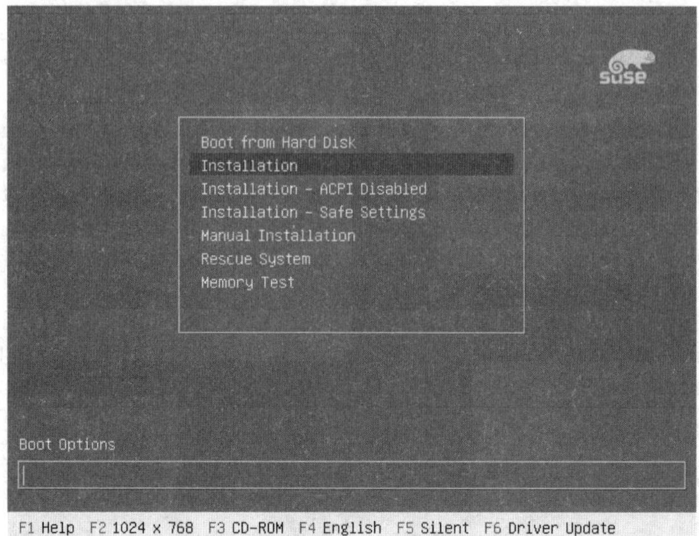

Figure 2.1: The Boot Screen

- **Manual Installation**: If the automatic loading of drivers causes problems with the installation, you can perform the installation manually. In a manual installation, drivers are not loaded automatically. However, this will not work if you use a USB keyboard on your machine.
- **Rescue System**: If you are unable to boot into your installed Linux system for some reason, you can boot the computer from the DVD or CD1 and select this item. This option starts a *rescue system* — a minimal Linux system without a graphical user interface, which allows experts to access disk partitions for troubleshooting and repairing an installed system. Less experienced users can alternatively use the System Repair tool supplied with YaST. Refer to Chapter 3 on page 45 for details.
- **Memory Test**: This tests your system RAM by means of repeated read and write cycles. This is done in an endless loop, as memory corruption often shows up very sporadically, so many read and write cycles might be necessary to detect it. If you suspect that your RAM might be defective, start this test and let it run for several hours. If no errors are detected after a longer time period, you can assume that the memory is intact. Terminate the test by rebooting.

A few seconds after starting the installation, SUSE LINUX loads a minimal ☞*Linux system*, which takes control and performs the installation. A number of messages and copyright notices are displayed then, at the end of the loading process, the YaST installation program is started. After a few more seconds, the screen should display the graphical interface that will guide you through the installation.

The YaST screens have a common format. All buttons, entry fields, and lists can be accessed with the mouse. If your mouse pointer does not move, the mouse has not been correctly detected. In this case, use the keyboard for navigation.

2.3 Language Selection

Select the language to use for SUSE LINUX and YaST. English is the default setting for the international distribution. If your mouse does not work, navigate with the arrow keys until the desired language is selected. After this, press (Tab) until 'Next' is highlighted. Then press (Enter) to confirm your language selection.

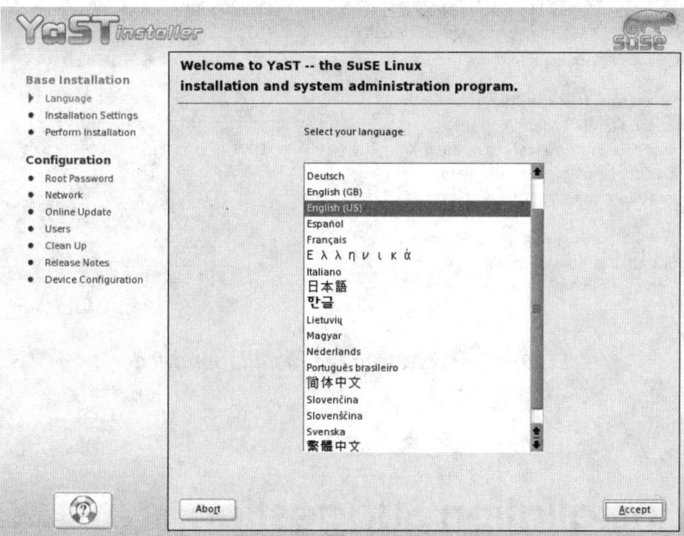

Figure 2.2: Selecting the Language

2.4 Installation Mode

Select between a 'New Installation' and an 'Update of an installed system'. The latter is only possible if a previous version of SUSE LINUX is already present. In this case, you can also boot this system with 'Boot Installed System'. If your installed system fails to boot, perhaps because some important system configuration has been corrupted, you can try to make the system bootable again with 'System Repair'. Without a previously-installed version of SUSE LINUX, it is only possible to perform a new installation.

The following sections describe the procedure of installing a new system. Detailed instructions for a system update can be found in Chapter 4.3.5 on page 66. A description of the system repair options can be found in Chapter 3 on page 45.

Click 'OK' to continue. See Figure 2.3.

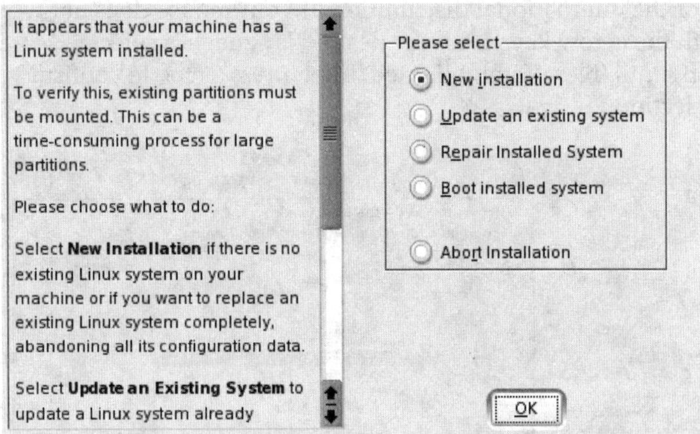

Figure 2.3: Selecting the Installation Mode

2.5 Installation Suggestion

After hardware detection, the suggestion window, shown in Figure 2.4 on the facing page, displays some information about the hardware recognized and proposes a number of installation and partitioning options. When selecting any of these items and configuring them in the corresponding dialogs, you are always returned to the suggestion window, which is updated accordingly. The individual settings are discussed in the following sections.

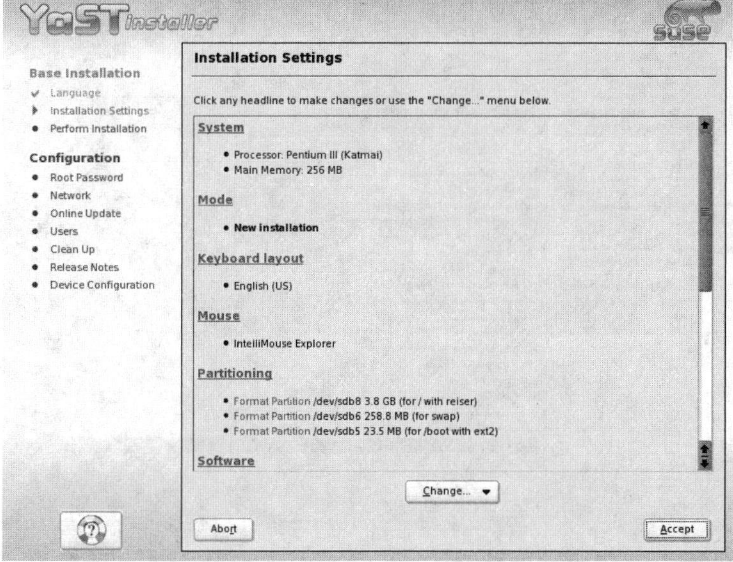

Figure 2.4: Suggestion Window

2.5.1 Installation Mode

Use this to change the installation mode. The options are the same as already described in Section 2.4 on the preceding page.

2.5.2 Keyboard Layout

Select the keyboard layout. By default, the layout corresponds to the selected language. After changing the layout, test Y, Z, and special characters to make sure the selection is correct. When finished, select 'Next' to return to the suggestion window.

2.5.3 Mouse

If YaST did not detect your mouse automatically, press Tab in the suggestion window several times until 'Mouse' is selected. Then use Space to open the dialog in which to set the mouse type. This dialog is shown in Figure 2.5.

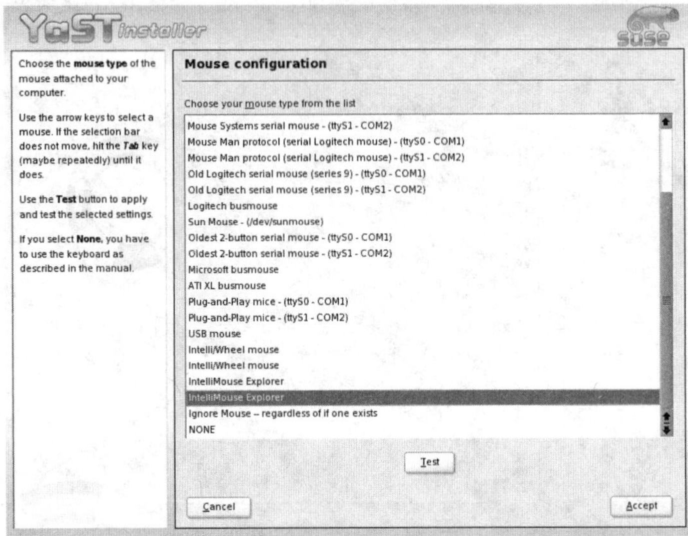

Figure 2.5: Selecting the Mouse Type

To select the mouse type, use ↑ and ↓. Consult the mouse documentation for information about the mouse type. After selecting a mouse type, use Alt + T to test whether the device works correctly without selecting it permanently. If the mouse does not behave as expected, use the keyboard to select another type and test again. Use Tab and Enter to make the current selection permanent.

2.5.4 Partitioning

In most cases, YaST proposes a reasonable partitioning scheme that can be accepted without change. If desired, modify this scheme to meet your needs or create a new one.

Partition Types

Every hard disk has a partition table with space for four entries. Each entry in the partition table can be a primary partition or an extended partition. Only *one* extended partition entry is allowed, however.

Primary partitions consist of a continuous range of cylinders (physical disk areas) assigned to a particular operating system. Using primary partitions, you could not set up more than four partitions per hard disk. More do not fit in the partition table.

This is why extended partitions are used. Extended partitions are also continuous ranges of disk cylinders, but an extended partition may itself be subdivided into *logical partitions*. Logical partitions do not require entries in the partition table. In other words, an extended partition is a container for logical partitions.

If you need more than four partitions, create an extended partition. This extended partition should span the entire remaining free cylinder range. Then create multiple logical partitions within the extended partition. The maximum number of logical partitions is fifteen on SCSI disks and 63 on (E)IDE disks.

It does not matter which type of partitions are used for Linux. Primary and logical partitions both work fine.

Required Disk Space

The amount of hard disk space needed depends on the intended use of the system. Available space limits what applications can be installed. The following hints give some guidelines for space requirements:

- Minimal system: 180 MB

  No graphical interface (X Window System) is installed, which means only console applications can be used. Also, only a very basic selection of software is installed.

- Minimal system with graphical interface: 500 MB

  This includes X and some applications.

- Graphical system with modern applications: between 1 GB and 2 GB

  This includes recent versions of graphical desktops, namely KDE and GNOME, and bigger application packages, such as OpenOffice.org and Netscape or Mozilla.

- For downloading movies and music with Linux: 2 GB

- Both items: 3 GB
- Burning CDs and the items listed above: 4 GB

These guidelines can help develop a partitioning scheme for your system:

- Under 500 MB:

  A swap partition and a root partition (/).

- Between 500 MB and 4 GB:

  A small boot partition located *within the first cylinders* of the hard disk (`/boot`, at least 8 MB or 1 cylinder) to hold the kernel and the boot loader. Also create a swap partition of approximately 256 MB then use the rest for the root partition (/).

- For more than 4 GB:

  Boot (`/boot`), swap, root (250 MB), home directories (`/home`) with about 200 MB for each user, and the rest for programs and data (`/usr`). You may also reserve an extra partition each for `/opt` and `/var`.

Some commercial programs install their data in `/opt`. If necessary, create a separate partition for `/opt` or make the root partition large enough. KDE and GNOME are also installed in `/opt`.

Note

Things should be fine if your partitioning setup is similar to that proposed by YaST. This is usually a small partition for `/boot` at the beginning of the hard disk (about 10 MB, or 1 cylinder on a large hard disk), a swap partition (between 128 and 256 MB), and the rest for /.

Note

Partitioning with YaST

When you select the partitioning item in the suggestion window for the first time, YaST displays a dialog listing the partition settings as currently proposed. Accept these current settings without change or change them before continuing. Alternatively, discard all the settings and start over from scratch.

Nothing in the partitioning setup is changed if you select 'Accept Suggested Partitioning Setup'. If you select 'Change Suggested Partitioning

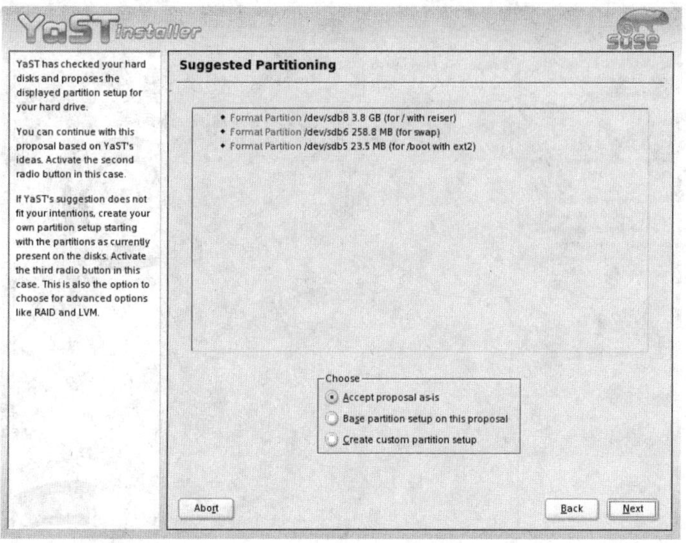

***Figure 2.6:** Editing the Partitioning Setup*

Setup', the 'Expert Partitioner' opens. It allows you to tweak the partition setup in every detail. This dialog is explained in Section 2.5.5 on the next page. The original setup as proposed by YaST is offered there as a starting point.

If you select 'Create custom partitioning setup', a dialog, like that in Figure 2.7 on the following page, opens in which to select a hard disk from those on your system. SUSE LINUX will be installed on the disk selected in this dialog.

The next step is to determine whether the entire disk should be used ('Use entire hard disk') or whether to use any existing partitions, if available, for the installation. If a Windows operating system was found on the disk or if there is some other FAT file system, select whether to delete or resize the partition. Before doing so, read Section 2.5.5 on page 25. If desired, go to the 'Expert Partitioner' dialog to create a custom partition setup at this point (see Section 2.5.5 on the following page).

Caution

If you choose 'Use entire hard disk', all data on that disk will be lost.

Caution

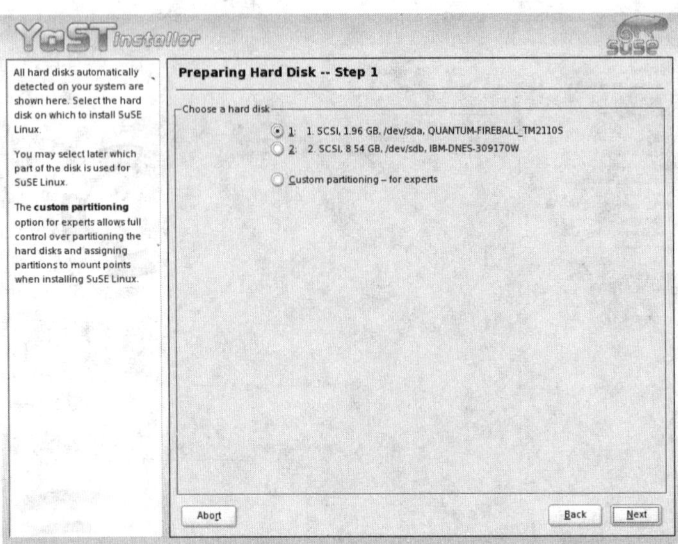

YaST installer
All hard disks automatically detected on your system are shown here. Select the hard disk on which to install SuSE Linux.
You may select later which part of the disk is used for SuSE Linux.
The custom partitioning option for experts allows full control over partitioning the hard disks and assigning partitions to mount points when installing SuSE Linux.
Preparing Hard Disk -- Step 1
Choose a hard disk
1: 1. SCSI, 1.96 GB, /dev/sda, QUANTUM-FIREBALL_TM2110S
2: 2. SCSI, 8.54 GB, /dev/sdb, IBM-DNES-309170W
Custom partitioning – for experts
Abort
Back
Next

***Figure** 2.7: Selecting the Hard Disk*

YaST checks during the installation whether the disk space is sufficient for the software selection made. If not, YaST automatically removes parts from the software selection as needed. The suggestion window then includes a notice to inform you about this. As long as there is sufficient disk space available, YaST simply accepts your settings and partitions the hard disk accordingly.

2.5.5 Expert Partitioning with YaST

With the expert dialog, shown in Figure 2.8 on the next page, manually modify the partitioning of your hard disk. Partitions can be added, deleted, or edited.

All existing or suggested partitions on all connected hard disks are displayed in the list of the expert dialog. Entire hard disks are listed as devices without numbers, such as `/dev/hda` or `/dev/sda`. Partitions are listed as parts of these devices, such as `/dev/hda1` or `/dev/sda1`. The size, type, file system, and mount point of the hard disks and their partitions are also displayed. The mount point describes where the partition is mounted in the Linux file system tree.

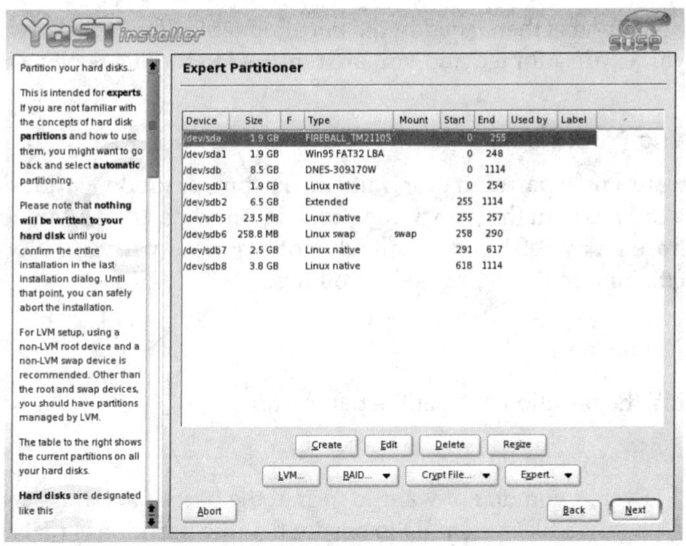

Figure 2.8: The YaST Partitioner in Expert Mode

Any free hard disk space is also listed and automatically selected. To allocate additional storage space to ☞*Linux*, free the needed space starting from the bottom toward the top of the list (starting from the last partition of a hard disk toward the first). For example, if you have three partitions, you cannot use the second exclusively for Linux and retain the third and first for other operating systems.

Creating a Partition

1. Select 'New'. If several hard disks are connected, a selection dialog appears in which to select a hard disk for the new partition. Then, specify the partition type (primary or extended). Create up to four primary partitions or up to three primary partitions and one extended partition. Within the extended partition, you can create several logical partitions (see Section 2.5.4 on page 19).

2. Select the file system to use to format the partition and a mount point, if necessary. YaST suggests a mount point for each partition created. Details of the parameters are provided in the next section.

3. Select 'OK' to apply your changes.

The new partition is then listed in the partition table. If you click 'Next', the current values are adopted and you are returned to the suggestion screen.

Partitioning Parameters

If you create a new partition or modify an existing partition, various parameters can be set in the partitioning tool. For new partitions, suitable parameters are set by YaST and usually do not require any modification. To perform manual settings, proceed as follows:

1. Select the partition.
2. 'Edit' the partition and set the parameters:
   - File System ID
     Even if you do not want to format the partition at this stage, assign it a file system ID to ensure that the partition is registered correctly. Possible values include 'Linux', 'Linux swap', 'Linux LVM' or 'Linux RAID'. Refer to the Administration Guide for details on LVM and RAID.
   - File System
     To format the partition immediately within the scope of the installation, specify one of the following file systems for the partition: 'Swap', 'Ext2', 'Ext3', 'ReiserFS', or 'JFS'.
     Swap is a special format that makes the partition usable as virtual memory. Every system should have at least one swap partition of at least 128 MB (see note 2.5.5 on the next page). ReiserFS is the default for Linux partitions. ReiserFS as well as JFS and Ext3 are journaling file systems. These file systems are able to restore your system very quickly after a system crash, as write processes are logged during the operation. Furthermore, ReiserFS is very fast in handling lots of small files. Ext2 is not a journaling file system. It is rock solid and good for smaller partitions, as it does not require too much disk space for management.
   - File System Options
     Here, specify various parameters for the selected file system. Depending on the file system used, various options are offered. Only make changes if you are absolutely sure what you are doing.
   - Encrypt File System

If you activate the encryption, all data is written to the hard disk in encrypted form. This increases the security of sensitive data, but reduces the system speed, as the encryption takes some time.

- fstab Options

  Here you can specify various parameters for the administration file of the file systems (`/etc/fstab`). Experienced users have the possibility to modify a number of options. Refer to the relevant chapter in the Administration Guide before changing anything.

- Mount Point

  This specifies the directory at which the partition should be mounted in the file system tree. Various YaST suggestions can be expanded at the respective entry field. If you accept these suggestions, the default file system structure is implemented. However, you can also specify any other names.

3. Select 'Next' to activate the partition.

Note

If you partition manually, create a swap partition. The swap partition is used to free the main memory from data that is not used at the present moment. This keeps the main memory free for the most frequently-used important data.

Note

Resizing a Windows Partition

If a hard disk containing a Windows FAT or NTFS partition was selected as installation target, YaST offers to delete or shrink this partition. In this way, you can install SUSE LINUX even if there is currently not enough space on the hard disk. This functionality is especially useful if the selected hard disk contains one Windows partition that covers the entire hard disk, which is often the case with preinstalled computers. If YaST sees that there is not enough space on the selected hard disk, but that space could be made available by deleting or shrinking a Windows partion, it will present a dialog in which to choose one of these two options.

If you select 'Delete Windows completely', the Windows partition will be marked for deletion, and the space will be used for the installation of SUSE LINUX.

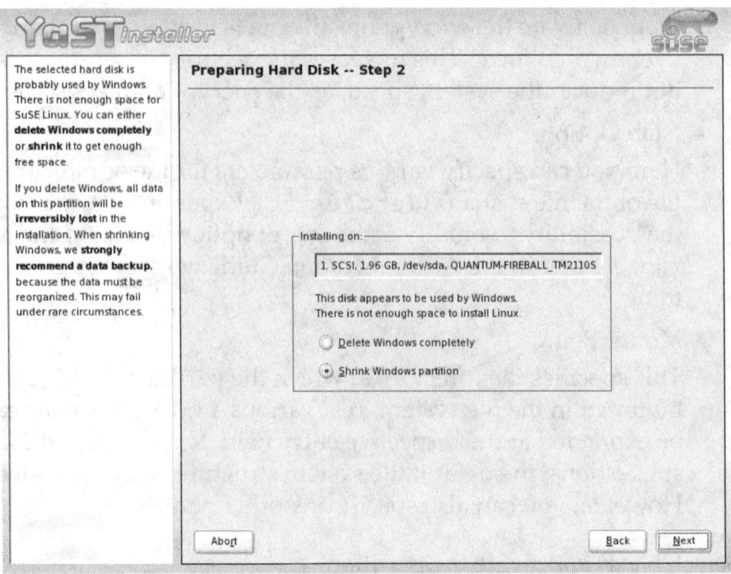

Figure 2.9: *Possible Options for Windows Partitions*

Caution

If you delete Windows, all data will be lost beyond recovery as soon as the formatting starts.

Caution

To shrink the Windows partition, interrupt the installation and boot Windows in order to prepare the partition from there. Although this step is not strictly required for FAT partitions, it speeds up the resizing process and also makes it safer. These steps are vital for NTFS partitions.

FAT file system In Windows, first run scandisk to make sure the FAT partition is free of lost file fragments and crosslinks. After that, run defrag to move files to the beginning of the partition. This will accelerate the resizing procedure in Linux.

Note

If you have optimized virtual memory settings for Windows in such a way that a contiguous swap file is used with the same initial (minimum) and maximum size limit, consider another step. With these Windows settings, the resizing might have the effect that the swap file is split into many small parts scattered all over the FAT partition. Also, the entire swap file would need to be moved during the resizing, which makes the process rather slow. It is therefore useful to unset these Windows optimizations for the time being and reenable them after the resizing has been completed.

Note

NTFS file system In Windows, run scandisk and defrag to move the files to the beginning of the hard disk. In contrast to the FAT file system, this *must* be done in NTFS to enable resizing.

Note

If you operate your system with a permanent swap file on an NTFS file system, this file may be located at the end of the hard disk and remain there despite defrag. Therefore, it may be impossible to shrink the partition sufficiently. In this case, temporarily deactivate the swap file (the virtual memory in Windows). After the partition has been resized, reconfigure the virtual memory.

Note

After these preparations, return to the Linux partitioning setup and select 'Shrink Windows Partition'. After a quick check of the partition, YaST opens a dialog with a suggestion for resizing the Windows partition. The first bar graph shows how much disk space is currently occupied by Windows and how much space is still available. The second bar graph shows how the space would be distributed after the resizing, according to YaST's current proposal (Figure 2.10 on the following page). Accept the proposed settings or use the slider to change the partition sizing (within certain limits).

If you leave this dialog by selecting 'Next', the settings will be stored and you will be taken back to the previous dialog. The actual resizing will take place later, before the hard disk is formatted.

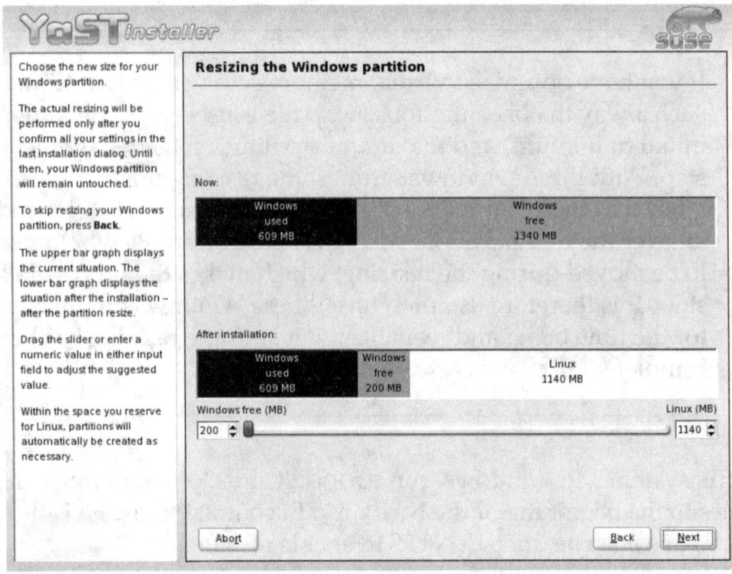

Figure 2.10: *Resizing the Windows Partition*

Note

Windows Systems Installed on NTFS Partitions

By default, the Windows versions NT, 2000, and XP use the NTFS file system. Unlike FAT file systems, NTFS file systems can (currently) only be read from Linux. Therefore, you can read your Windows files from Linux, but you cannot edit them. If you want write access to your Windows data and do not need the NTFS file system, reinstall Windows on a FAT32 file system. In this case, you will have full access to your Windows data from SUSE LINUX.

Note

More Partitioning Tips

If the partitioning is performed by YaST and other partitions are detected in the system, these partitions are also entered in the file `/etc/fstab` to enable easy access to this data. This file contains all partitions in the system with their properties (parameters), such as the file system, mount point, and user permissions.

Example 2.1: /etc/fstab: Partition Data

```
/dev/sda1      /data1  auto    noauto,user 0 0
/dev/sda8      /data2  auto    noauto,user 0 0
```

The partitions, regardless of whether they are Linux or FAT partitions, are specified with the options `noauto` and `user`. This allows any user to mount or unmount these partitions as needed. For security reasons, YaST does not automatically enter the `exec` option here, which is needed for executing programs from the respective location. However, to run programs from there, you can enter this option manually. This measure is necessary if you encounter system messages such as `bad interpreter` or `Permission denied`.

Detailed background information and tips for partitioning are provided in the Administration Guide.

2.5.6 Software

SUSE LINUX contains a number of software packages for various application purposes. As it would be burdensome to select the needed packages one by one, SUSE LINUX offers three system types with various installation scopes. Depending on the available disk space, YaST selects one of these basic systems and displays it in the suggestion screen.

- Minimum System (only recommended for special purposes)

  This installs the operating system with various services without the graphical user interface. The machine can only be operated by way of the ASCII consoles. This system type is especially suitable for server applications requiring little direct user interaction.

- Minimum Graphical System (without KDE)

  If you do not want the KDE desktop or if the disk space is insufficient, install this system type. The installed system includes an elementary graphical user interface with terminal windows, but no real desktop with the usual functionality. You can use all programs that have their own graphical user interfaces (such as Netscape). No office programs are installed.

- Default System (with KDE and office package)

  This is the largest of all offered basic systems. It contains the KDE desktop together with most of the KDE programs and the office programs. This is the most suitable system type for normal stand-alone machines. If possible, YaST selects this system type.

Click 'Software Selection' in the suggestion screen to open a dialog in which to select one of the basic systems. To start the software installation modules (package manager) and modify the installation scope, click 'Detailed Selection' (see Figure 2.11).

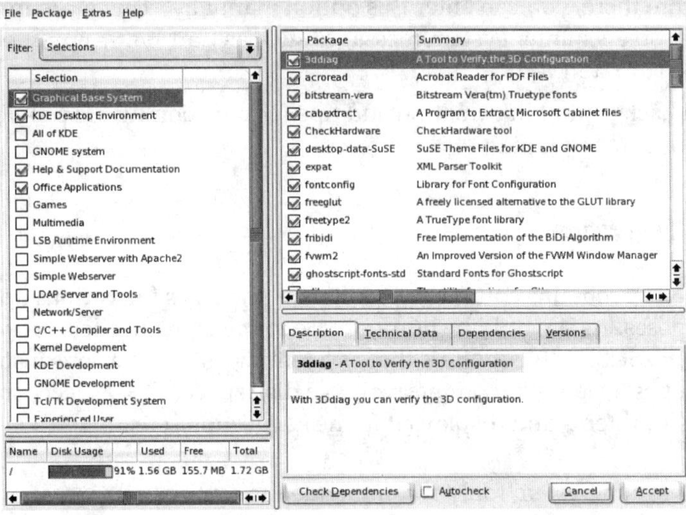

Figure 2.11: Installing and Removing Software with the YaST Package Manager

Changing the Installation Scope

If you install the default system, there is usually no need to add or remove individual packages. This basic system consists of a software selection that meets most requirements without any changes. If you have specific needs, modify this selection with the package manager. It offers various filter criteria for determining a selection from the numerous packages in SUSE LINUX.

The filter selection box is located at the top left under the menu bar. At start-up, the 'Selections' filter is active. This filter groups the program packages by their application purpose, such as multimedia or office applications. The various groups of the Selections filter are listed under the filter selection box. The packages included in the selected system type are preselected. Click the respective check boxes to select or deselect entire selections for installation.

The right part of the window displays a table listing the individual packages included in the current selection. The leftmost table column shows the current status of each package. Two status flags are especially relevant for the installation: *Install* (the box in front of the package name is checked) and *Do Not Install* (the box is empty). To select or deselect individual software packages, click the status box until the desired status is displayed.

Alternatively, right-click the package line to access a pop-up menu listing various status options. However, the other status settings are not needed for the installation. They are described in detailed in Section 4.3.4 on page 59.

Other Filters

Click the filter selection box to view the range of possible filters. The selection according to 'Package Groups' can also be used for the installation. This filter sorts the program packages by subjects in a tree structure to the left. The more you expand the branches, the more specific the selection of packages is and the fewer packages that are displayed in the list of associated packages to the right.

Use 'Search' to search for a specific package. This is explained in detail in Section 4.3.4 on page 59.

Package Dependencies and Conflicts

Instead of rewriting the same basic functions in each software package, programmers access the functions of other packages. For this reason, many packages require that other packages are installed for the programs to function. In rare cases, programs interfere with each other, causing conflicts. When selecting and deselecting software packages in this dialog, alerts about unresolved package dependencies or conflicts may be displayed. If you install SUSE LINUX for the first time or if you do not understand the alerts, read Section 4.3.4 on page 59, which provides detailed information about the operation of the package manager and a brief summary of the software organization in Linux.

Caution

The software preselected for installation is based on long-standing experience and is usually suitable for the needs of most newcomers and advanced home users. In general, there is no need to change anything here. However, if you decide to select or deselect any packages, you should be aware of the consequences. In particular, observe any warnings and avoid deselecting any packages of the base system.

Caution

Exiting the Software Selection

When satisfied with your software selection and there are no more unresolved package dependencies or conflicts, click 'Accept' to apply your changes and exit the program. If this module is started in the installed system, the changes are applied immediately. During the installation, however, the changes are recorded internally and applied later when the actual installation starts.

2.5.7 Boot Configuration (Boot Loader Installation)

During the installation, YaST proposes a boot configuration for your system. Normally, you should leave these settings unchanged. However, if you need a custom setup, modify the proposal for your system.

One possibility is to configure the boot mechanism to rely on a special boot floppy. Although this has the disadvantage of requiring the boot floppy in the drive for boot, it allows you to leave an existing boot mechanism untouched. This should not normally be necessary, however, because YaST can configure the boot loader to boot existing operating systems as well. Another possibility with the configuration is to change the location of the boot mechanism on the hard disk.

To change the boot configuration proposed by YaST, select 'Booting' to open a dialog in which to change many details of the boot mechanism. For information, read Section 4.8.4 on page 120.

Note

The boot method should only be changed by experienced computer users.

Note

2.5.8 Time Zone

In this dialog, shown in Figure 2.12, choose between `Local Time` and `UTC` under 'Hardware clock set to'. The selection depends on how the hardware (BIOS) clock is set on your machine. If it is set to `GMT`, which corresponds to UTC, your system can rely on SUSE LINUX to switch from standard time to daylight savings time and vice versa.

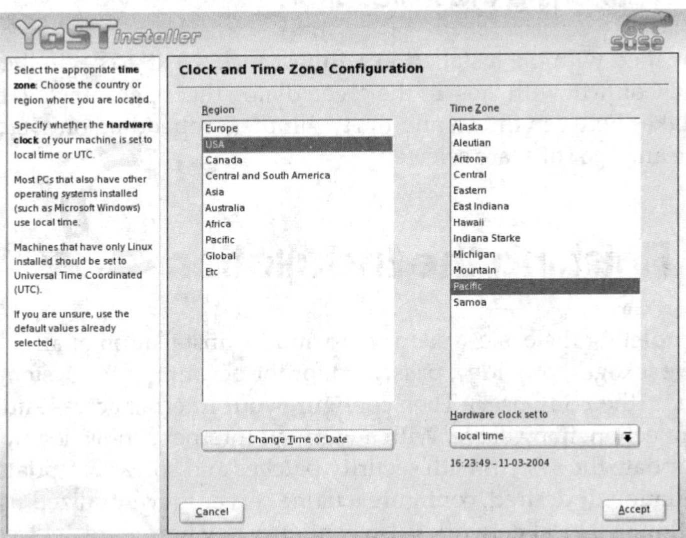

Figure 2.12: Selecting the Time Zone

2.5.9 Language

The language was already selected at the beginning of the installation (see Section 2.3 on page 15. If you want to change this setting, you can do this here. Furthermore, advanced users can use the 'Details' button to set the language for the user `root`. The drop-down menu offers three options:

ctype The value of the variable `LC_CTYPE` in the file `/etc/sysconfig/language` is adopted for the user `root`. This sets the localization for language-specific function calls.

yes The user `root` has the same language settings as the local user.

no The language settings for the user `root` are not affected by the language selection.

Click 'OK' to complete the configuration or 'Discard' to undo your changes.

2.5.10 Launching the Installation

When satisfied with the installation settings, click 'Next' to begin the installation. Confirm with 'Yes' in the green dialog that opens. Installation usually takes between fifteen and thirty minutes, depending on system performance and the software selected.

2.6 Finishing the Installation

After completing the basic system setup and the installation of all selected software packages, provide a password for the account of the system administrator (the `root` user). Then configure your Internet access and network connection, if available. With a working Internet connection, it is possible to update the system with security patches and software updates during installation. If desired, configure a name server for centralized user administration in a local network. Also configure any hardware devices, such as printers and scanners.

2.6.1 root Password

☞*root* is the name of the superuser, the administrator of the system. Unlike regular users, which may or may not have permission to do certain things on the system, `root` has unlimited power to do anything: change the system configuration, install programs, and set up new hardware. If users forget their passwords or have other problems with the system, `root` can help. The `root` account should only be used for system administration, maintenance, and repair. Logging in as `root` for daily work is rather risky: a single mistake could lead to many system files being irretrievably lost.

Figure 2.13 on the facing page shows the relevant dialog. For verification purposes, the password for `root` must be entered twice. Do not forget the `root` password. It cannot be retrieved later.

Caution

The user `root` has all the permissions needed to make changes to the system. To carry out such tasks, the `root` password is required. You cannot carry out any administrative tasks without this password.

Caution

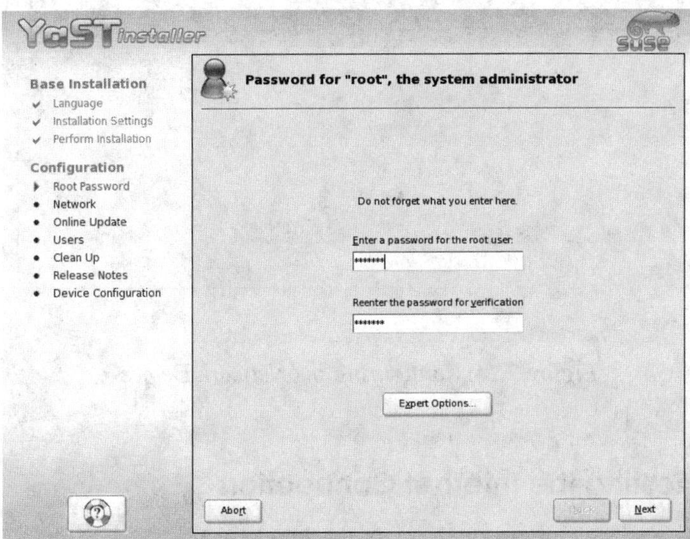

Figure 2.13: Setting the root Password

2.6.2 Network Configuration

In this step, configure network devices for a connection to the outside world. If you have these devices, such as network cards, modems, and ISDN or DSL hardware, it is a good idea to configure them now. An Internet connection allows YaST to retrieve any available SUSE LINUX updates.

To configure your network hardware here, refer to the relevant parts of Section 4.5 on page 94. Otherwise choose to 'Skip Network Setup' and confirm this with 'Continue'. The network hardware can also be configured after system installation has completed.

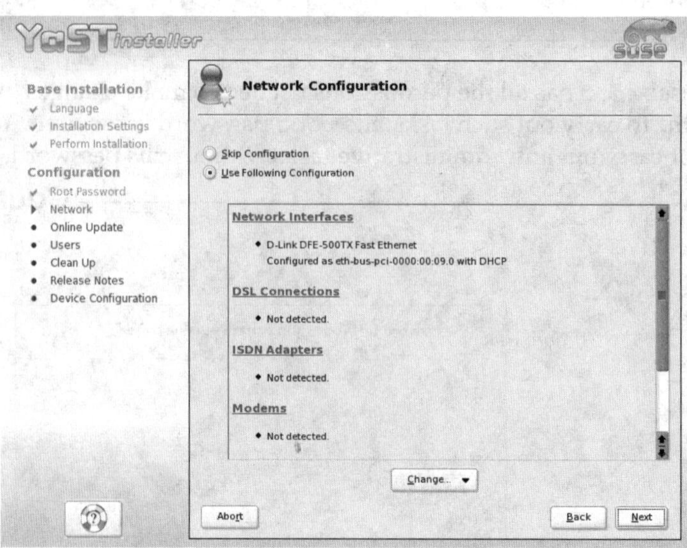

Figure 2.14: Configuring the Network Devices

2.6.3 Testing the Internet Connection

If you configured an Internet connection, you can test it right now. For this purpose, YaST establishes a connection to the SUSE server and checks if any product updates are available for your version of SUSE LINUX. Also, the latest release notes are downloaded. Any available updates can be installed in the next step.

If you do not want to test the connection at this point, select 'Skip Test' then 'Next'. This also skips downloading product updates and release notes.

2.6.4 Loading Software Updates

If YaST was able to connect to the SUSE servers, select whether to perform a YaST online update. If there are any patched packages available on the servers, you can download and install them now to fix known bugs or security issues.

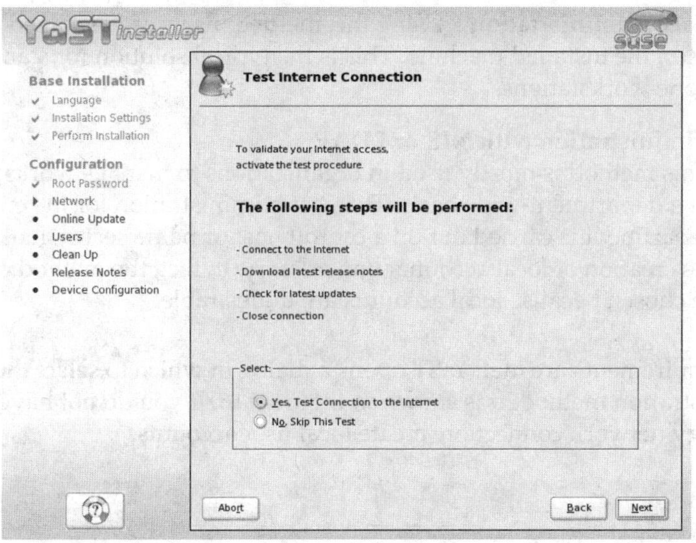

Figure 2.15: Testing the Internet Connection

Note

The download of updates might take quite some time, depending on the bandwidth of the Internet connection and on the size of the update files.

Note

To perform a software update immediately, select 'Perform Update Now' and click 'OK'. This opens YaST's online update dialog with a list of the available patches (if any), which can be selected and loaded. To learn about the process, read Section 4.3.2 on page 56. This kind of update can be performed at any time after the installation. If you prefer not to update now, select 'Skip Update' then click 'OK'.

2.6.5 User Authentication

If the network access been configured successfully during the previous steps of the installation, you now have two different possibilities for managing user accounts on your system.

Local User Administration Using this method, users are managed locally — on the installed machine. This is the typical solution for stand-alone workstations.

User Administration with NIS or LDAP
This method is mostly used in organizations to manage workstations on a department-wide basis. The user administration for the entire department is carried out on a central host or name server, making the creation of local accounts unnecessary. In fact, the method could be chosen because local accounts are undesirable.

If all requirements are met, YaST opens a dialog in which to select the user administration method. It is shown in Figure 2.16. If you do not have the necessary network connection, create local user accounts.

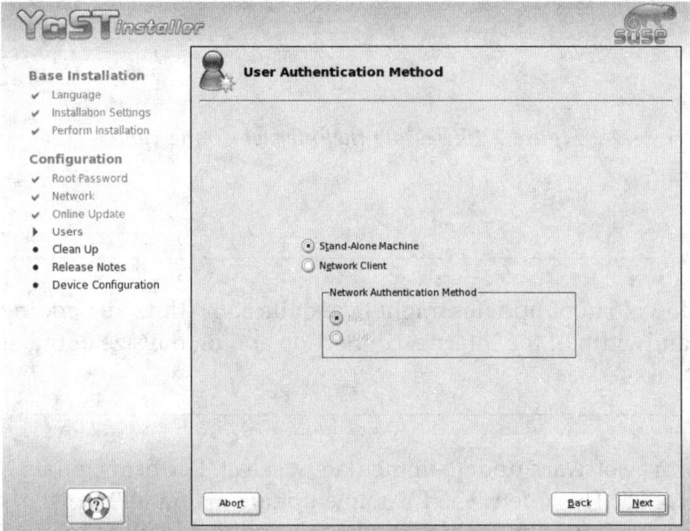

Figure 2.16: User Authentication

2.6.6 Configuring the Host as a NIS Client

If you have decided to manage user accounts through NIS, configure the host as a NIS client. A NIS-enabled network requires some expert knowledge. The details of NIS are explained in the Administration Guide. The following only explains the basic setup of the client side.

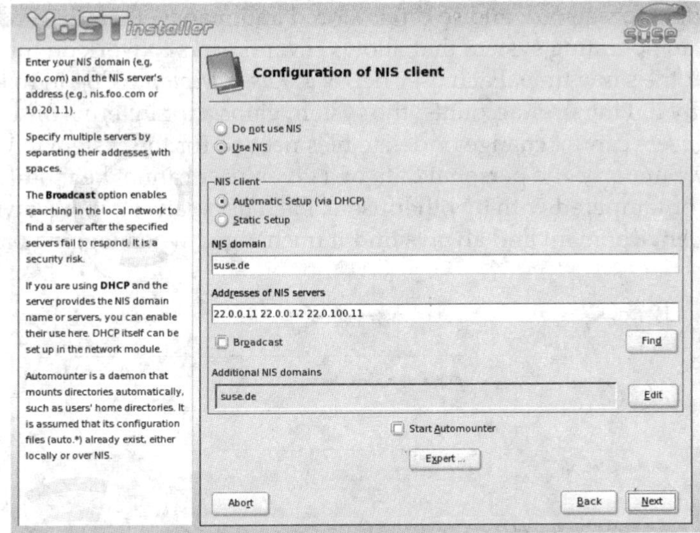

***Figure 2.17:** NIS Client Configuration*

In the following dialog, shown in Figure 2.17, first select whether the host has a fixed IP address or gets one via DHCP. DHCP also provides the NIS domain and the NIS server. For information about DHCP, see the *Administration Guide*. If a static IP address is used, specify the NIS domain and the NIS server manually.

To search for NIS servers broadcasting in the network, check the relevant option. You can also specify several NIS domains and set a default domain. For each domain, select 'Edit' to specify several server addresses or enable the broadcast function on a per-domain basis.

In the expert settings, use 'Answer to the Local Host Only' to prevent other network hosts from being able query which server your client is using. If you activate 'Broken Server', responses from servers on unprivileged ports are also accepted. For more information, refer to the man page of `ypbind`.

2.6.7 Creating Local User Accounts

When user accounts are created locally, any data related to user accounts (name, login, password, and so on) is stored and managed on this host. Linux is an operating system that allows several users to work on the same system at the same time. Each user needs a ☞*user account* to log in to the system. By having user accounts, the system gains a lot in terms of security. Regular users cannot change or delete files needed for the system to work properly. Similarly, the personal data of a given user cannot be modified, viewed, or tampered with by other users. Each user can set up his own working environment and always find it unchanged when logging back in.

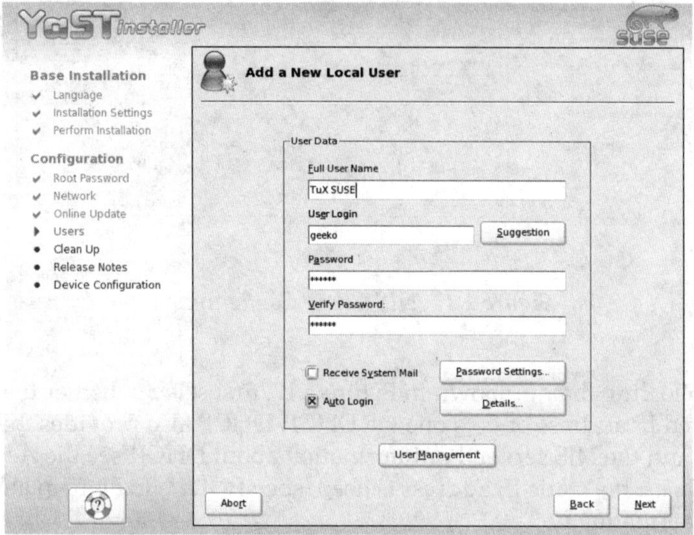

Figure 2.18: *Entering the User Name and Password*

A user account can be created using the dialog shown in Figure 2.18. After entering the first name and last name, specify the user name (login). If you cannot think of a suitable user name, click 'Suggestion' for the system to generate one automatically.

Finally, enter a password for the user. Reenter it for confirmation (to ensure that you did not type something else by mistake). The user name tells the system who a user is and the password is used to verify this identity.

Caution

Remember both your user name and the password because they are needed each time you log in to the system.

Caution

To provide effective security, a password should be between five and eight characters long. The maximum length for a password is 128 characters. However, if no special security modules are loaded, only the first eight characters are used to discern the password. Passwords are case-sensitive. Special characters like umlauts are not allowed. Other special characters (7-bit ASCII) and the digits 0 to 9 are allowed.

Two options are available for local users:

'Receive system messages via e-mail' Checking this box sends the user messages created by the system services. These are usually only sent to `root`, the system administrator. This option is useful for the prominently-used user account, because it is highly recommended to log in as `root` only in special cases.

'Automatic login' This option is only available if KDE is used as the default desktop. It automatically logs the current user into the system when it starts. This is mainly useful if the computer is operated by only one user.

Note

No authentication is performed during system start-up with automatic login. Do not check this option for systems containing sensitive data or to which other people have access.

Note

2.6.8 Reading the Release Notes

After completing the user authentication setup, YaST displays the release notes. They contain important up-to-date information not available when the manuals were printed. If you have installed update packages, the most recent version of the release notes is available.

2.7 Hardware Configuration

Configure the graphics card and, if desired, other hardware devices, such as the printer and the sound card. Just click a component to start its configuration. For the most part, YaST then detects and configures the devices automatically.

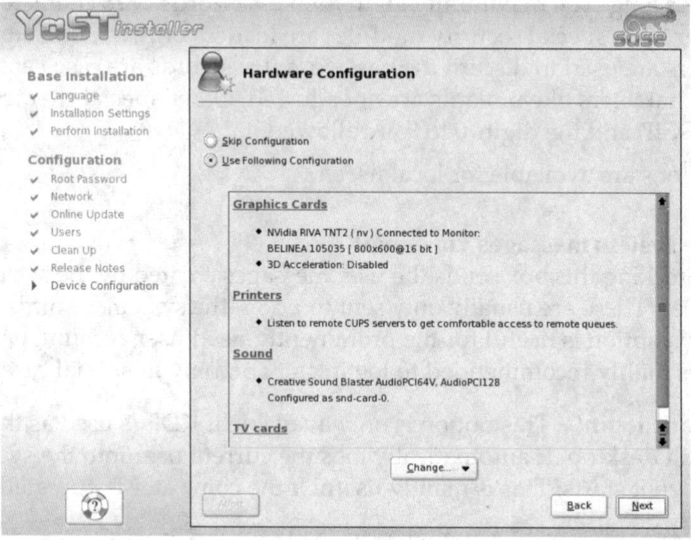

Figure 2.19: Configuring the System Components

You may skip any peripheral devices and configure them later. However, you should configure the graphics card right away. Although the display settings as autoconfigured by YaST should be generally acceptable, most users have very strong preferences as far as resolution, color depth, and other graphics features are concerned. To change these settings, select 'X Configuration'. The configuration is explained in Section 4.4.4 on page 79. When finished, click 'Finish Installation'.

After YaST has written the configuration data, you can finish the installation of the SUSE LINUX with 'Finish' in the final dialog.

2.8 Graphical Login

SUSE LINUX is now installed. You can start right away without passing the login procedure if you checked automatic login in the local user administration module. If not, the graphical ☞*Login* window shown in Figure 2.20 is displayed on your screen. Enter a previously determined user name and password to log in to the system.

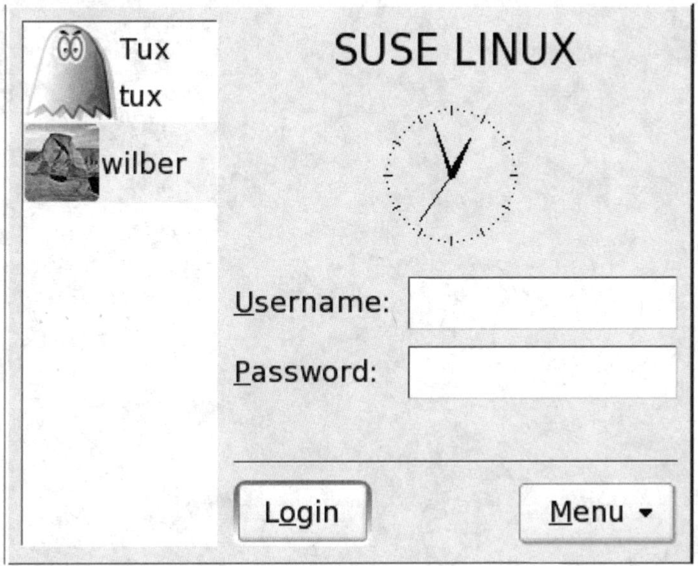

***Figure 2.20:** The Login Screen*

YaST System Repair

Despite its robustness, the SUSE LINUX system can be damaged by configuration blunders or other "accidents". While this is quite unlikely when logged in as a regular user, the superuser `root` is allowed to change all system files and configuration, making it possible for him to accidentally cause damage. There are good chances of putting the system back on track with the YaST System Repair in such a case. It is impossible to correct all imaginable defects, but many of the common problems can be solved.

3.1 Starting YaST System Repair

Because it cannot be assumed that a damaged system can boot by itself and a running system cannot be easily repaired, the YaST System Repair utility is run from the SUSE LINUX installation CD or DVD. Follow the steps outlined in Chapter 2 on page 11 to get to the dialog page offering the various installation options and select 'Repair Installed System'. See Figure 3.1.

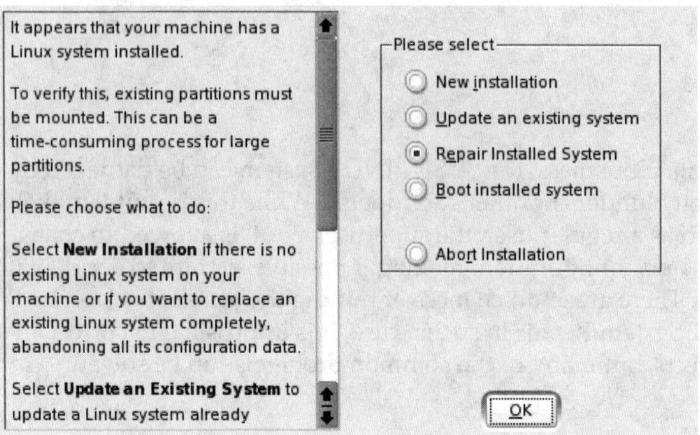

Figure 3.1: Selecting the YaST System Repair Utility

Note

Because the test and repair procedure is loaded from CD or DVD, it is essential to run it from an installation medium that *exactly* corresponds to your installed version of SUSE LINUX.

Note

In the next step, choose how the system repair should be performed. The following options are available and are described below:

- Automatic repair
- User-defined repair
- Expert tools

3.2 Automatic Repair

This method is best suited to restoring a damaged system with unknown cause. Selecting it starts an extensive analysis of the installed system, which will take quite some time due to the large amount of tests and examinations. The progress of the procedure is displayed at the bottom of the screen with two progress bars. The upper bar shows the progress of the currently running test. The lower bar shows the overall progress of the analysis process. The log window above allows tracking of the currently running activity and its test result. See Figure 3.2 on the following page. The following main test runs are performed with every run. They contain, in turn, a number of individual subtests.

Partition tables of all hard disks The validity and coherence of the partition tables of all detected hard disks are checked.

Swap partitions The swap partitions of the installed system are detected, tested, and offered for activation where applicable. The offer should be accepted for the sake of a higher system repair speed.

File systems All detected file systems are subjected to a file system–specific check.

Entries in the file `/etc/fstab` The entries in the file are checked for completeness and consistence. All valid partitions are mounted.

Boot loader configuration The boot loader configuration of the installed system (GRUB or LILO) is checked for completeness and coherence. Boot and root devices are examined and the availability of the initrd modules is checked.

Package database This checks whether all packages necessary for the operation of a minimal installation are present. While it is optionally possible to also analyze the base packages, this takes a long time because of their vast number.

Whenever an error is encountered, the procedure is stopped and a dialog opens, offering details and possible solutions. It is not possible to describe all these cases. Read the notifications on the screen carefully and choose the desired action from the list options. It is also possible to decline the offered repair action in cases of doubt. The system remains unaltered in this aspect and no repair is ever performed automatically and without prompting the user.

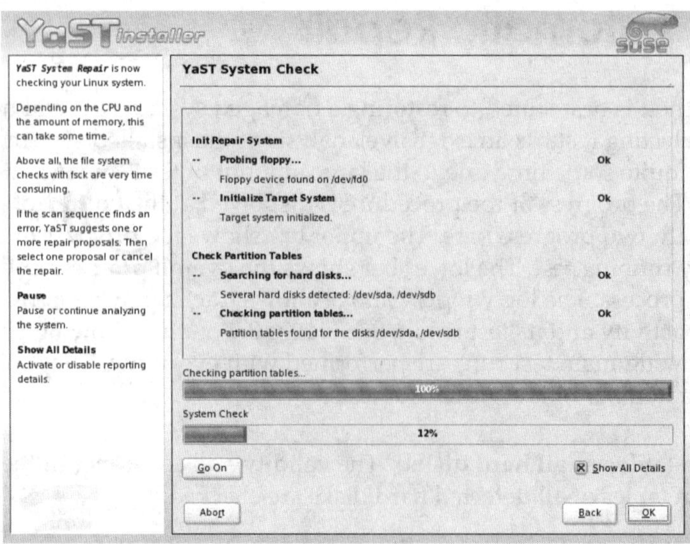

Figure 3.2: Automatic Repair Mode

3.3 User-Defined Repair

The automatic repair explained in the preceding section categorically performs all tests. This is useful if the extent of the system damage is unkown. However, if you already know what part of the system is affected, the range of the applied tests can be narrowed. Choosing 'User-defined repair' shows a list of test runs that are all marked for execution at first. The total range of tests matches that of automatic repair. If you already know where *no* damage is present, unmark the corresponding tests. Clicking 'Continue' then starts a narrower test procedure that probably has a significantly shorter running time.

Not all test groups are applicable individually. The analysis of the fstab entries is always bound to an examination of the file systems, including existing swap partitions. YaST automatically satisfies such dependencies by selecting the smallest amount of necessary test runs.

3.4 Expert Tools

If you are knowledgeable with SUSE LINUX and already have a very clear idea of what needs to be repaired in your system, directly apply the tools necessary for repairing it by choosing 'Expert tools'.

Install new boot loader This starts the YaST boot loader configuration module. Details can be found in Section 4.8.4 on page 120

Run partitioning tool This starts the expert partitioning tool in YaST. Details can be found in Section 2.5.5 on page 22

Fix file system This allows checking the file systems of your installed system. You are first offered a selection of all detected partitions and can then choose the ones to check.

Restore lost partitions It is possible to attempt a reconstruction of damaged partition tables. A list of detected hard disks is presented first for selection. Clicking 'OK' starts the examination. This can take a while depending on the processing power and size of the hard disk.

Note

The reconstruction of a partition table is tricky. YaST attempts to recognize lost partitions by analyzing the data sectors of the hard disk. The lost partitions are added to the rebuilt partition table upon successful recognition. This is, however, not successful in all imaginable cases.

Note

Save system settings to disk This option allows saving important system files to a floppy disk. Should one of these files become damaged, it can be restored from disk.

Check installed software This checks the consistency of the package database and the availability of the most important packages. Any damaged installed packages can be reinstalled with this tool.

Part II

Configuration

4

YaST — Configuration

YaST, the setup tool used for the installation, is also the configuration tool for SUSE LINUX. This chapter covers the configuration of your system with YaST. This includes most of the hardware, the graphical user interface, Internet access, security settings, user administration, installation of software, system updates, and system information. This chapter also provides instructions for using YaST in text mode.

4.1 Starting YaST

System configuration with YaST uses various YaST modules serving different purposes, such as the configuration of the keyboard or the selection of the system language. These modules can be accessed in various ways. An overview of all modules is available in the YaST Control Center, which can be started from the 'SUSE' menu, the SUSE icon at the bottom left of your KDE panel. Select 'SUSE' -> 'System' -> 'YaST'. The individual modules can also be accessed from the KDE Control Center. If you use KDE, you can also start YaST by pressing Alt + F2. In the window that opens, enter `kdesu /sbin/yast2` and confirm with Enter. If you do not want to start the graphical version of YaST, enter `/sbin/yast` instead of `/sbin/yast2`. YaST then runs in console mode as described in Section 4.10 on page 129.

As these start methods are usually used by a normal user, YaST opens a small dialog for entering the `root` password. `root` privileges are required for all YaST modules, as only this user is permitted to modify the Linux system files.

If, for any reason, YaST cannot be started as described above, it can be started from the command line. In the shell, change to the user `root` with `sux`. Enter the root password and run the command `yast2`.

Note

To change the language of YaST, select 'System' -> 'Select Language' in the YaST Control Center. Choose a language, exit the YaST Control Center, log out from your computer, then log in and restart YaST.

Note

4.2 The YaST Control Center

When you start YaST in the graphical mode, the YaST Control Center, as shown in Figure 4.1 on the facing page, opens. The left frame features the categories 'Software', 'Hardware', 'Network Devices', 'Network Services', 'Security & Users', 'System', and 'Miscellaneous'. If you click one of icons, the respective contents are listed on the right-hand side. For example, if you select 'Hardware' and click 'Sound' to the right, a configuration dialog opens for the sound card. The configuration of the individual items usually comprises several steps. Press 'Next' to proceed to the following step.

The left frame displays a help text for the respective topic, explaining the required entries. After making the needed settings, complete the procedure by pressing 'Finish' in the last configuration dialog. The configuration is then saved.

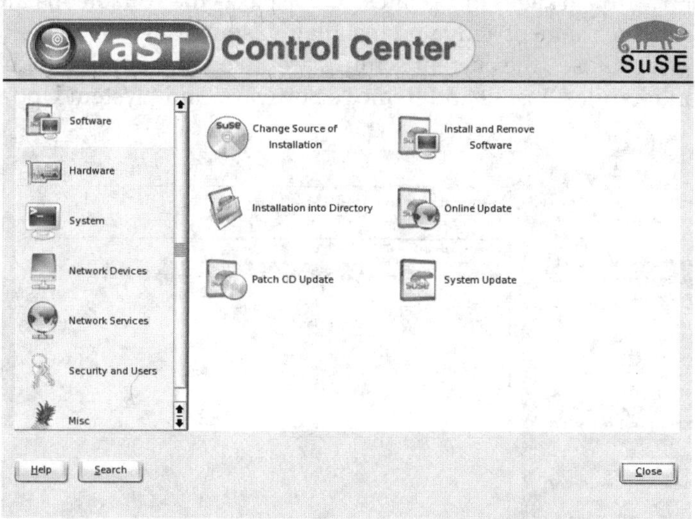

Figure 4.1: The YaST Control Center

4.3 Software

4.3.1 Change Installation Source

The installation source is the medium containing the software to install. YaST can administer a number of different installation sources. It enables their selection for installation or update purposes.

When this module is started, a list displaying all previously registered sources is displayed. Following a normal installation from CD, only the installation CD is listed. Click 'Add' to include additional sources in this list. You can add removable media, such as CDs and DVDs, and network servers, such as NFS and FTP. Even directories on the local hard disk can be selected as the installation medium. See the detailed YaST help text.

During the installation or update, YaST can take multiple installation sources into consideration. Therefore, all registered sources have an activation status in the first column of the list. Click 'Activate or Deactivate' to activate or deactivate individual installation sources. During the installation of software packages or updates, YaST selects the suitable installation source from the range of activated installation sources. When you exit the module with 'Close', the current settings are saved and applied to the configuration modules 'Install and Remove Software' and 'System Update'.

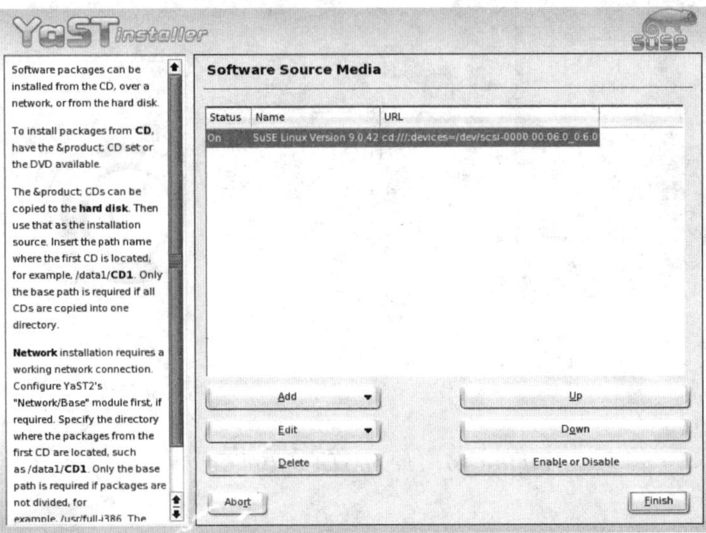

Figure 4.2: Change Installation Source

4.3.2 YaST Online Update

The YaST Online Update (YOU) enables the installation of important updates and improvements. The respective patches are available for download on the SUSE FTP server and various mirror servers. Under 'Installation Source', select one of the various servers. When you select a server, the respective URL is copied to the input field below, where it can be edited. You can also specify local URLs in the form "file:/my/path" or simply "/my/path". Expand the existing list with additional servers using 'New Server'. Click 'Edit Server' to modify the settings of the currently selected server.

When the module starts, 'Manual Selection of Patches' is active, enabling determination of whether individual patches should be fetched. To apply all available update packages, deactivate this option. However, depending on the bandwidth of the connection and the amount of data to transmit, this can result in long download times.

If you activate 'Download All Patches Again', all available patches, installable packages, and descriptions are downloaded from the server. If this box is not activated (default), only retrieve patches not yet installed on your system.

Additionally, there is a possibility to update your system automatically. Click 'Configure Fully Automatic Update' to configure a process that automatically looks for updates and applies them on a daily basis. This procedure is fully automated and does not require any interaction. This only works if a connection to the update server, such as an Internet connection, exists at the time of the update.

If you decide to perform a manual update (default), click 'Next' to load a list of all available patches and start the package manager, described in Section 4.3.4 on page 59. In the package manager, the filter for YOU patches is activated, enabling selection of updates to install. Patches recommended for installation are preselected. Normally, you should accept this suggestion.

After making your selection, click 'Accept' in the package manager. All selected updates are then downloaded from the server and installed on your machine. Depending on the connection speed and hardware performance, this may take some time. Any errors are displayed in a window. If necessary, skip the respective package. Prior to the installation, some patches may open a window displaying details, allowing you to confirm the installation or skip the package.

While the updates are downloaded and installed, track actions in the log window. Following the successful installation of all patches, exit YOU with 'Finish'. If you do not need the update files after the installation, delete them with 'Remove Source Packages after Update'. Finally, SuSEconfig is executed to adapt the system configuration to the new circumstances.

In addition to the common operation from the YaST interface, experts can also run the YaST Online Update from the command line of a console window. The desired actions are, in this case, passed as command line parameters: `online_update[command line parameter]`. The available parameters are displayed in the following list along with their purpose.

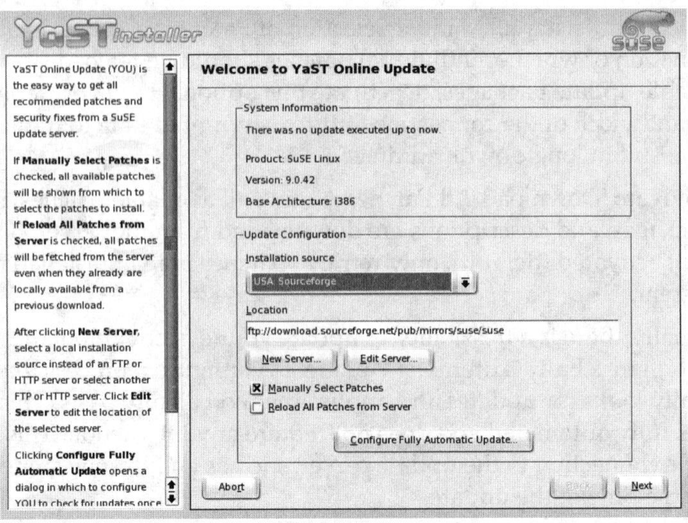

Figure 4.3: YaST Online Update

`-u URL` Base URL of the directory tree from which the patches should be fetched.

`-g` Download the patches without installing them.

`-i` Install already fetched patches without downloading anything.

`-k` Check for existing new patches.

`-c` Show current configuration without further action.

`-p product` Product for which patches should be fetched.

`-v version` Product version for which patches should be fetched.

`-a architecture` Base architecture for which patches should be fetched.

`-d` "Dry run" cycle. Fetch patches and simulate installation for test purposes. The system remains unchanged.

`-n` No signature checking of the fetched files.

`-s` Display list of available patches.

-V Verbose mode. Print progress messages.

-D Debug mode for experts and for troubleshooting.

4.3.3 Patch CD Update

The Patch CD Update is for SUSE LINUX Enterprise Server customers. Patches are installed from CD instead of from an FTP server.

4.3.4 Installing and Removing Software

This module enables installation, uninstallation, and update of software on your machine.

In Linux, software is available in the form of packages. Normally, a package contains everything needed for a program (such as an editor or a compiler). Usually, this includes the actual program, associated configuration files, and documentation. A package containing the source files for the respective program is normally available as well. The sources are not needed for running the program. However, you may want to install the sources to compile a custom version of the program. In Linux, this is possible and permitted.

Some packages depend on other packages. This means that the software of the respective package only works properly if another package is also installed (package dependency). Furthermore, the installation (not only the operation) of some packages is only possible if certain other packages are installed, perhaps because the installation routine needs specific tools. Accordingly, such packages must be installed in the correct sequence. Moreover, there are some packages with identical or similar functionalities. If these packages use the same system resource, they should not be installed concurrently (package conflict). Dependencies and conflicts can occur between two or more packages and are sometimes very complex. The fact that a specific package version may be required for smooth interaction can make things even more complicated.

All these factors must be taken into consideration when installing, uninstalling, and updating software. Fortunately, YaST provides an extremely efficient tool for this purpose: the software installation module, usually referred to as the package manager. When the package manager is started, it examines the system and displays installed packages. If you select additional packages for installation, the package manager automatically checks the dependencies and selects any other needed packages (resolution of dependencies). If you unknowingly select conflicting packages, the package manager indicates this and submits suggestions for solving the problem (resolution of conflicts). If a package needed by other installed packages is accidentally marked for deletion, the package manager issues an alert with detailed information and alternative solutions.

Apart from these purely technical aspects, the package manager provides a well-structured overview of the range of packages in SUSE LINUX. The packages are arranged by subjects and the display of these groups is restricted by means of suitable filters. Thus, the package manager facilitates the management of software packages and is a valuable tool for maintaining your system.

The Package Manager

To change the software selection on your system with the package manager, select 'Install or Remove Software' in the YaST Control Center. The dialog window of the package manager is shown in Figure 4.4.

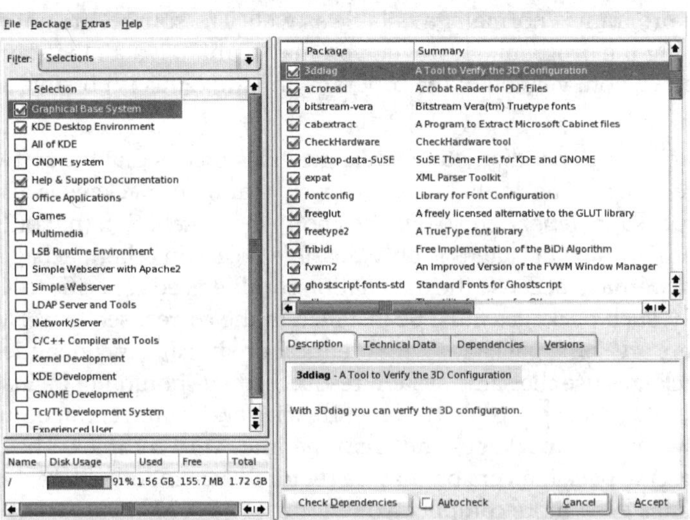

Figure 4.4: YaST Package Manager

The window comprises various frames. The frame sizes can be modified by clicking and moving the lines separating the areas. The contents of the frames and their uses are described below.

The Filter Window

Selecting all packages of an installation one by one would be vary laborious and time-consuming.

Therefore, the package manager offers various filter methods for arranging the packages in categories and limiting the number of displayed packages. The filter window is located to the left under the menu bar. It controls and displays various filter methods. The filter selection box at the top determines what will be displayed in the lower part of the filter window. Click the filter selection box to select a filter from the list of available filters.

The Selections Filter At start-up, the 'Selections' filter is active. This filter groups the program packages according to their application purpose, such as "Multimedia" or "Office Applications." The various groups of the 'Selections' filter are listed under the filter selection box. The packages already installed on the system are preselected. Click the status box at the beginning of a line to toggle the status flags of a selection. You can also select a status directly by right-clicking the selection and using the context menu. The individual package window to the right displays the list of packages included in the current selection, enabling selection and deselection of individual packages.

The Package Groups Filter The 'Package Groups' filter provides a more technical overview of the range of packages and is suitable for users who are familiar with the package structure of SUSE LINUX. This filter sorts the program packages by subjects, such as "Applications," "Development," and "Hardware," in a tree structure to the left. The more you expand the branches, the more specific the selection is and the fewer packages are displayed in the individual package window to the right. The filter additionally provides the possibility to display all packages in alphabetic order. To do this, select 'zzz All' in the top level. As SUSE LINUX contains a large number of packages, it may take some time to display this long list.

The Search Function The 'Search' function is the easiest way to find a specific package. By specifying various search criteria, restrict the filter so much that often only one package is displayed in the individual package window. Enter a search string and use the check boxes to determine where to search for this string (in the name, in the description, or in the package dependencies). Advanced users can even define special search patterns using wild cards and regular expressions and search the package dependencies in the "Provides" and "Requires" fields. For example, software developers who download source packages from the Internet can use this function to determine which package contains a specific library needed for compiling and linking this package.

Note

In addition to the 'Search' filter, all lists of the package manager feature a quick search for the current list content. For example, simply enter the initial letter of a package name to move the cursor to the first package in the list whose name begins with this letter. The cursor must be in the list (by clicking the list).

Note

Installation Summary After selecting the packages for installation, update, or deletion, use the filter selection to view the installation summary. It shows what will happen with packages when you click 'Accept'. Use the check boxes to the left to filter the packages to view in the individual package window. If, for example, you merely want to check which packages are already installed, start the package manager and deactivate all check boxes except 'Keep'. Of course, the package status in the individual package window can be changed as usual. However, the respective package may no longer meet the search criteria. To remove such packages from the list, update the list with 'Update list'.

The Individual Package Window

As mentioned above, a list of individual packages is displayed to the right in the individual package window. The content of this list is determined by the currently selected filter. If, for example, the 'Selection' filter is selected, the individual package window displays all packages of the current selection.

In the package manager, each package has a status that determines what to do with the package, such as "Install" or "Delete". This status is shown by means of a symbol in a status box at the beginning of the line. Toggle the status by clicking or select it from the menu that opens when the item is right-clicked. Depending on the current situation, some of the possible status flags may not be available for selection. For example, a package that has not yet been installed cannot be set to "Delete." View the available status flags with 'Help' -> 'Symbols'.

The package manager offers the following package status flags:

Do Not Install This package is not installed and will not be installed.

Install This package is not yet installed but will be installed.

Keep This package is already installed and will not be changed.

Update This package is already installed and will be replaced by the version on the installation medium.

Delete This package is already installed and will be deleted.

Taboo — Never Install This package is not installed and will never be installed. It will be treated as if it does not exist on any of the installation media. If a package would automatically be selected to resolve dependencies, this can be prevented by setting the package to "Taboo." However, this may result in inconsistencies that must be resolved manually (dependency check). Thus, "Taboo" is mainly intended for expert users.

Protected This package is installed and should not be modified, as unresolved dependencies from other packages exist or could arise. Third-party packages (packages without SUSE signature) are automatically assigned this status to prevent them from being overwritten by later versions existing on the installation media. This may cause package conflicts that must be resolved manually (for experts).

Automatic Installation This package has been automatically selected for installation, as it is required by another package (resolution of package dependencies).

> **Note**
>
> To deselect such a package, you may need to use the status "Taboo".
>
> **Note**

Automatic Update This package is already installed. However, as another package requires a newer version of this package, the installed version will automatically be updated.

Delete Automatically This package is already installed, but existing package conflicts require this package be deleted. For example, this may be the case if the current package has been replaced by a different package. However, this does not happen very often.

Automatic Installation (after selection)
This packages has been automatically selected for installation because it is part of a predefined selection, such as "Multimedia" or "Development."

Automatic Update (after selection)
This package is already installed, but a newer version exists on the installation media. This package is part of a predefined selection, such as "Multimedia" or "Development," selected for update and will automatically be updated.

Delete Automatically (after selection)
This package is already installed, but a predefined selection (such as "Multimedia" or "Development") requires this package be deleted. This does not happen very often.

Additionally, decide to install or not to install the sources for a package. This information complements the current package status and cannot be toggled with the mouse or selected directly from the context menu. Instead, a check box at the end of the package line enables selection of the source packages. This option can also be accessed under 'Package'.

Install Source Also install the source code.

Do Not Install Source The sources will not be installed.

The font color used for various packages in the individual package window provides additional information. Installed packages for which a newer version is available on the installation media are displayed in blue. Installed packages whose versions numbers are higher than those on the installation media are displayed in red. However, as the version numbering of packages is not always linear, the information may not be perfect, but should be sufficient to indicate problematic packages. If necessary, check the version numbers in the information window.

The Information Window

The tabs in the bottom right frame provide various information about the selected package. The description of the selected package is automatically active. Click the other tabs to view technical data (package size, group, etc.), the list of dependencies from other packages, or the version information.

The Resource Window

The resource window at the bottom left displays the disk space needed for your current selection of software on all currently mounted file systems. The colored bar graph grows with every selection. As long as it remains green, there is sufficient space. The bar color slowly changes to red as you approach the limit of disk space. If you select too many packages for installation, an alert is displayed.

The Menu Bar

The menu bar at the top left of the window provides access to most of the functions described above and a number of other functions that cannot be accessed in any other way. It contains the following four menus:

File Select 'File' -> 'Export' to save a list of all installed packages in a text file. This is recommended if you want to replicate a specific installation scope at a later date or on another system. A file generated in this way can be imported with 'Import' and generates the same package selection as was saved. In both cases, define the location of the file or accept the suggestion. To exit the package manager without saving changes to the package selection, click 'Exit — Discard Changes'. To save your changes, select 'Quit — Save Changes'. In this case, all changes are applied and the program is terminated.

Package The items in the 'Package' menu always refer to the package currently displayed in the individual package window. Although all status flags are displayed, you can only select those possible for the current package. Use the check boxes to determine whether to install the sources of the package. 'All in This List' opens a submenu listing all package status flags. However, these do not merely affect the current package, but all packages in this list.

Extras The 'Extras' menu offers options for handling package dependencies and conflicts. If you have already manually selected packages for installation, click 'Show Automatic Package Changes' to view the list of packages that the package manager automatically selected to resolve dependencies. If there are still unresolved package conflicts, an alert is displayed and solutions suggested. If you set package conflicts to 'Ignore', this information will be saved permanently in the system. Otherwise, you would have to set the same packages to 'Ignore' each time you start the package manager. To unignore dependencies, click 'Reset Ignored Dependency Conflicts'.

Help 'Help' -> 'Overview' provides a brief explanation of the package manager functionality. A detailed description of the various package flags is available under 'Symbols'. If you prefer to operate programs without using the mouse, click 'Keys' to view a list of shortcuts.

Dependency Check

'Check Dependencies' and 'Autocheck' are located in the information window. If you click 'Check Dependencies', the package manger checks if the current package selection results in any unresolved package dependencies or conflicts. In the event of unresolved dependencies, the required additional packages are selected automatically. For package conflicts, the package manager opens a dialog that shows the conflict and offers various options for solving the problem.

If you activate 'Autocheck', any change of a package status triggers an automatic check. This is a useful feature, as the consistency of the package selection is monitored permanently. However, this process consumes resources and can slow down the package manager. For this reason, the autocheck is not activated by default. In either case, a consistency check is performed when you confirm your selection with 'Accept'.

In the following example, `sendmail` and `postfix` may not be installed concurrently. Figure 4.5 on the next page shows the conflict message prompting you to make a decision. `postfix` is already installed. Accordingly, you can refrain from installing `sendmail`, remove `postfix`, or take the risk and ignore the conflict.

Caution

Ignoring a conflict is strongly discouraged, as the stability and operability of your system can no longer be guaranteed under these conditions.

Caution

4.3.5 System Update

This module enables an update of the version installed on your system. During operation, you can only update application software, not the SUSE LINUX base system. To update the base system, boot the computer from an installation medium, such as the CD. When selecting the installation mode in YaST, select 'Update an Existing System' instead of 'New Installation'.

The procedure for updating the system is similar to the new installation. Initially, YaST examines the system, determines a suitable update strategy,

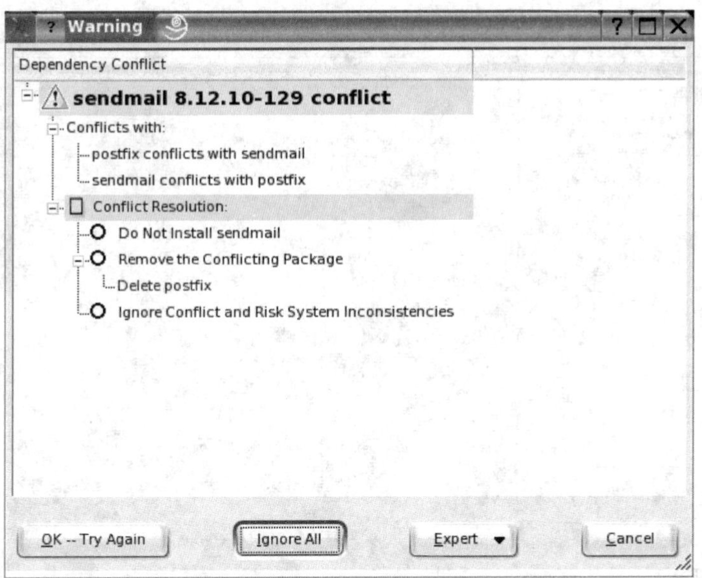

Figure 4.5: Conflict Management of the Package Manager

and presents the results in a suggestion dialog like that in Figure 4.6 on the following page. Click the individual items with the mouse to change any details. Some items, such as 'Language' and 'Keyboard Layout', are covered in the section explaining the installation procedure. Therefore, the following paragraphs only cover update-specific settings.

Selected for Update

In case several versions of SUSE LINUX are installed on your system, this item enables selection of a partition for the update from the list.

Update Options

Here, set the update method for your system. Two options are available. See Figure 4.7 on page 69.

Update with Installation of New Software
To update the entire system to the latest software versions, select one of the predefined selections. These selections are the same as those

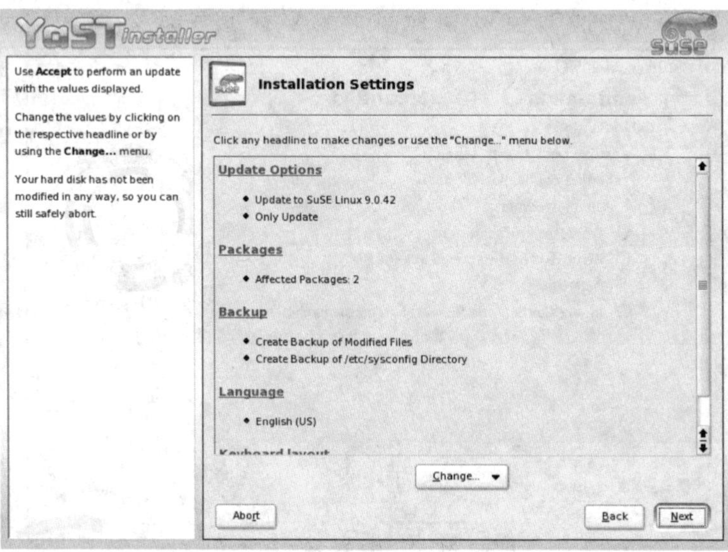

Figure 4.6: *Suggestion Dialog for Updates*

offered during the installation. They make sure new packages that did not exist previously are also installed.

Only Update Installed Packages This option merely updates packages that already exist on the system. No new features will be installed.

Additionally, you can use 'Delete Outdated Packages' to remove packages that do not exist in the new version. By default, this option is preselected to prevent outdated packages from unnecessarily occupying hard disk space.

Packages

Click 'Packages' to start the package manager and select or deselect individual packages for update. Any package conflicts should be resolved with the consistency check. The use of the package manager is covered in detail in Section 4.3.4 on page 59.

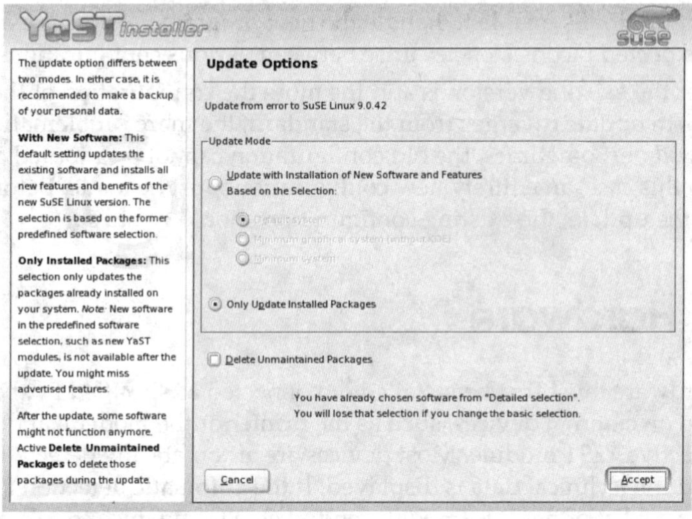

YaST installer
The update option differs between two modes. In either case, it is recommended to make a backup of your personal data.
With New Software: This default setting updates the existing software and installs all new features and benefits of the new SuSE Linux version. The selection is based on the former predefined software selection.
Only Installed Packages: This selection only updates the packages already installed on your system. Note: New software in the predefined software selection, such as new YaST modules, is not available after the update. You might miss advertised features.
After the update, some software might not function anymore. Active Delete Unmaintained Packages to delete those packages during the update.
Update Options
Update from error to SuSE Linux 9.0.42
Update Mode
Update with Installation of New Software and Features Based on the Selection:
Only Update Installed Packages
Delete Unmaintained Packages
You have already chosen software from "Detailed selection".
You will lose that selection if you change the basic selection.
Cancel
Accept

Figure 4.7: Update Options

Backup

During the update, the configuration files of some packages may be replaced by those of the new version. As you may have modified some of the files in your current system, the package manager normally makes backup copies of the replaced files. With this dialog, determine the scope of these backups.

Caution

This backup does not include the software. It only contains configuration files.

Caution

Important Information about Updates

The system update is a very complex procedure. For each program package, YaST must check which version is installed on the computer and what needs to be done to replace the old version with the new version correctly. YaST also tries to adopt any personal settings of the installed packages. However, some configurations may cause problems after the update if the old configuration is unable to handle the new program version as expected or if unexpected inconsistencies arise between various configurations.

The older the existing version is and the more the configuration of the packages to update diverges from the standard, the more problematic the update will be. Sometimes, the old configuration cannot be adopted correctly. In this case, an entirely new configuration must be made. Before starting the update, the existing configuration should be saved.

4.4 Hardware

New hardware must first be installed or connected as specified by the vendor. Turn on external devices, such as the printer or the modem, and start the respective YaST module. Most devices are automatically detected by YaST and the technical data is displayed. If the automatic detection fails, YaST offers a list of devices (model, vendor, etc.) from which to select the suitable device. Consult the documentation enclosed with your hardware for more information.

Note

If your model is not included in the device list, try a model with a similar designation. However, in some cases the model must match exactly, as similar designations do not always indicate compatibility.

Note

4.4.1 CD-ROM Drives

Within the scope of the installation, all detected CD-ROM drives are integrated in the installed system by means of entries in the file `/etc/fstab`. The respective subdirectories are created in `/media`. Use this YaST module to integrate additional drives in the system.

When the module is started, a list of all detected drives is displayed. Mark your new drive using the check box at the beginning of the line and complete the integration with 'Finish'. The new drive will be integrated in the system.

4.4.2 Printer

A Linux system manages printers through printer queues. Before any data is printed, it is sent to a printer queue for temporary storage. From there, it is retrieved by a print spooler, which sends it to the printer device in the required order.

However, for the most part this data is not available in a form that can be processed by the printer. A graphical image, for instance, first needs to be converted into a format the printer can understand. This conversion into a printer language is achieved with a printer filter, a program called by the print spooler to translate data as needed, so the printer can handle it.

Some Standard Printer Languages

- ASCII text

  Every normal printer should at least be able to print ASCII text directly. However, there are devices that cannot print ASCII text directly, but are able to handle one of the other standard printer languages mentioned below.

- PostScript

  PostScript is the established printer language on Unix and Linux systems. Many programs produce PostScript output that can then be directly printed by a PostScript printer.

- PCL3, PCL4, PCL5e, PCL6, ESC/P, ESC/P2, and ESC/P raster

  If a PostScript printer is not available, the print filter can use the program Ghostscript to convert PostScript data into one of these other standard printer languages. Ghostscript uses different drivers for different printers to make use of specific features, such as color settings, offered by the various models as much as possible.

Processing a Print Job

1. The user or an application generates a new print job.
2. The print data is temporarily stored in the print queue. The print spooler sends it from there to the printer filter.
3. Now the printer filter performs the following steps:
   (a) It determines the type of print data.
   (b) The print data is converted into PostScript, if not in PostScript already. ASCII text, for example, is normally converted into PostScript by the filter program a2ps.

(c) If necessary, the PostScript data is converted to another printer language.
   - If the printer is a PostScript model, the PostScript data is sent directly to the printer.
   - If the printer is not a PostScript model, Ghostscript uses a driver suitable for the respective printer to generate the printer-specific data that is subsequently sent to the printer.

4. After the entire print job has been sent to the printer, the print spooler removes the print job from the print queue.

Available Printing Systems

SUSE LINUX supports two different printing systems:

LPRng and lpdfilter This is a traditional printing system that consists of the print spooler LPRng and the printer filter lpdfilter. The entire configuration of this printing system is left to the system administrator. Regular users can only choose between the different print queues that have already been set up. To allow users to choose between different options for a given printer, a number of print queues must be defined, each with a different printer configuration.

CUPS In the CUPS printing system, users can determine individual printing settings, as the entire configuration of a queue is not defined by the system administrator. Rather, printer-specific settings are stored in a PPD (PostScript Printer Description) file for each queue and can be offered to users in a print dialog.

Because of conflicts between these two printing systems, you cannot have both installed at the same time. More information about CUPS is available at `http://www.cups.org/` and in the Administration Guide.

Queues

In most cases, more than one print queue is required. Different printer devices must be addressed through different print queues. The printer filter can be configured differently for each print queue. By having different queues for one printer, it can be operated with a different set of options. However, this is not required when using the CUPS printing system, because CUPS allows users to set options individually for each print job.

One standard configuration is sufficient for plain black-and-white printers, such as most laser printers. However, color ink jet printers usually require at least two configurations (two queues):

- A standard `lp` configuration for quick and inexpensive black-and-white printouts.
- A `color` queue for color printing.

Supported Printers

Because most Linux printer drivers are not written by the maker of the hardware, it is crucial that the printer can be driven through one of the generally known languages. Normal printers understand at least one of these common languages. In the case of a GDI printer, however, the manufacturer has built a device that relies on its own special control sequences. Many inexpensive ink jet models belong to this group. Such a printer only runs out of the box under the versions of the operating systems for which the manufacturer has included a driver. As the device cannot be operated through one of the standard languages, it cannot be used with Linux or can only be used with difficulties.

Nevertheless, a number of these printers are supported by SUSE LINUX. However, their use is often rather problematic and some features might not be available at all, for example, the printer could be limited to low resolution monochrome printing. The following list includes the GDI models that can be directly configured with YaST. Because SUSE does not test GDI printers, there is no guarantee that the list is correct.

- Brother HL 720/730/820/1020/1040, MFC 4650/6550MC/9050, and compatible models
- HP DeskJet 710/712/720/722/820/1000 and compatible models
- Lexmark 1000/1020/1100/2030/2050/2070/3200/5000/5700/7000/7200, Z11/42/43/51/52, and compatible models:
  Linux drivers from Lexmark are available at
  `http://www.lexmark.com/printers/linuxprinters.html`.
- Oki Okipage 4w/4w+/6w/8w/8wLite/8z/400w and compatible models
- Samsung ML-200/210/1000/1010/1020/1200/1210/1220/4500/5080/6040 and compatible models

To our knowledge, the following GDI printers are not supported by SUSE LINUX. This list is by no means complete.

- Brother DCP-1000, MP-21C, WL-660

- Canon BJC 5000/5100/8000/8500, LBP 460/600/660/800, MultiPASS L6000
- Epson AcuLaser C1000, EPL 5500W/5700L/5800L
- HP LaserJet 1000/3100/3150
- Lexmark Z12/22/23/31/32/33/82, Winwriter 100/150c/200
- Minolta PagePro 6L/1100L/18L, Color PagePro L, Magicolor 6100DeskLaser/2DeskLaserPlus/2DeskLaserDuplex
- Nec SuperScript 610plus/660/660plus
- Oki Okijet 2010
- Samsung ML 85G/5050G, QL 85G
- Sharp AJ 2100, AL 1000/800/840/F880/121

Configuration with YaST2

To set up a printer, go to 'Hardware' in the YaST Control Center then select 'Printer'. This opens the main printer configuration window in which the detected devices are listed in the upper part. The lower part lists any queues already configured. If your printer was not detected, restart the autodetection. If it fails again, select 'Configure' to configure the printer manually. Not every printer can be configured for both printing systems. Certain configurations are only supported by either CUPS or LPRng and lpdfilter. YaST informs you about this whenever necessary.

Note

In SUSE LINUX, the default printing system is CUPS, but you can switch from CUPS to LPRng and back at any time. To do so, select 'Change' -> 'Advanced' in the YaST printer configuration module. Then select either printing system and configure it.

Note

Automatic Configuration

YaST configures the printer automatically if these requirements are met:

1. The parallel or USB port can be set up automatically in the correct way and the connected printer can be autodetected.

2. The ID string of the printer, as supplied to YaST during hardware autodetection, is included in the printer database. As this ID may be different from the actual name of the model, you may need to select the model manually.

To make sure everything works properly, each configuration should be checked with the print test function of YaST. The YaST test page also provides important information about the configuration selected.

Manual Configuration

If one of the requirements for automatic configuration is not met or if you want a custom setup, configure the printer manually. Depending on how successful the autodetection is and how much information about the printer model is found in the database, YaST may be able to determine the right settings automatically or at least make a reasonable preselection.

The following parameters must be configured:

Hardware Connection (Port) The configuration of the hardware connection depends on whether YaST has been able to find the printer during hardware autodetection.

- If YaST is able to detect the printer model automatically, it can be assumed that the printer connection works on the hardware level and no settings need to be changed in this respect.
- If YaST is unable to autodetect the printer model, there may be some problem on the hardware level and some manual intervention is required to configure the connection. To learn about the steps involved in this, refer to the Administration Guide.

Name of the Queue The queue name is used when issuing print commands. The name should be relatively short and consist of lowercase letters and numbers only.

Ghostscript Driver or Printer Language (Printer Model)
The Ghostscript driver and the printer language depend on your printer model. YaST lets you select a predefined configuration suitable for the model. Selecting a manufacturer and a model basically means selecting a printer language and a Ghostscript driver suitable for this language with some default settings for the driver. These settings may then be changed in an additional dialog as needed.

For non-PostScript models, all printer-specific data is produced by the Ghostscript driver. The driver configuration — both choosing the right driver and the correct options for it — is the single most important factor determining the output quality. The settings made at this point affect the printout on a queue-by-queue basis.

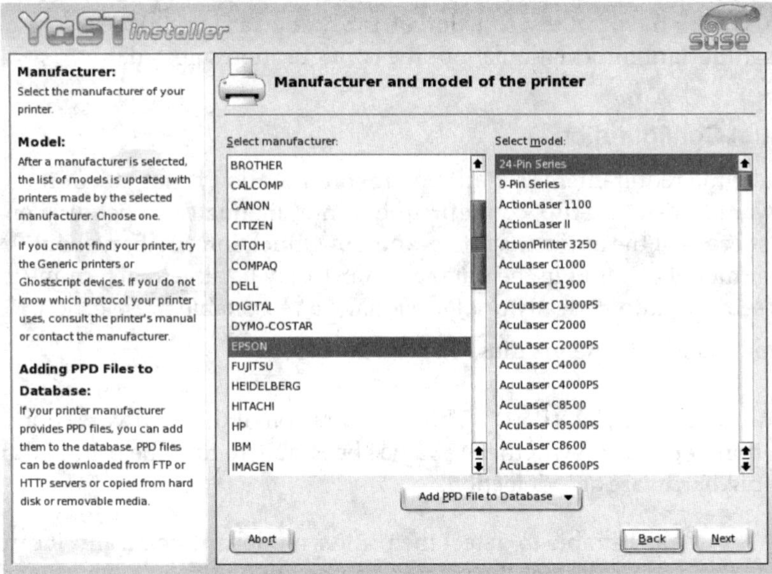

Figure 4.8: Selecting the Printer

If your printer was autodetected (using the printer database) or if the model has been selected manually, YaST presents a choice of suitable Ghostscript drivers, usually with a number of predefined configurations for each of them, for instance:

- monochrome
- color 300 dpi
- photo 600 dpi

A predefined configuration includes a suitable Ghostscript driver and, if available, a set of options for the driver related to output quality. Not all selectable combinations of driver settings work with every printer model. This is especially true for higher resolutions. Always check whether your settings work as expected by printing the test page. If the output is garbled, for example, with several pages almost empty, you should be able to stop the printer by first removing all paper then stopping the print test from YaST. However, in some cases the printer will refuse to resume work if you do so. It may then be better to stop the print test first and wait for the printer to eject all pages by itself.

If the printer model is not listed in the printer database, YaST offers a selection of standard drivers for the standard printer languages.

Advanced Settings Use this dialog to access some additional hardware-dependent (driver-specific) and hardware-independent options. If needed, change special queue settings or restrict access to the printer. However, normally there should be no need change anything here. Details about the possible settings are provided in the printing chapter of the Administration Guide.

Configuration for Applications

Applications rely on the existing printer queues in the same way as any command-line tools do. There is usually no need to reconfigure the printer for a particular application and you should be able to print from applications using the available queues.

Printing from the Command Line Print from the command line using the command `lpr -Plp filename`, where `filename` is the name of the file to send to the printer. In this example, the default printer queue `lp` is used, but the `-P` option allows you to specify another queue. For instance, the command `lpr -Pcolor filename` tells the printing system to use the `color` queue.

Using the LPRng Printing System With this printing system, applications use the `lpr` command for printing. In the application, select the name of an existing queue (such as `color`) or enter the respective print command (such as `lpr -Pcolor`) in the print dialog of the application.

Using the CUPS Printing System The CUPS printing system provides command-line tools, such as the `lpr` command, so the approach as described above works with CUPS, too. To enable the above for KDE programs, it is necessary to use the 'Print through an external program' option in the print dialog. There are also several graphical tools, such as xpp and the KDE program kprinter, which provide a graphical interface to choose among queues and to change both CUPS standard options and printer-specific options as made available through the PPD file.

If desired, configure applications to use kprinter as the standard printing interface by specifying kprinter or kprinter --stdin as the printing command in the respective dialogs of these applications. Which of the two commands to use depends on the behavior of the application itself. If this is set up correctly, the application should call the kprinter dialog whenever a print job is issued from it, so you can use kprinter to select the queue and to set other options. This requires that the application's own print setup does not conflict with that of kprinter and that the setup is left unchanged after kprinter has been enabled.

Troubleshooting

If there is some kind of error in the communication between the computer and the printer, the printer may no longer be able to interpret data correctly. This can cause the output to be garbled and use up large amounts of paper.

1. To stop the printing, take out all paper or open the paper trays.
2. As the print job will be removed from the printer queue only after having been sent completely to the printer, it will usually still be there. Even a reboot will not remove it. To delete the print job, use a tool like kprinter. Instructions for managing print jobs from the command line are provided in the Administration Guide.
3. It is possible that some data is still transmitted to the printer even though the print job has been deleted from the queue. To stop all processes still using the printer device, use the `fuser` command. For a printer connected to the first parallel port, enter `fuser -k /dev/lp0`. To achieve the same for a USB printer, enter `fuser -k /dev/usb/lp0`.
4. Do a complete reset of the printer by switching it off. Wait a few seconds before putting the paper back into the trays and switching the device back on. The printer should now be ready to accept new jobs.

For More Information

Details about the Linux printing systems are provided in the printing chapter in the Administration Guide, which should already be installed on your system. To read the manual, start SuSE Help and click Administration Guide. The PDF file is also available in `/usr/share/doc/packages/suselinux-reference_en` and can be opened with a browser.

If you have problems with your printer, check the Support Database articles *Installing a Printer* and *Printer Configuration with SuSE Linux 9.0 and Later*, which you can find by searching for the keyword installation or online at:

`http://sdb.suse.de/de/sdb/html/jsmeix_print-einrichten.html`

`http://sdb.suse.de/de/sdb/html/jsmeix_print-einrichten-82.html`

The most important problems are summarized in a central article:
`http://portal.suse.de/sdb/en/2004/02/bugs91.html`

4.4.3 Hard Disk Controller

Normally YaST configures the hard disk controller of your system during the installation. If you add controllers, integrate these into the system with this YaST module. You can also modify the existing configuration, but this is generally not necessary.

The dialog presents a list of detected hard disk controllers and enables the assignment of the suitable kernel module with specific parameters. Use 'Test Loading of Module' to check if the current settings work before they are saved permanently in the system.

Caution

This is an expert tool. Do not modify the settings unless you know what you are doing. Your system may no longer boot if you make incorrect settings. In any case, you should make use of the test option.

Caution

4.4.4 Graphics Card and Monitor (SaX2)

The graphical user interface, or X server, handles the communication between hardware and software. Desktops, like KDE and GNOME, and the wide variety of window managers use the X server for interaction with the user.

The graphical user interface is initially configured during installation. To change the settings afterwards, run this YaST module. In the configuration dialog, choose between 'Text Mode Only' and the graphical user interface. The current settings are saved and you can reset to them at any time. The current values are displayed and offered for modification: the screen resolution, the color depth, the refresh rate, and the vendor and type of your monitor, if it was autodetected. If you have just installed a new graphics card, a small dialog appears asking whether to activate 3D acceleration for your graphics card.

Click 'Edit'. SaX2, the configuration tool for the input and display devices, is started in a separate window. This window is shown in Figure 4.9.

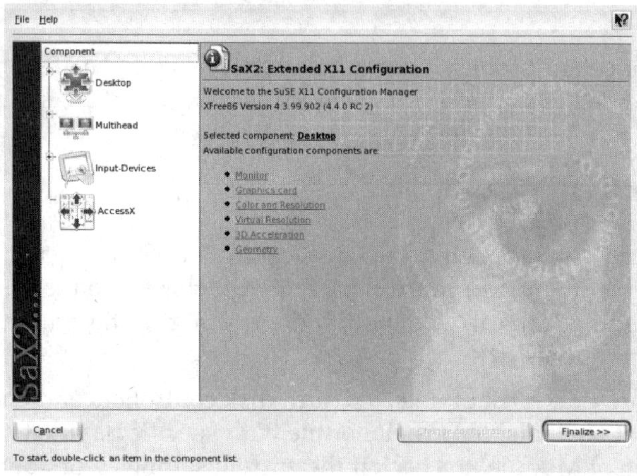

Figure 4.9: *The Main Window of the New SaX2*

SaX2 — Main Window

In the left navigation bar, there are four main items: 'Display', 'Input devices', 'Multihead', and 'AccessX'. Configure your monitor, graphics card, color depth, resolution, and the position and size of the screen under 'Display'. The keyboard, mouse, touchscreen monitor, and graphics tablet can be configured under 'Input devices'. Use 'Multihead' to configure multiple screens (see Section 4.4.4 on page 85). 'AccessX' is a useful tool for controlling the mouse pointer with the number pad.

Select your monitor and graphics card. Usually, the monitor and graphics card are autodetected by the system. In this case, no manual settings are required.

If your monitor is not autodetected, you will automatically be taken to the monitor selection dialog. Select your monitor from the extensive list of vendors and devices or manually enter the monitor values specified in the monitor manual. Alternatively, select one of the preconfigured VESA modes.

After you click 'Finish' in the main window following the completion of the settings for your monitor and your graphics card, test your settings. This ensures that your configuration is suitable for your devices. If the image is not steady, terminate the test immediately by pressing (Esc) and reduce the refresh rate or the resolution and color depth. Regardless of whether you run a test, all modifications are only activated when you restart the X server.

Display

With 'Edit configuration' -> 'Properties', a window with the tabs 'Monitor', 'Frequencies', and 'Expert' appears.

- 'Monitor' — In the left part of the window, select the vendor. In the right part, select your model. If you have floppy disks with Linux drivers for your monitor, install these by clicking 'Driver disk'.
- 'Frequencies' — Here, enter the horizontal and vertical frequencies for your screen. The vertical frequency is another designation for the image refresh rate. Normally, the acceptable value ranges are read from the model and entered here. Usually, they do not need to be changed.
- 'Expert' — Here, enter some options for your screen. In the upper selection field, define the method to use for the calculation of the screen resolution and screen geometry. Do not change anything unless the monitor is addressed incorrectly and the display is not stable. Furthermore, you can change the size of the displayed image and activate the power saving mode DPMS.

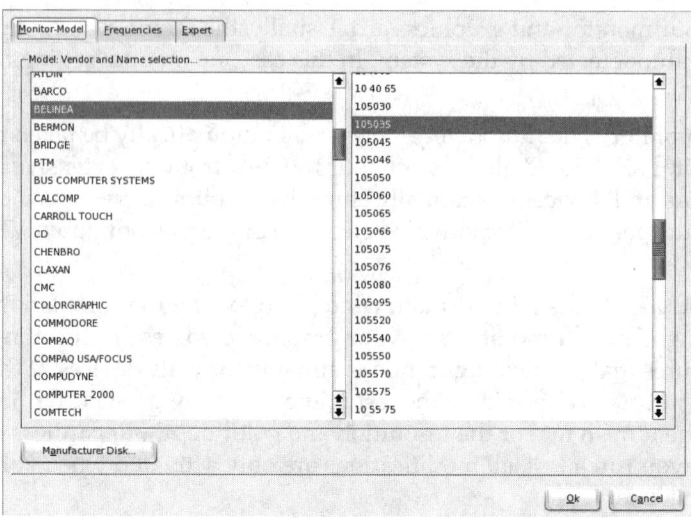

Figure 4.10: Monitor Selection

Caution

There are safety mechanisms, but you should still be very careful when manually changing the allowed frequencies. False values may destroy your monitor. If in doubt, refer to the manual of the monitor.

Caution

Graphics Card

The graphics card dialog has two tabs: 'General' and 'Expert'. In 'General', select the vendor of your graphics card on the left side and the model on the right.

'Expert' offers more advanced configuration possibilities. On the right side, turn your screen to the left or to a vertical position (useful for some turnable TFT screens). The entries for the BusID are only relevant if you operate several screens. Normally, nothing needs to be changed here. You should not modify the card options unless you have experience in this field and know what the options mean. If necessary, check the documentation of your graphics card.

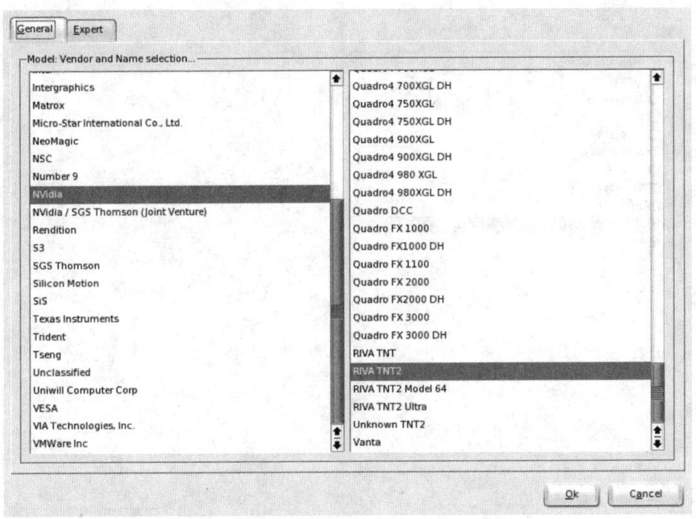

Figure 4.11: Selecting the Graphics Card

Colors and Resolutions

Here, three tabs, 'Colors', 'Resolution', and 'Expert', are available.

- 'Colors' — Depending on the hardware used, select a color depth of 16, 256, 32768, 65536, or 16.7 million colors (4, 8, 15, 16, or 24 bit). For a reasonable display quality, set at least 256 colors.
- 'Resolution' — When the hardware is detected, the resolution is queried. Therefore, the module usually only offers resolution and color depth combinations that your hardware can display correctly. This keeps the danger of damaging your hardware with incorrect settings very low in SUSE LINUX. If you change the resolution manually, consult the documentation of your hardware to make sure the value set can be displayed.
- 'Expert' — In addition to the resolutions offered in the previous tab, this tab enables you to add your own resolutions, which will subsequently be included for selection in the tab.

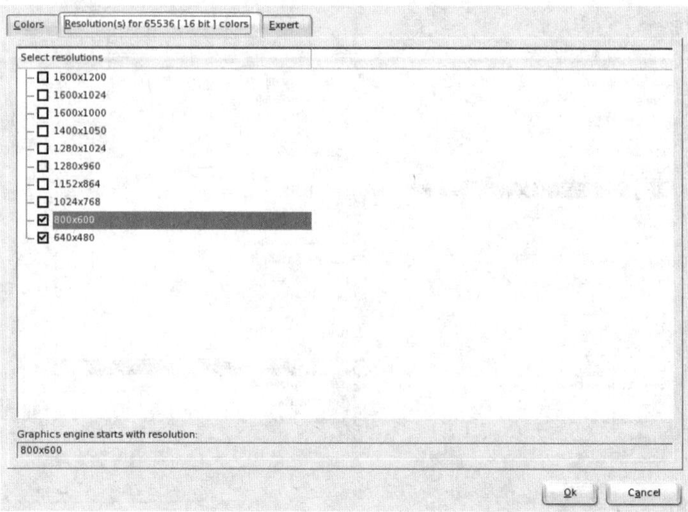

Figure 4.12: Configuring the Resolution

Virtual Resolution

Every desktop has a certain resolution that is displayed over the full screen of the monitor. Additionally, it is possible to set the resolution larger than the visible area of the screen. If you move the mouse beyond the margins of the desktop, the virtual part of the desktop is displayed on screen. This increases the available work space.

The virtual resolution can be set in two different ways:

- 'By Drag&Drop' – Move the mouse pointer over the monitor image and the mouse will turn into crosshairs. Keep the left mouse button pressed and move the mouse to enlarge the raster image, which corresponds with the virtual resolution. This method is best if you are not quite sure how much virtual space you want on your desktop.
- 'By selection from the pop-up menu' — In the pop-up menu in the middle of the raster image, the currently used virtual resolution is displayed. To use one of the default virtual resolutions, select one from the menu.

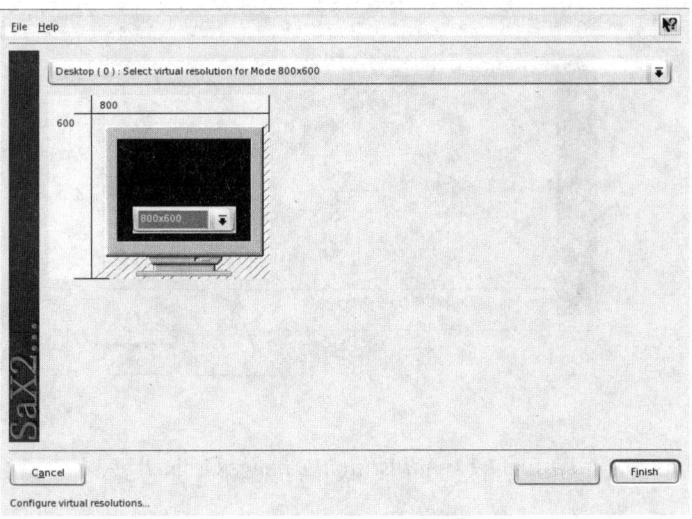

Figure 4.13: Configuring the Virtual Resolution

3D Acceleration

Optionally, activate the 3D acceleration of your graphics card. A dialog is displayed in which to activate the 3D properties of your graphics card.

Image Position and Size

Under these two tabs, precisely adjust the size and the position of the image with the arrows. See Figure 4.14 on the next page. If you have a multihead environment (more than one screen), use 'Next screen' to switch to the other monitors to adjust their size and position. Press 'Save' to save your settings.

Multihead

If you have installed more than one graphics card in your computer or a graphics card with multiple outputs, you can connect more than one screen to your system. If you operate two screens, this is referred to as *dualhead*. More than two is referred to as *multihead*. SaX2 automatically detects multiple graphics cards in the system and prepares the configuration accordingly. Set the multihead mode and the arrangement of the screens in the

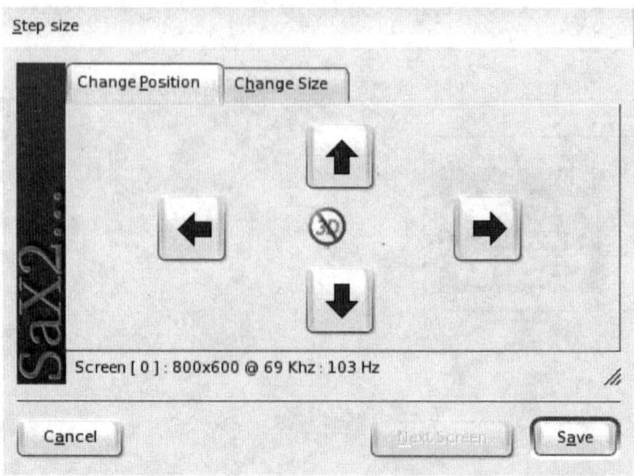

Figure 4.14: Adjusting the Image Geometry

multihead dialog. Three modes are offered: 'Traditional' (default), 'One screen (Xinerama)', and 'Clone mode'.

- 'Traditional multihead' — Each monitor represents an individual unit. The mouse pointer can switch between the screens.
- 'Cloned multihead' — In this mode, all monitors display the same contents. The mouse is only visible on the main screen.
- 'Xinerama multihead' — All screens combine to form a single large screen. Program windows can be positioned freely on all screens or scaled to a size that fills more than one monitor.

The layout of a multihead environment describes the arrangement of and the relationship between the individual screens. By default, SaX2 configures a standard layout that follows the sequence of the detected graphics cards, arranging all screens in a row from left to right. In the 'Layout' dialog of the multihead tool, determine the way the monitors are arranged by using the mouse to move the screen symbols in the grid. After you have completing the layout dialog, verify the new configuration by clicking 'Test'.

Linux currently does not offer 3D support for Xinerama multihead environments. In this case, SaX2 deactivates the 3D support.

Input Devices

Mouse If the mouse already works, you do not need to do anything. However, if the mouse does not work, control it with the number pad of the keyboard as described in Section 4.4.4 on the following page. If the automatic detection fails, use this dialog to configure your mouse manually. Refer to the documentation of your mouse for a description of the model. Select your model from the list of supported mouse types and confirm by pressing ⑤ on the number pad.

Keyboard Use the selection field at the top of this dialog to specify the kind of keyboard to use. Then select the language for the keyboard layout (the country-specific position of the keys). Use the test field to check if special characters are displayed correctly. The status of the check box used for activating and deactivating the entry of accented letters depends on the respective language and does not need to be changed. Click 'Finish' to apply the new settings to your system.

Touchscreen Currently, XFree86 only supports Microtouch and Elo TouchSystems touchscreens. SaX2 can only autodetect the monitor, not the toucher. The toucher is treated as an input device. To configure the toucher, start SaX2 and select 'Input devices' -> 'Touchscreens'. Click 'Add' and add a touchscreen. Save the configuration by clicking 'Finish'. You do not need to test the configuration. Touchscreens feature a variety of options and usually must be calibrated first. Unfortunately, there is no general tool for this purpose in Linux. The standard configuration contains suitable default values for the dimensions of the touchscreen. Normally, no additional configuration is required.

Graphics Tablet Currently, XFree86 only supports a limited number of graphics tablets. SaX2 enables the configuration of graphics tablets connected to the USB port or the serial port. From the configuration perspective, a graphics tablet is just an input device like a mouse. Start SaX2 and select 'Input devices' -> 'Graphics tablet'. Click 'Add', select the vendor from the following dialog, and add a graphics tablet from the selection list. Mark the check boxes to the right if you have connected a pen or eraser. If your tablet is connected to the serial port, verify the port. `/dev/ttyS0` refers to the first serial port. `/dev/ttyS1` refers to the second. Additional ports use similar notation. Save the configuration by clicking 'Finish'.

AccessX

If you do not use a mouse on your computer, start SaX2 and activate AccessX to be able to control the mouse pointer with the keys on the numeric keypad. (See Table 4.1).

Table 4.1: AccessX — Operating the Mouse with the Numeric Keypad

Key	description
÷	selects the left mouse button
×	selects the middle mouse button
−	selects the right mouse button
5	invokes a click event of the previously selected mouse button. The left mouse button is preset if no other button was selected.The selection is reset to its default after the event.
+	acts like 5 except is a double-click event
0	acts like 5 except is a click-and-hold event
Del	releases the click-and-hold event previously invoked with 0
7	moves the cursor toward the upper left
8	moves the cursor straight upwards
9	moves the cursor towards the upper right
4	moves the cursor towards the left
6	moves the cursor towards the right
1	moves the cursor towards the lower left
2	moves the cursor straight downwards
3	moves the cursor towards the lower right

With the slider, set the speed of the mouse pointer movement when a key is pressed.

For More Information

For more information about the X Window System and its properties, refer to the Administration Guide.

4.4.5 Hardware Information

YaST detects hardware for the configuration of hardware components. The detected technical data is displayed in this screen. This is especially useful, for example, if you want to submit a support request for which you need information about your hardware.

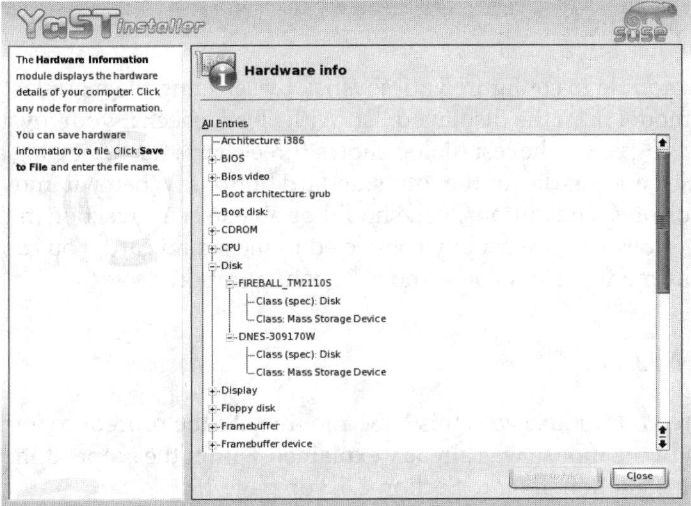

Figure 4.15: Displaying Hardware Information

4.4.6 IDE DMA Mode

With this module, activate and deactivate the DMA mode for your IDE hard disks and your IDE CD and DVD drives in the installed system. This module does not have any effect on SCSI devices. DMA modes can substantially increase the performance and data transfer speed in your system.

During the installation, the current SUSE LINUX kernel automatically activates DMA for hard disks but not for CD drives, as default DMA activation for all drives often caused problems with CD drives. Use the DMA module if you want to activate DMA for your drives. If the drive supports the DMA mode without any problems, the data transfer rate of your drive can be increased by activating DMA.

Note

DMA (Direct Memory Access) means that your data can be transferred directly to the RAM, bypassing the processor control.

Note

4.4.7 Joystick

Use this module to configure your joystick by selecting the manufacturer and the model from the displayed list. With 'Test', check if your joystick responds correctly. The test dialog shows three charts for the analog axes of the joystick and marks for the four standard buttons. When you move the joystick or press the buttons, you should be able to see a reaction in the test dialog. As joysticks are usually connected to the sound card, you can also access this module from the sound card configuration.

4.4.8 Mouse

Configure your mouse with this YaST module. As the procedure for the selection of the mouse was already explained within the scope of the user-defined installation, refer to Section 2.5.3 on page 18.

4.4.9 Scanner

If your scanner is connected and switched on, it should be detected automatically when this YaST module is started. In this case, the dialog for the installation of the scanner appears. If no scanner is detected, the manual configuration dialog appears. If you have already installed one or several scanners, a list of existing scanners that can be modified or deleted is displayed. Press 'Add' to configure a new device.

Next, an installation is performed with default settings. If the installation is successful, a corresponding message will appear. Now, test your scanner by inserting a document and clicking 'Test'.

Scanner Not Detected

Only supported scanners can be autodetected. Scanners connected to another network host will not be detected. The manual configuration distinguishes three types of scanners: USB scanners, SCSI scanners, and network scanners.

- USB scanner: Specify the vendor and model. YaST then attempts to load USB modules. If your scanner is very new, the modules may not be loaded automatically. In this case, continue automatically to a dialog in which to load the USB module manually. Refer to the YaST help text for more information.
- SCSI scanner: Specify the device (such as `/dev/sg0`). SCSI scanners should not be connected or disconnected when the the system is running. Shut the system down first.
- Network scanner: Enter the IP address or the host name.

You can use a scanner that is connected to a host in your network and configured as a network scanner. To configure a network scanner, refer to the Support Database article Scanning in Linux (`http://sdb.suse.de/en/`, keyword scanner). When selecting a network scanner, enter the host name or the IP address of the host to which the scanner is connected.

If your scanner was not detected, the device probably is not supported. However, sometimes even supported scanners are not detected. If that is the case, proceed with the manual scanner selection. If you can identify your scanner in the list of vendors and models, select it. If not, select 'Cancel'. Information about scanners that work with Linux is provided at `http://cdb.suse.de/index.php?LANG=en`, `http://sdb.suse.de/en/`, and `http://www.mostang.com/sane`.

Caution

Only assign the scanner manually if you are absolutely sure. Incorrect selection could damage your hardware.

Caution

Troubleshooting

Your scanner may not have been detected for one of the following reasons:

- The scanner is not supported. Check `http://sdb.suse.de/en/` for a list of Linux-compatible devices.
- Your SCSI controller was not installed correctly.
- There are termination problems with your SCSI port.
- Your SCSI cable is too long.

- Your scanner has a SCSI Light Controller that is not supported by Linux.
- Your scanner is defective.

Caution

SCSI scanners should not be connected or disconnected when the the system is running. Shut the system down first.

Caution

For more information about scanning, refer to Chapter 23 on page 351.

4.4.10 Sound

When the sound configuration tool is started, YaST tries to detect your sound card automatically. Configure one or multiple sound cards. To use multiple sound cards, start by selecting one of the cards to configure. Press 'Configure' to enter the 'Setup' dialog. 'Edit' opens a dialog in which to edit previously configured sound cards. 'Finish' saves the current settings and completes the sound configuration. If YaST is unable to detect your sound card automatically, press 'Add Sound Card' in 'Sound Configuration' to open a dialog in which to select a sound card and module.

Setup

With 'Quick Automatic Setup', you are not required to go through any of the further configuration steps and no sound test is performed. The sound card is configured automatically. With 'Normal Setup', you have the possibility to adjust the output volume and play a test sound. With 'Options', manually customize the sound card options.

Set up your joystick by clicking the respective check box. Select the joystick type in the following dialog and click 'Next'. The same dialog appears when you click 'Joystick' in the YaST Control Center.

Sound Card Volume

Test your sound configuration in this test screen. Use '+' and '–' to adjust the volume. Start at about ten percent to avoid damage to your speakers or hearing. A test sound should be audible when you press 'Test'. If you cannot hear anything, increase the volume. Press 'Continue' to complete the sound configuration. The volume setting will be saved.

Sound Configuration

Use 'Delete' to remove a sound card. Existing entries of configured sound cards are deactivated in the file /etc/modules.conf. Click 'Options' to open a dialog in which to customize the sound module options manually. In 'Volume', configure the individual settings for the input and output of each sound card. 'Next' saves the new values and 'Back' restores the default configuration. Under 'Add Sound Card...', configure additional sound cards. If YaST detects another sound card, continue to 'Configure a Sound Card'. If YaST does not detect a sound card, automatically be directed to 'Manual Sound Card Selection'.

If you use a Creative Soundblaster Live or AWE sound card, automatically copy SF2 sound fonts to your hard disk from the original Soundblaster driver CD-ROM with 'Install Sound Fonts'. The sound fonts will be saved in the directory /usr/share/sfbank/creative/.

Enable or disable the start-up of ALSA when booting the machine with 'Start ALSA'. For playback of MIDI files, activate 'Start Sequencer'. This way, the sound modules required for sequencer support are loaded along with the ALSA modules.

The volume and configuration of all sound cards installed will be saved when you click 'Finish'. The mixer settings are saved to the file /etc/asound.conf and the ALSA configuration data is appended at the end of the file /etc/modules.conf.

Configuring a Sound Card

If multiple sound cards were detected, select your preferred card under 'List of Automatically Recognized...'. Continue to 'Setup' with 'Next'. If the sound card was not automatically detected, click 'Select from List' and, with 'Next', proceed to 'Manual Sound Card Selection'.

Manual Sound Card Selection

If your sound card was not automatically detected, a list of sound card drivers and models are shown from which to choose. With 'All', see the entire list of supported cards.

Refer to your sound card documentation for the information required. A reference list of sound cards supported by ALSA with their corresponding sound modules is available in /usr/share/doc/packages/alsa/cards.txt and at http://www.alsa-project.org/~goemon/. After making your selection, click 'Next' to return to 'Setup'.

4.4.11 TV and Radio Cards

After starting and initializing this YaST module, the 'TV and Radio Cards' dialog appears. If your card was automatically detected, it is displayed at the top of the list. In this case, highlight the line with the mouse and select 'Configure'. If your card was not detected, select 'Other (not recognized)'. Press 'Configure' to proceed with the manual selection in which to select your card from the list of vendors and models.

If you have already configured TV or radio cards, modify existing configurations with 'Change'. In this case, a dialog presents a list of all configured cards. Select a card and start the manual configuration with 'Edit'.

During the automatic hardware detection, YaST attempts to assign the correct tuner to your card. If you are not sure, simply keep the setting 'Default (recognized)' and check whether it works. If you are not able to set all channels, this might be due to a failure of the automatic detection of the tuner type. In this case, click 'Select Tuner' and highlight the correct tuner type in the list.

If you are familiar with the technical details, you can use the expert dialog to specify settings for a TV or radio card. Select a kernel module and its parameters in this dialog. Also check all parameters of your TV card driver. To do this, select the respective parameters and enter the new value in the parameter line. Confirm the new values with 'Apply' or restore the default values with 'Reset'.

The dialog 'TV and Radio Cards, Audio' enables you to connect your TV or radio card with the installed sound card. You must use a cable to connect the output of the TV or radio card with the external audio input of the sound card. This only works if the sound card is already configured and the external input is active. If you have not yet configured your sound card, select 'Configure Sound Card' to go to the respective dialog, described in Section 4.4.10 on page 92.

If your TV or radio card has speaker jacks, you can also connect the speakers directly without configuring the sound card. There are also TV cards without any sound function, which do not require an audio configuration (e.g., for CCD cameras).

4.5 Network Devices

All the machines connected to the Internet form a large network in which various operating systems run with different hardware. The Internet uses a standard communication protocol that can be understood regardless of the hardware or software used. This is made possible by means of the Internet Protocol (IP) together with the Transmission Control Protocol (TCP), the User Datagram Protocol (UDP), and the Internet Control Message Protocol (ICMP). These protocols comprise the common language used by all machines on the Internet. The abbreviation for this is TCP/IP.

Every machine on the Internet has an ID number — the IP address. It can only be addressed by TCP/IP with this number. Normally, a machine also has a text name. The Domain Name System (DNS) is responsible for converting the IP address to a text name. This particular service is offered by name servers. A machine or an application offering a service is called a server (for example, a DNS server) and a machine or application making use of a service is called a client.

Under TCP/IP, there are various standardized protocols for forwarding the appropriate TCP/IP data transfers to the given transmission method. For network connections via a network card, the ethernet protocol is used. For modem and ISDN telephone connections, it is the point-to-point protocol (PPP). For ADSL and T-DSL connections, the point-to-point over ethernet Protocol (PPPoE) is used.

To establish an Internet connection, the ethernet, PPP, or PPPoE connection between your host and a host of the Internet provider must be established first. Then the TCP/IP connection must be established. Various standardized protocols work on top of TCP/IP for proper data transfer to the application:

- The HyperText Transfer Protocol (HTTP) is used for the transfer of web sites in HyperText Markup Language (HTML) format.
- The Simple Mail Transfer Protocol (SMTP) is responsible for sending e-mails to another machine and the Post Office Protocol (POP3) for downloading e-mails from a mail server.
- The File Transfer Protocol (FTP) is used to transfer files.

For several application programs, such as a web browser and an e-mail program, to use the same Internet connection at the same time, separate TCP/IP connections are used for each application. Large amounts of TCP/IP data are also divided into small packets, so HTTP packets from the web browser can be sent over its TCP/IP connection while alternating with SMTP or POP3 packet transfers from the e-mail program via other TCP/IP connections.

As several applications use the same Internet connection, the IP address, which only identifies the machine, is not sufficient. A port number is needed to sort out which TCP/IP data belongs to which application. These standard services are usually provided on servers at the following port numbers:

- DNS on port 53
- HTTP on port 80
- SMTP on port 25 and POP3 on port 110
- FTP on ports 20 and 21

The client can only use services if it addresses the correct port number on the server.

4.5.1 Information about the Internet Dial-Up

If you activate 'Dial on Demand' or 'Automatic Dial-Up' in the YaST modules, the Internet connection is established automatically whenever necessary, for example, when an external URL is entered in the browser or when e-mail is sent and fetched. 'Dial on demand' or 'automatic' is only advisable if you have a flat rate for Internet access. With 'manual', the computer only establishes a connection to the Internet when you want it to do so. Background processes, such as fetching e-mail in regular intervals, frequently establish connections to the Internet, which can be expensive. To connect to the Internet, you can use the KDE program KInternet, described in Section 5.4.1 on page 154.

4.5.2 Network Card

When the YaST module is started, an overview of the network configuration is displayed. The upper part of the dialog lists all network cards that were automatically detected or manually configured. If your card was detected correctly when the system was booted, the name of the card appears here. Devices that were not recognized are listed as 'Other (not detected)'. The lower part of the screen lists configured devices including the network type and the address. You can configure new network cards or modify the configuration of a configured device.

Manual Configuration of the Network Card

Make the following basic settings to configure a network card that was not recognized:

Network Interface Specify the network type and the device number.

Support for Wireless Connections If you are located in a wireless LAN and your network card supports this connection type, use 'Wireless Device' to access the 'Wireless Settings' dialog in which to configure the operating mode, network name (ESSID), network ID (NWID), encryption key, and nickname. Press 'OK' to complete the configuration of your card.

Kernel Module and Selection of the Network Card
If your network card is a PCMCIA or USB device, activate the respective check boxes and exit the dialog with 'Next'. If not, select the network card model with 'Select from list'. YaST automatically selects a suitable kernel module. Exit this dialog with 'Next'.

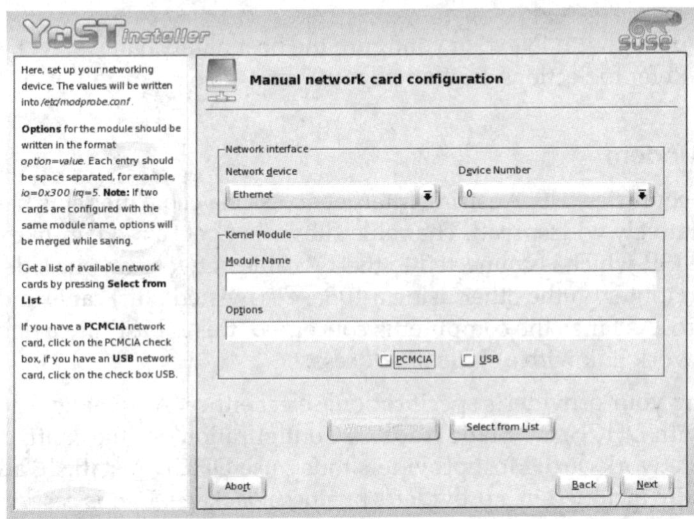

Figure 4.16: Configuration of the Network Card

Configuration of the Network Address

Specify the address assignment method for your network card:

'Automatic Address Setup (with DHCP)'
If a DHCP server exists in your network, automatically retrieve the configuration data for your network card from there. Activate the address assignment with DHCP if your DSL provider has not given you a static IP address for your system. Click 'DHCP Client Options' to access the client configuration. Here, specify whether the DHCP server should always respond to a broadcast. Additionally, you can specify an ID. By default, the host is identified by means of the hardware address of the network card. However, if you have several virtual machines using the same network card, distinguish them by means of various IDs.

'Static Address Configuration' If you have a static IP address, activate the respective check box. Enter the IP address and the correct subnet mask for your network. The preset value for the subnet mask should meet the requirements of a typical home network.

Exit this dialog with 'Next' or configure the host name, name server, and routing. Refer to Sections 4.6.1 on page 107 and 4.6.6 on page 109.

Cable Modem

In some countries (US, Austria), Internet access via cable modems has become relatively widespread. The cable subscriber gets a modem-like device from the ISP, which is connected to the TV cable network on one side and to the computer on the other using a 10BaseT (twisted pair) cable and a network card. As far as the computer is concerned, this is basically a permanent network link with a static IP address.

Following your provider's specification, select either 'Automatic Address Setup (with DHCP)' or 'Static Address Configuration' for the configuration of your network card. Most providers today use DHCP. A static IP address is generally included in a provider's business package. In this case, the provider should have assigned a static IP address. Regarding the setup and configuration of cable modems, refer to the Support Database article available online at `http://sdb.suse.de/en/sdb/html/cmodem8.html`.

4.5.3 Modem

In the YaST Control Center, the modem configuration is available under 'Network Devices'. If the autodetection fails, select the manual configuration. In the dialog that opens, enter the port under 'Device'.

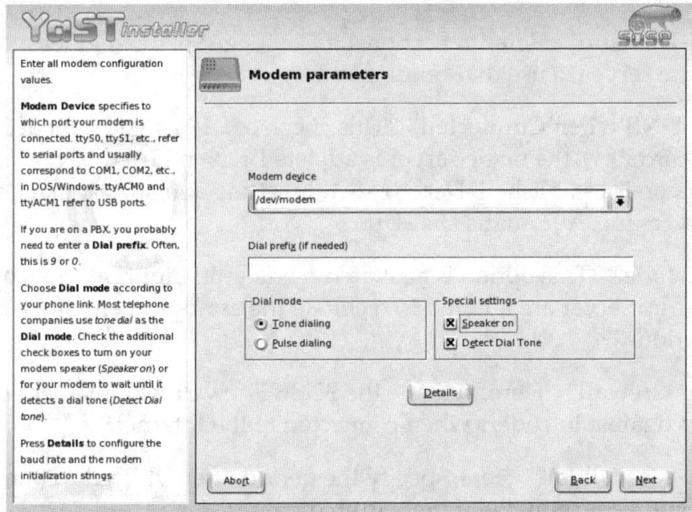

Figure 4.17: *Modem Configuration*

If a PBX is interposed, you may need to enter an extra number to dial external numbers (usually a zero, but you can find this out in the operation instructions for your telephone system). Also decide between tone and pulse dialing, whether the speaker should be switched on, and whether it should wait for the dial tone. The last option should not be used if your modem is connected to a PBX.

The baud rate and the initialization string settings for the modem can be specified under 'Details'. Only make changes if your modem has not automatically been recognized and special settings must be made for data transfer. This is primarily the case for ISDN terminal adapters. Exit this dialog with 'OK'.

Select the ISP (Internet Service Provider) in the following dialog. To select your provider from a list of preconfigured providers in your country, activate 'Countries'. Configure the ISP parameters manually by pressing 'New'. In the dialog that opens, enter the name of the dial-up connection, the provider, and the provider's phone number. Furthermore, enter the user name and the password assigned by your provider. Activate 'Always ask for password' to be prompted for the password every time a connection is established.

Enter the connection parameters in the final dialog:

'Dial-on-Demand' Refer to Section 4.5.1 on page 96. Enter at least one name server to use dial-on-demand.

'Modify DNS when Connected' This check box is activated by default. Accordingly, the name server is adjusted each time a dial-up connection is established. Deactivate this setting and specify static name servers for 'Automatic Dial-Up'.

'Stupid Mode' This option is activated by default. Input prompts by the dial-up server are ignored to facilitate the establishment of the connection.

'Activate Firewall' Here, activate the SUSE Firewall to implement protection against intruders when connected to the Internet.

'Idle Time (seconds)' Here, specify the period after which the connection should be terminated if there is no data transfer.

IP Details With this button, enter the address configuration dialog. If your provider has not assigned a dynamic IP address, deactivate 'Dynamic IP Address' and enter the local IP address of your host and the remote IP address. Contact your provider for information about these settings. Leave the 'Default Route' setting active and exit the dialog with 'OK'.

Press 'Next' to return to the overview and view the configuration. Complete the configuration with 'Finish'.

4.5.4 DSL

The YaST module 'DSL' in the category 'Network Devices' is designed for the configuration of DSL. Several dialogs enable you to enter the data for your DSL access. YaST supports the configuration of DSL based on the following protocols:

- PPP over ethernet (PPPoE) — Germany

- PPP over ATM (PPPoATM) — England
- CAPI for ADSL (Fritz cards)
- Tunnel protocol for point-to-point (PPTP) — Austria

The configuration of your DSL access with PPPoE and PPTP is only possible if your network card is configured correctly. If this has not been done, select 'Configure Network Cards' to access the dialog for configuring your network card. See Figure 4.5.2 on page 96. The DHCP protocol is not used for the automatic assignment of IP addresses for DSL. Therefore, do not use 'Automatic address setup (with DHCP)'. Instead, use a static dummy IP address like `192.168.22.1`. In 'Subnet mask', enter `255.255.255.0`. For a stand-alone system, do not make any entries in the 'Default gateway' field.

Note

The values for the 'IP address' of your host and 'Subnet mask' are merely placeholders. They are not used for establishing a connection with DSL and are only needed for activating the network card.

Note

At the beginning of the configuration, as shown in Figure 4.18 on the following page, select the PPP mode and the ethernet card to which your modem is connected (usually `eth0`). With'Device Activation', determine whether the DSL connection should be established automatically when the system is booted or established manually. Subsequently, select your country and provider. The contents of the following dialogs depend on the previously selected settings. If you are not sure about some options, read the detailed help texts in the dialogs.

To use 'Dial on demand' (see Section 4.5.1 on page 96) for a stand-alone system, configure a DNS server. Today, most providers support dynamic DNS assignment, so a valid IP address of the name server is provided each time a connection is established. Nevertheless, a suitable dummy DNS must be entered in this dialog, such as `192.168.22.99`. If you are not dynamically assigned a name server, specify the IP addresses of your provider's name server here.

'Idle time-out (seconds)' allows you to set an idle time after which the connection is terminated automatically. A value between 60 and 300 seconds is recommended.

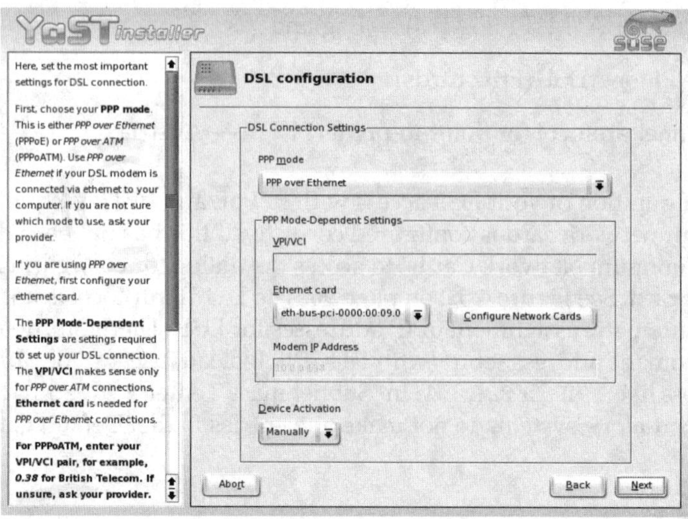

Figure 4.18: *DSL Configuration*

Note

If you select 'Dial on Demand', the connection is not terminated completely after the time-out, but remains in a standby mode that enables the automatic establishment of a connection as soon as data needs to be transferred. If you do not use 'Dial on Demand', the connection is terminated completely, requiring the manual establishment of a connection before data can be transmitted. For this case, block automatic establishment of a connection by setting the idle time to 0.

Note

The configuration of T-DSL (German Telecom) is similar to ADSL. If you select the provider 'T-Online', continue automatically to the configuration dialog for T-DSL. Furthermore, you need the connection ID, T-Online number, user ID, and personal password specified in your T-DSL registration documents.

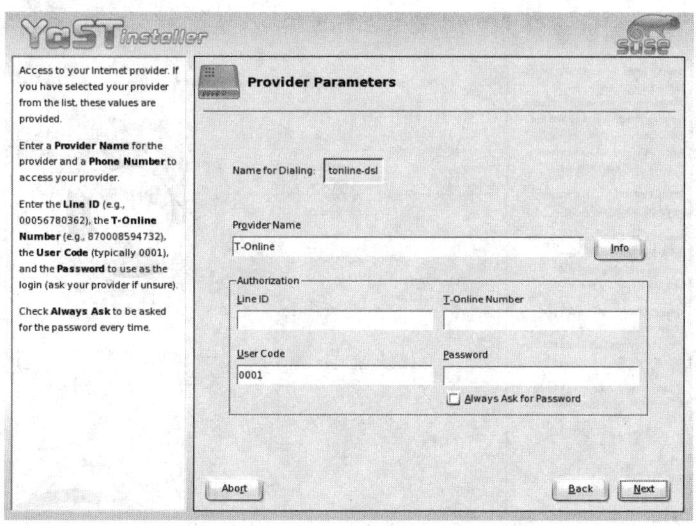

Figure 4.19: *T-DSL Configuration in Germany*

4.5.5 ISDN

This module enables the configuration of one or several ISDN cards in your system. If the ISDN card is not automatically detected by YaST, select the card manually. Theoretically, you can configure several interfaces. However, this is usually not necessary for home users, as several providers can be configured for one interface. The following dialogs provide for the configuration of the various ISDN parameters for operating the card.

The next dialog, shown in Figure 4.20 on the following page, is used for the 'Selection of ISDN protocol'. The standard setting for Europe is 'Euro-ISDN (EDSS1)' (refer to scenarios 1 and 2a below). '1TR6' is a protocol used by older or large phone systems (refer to scenario 2b below). The standard setting for the US is 'NI1'. Select the country code from the selection box. In the adjacent input field, enter the area code for your location (e.g., 212 for New York). If necessary, enter the prefix for external calls.

Use 'Start Mode' to set the start mode for the current ISDN card. 'On Boot' initializes the ISDN driver to when the system is booted. With 'Manual', the ISDN driver must be initialized manually by the user `root` with `rcisdn start`. 'Hotplug' loads the driver when the PCMCIA card or USB device is connected. Complete all settings and click 'OK'.

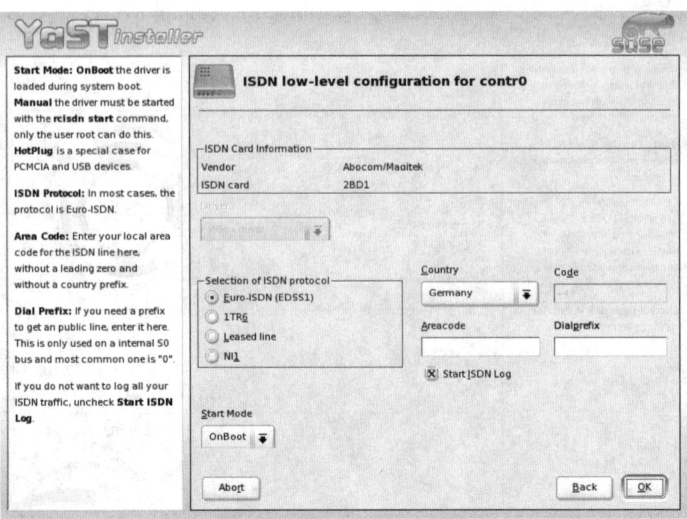

Figure 4.20: ISDN Configuration

In the following dialog, define the interface for your ISDN card or add further providers to existing interfaces. Set up the interfaces with the `SyncPPP` or `RawIP` modes. Most Internet providers use `SyncPPP`, which is described below.

Depending on the connection scenario, specify one of the following for 'Your Phone Number':

1. **The ISDN card is connected directly to the socket**

   By default, ISDN offers three numbers (MSN — multiple subscriber number). On request, up to ten numbers can be made available for your line. Assign one of the MSN numbers to your ISDN card. Enter the number without the prefix. If you enter an incorrect number, your telecom provider will automatically use the first MSN assigned to your ISDN line.

2. **The ISDN card is connected to a PBX**

   Various specifications are required depending on the constellation.

   (a) For private use: Usually the Euro-ISDN or EDSS1 protocol is used for the internal ports of small phone systems. These phone

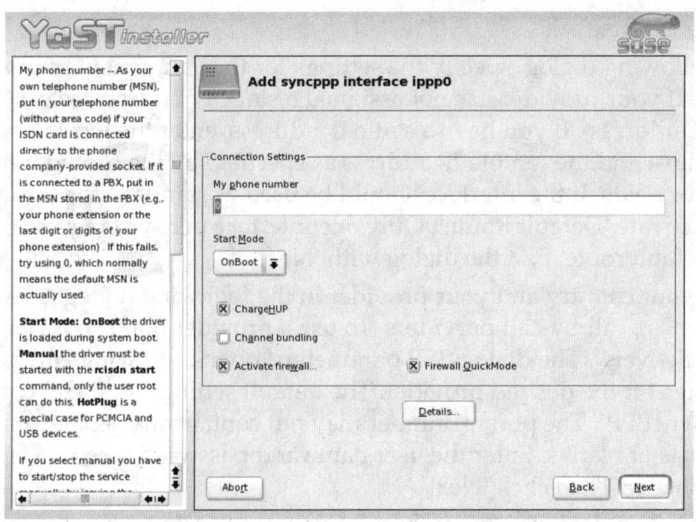

***Figure 4.21:** ISDN Interface Configuration*

systems use an internal S0 bus and use internal numbers for the connected devices.

Use one of the internal numbers to specify the MSN. One of the MSNs of your phone system should work, provided external access is possible with this MSN. As a final resort, a single zero might work. For more information, refer to the documentation of your phone system.

(b) For commercial use: Normally, the 1TR6 protocol is used for the internal ports of large phone systems. Here, the MSN is called EAZ and is usually the extension. For the Linux configuration, the last digit of the EAZ is normally sufficient. If this does not work, try the digits 1 to 9.

By means of a check box, determine whether existing connections should be terminated prior to the next charge increment ('ChargeHUP'). However, this does not yet work with all providers. For 'Channel bundling' (multi-link PPP), activate the respective check box. To start SUSEfirewall2, mark 'Activate firewall'.

'Details' opens a dialog that enables the implementation of more complex connection scenarios. Normal home users do not need this dialog. Exit the dialog with 'Next'.

In the following dialog, specify the settings for the assignment of the IP address. If your provider has not assigned a static IP address, select 'Dynamic IP address'. If you have a static IP address, enter the local IP address of your host and the remote IP address as specified by the provider in the respective fields. If the interface should be used as standard route to the Internet, activate 'Default Route'. Only one interface per system can be used as the default route. Exit the dialog with 'Next'.

Specify your country and your provider in the following dialog. The listed providers are call-by-call providers. To use a provider that is not listed here, click 'New'. The dialog 'ISP parameters' opens, allowing entry of all settings for the desired provider. The default setting for 'ISDN type' is 'ISDN SyncPPP'. The phone number may not contain any separators, such as commas or blanks. Enter the user name and password received from your provider. Then click 'Next'.

To use 'Dial on demand' (see page 4.5.1 on page 96) if you have a standalone system, enter a name server. Most providers today support dynamic DNS assignment, so a current IP address is forwarded to the name server each time the connection is set up. However, a suitable dummy name server IP must be entered in this dialog, for example, `192.168.22.99`. If you do not receive a dynamic name server assignment, enter the IP addresses of the name servers of your provider here. Also set the time after which the connection should be terminated automatically if no data exchange has occurred. Finally, confirm your settings with 'Next' to continue to the overview of the configured interfaces. Activate your settings with 'Finish'.

4.6 Network Services

This group mostly contains tools for professionals and system administrators. If you have SUSE LINUX Personal Edition, some of the tools covered in this section are not available, as they are only installed in the Professional Edition.

Note

The tools 'LDAP Client', 'NIS Server', 'NIS Client', 'NIS+ Client', and 'Proxy' are not addressed here, as these are genuine expert tools that are usually only used in company networks. More information about these modules is provided in the Administration Guide.

Note

4.6.1 Host Name and DNS

The host name and the domain name can be changed here. If the provider has been configured correctly for DSL, modem, or ISDN access, the list of name servers contains entries made automatically, as they were extracted from the provider data. If you are located in a local network you might receive your host name via DHCP, in which case you should not modify the name.

4.6.2 NFS Client and NFS Server

You need these two tools only if you are located in a network. In this case, you have the possibility to operate a file server that can be accessed by members of your network. On this file server, you can make programs, files, or storage space available for users. Use the 'NFS Server' module to set up your computer as an NFS server and to determine the directories to export for use by the network users. The NFS server should be set up by an expert. To configure an NFS server, refer to the brief instructions in the Administration Guide.

Subsequently, any user (with the needed permissions) can mount these directories in his own file tree. The easiest way to do this is by means of the 'NFS Client' module in which the user merely needs to enter the host name of the computer acting as NFS server and the mount point on his computer. To do this, select 'Add' in the first dialog and enter the needed data. See Figure 4.22.

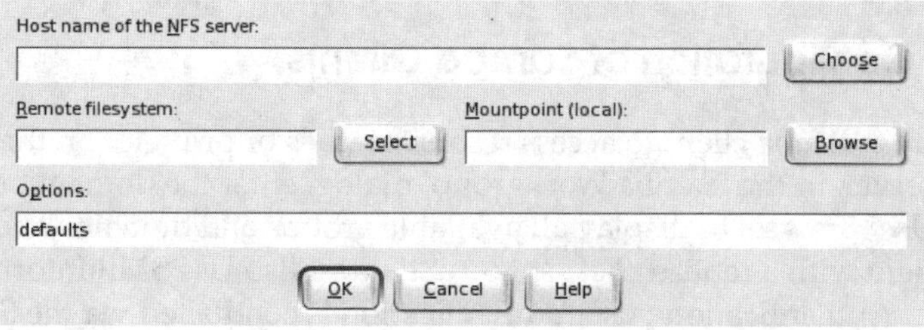

Figure 4.22: Configuration of NFS Clients

4.6.3 Configuration of a Samba Server

Set up a Samba server to share resources such as files or printers with Windows hosts. In the first dialog, define the role of the Samba server. You can deactivate it, use it as a file and print server, or use it as a backup or primary domain controller. A file and print server makes directories and printers available. A domain controller enables its clients to log in to a Windows domain. The primary domain controller manages users and passwords. A backup domain controller uses another domain controller for authenticating the users. More information about Samba is available in the Administration Guide.

After determining the use, enter the Windows domain or workgroup. Use 'Browse' to display all existing domains and workgroups. Under 'Server Description', enter a text to display to all clients. Use 'Authentication Details' to enter an advanced configuration dialog in which to set the user authentication mode. If you activate 'smbpasswd', all users and their passwords are saved in the file `smbpasswd`. If you opt for LDAP, the user information is stored on an LDAP server. Specify the LDAP server by entering the server name, Base DN, and Administration DN. Detailed information about LDAP is available in the Administration Guide. Test the LDAP connection with the respective button. Enter the LDAP administration password when required to do so.

Complete all settings and click 'Next'. In the following dialog, define the resources. If you activate 'Share homes', the home directories of the users appear as Windows shares on the clients. If you activate 'Share printers', use 'Select' to share individual printers.

4.6.4 Configuration of Samba Clients

Configure a Samba client to access resources (files or printers) on the Samba server. In the 'Samba Workgroup' dialog, enter the domain or workgroup. Use 'Browse' to display all available groups and domains and select one of them with a mouse click. If you activate 'Also Use SMB Information for Linux Authentication', user authentication is conducted via the Samba server. After specifying all settings, click 'Finish' to complete the configuration.

4.6.5 NTP Client

NTP (Network Time Protocol) is a protocol for synchronizing the clocks of network hosts. In the respective YaST module, select a type with 'Add'.

Several options are then displayed. 'Server' and 'Radio clock' are the most frequently-used options. 'Radio clock' requires special hardware.

If you select 'Server', enter the address of an NTP server when prompted. Normally, your system administrator does this for you. However, you can also enter one of the public NTP servers listed at `http://www.eecis.udel.edu/~mills/ntp/servers.html`. Confirm with 'OK'.

To start the NTP daemon when the system is booted, select 'When booting system'. Save your settings with 'Finish'. Consult the Administration Guide for more information.

4.6.6 Routing

This tool is only needed if you are located in a local network or are connected to the Internet by way of a network card, as is the case with DSL. As indicated in Section 4.5.4 on page 100, for DSL the gateway data is only needed to configure the network card correctly. However, the entries are dummies that do not have any function. The value is important only if you are located in a local network and use your own computer as gateway (the gateway to the Internet).

4.6.7 Mail Transfer Agent

This configuration module allows you to adapt your mail settings if you send your e-mail with sendmail, postfix, or the SMTP server of your provider. You can fetch mail via the fetchmail program, for which you can also enter the details of the POP3 server or IMAP server of your provider.

You can also use a mail program of your choice, such as KMail (see Section 16 on page 257) or Evolution, to set your POP and SMTP access data as usual (to receive mail with POP3 and send mail with SMTP). In this case, you do not need this module.

Connection Type

If you want to configure your mail with YaST, specify the desired type of connection to the Internet in the first dialog of the e-mail configuration module. Choose one of the following options:

'Permanent' Select this option if you have a dedicated line to the Internet. Your machine will be online permanently, so no dial-up is required. If your system is part of a local network with a central e-mail server, select this option to ensure permanent access to your e-mail messages.

'Dial-up' This item is relevant for all users who have a computer at home, are not located in a network, and establish dial-up connections with the Internet occasionally via modem, DSL, or ISDN.

No connection If you do not have access to the Internet and are not located in a network, you cannot send or receive e-mail.

Furthermore, you can activate virus scanning for your incoming and outgoing e-mail with AMaViS by activating the respective check box. The package is installed automatically as soon as you activate the mail filtering feature. In the following dialogs, specify the outgoing mail server (usually the SMTP server of your provider) and the parameters for incoming mail. If you use a dial-up connection, you can specify diverse POP or IMAP servers for mail reception by various users. By means of this dialog, you can also assign aliases, use masquerading, or set up virtual domains. Click 'Finish' to exit the mail configuration.

4.6.8 Network Services (inetd)

This tool allows you to determine which network services (such as telnet, finger, talk, and ftp) should start when SUSE LINUX boots. These services enable external hosts to connect to your computer. You can also configure various parameters for each service. By default, the master service that manages the individual services (inetd or xinetd) is not started.

When this module starts, choose which of the two services to configure. The selected daemon can be started with a standard selection of network services. If desired, 'Add', 'Delete', or 'Edit' services to compose your own selection of services.

Caution

This is an expert tool. Only make modifications if you are familiar with network services.

Caution

4.7 Security and Users

A basic aspect of Linux is its multiuser capability. Consequently, several users can work independently on the same Linux system. Each user has a user account identified by a login name and a personal password for logging in to the system. All users have their own home directories where personal files and configurations are stored.

4.7.1 User Administration

Use the check boxes to select to edit users. YaST provides an overview of all local users in the system. If you are part of an extensive network, click 'Set Filter' to list all system users (e.g., `root`) or NIS users. You can also create user-defined filter settings. Instead of switching between individual user groups, combine them according to your needs. To add new users, fill in the required blanks in the following screen. Subsequently, the new user can log in to the host with the login name and password. The user profile can be fine-tuned with 'Details'. You can manually set the user ID, the home directory, and the default login shell. Furthermore, the new user can be assigned to specific groups. Configure the validity of the password in 'Password settings'. Click 'Edit' to change these settings whenever necessary. To delete a user, select the user from the list and click 'Delete'.

For advanced network administration, use 'Expert Options' to define the default settings for the creation of new users. Select the authentication method (NIS, LDAP, Kerberos, or Samba) as well as the algorithm for the password encryption. These settings are relevant for large (corporate) networks.

4.7.2 Group Administration

Start the group administration module from the YaST Control Center or click 'Groups' in the user administration. Both dialogs have the same functionality, allowing you to create, edit, or delete groups.

YaST provides a list of all groups. To delete a group, select it from the list (the line will be highlighted dark blue) and click 'Delete'. Under 'Add' and 'Edit', enter the name, group ID (gid), and members of the group in the respective YaST screen. If desired, set a password for the change to this group. The filter settings are the same as in the 'User Administration' dialog.

4.7.3 Security Settings

In 'Local security configuration', which can be accessed under 'Security&Users', select one of the following four options: Level 1 is for stand-

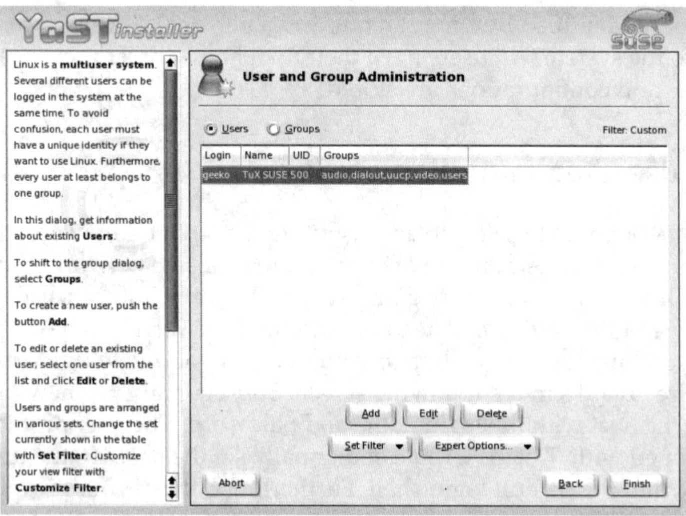

Figure 4.23: User Administration

alone computers (preconfigured). Level 2 is for workstations with a network (preconfigured). Level 3 is for a server with a network (preconfigured). Use 'Custom Settings' for your own configuration.

If you click one of the first three items, incorporate one of the levels of preconfigured system security options. To do this, simply click 'Finish'. Under 'Details', access the individual settings that can be modified. If you choose 'Custom settings', proceed to the different dialogs with 'Next'. Here, find the default installation values.

'Password Settings' For new passwords to be checked by the system before they are accepted, mark 'Checking new passwords' and 'Plausibility test for password'. Set the minimum and maximum length of passwords for newly created users. Define the period for which the password should be valid and how many days in advance an expiration alert should be issued when the user logs in to the text console.

'Boot settings' Specify how the key combination Strg + Alt + Del should be interpreted by selecting the action from the drop-down list.

Usually, this combination, entered in the text console, causes the system to reboot. Do not modify this setting unless your machine or

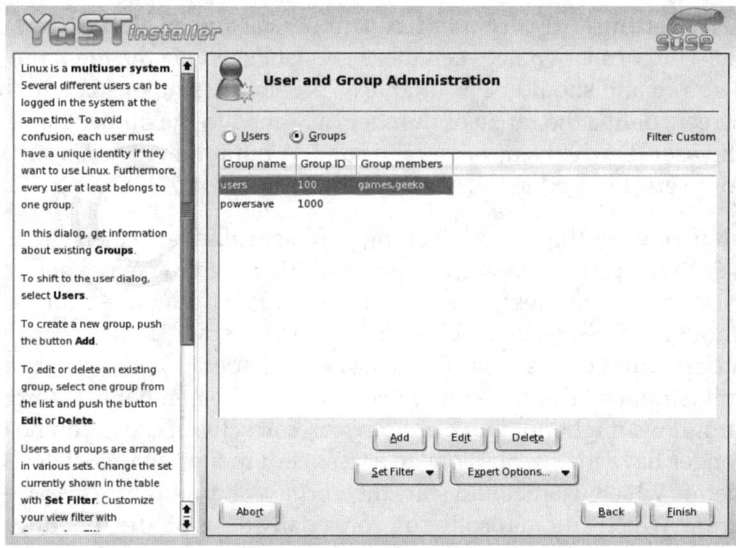

Figure 4.24: *Group Administration*

server is publicly accessible and you are afraid someone could carry out this action without authorization. If you select 'Stop', this key combination causes the system to shut down. With 'Ignore', this key combination is ignored.

Specify the 'Shutdown Behavior of KDM' by granting permission to shut down the system from the KDE Display Manager, the graphical login of KDE. 'Only root' (the system administrator), 'All users', 'Nobody', or 'Local users'. If 'Nobody' is selected, the system can only be shut down via the text console.

'Login Settings' Typically, following a failed login attempt, there is a waiting period lasting a few seconds before another login is possible. The purpose of this is to make it more difficult for password sniffers to log in. In addition, you have the option of activating 'Record failed login attempts' and 'Record successful login attempts'. If you suspect someone is trying to discover your password, check the entries in the system log files in `/var/log`. By means of the 'Allow remote graphical login', other users are granted access to your graphical login screen via the network. However, as this access possibility represents a potential security risk, it is inactive by default.

'Add User Settings' Every user has a numerical and an alphabetical user ID. The correlation between these is established via the file `/etc/passwd` and should be as unique as possible. Using the data in this screen, define the range of numbers assigned to the numerical part of the user ID when a new user is added. A minimum of 500 is suitable for users. Proceed in the same way with the group ID settings.

'Miscellaneous Settings' For 'Setting of file permissions', there are three selection options: 'Easy', 'Secure', and 'Paranoid'. The first one should be sufficient for most users. The YaST help text provides information about the three security levels. The setting 'Paranoid' is extremely restrictive and can serve as the basic level of operation for system administrator settings. If you select 'Paranoid', remember that some programs might not work or not work correctly, because you no longer have the permissions to access certain files. In this dialog, also define which user should start the `updatedb` program. This program, which automatically runs on a daily basis or after booting, generates a database (locatedb) where the location of each file on your computer is stored (locatedb can be searched by running the `locate` command). If you select 'Nobody', any user can find only the paths in the database that can be seen by any other (unprivileged) user. If `root` is selected, all local files are indexed, because the user `root`, as superuser, may access all directories.

Finally, make sure the option 'Current directory in root's path' is deactivated (default).

Press 'Finish' to complete your security configuration.

4.7.4 Firewall

Use this module to configure SuSEfirewall2 to protect your machine against attacks from the Internet. When the module is started, four dialogs appear consecutively. In the first dialog, select the interface to protect. See Figure 4.26 on page 116. 'External interface' is the interface facing the Internet. 'Internal interface' is only required if you are located in an internal network and intend to use the firewall to protect your computer against internal attacks. In this case, your computer would be in a *demilitarized zone* (DMZ). Normally, a configuration with DMZ is only used for company networks.

After selecting your interface, activate the individual services of your computer for which to allow access from the Internet. See Figure 4.27. If you do

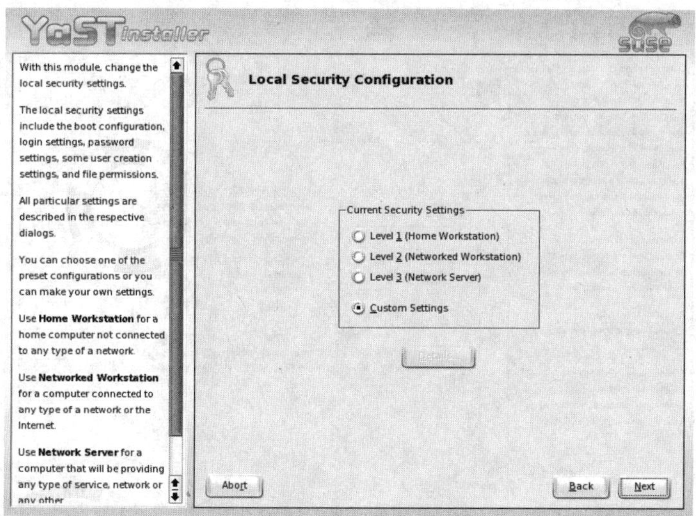

Figure 4.25: Security Settings

not offer any server services but only use your computer for surfing the Internet and sending and receiving e-mail, skip this dialog without activating any of the services.

If you are not familiar with the terms masquerading and traceroute, simply accept the third dialog without any modifications. You can also accept the final dialog, as the default log options are usually sufficient.

When you click 'Next', a small window asks for confirmation. Then the new configuration is saved to the hard disk. The next time your Internet connection is started, your computer will be protected effectively against attacks. For more information about the SUSE Firewall, refer to the Administration Guide.

4.8 System

4.8.1 Backup Copy of the System Areas

The YaST backup module enables you to create a backup of your system. The backup created by the module does not comprise the entire system,

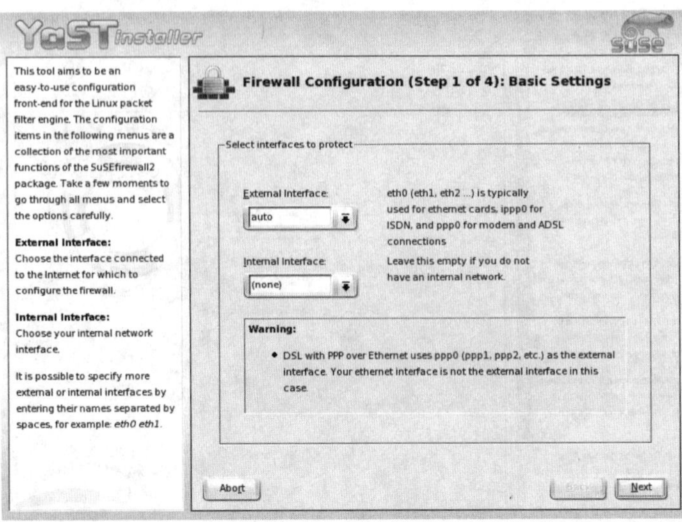

Figure 4.26: SUSE Firewall: Selecting the Interfaces to Protect

but only saves information about changed packages and copies of critical storage areas and configuration files.

Define the kind of data to save in the backup. By default, the backup includes information about any packages changed since the last installation. In addition, it may include data that does not belong to packages themselves, such as many of the configuration files in `/etc` or the directories under `/home`. Apart from that, the backup can include important storage areas on your hard disk that may be crucial when trying to restore a system, such as the partition table or the master boot record (MBR).

4.8.2 Restoring the System

The restore module, shown in Figure 4.28 on page 118, enables restoration of your system from a backup archive. Follow the instructions in YaST. Press 'Next' to proceed to the individual dialogs. First, specify where the archives are located (removable media, local hard disks, or network file systems). As you continue, a description and the contents of the individual archives are displayed, enabling you to decide what to restore from the archives.

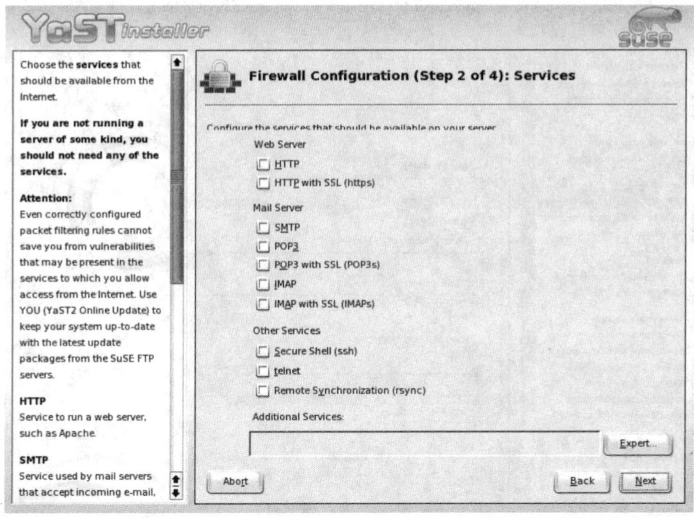

Figure 4.27: SuSE Firewall: Externally Accessible Services

Additionally, there are two dialogs for uninstalling packages that were added since the last backup and for the reinstallation of packages that were deleted since the last backup. These two steps enable you to restore the exact system state at the time of the last backup.

Caution

As this module normally installs, replaces, or uninstalls many packages and files, use it only if you have experience with backups, as otherwise you may lose data.

Caution

4.8.3 Creating a Boot, Rescue, or Module Disk

Use this YaST module to create boot disks, rescue disks, and module disks. These floppy disks are helpful if the boot configuration of your system is damaged. The rescue disk is especially necessary if the file system of the root partition is damaged. In this case, you might also need the module disk with various drivers to be able to access the system (e.g., to access a RAID system).

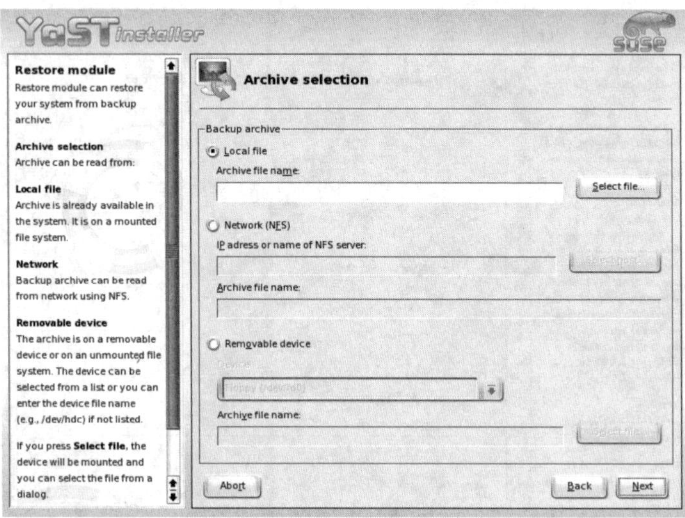

Figure 4.28: Start Window of the Restore Module

'Standard boot disk' Use this option to create a standard boot disk with which to boot an installed system. This disk is also needed for starting the rescue system.

'Rescue disk' This disk contains a special environment that allows you to perform maintenance tasks in your installed system, such as checking and repairing the file system and updating the boot loader. To start the rescue system, boot with the standard boot disk then select 'Manual Installation' -> 'Start Installation or System' -> 'Rescue System'.

You will then be prompted to insert the rescue disk. If your system was configured to use special drivers (such as RAID or USB), you might need to load the respective modules from a module disk.

'Module disks' Module disks contain additional system drivers. The standard kernel only supports IDE drives. If the drives in your system are connected to special controllers (such as SCSI), load the needed drivers from a module disk. If you select this option and click 'Next', you will be taken to a dialog for creating various module disks.

- USB modules

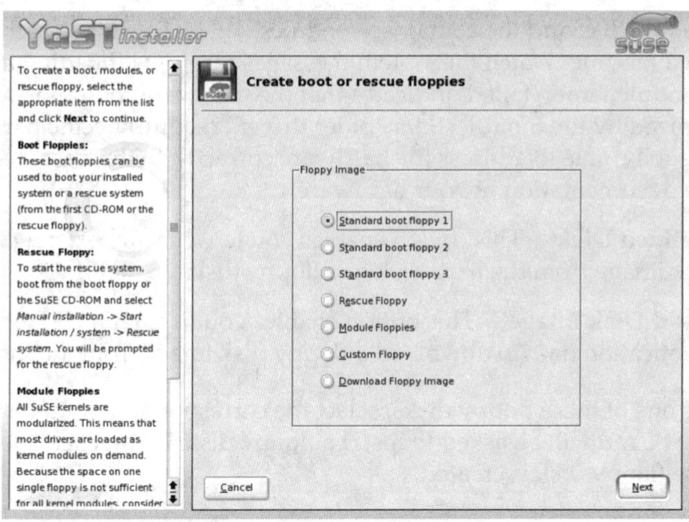

Figure 4.29: *Creating a Boot, Rescue, or Module Disk*

This floppy disk contains the USB modules you might need if USB drives are connected.

- IDE, RAID, and SCSI modules
  As the standard kernel only supports normal IDE drives, you will need this module disk if you use special IDE controllers. Furthermore, all RAID and SCSI modules are provided on this disk.
- Network modules
  If you need access to a network, load the suitable driver module for your network card from this floppy disk.
- PCMCIA, CD-ROM (non-ATAPI), FireWire, and file systems
  This floppy disk contains all PCMCIA modules used especially for laptop computers. Furthermore, the modules for FireWire and some less common file systems are available here. Older CD-ROM drives that do not comply with the ATAPI standard can also be operated with drivers from this floppy disk.

To load drivers from a module disk to the rescue system, select 'Kernel Modules (hardware drivers)' and the desired module category (SCSI, ethernet, etc.). You will be prompted to insert the respective module disk and the contained modules will be listed. Select the desired module. Watch the system messages carefully: 'Loading module <modulename> failed' indicates that the hardware could not be recognized by the module. Some older drivers require specific parameters to be able to address the hardware correctly. In this case, refer to the documentation of your hardware.

'User-Defined Disk' This option enables you to write any existing floppy disk image from the hard disk to a floppy disk.

'Download Disk Image' This option enables you to enter a URL and authentication data to download a floppy disk image from the Internet.

To create one of these floppy disks, select the corresponding option and click 'Next'. You will be asked to insert a floppy disk. If you click 'Next' again, the floppy disk is created.

4.8.4 Configuring the Boot Loader with YaST

This YaST module simplifies the configuration of the boot loader. However, you should not experiment with this module unless you understand the concepts behind it. Read the corresponding parts of the Administration Guide before changing the boot loader configuration. The following discussion mainly covers the default boot loader GRUB.

Note

Do not change the boot method of a running system unless you really know what you are doing.

Note

In the YaST Control Center, select 'System'-> 'Boot Loader Configuration'. The current boot loader configuration of your system will be displayed, enabling you to make any needed changes (see Figure 4.30 on the next page).

The Main Window

The table listing the configuration data consists of three columns. Under 'Changed' (to the left), flags mark the changed options listed in the center column. To add an option, click 'Add'. To change the value of an existing option, select it with a mouse click and click 'Edit'. If you do not want to use an existing option at all, select it and click 'Delete'.

'Reset' to the right under the configuration window offers the following options:

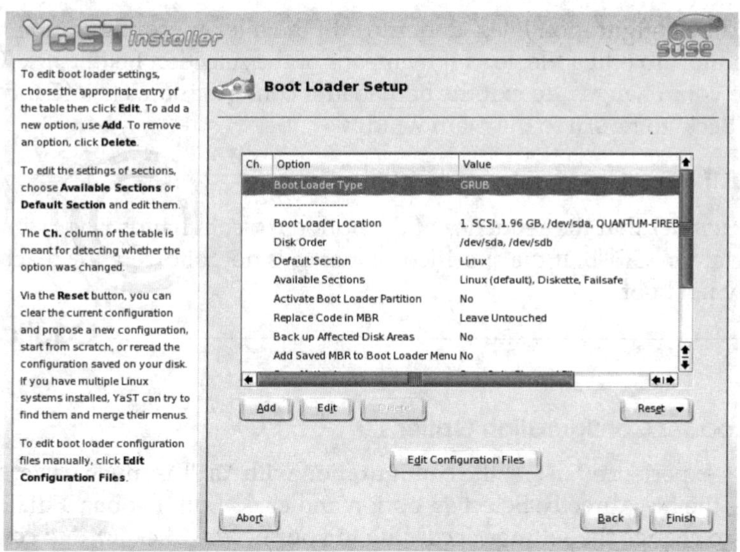

Figure 4.30: Configuring the Boot Loader with YaST

Propose New Configuration Generates a new configuration suggestion. Older Linux versions or other operating systems found on other partitions will be included in the boot menu, enabling you to boot Linux or its old boot loader. The latter takes you to a second boot menu.

Start from Scratch Enables you to create the entire configuration from scratch. No suggestions will be generated.

Reread Configuration from Disk If you already performed some changes and are not satisfied with the result, you can reload your current configuration with this option.

Propose and Merge with Existing GRUB Menus
If another operating system and an older Linux version are installed in other partitions, the menu will be generated from an entry for the new SUSE LINUX, an entry for the other system, and all entries of the old boot loader menu. This procedure might take some time. This is not possible if LILO is used.

Restore MBR from Hard Disk The MBR saved on the hard disk will be written back.

Use 'Edit Configuration Files' under to edit the relevant configuration files in an editor. To edit a file, load it by means of the selection field. Click 'OK' to save your changes. To exit the boot loader configuration, click 'Cancel'. Click 'Back' to return to the main window.

Caution

Remember that the sequence of the options or commands is very important in GRUB. If the specified sequence is not followed, the machine may not boot.

Caution

Boot Loader Configuration Options

For less experienced users, the configuration with YaST is much easier than editing the files directly. Select an option and click 'Edit' to open a dialog in which to change the settings according to your needs. Click 'OK' to confirm the changes and return to the main menu, where you can edit other options. The available options depend on the boot loader used. The following list introduces some options of the boot loader GRUB:

Boot Loader Type Use this option to switch between GRUB and LILO. You will be taken to another dialog in which to specify the way in which this change should be performed. For instance, convert the current GRUB configuration into a similar LILO configuration. However, some settings may be lost if no equivalent options are available. You can also create a new configuration from scratch or generate and edit a suggestion for a configuration. If you start the boot loader configuration in the running system, you can load the configuration from the hard disk. If you decide to return to the original boot loader, you can load its configuration by means of the last option. However, this possibility only exists as long as you do not close the boot loader module.

Boot Loader Location Use this dialog to define where to install the boot loader: in the master boot record (MBR), in the boot sector of the boot partition (if available), in the the boot sector of the root partition, or on a floppy disk. Use 'Others' to specify a different location. Refer to the information about GRUB in the Administration Guide.

Disk Order If your computer has more than one hard disk, specify the boot sequence of the disks as defined in the BIOS setup of the machine.

Default Section With this option, set which kernel or operating system to boot by default, if no other entry is selected in the boot menu. The default system is booted after the time-out. Click this option and 'Edit' to see a list of all boot menu entries. Then select one entry from the list and click 'Set as Default'. Click 'Edit' to modify an entry. The dialog that opens allows changing the order of entries in the boot menu, adding, modifying, and deleting entries, and setting a default entry.

Available Sections The existing entries of the boot menu are listed under this option in the main window. If you select this option then click 'Edit', a dialog opens that is identical to the 'Default Entry' dialog.

Make Boot Loader Partition Active
Use this option to activate the partition whose boot sector holds the boot loader, independently from the partition on which the directory with the helper files of the boot loader are stored (`/boot` or the root directory /).

Replace Code in MBR Specify whether to overwrite the MBR, which may be necessary if you have changed the location of the boot loader.

Backing up Files and Parts of Hard Disks
Backs up the changed hard disk areas.

Add Saved MBR to Boot Loader Menu
Adds the saved MBR to the boot loader menu.

Using 'Time-out', define for how many seconds the boot loader should wait for entries before the default system is booted. A number of other options can be specified with 'Add'. However, the use of these options requires a deeper understanding and is not covered here. Refer to the relevant chapter in the Administration Guide and the manual pages of GRUB and LILO (`man grub`, `man lilo`, and `man lilo.conf`). Additionally, a detailed online manual for GRUB is available at `http://www.gnu.org/software/grub/`.

4.8.5 LVM

The Logical Volume Manager (LVM) is a tool for individually partitioning hard disks by means of logical drives. As this is a genuine expert tool, no additional information is provided within the scope of this user guide. For information, refer to the Administration Guide.

4.8.6 Partitioning

Although it is possible to modify the partitions in the installed system, this should be handled by experts who know exactly what they are doing, as otherwise the risk of losing data is very high. If you decide to use this tool, refer to the description in Section 2.5.4 on page 18 (the partitioning tool during the installation is the same as in the installed system).

4.8.7 Profile Manager (SCPM)

The SCPM (System Configuration Profile Management) module offers the possibility of creating, managing, and switching among system configurations. This is especially useful for mobile computers that are used in different locations (in different networks) and by different users. Nevertheless, this feature is useful even for stationary machines, as it enables the use of various hardware components or test configurations. Although the module with the accompanying help is easy to use, the configuration of profiles is a task that should be performed by experts or system administrators. For more information about SCPM basics and handling, refer to the respective sections in the Administration Guide.

4.8.8 Runlevel Editor

SUSE LINUX can be operated in several runlevels. By default, the system boots to runlevel 5, which offers multiuser mode, network access, and the graphical user interface (X Window System). The other runlevels offer multiuser mode with network but without X (runlevel 3), multiuser mode without network (runlevel 2), single-user mode (runlevel 1 and S), system halt (runlevel 0), and system reboot (runlevel 6).

The various runlevels are useful if problems are encountered in connection with a particular service (X or network) in a higher runlevel. In this case, the system can be booted to a lower runlevel to repair the service. Many servers operate without a graphical user interface and must be booted in a runlevel without X, such as runlevel 3.

Usually home users only need the standard runlevel (5). However, if the graphical user interface freezes at any time, you can restart the X Window system by switching to a text console with Ctrl + Alt + F1, logging in as root, and switching to runlevel 3 with the command `init 3`. This shuts down your X Window System, leaving you with a text console. To restart the graphical system, enter `init 5`.

In a default installation, runlevel 5 is selected. To start a different

runlevel when the system is booted, change the default runlevel here. With 'Runlevel properties', determine which services are started in which runlevel.

Caution

Incorrect settings for system services and runlevels can render your system useless. To retain the operability of your system, consider the possible consequences before modifying any of these settings.

Caution

For more information about the runlevels in SUSE LINUX, refer to the Administration Guide.

4.8.9 Sysconfig Editor

The directory `/etc/sysconfig` contains the files with the most important settings for SUSE LINUX (formerly centrally administered in the file `/etc/rc.config`). The sysconfig editor displays all settings in a well-arranged form. The values can be modified and saved to the individual configuration files. Generally, manual editing is not necessary, as the files are automatically adapted when a package is installed or a service is configured.

Caution

Do not edit the files in `/etc/sysconfig` if you do not know exactly what you are doing, as this could seriously inhibit the operability of your system.

Caution

More information is provided in the Administration Guide.

4.8.10 Time Zone Selection

The time zone was already set during the installation, but you can make changes here. Click your country or region in the list and select 'Local time' or 'GMT' (Greenwich Mean Time). 'GMT' is often used in Linux systems. Machines with additional operating systems, such as Microsoft Windows, mostly use local time.

4.8.11 Language Selection

Here, select the language for your Linux system. The language can be changed at any time. The language selected in YaST applies to the entire system, including YaST and the desktop environment KDE 3.

4.8.12 Keyboard Layout Selection

Note

Only use this module if you work on a system without the X Window System and a graphical user interface. If you use a graphical system (such as KDE), set up the keyboard with the module 'Display and Input Devices'. See Section 4.4.4 on page 79.

Note

The desired keyboard layout usually matches the selected language. Use the test field to see if special characters, such as the pipe symbol `|`, are displayed correctly.

4.9 Miscellaneous

4.9.1 Submitting a Support Request

By purchasing SUSE LINUX, you are entitled to free installation support. For information about the support scope, address, and phone numbers, visit our web site at `www.suse.de/en/`.

YaST offers the possibility to send a support request directly by e-mail to the SUSE team. Registration is required first. Start by entering the required data — your registration code is located at the back of the CD cover. Regarding your query, select the problem category in the following window and provide a description of the problem (Figure 4.31 on the following page). Also read the YaST help text, which explains how best to describe the problem so the support team can help you.

Note

If you need advanced support (such as for special problems), consider using the SUSE Professional Services. Refer to `http://www.suse.de/en/support/` for details.

Note

4.9.2 Boot Log

The boot log contains the screen messages displayed when the computer is started. It is logged to `/var/log/boot.msg`. Use this YaST module to

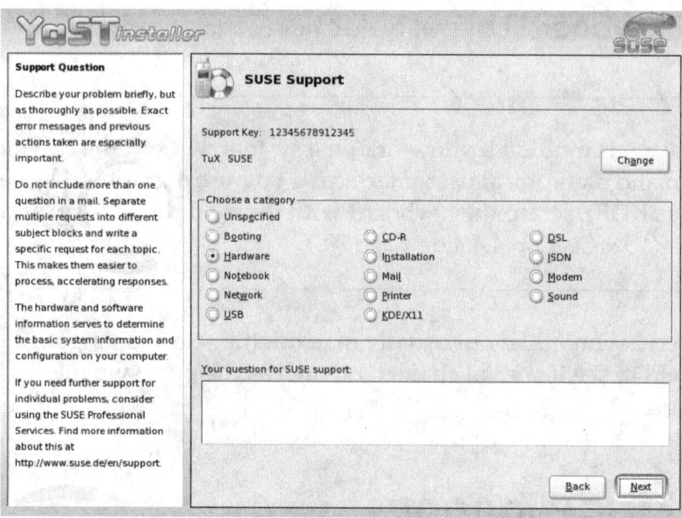

Figure 4.31: Submitting a Support Request

view the log, for example, to check if all services and functions were started as expected.

4.9.3 System Log

The system log logs the operations of your computer to `/var/log/messsages`. Kernel messages are recorded here, sorted according to date and time.

4.9.4 Loading a Vendor's Driver CD

With this module, automatically install device drivers from a Linux driver CD that contains drivers for SUSE LINUX. When installing SUSE LINUX from scratch, use this YaST module to load the required drivers from the vendor CD after the installation.

4.10 YaST2 in Text Mode (ncurses)

YaST can also be controlled by means of a text-based terminal. This is especially useful in the case of systems that cannot run the X Window System or where X is unneeded, as in dedicated server or firewall machines. It is also good for administrators remotely accessing a system.

4.10.1 Controls

The usage may be unfamiliar, but is very simple. Basically, the entire program can be controlled with Tab, Alt + Tab, Space, the arrow keys (↑ and ↓), Enter, and shortcuts. The YaST Control Center appears first, as shown in Figure 4.32.

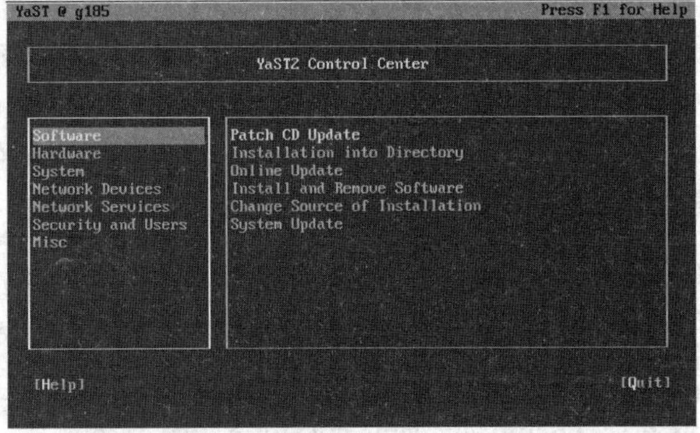

Figure 4.32: The Main Window of YaST2 ncurses

The left frame, which is surrounded by a thick white border, features the categories to which the various modules belong. The active category is indicated by a colored background. The right frame, which is surrounded by a thin white border, provides an overview of the modules contained in the active category. The bottom frame contains the buttons for 'Help' and 'Exit'.

When the YaST Control Center is started, the category 'Software' is selected automatically. Use ↓ and ↑ to change the category. To start a module from the selected category, press →. The module selection then appears with a thick border. Use ↓ and ↑ to select the desired module. Keep the arrow keys pressed to scroll through the list of available modules. When a module is selected, the module title appears with a colored background and a brief description is displayed in the bottom frame.

Press Enter to start the desired module. Various buttons or selection fields in the module contain a letter with a different color (yellow by default). Use Alt + yellow letter to select the respective button directly without navigating there with Tab. Exit the YaST Control Center by pressing 'Exit' or by selecting 'Exit' in the category overview and pressing Enter.

4.10.2 Restriction of Key Combinations

If you have system-wide Alt key combinations when the X server is running, the Alt combinations in YaST might not work. Furthermore, keys like Alt or Shift might be occupied by the settings of the terminal.

Replacing Alt with Esc: Alt shortcuts can be executed with Esc instead of Alt. For example, Esc-H replaces Alt-H.

Replacing backward and forward navigation with Ctrl-F and Ctrl-B: If the Alt and Shift combinations are occupied by the window manager or the terminal, the combinations Ctrl-F (forward) and Ctrl-B (backward) can be used instead.

Restricted function keys: The F keys are also used for functions. Certain function keys can be occupied by the terminal so might not be available for YaST. However, the Alt key combinations and the F keys should always be fully available on a pure text console.

The following paragraphs assume that the Alt key combinations are functional.

4.10.3 Module Operation

Navigating Buttons and Selection Lists
Tab and Alt-Tab navigate among buttons and frames.

Navigating in Selection Lists ↑ and ↓ always navigate among the single items within an activated frame containing a selection list. These can, for instance, be the single modules of a module group in the control center.

Checking Radio Buttons and Check Boxes
Buttons with empty square brackets (check boxes) or empty parentheses (radio buttons) can be selected with Space or Enter. The buttons at the bottom of the individual modules are activated with Enter when selected (green background) or with the combination Alt + yellow letter. Refer to Figure 4.33.

The Function Keys Various functions are mapped to the F keys (F1 to F12). Which keys are actually mapped to functions depends on which YaST module is active, because the different modules offer different buttons (such as details, info, add, and delete). The buttons 'OK', 'Next', and 'Finish' are mapped to F10. The YaST help, which can be accessed with F1, provides information about the functions of the individual F keys.

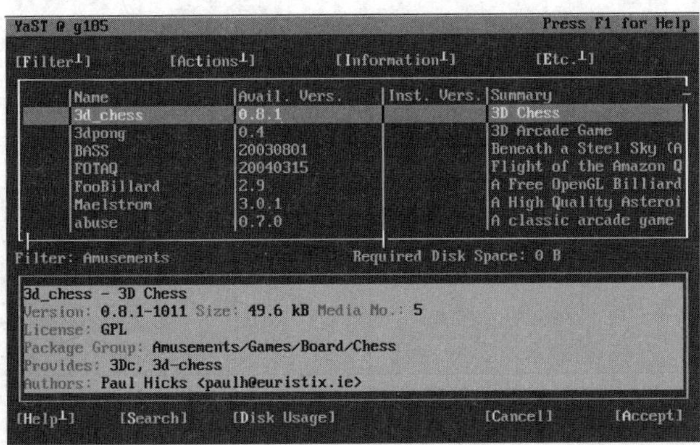

Figure 4.33: The Software Installation Module

4.10.4 Starting Individual Modules

To save time, the individual YaST modules can also be started directly. To start the modules, enter `yast` followed by the name of the module.

The KDE Desktop

KDE is the default desktop in a standard installation of SUSE LINUX. It is easy to use and highly configurable. The following sections introduce the basic desktop and customization of the desktop. Konqueror is essential for file management. A number of additional applications are also described.

5.1 Desktop Components

The graphical desktop environment should not pose any problems for former Windows or Macintosh users. The main components are the icons on the desktop and the panel at the bottom of the screen. The mouse is your most important tool. Click a symbol or an icon once to start the associated program or the file manager Konqueror. If you right-click an icon, different menus appear, depending on the program. As well as the icons, there are two desktop menus.

5.1.1 The Desktop Menus

If you middle-click the desktop (if your mouse only has two buttons, press both buttons at the same time), a window and desktop management menu are displayed. If you keep the mouse button pressed, select a menu item directly. Alternatively, release the mouse button and click the respective menu item.

Unclutter Windows If you have several windows on your desktop, they are placed next to each other and aligned with the top left corner.

Cascade Windows Starting from the top left corner, the windows on the desktop are placed on top of each other in such a way that only the top and left borders of the lower windows are visible.

Desktop 1 Desktop 1 is your default desktop. All open windows are listed under this menu item. Click windows to move them to the foreground.

additional desktop You can use additional virtual desktops. Switch to another desktop with the menu or the panel. All functions are available on all desktops. This limits the number of programs and associated windows that need to be arranged on one desktop. These virtual desktops resemble additional desks in your office.

If you right-click the desktop, a more complex menu is displayed, allowing you to customize your desktop.

Create New Enables creation of new elements, such as directories, files, or URLs, on the desktop. A list of possible elements is provided for selection in a submenu.

Bookmarks This item opens the bookmark editor KEditBookmarks. With it, create, group, change, or delete bookmarks. The browser and file manager Konqueror can access these bookmarks.

Undo This option allows you to undo the last action. For example, if you just created a new directory on the desktop, clicking this item reverts the creation so the directory disappears.

Paste To have a desktop icon for a folder or document, copy the icon from the file manager by right-clicking and selecting 'Copy' then moving the mouse to the desired location on the desktop. Right-click again and select 'Paste'. The icon is now available on your desktop and can be moved around by dragging it with the left mouse button pressed.

Icons Rearranges the symbols on the desktop. You can also change the order of the icons.

Windows The windows on the desktop are either placed on top of each other at the top left corner or next to each other.

Configure Desktop This menu item starts a configuration dialog with which to configure the appearance of the desktop. Details about the configuration of the desktop are provided in Section 5.2 on page 141.

Help Use this submenu to open the KDE manual or write a bug report to the developers via the KDE web site. You can also start an information page about KDE.

Lock Screen If you leave your workstation and do not log out, you should use this function to prevent others from gaining access to your files. Depending on the setting, the screen either turns black or a screensaver starts. To continue using the computer, enter your password.

Logout User Log out from your system if you are not going to use the system for some time.

5.1.2 The Trash Bin

The trash bin is a directory for files marked for deletion. Drag icons from the file manager or the desktop to the trash bin icon by keeping the left mouse button pressed then release to drop them there. Alternatively, right-click an icon and select 'Move to Trash' from the menu. Click the trash bin icon to view its contents. You can retrieve an item from the trash if desired.

Files removed with 'Delete' are not moved to the trash bin, but deleted completely. To delete the files in the trash bin completely, right-click the trash bin icon and select 'Empty Trash Bin'.

5.1.3 CD-ROM, DVD-ROM, and Floppy Disks

If you click the floppy disk icon when a floppy disk is inserted, the file manager starts and displays the content of the floppy disk. Display a context menu with various options by right-clicking the individual icons on the floppy disk. It is also possible to move the icon to a different location, such as the desktop or your home directory, by simply keeping the left mouse button pressed and dragging it to the appropriate icon. You will be asked whether you want to move or copy the file or create a link. You can also copy or move files from your home directory to the floppy disk.

Right-click the floppy disk icon to access the context menu. 'Unmount' is a very important option. Be sure to unmount the drive before removing a floppy disk from the drive, as this is necessary to trigger the actual writing of the data to the floppy disk.

The handling of CDs and DVDs is similar, with the only difference that these media are not writable. Nevertheless, you must unmount CD and DVD drives, because otherwise you will not be able to eject the CD. You can also select 'Eject', which causes the medium to be unmounted and ejected. Both methods only work if the CD or DVD is no longer accessed and any file manager window displaying the content of the CD or DVD has been closed.

5.1.4 The Printer Icon

Click the printer icon on the desktop to start KPrinter. This program enables you to adjust a number of settings and send print jobs directly. The upper part of the main window, like that in Figure 5.1 on the facing page, shows the selected printer and allows selection of a different printer. Click the black arrow next to the printer name to display a list of all available printers and select the desired printer.

To configure the selected printer, click 'Properties'. A configuration dialog like that shown in Figure 5.2 on page 138 opens, enabling you to change the paper format (e.g., from A4 to letter) or change between multiple paper trays. The latter is especially useful if one of the trays contains letterhead paper and another contains plain white paper.

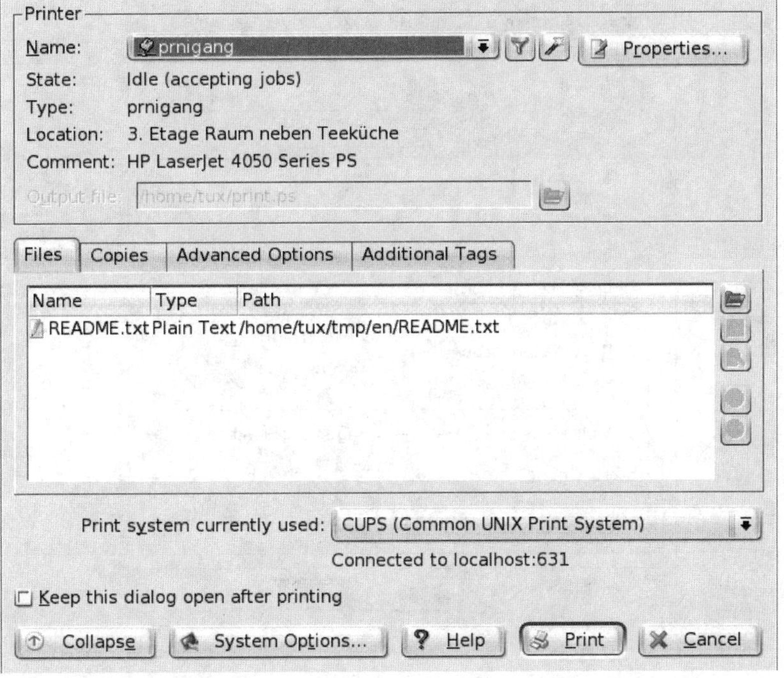

Figure 5.1: The Main Window of KPrinter

Under 'Orientation', choose between 'Portrait' and 'Landscape'. To the right of 'Orientation', specify the settings for two-sided printing. If 'None' is selected, only one page is printed per sheet. If you click the circle preceding 'Long side', the front and back will be printed like in a book. With 'Short side', the back is printed reversely and you have to turn the sheet up to view the text correctly. Under 'Start/End', mark your document with headlines and subtitles, such as "confidential" or "secret". Under 'Pages per Sheet', select to print two or four pages on one sheet. For this purpose, the pages are downsized accordingly. If you click 'Save', your settings are adopted for other print jobs, too. However, if you click 'OK', the settings only apply to the current job. If you terminate the dialog with 'Cancel', all changes are discarded.

After making all settings, click 'Expand'. The second part of the window now becomes visible. Click the blue folder icon. By default, your home directory is displayed. Select a file and confirm with 'OK'. You can also se-

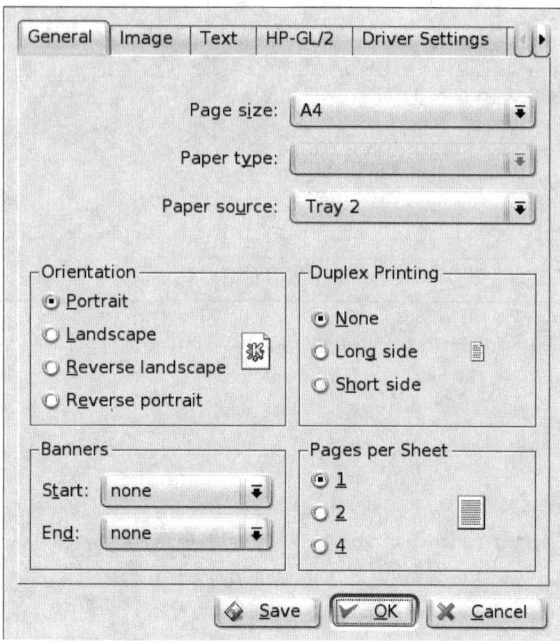

***Figure 5.2:** Settings in KPrinter*

lect the file by double-clicking it. The respective file then appears in the overview of the main window, together with the name, type, and path specification. Now click 'Print' to send the job to the printer. The job is placed in the queue and can be monitored with KJobViewer. On the other hand, if you click the document, two additional buttons become active to the right. Use the X button to remove the document from the selection or use the magnifying glass icon to display, edit, and save the file with Kwrite or OpenOffice.org (depending on the document type). Afterwards, simply close the editing program and click 'Print' in the KPrinter dialog. Your changes are then adopted for printing.

All KDE applications use KPrinter for printing. For example, if you click the printer icon in KWrite, the KPrinter dialog appears. The file to print is already preselected.

5.1.5 The Panel

The panel at the lower edge of the screen consists of several areas. By default, the icon for the main menu is located to the far left. Other icons are lined up alongside it. The house icon provides quick access to your home directory with all subdirectories. The other icons start applications, such as OpenOffice.org, K-Mail, and the web browser Konqueror, if these programs were installed.

Next to these icons are the numbered buttons with which to switch desktops. These multiple desktops enable you to organize your work if you use many programs simultaneously, as if you had several desks for various tasks.

The taskbar is located next to the virtual desktops. All started applications are displayed in the taskbar. If you click a window title in the taskbar, the application is moved to the foreground. If it is already in the foreground, clicking minimizes the application. If you click it again, it reopens. Next to the taskbar, find applets, such as the clipboard Klipper, SuSEwatcher, and any other applets you have started. The clock helps you keep track of the time.

If you right-click an empty space in the panel, a menu providing the usual help and configuration options for the panel is displayed. Use the menu to change the size of the panel and add and remove applications. To add an application, search for the respective application in the menu and select it. Remove applications or applets by right-clicking the corresponding icon and selecting 'Remove' from the displayed menu.

5.1.6 The Main Menu

Access the main menu by means of the icon to the far left of the panel. By default, this menu contains entries for logging out from the system, locking the screen, executing commands, and starting the quick browser and the bookmark manager. Use the file manager to display your home directory, search for files, or start the Control Center for the purpose of customizing the desktop. The other menu entries allow you to start a variety of programs sorted by subjects. The following section provides information about selected functions that you can start by means of the main menu. Detailed information about the Control Center is available in Section 5.2 on page 141.

Logout User You can log out from the system by means of this menu item. However, first you will be asked what should happen after the logout. If you select the 'Login as different user', the login screen is displayed, allowing you or another user to log in to the system. You can also turn off or restart the computer. Confirm your selection with 'OK' or remain logged in by clicking 'Cancel'.

Lock Screen If you leave your workstation, you can blacken your screen or start a screensaver. To restore the session view, enter your normal login password. In this way, make sure no one reads or manipulates your documents or e-mail messages.

Start New Session To start a second session with a graphical user interface on your machine, select 'Start New Session' from the main menu. Your current session remains active while you are taken to the login screen. Log in. You can also start another window manager. Access the first session by pressing Ctrl + Alt + F7. Press F8 instead of F7 to access the new session. Additional sessions can be accessed by pressing Ctrl + Alt + F9 to F12.

Run Command Enter a command in the dialog that opens. In this way, easily start applications whose name you know without having to navigate through the menu.

Bookmarks By way of this menu, start the bookmark editor with 'Edit Bookmarks' to manage your bookmarks. If you select a bookmark from the menu, the browser starts and loads the desired URL.

Search 'Search' starts the program KFind. Use 'Help' to access the program manual, which provides information about all details. If you forget where a certain file is, enter it in the 'Named' field and start a search in your home directory. This default setting can be changed to a different directory, such as `Documents`, by clicking 'Browse'. If you are not sure what the exact file name is, use wild cards. If you can remember that the file name contains the character string `blubb`, simply enter `*blubb*`. This tells the program that `blubb` can be preceded and followed by any characters.Use the tabs at the top left of the window to change to 'Contents' and 'Properties'. In 'Contents', use 'File type' to limit the search to files or directories or search for the content of the document. If you enter a keyword of the document to find in 'Containing text', all texts containing this word are displayed. Click the desired file to load it directly. With 'Save as...', save the file under a new name in a different directory. The original file is retained.Search criteria can be specified in the 'Properties' dialog. You can limit your search to files that were modified or created recently or to files that belong to a specific user or group.

5.1.7 The Windows

The windows of all KDE applications have the same structure. The title bar features four buttons in the right corner. The question mark provides access to context help. If you click the question mark then an icon of the application, a short help text is displayed. The button with the black dash minimizes the window. A minimized window is placed in the panel but not terminated. Display it and continue to use it by clicking the icon in the taskbar. The button with the square maximizes the window over the entire screen area. Another click on this symbol restores the window to its former size. The X closes the window and terminates the application.

Windows can be moved, enlarged, or downsized. Click the title bar and keep the left mouse button pressed to move the window on your screen. If you right-click the top bar, a configuration menu is displayed. To change the size of the window, move the mouse pointer along one of the four edges of the window until the mouse pointer symbol changes to a double arrow. Then keep the left mouse button pressed while moving this edge. Another possibility is to move the mouse pointer to one of the four corners and resize two edges of the window at the same time.

5.2 Settings

The KDE desktop can be customized according to your preferences and needs. 'Control Center' in the main menu opens the configuration dialog for your KDE desktop. The following section introduces a number of modules.

5.2.1 Peripherals

This opens the configuration dialogs for the mouse, keyboard, and printer administration.

Keyboard

Keyboard repeat Keeping a key pressed causes the associated character to be printed repeatedly as long as the key is pressed. The option is activated by default.

Key click volume If you want to hear a sound when a key is clicked, activate this option and adjust the volume with the slider.

Use sticky keys, slow keys, or bounce keys
These options are the same as those listed in Section 5.2.5 on page 149, where they are described in detail.

NumLock on KDE startup Here, determine whether the number pad of your keyboard should be active when KDE is started.

Mouse

The mouse configuration comprises three tabs:'General', 'Advanced', and 'Mouse Navigation'. The configuration options of the 'General' tab are:

Button Mapping Here, specify right-handed or left-handed use of your mouse.

Icons Determine how the system should react to clicks and double-clicks. The default setting for the KDE desktop is a single click for opening files or folders and a mouse pointer that changes its appearance when it is moved over icons. If you want icons to be selected automatically in addition to the single click, activate the respective option and set the delay for this selection.

To use double-click for opening files and folders, select 'Double-click to open files and folders (select icons on first click)'. Finally, set the size and color of the pointer and the visual feedback on activation.

Configuration options of the 'Advanced' tab:

Pointer Acceleration and Pointer Threshold
The pointer acceleration defines the relation between the movement speed of the input device (mouse) and the speed of the pointer on the screen. The higher the selected factor is, the more difficult it is to control the screen pointer. The threshold (in pixels) specifies the distance the pointer must cover before the indicated pointer acceleration is activated. In this way, control the mouse pointer easily when covering small distances and cover large distances on the screen with small movements.

Double Click Interval Here, set the maximum interval between two mouse clicks that should still be interpreted as a double-click.

Drag Start Time and Drag Start Distance
The object selected with a click is moved if you move it by the distance in pixels specified in 'Drag start distance' within the period specified in 'Drag start time'.

Mouse Wheel Scrolls By If you have a wheel mouse, specify the number of lines the image should scroll per wheel "tooth".

To be able to navigate the mouse pointer with the arrow keys of the number pad, activate this function under 'Mouse Navigation' and customize the parameters according to your needs.

Printers

The printer administration module mainly consists of three parts. The top frame lists all printers available in the network. The center part features a configuration and information zone comprising four tabs. The lower part indicates the current print system type. The following description only covers the configuration part.

Note

The configuration options relevant for your daily work with the system can be accessed under 'Jobs' and 'Instances'. 'Information' and 'Properties' mainly provide information or are used for system administration.

Note

Depending on which printer is currently selected in the overview, view and modify status and model information and configuration options in the following four tabs at the center of the dialog window:

Information This tab provides general and unmodifiable information about the printer, such as the printer type, its status, location, and designation.

Jobs This tab corresponds to KJobViewer, described in Section 5.4.5 on page 158.

Properties All settings related to the printer are available here: general information, drivers, interfaces, separator pages, quotas, and user accesses.

Instances Depending on the document type, you may have diverse requirements for the printouts (page format, duplex printing, orientation, print quality, and banners). Combine the characteristic settings for each type in *instances*. To create a new profile, select 'New' and enter a name for the profile. Click 'Settings...' to open a configuration dialog in which to specify these settings. To save the settings and exit the dialog, click'OK'. To define one of your custom profiles as the default for this printer, click 'Set as Default'. Your default profile is used when printing from applications. You can only switch between the individual profiles in the printer administration module.

5.2.2 Desktop

Under 'Appearance', set the standard font, font size, background colors, and underlining on the desktop. Under 'Window Behavior', configure the behavior of the windows and their activation. For example, set the focus to follow the mouse. In this case, you do not need to click a window to activate it.

The taskbar in the panel displays the applications currently started on your system. In this module, determine to what extent started programs and virtual desktops should be displayed in the taskbar and which actions should be associated with mouse clicks in the taskbar.

Under 'Panels', set the position and size of the panels and configure their hiding mode. You can also place additional menus in the panel. If the standard number of virtual desktops is not sufficient, set up additional virtual desktops under 'Multiple Desktops' and assign them names.

5.2.3 Sound & Multimedia

Here, perform all settings for the playback of audio CDs and for the sound system. Under 'System Bell', switch from system notification to a system bell and specify the volume, pitch, and duration of the bell.

By default, system notifications are used. Use this module to determine how the system should inform you in the event of a problem, when a task is performed, or if an event requiring your immediate attention occurs.

In the upper part of the dialog, select the application for which to configure the system notifications. As soon as you select a program, all events the application can send to the user are listed in the lower window. Determine the notification type for each notification in the 'Actions' dialog.

The standard view of the system notification dialog only offers the activation of a 'Play a sound' check box for audible notification. Click 'More Options' to access other action modes. You can log the notification to a file, execute a program, or show the message in a pop-up window. In the lower part of the dialog under 'Quick Controls', globally activate or deactivate the actions for all programs.

5.2.4 Appearance & Themes

This item features all fine tuning options for the appearance of your desktop.

Screen saver

The module for selecting and configuring the screensaver consists of three parts. Select a suitable screensaver from the list to the left. The preview to the right shows how the selected program looks. Use 'Setup' and 'Test' to test the screensaver in the running system and configure it.

Start screen saver automatically For the screensaver to be activated automatically, select this check box and specify the time (in minutes) after which the screensaver should be activated.

Require password to stop screen saver The screensaver can block your workstation and require a password for the release.

Priority Use the slider to set the priority of the screensaver in relation to other processes. If you use a graphically complicated screensaver that generates a high processor load, set the priority higher to achieve a smooth display quality. In this case, the priority of other processes is reduced accordingly. However, if you frequently let your machine work while you do other things, you should refrain from running a complex screensaver with a high priority.

Colors

Use this module to manage and edit color schemes for your desktop. Select one of the many existing schemes. The preview window displays all desktop elements in the defined colors. To change the color of one or several widgets, select the name of the widget from the drop-down menu under 'Widget Color' and click the color bar below to choose a suitable color in the color editor. Finally, adjust the contrast settings and save the modified scheme under a name of your choice. To apply this scheme globally, activate 'Apply colors to non-KDE applications'.

Window Decorations

Select a decoration style for your application windows from the list under the 'General' tab. Click 'Apply' to test the selected style. To position or move individual elements of the title bar, activate 'Use custom titlebar button positions' and rearrange the elements under the 'Buttons' tab. If additional configuration options are available for the selected style, access these under the 'Configure' tab.

Background

Determine a background for your desktop. By default, your modifications are applied to all virtual desktops. To configure the backgrounds separately for the individual virtual desktops, deactivate 'Common Background'. The effect of your configuration can be seen in the preview at the top right of the dialog window.

The background colors can be selected under the 'Background' tab. To modify the color components, click the color bar next to 'Color 1' or 'Color 2' to open a color editor. Here, change the color settings as desired or use the pipette to adopt a color from any desktop element or a loaded image or web page. Select special gradient effects under 'Mode'.

To use an image as a background for one or several backgrounds, activate 'Single Wallpaper'. Then select the scaling mode or the position of the wallpaper on your desktop and designate a suitable wallpaper with the drop-down menu or the 'Browse...' button. Alternatively, drag and drop image files from your file manager (see Section 5.3 on page 150) or the desktop to the preview image. For wallpaper variety, activate 'Multiple Wallpapers' and proceed with the further configuration using 'Setup Multiple...'.

The 'Advanced' tab features some special settings that usually do not need to modified.

Fonts

All fonts and font attributes used on the desktop can be configured here. Click 'Choose...' then specify your settings in the dialog that opens. By default, antialiasing is activated for all fonts. To deactivate or customize antialiasing, select the respective check boxes.

Note

Changes to the antialiasing settings are only applied to newly-started programs. Programs already open are not affected by the changes.

Note

Style

Here, select the style for all widgets (elements of the graphical interface) in KDE applications. The configuration contains three tabs. Select the style under 'Style', using the preview in the lower part of the window. Use 'Effects' to configure various GUI effects and transparency types, if supported by the respective style.

5.2.5 Regional & Accessibility

Country/Region & Language

The settings in this module only apply to KDE applications. Other applications, such as OpenOffice.org, may need to be configured separately. All regional system settings can be configured under five tabs.

Locale Use the drop-down menu to select the desired country from the list. Settings, such as the language, numbers, currency, time, and date are automatically set to suitable values. A preview of all current regional settings is displayed in the lower part of the dialog. For example, to use the regional settings for the US but use Spanish as the system language, click 'Add Language' to select this language and add it to the list of available system languages. To remove a language, mark it in the list and click 'Remove Language'.

Numbers To use different number settings than the default settings associated with the country selected under 'Locale', configure the decimal symbol, thousands separator, positive sign, and negative sign in this dialog. The decimal symbol and the thousands separator for currencies are configured separately under the 'Money' tab. The default setting on a US system is "." for the decimal symbol, an optional "," for the thousands separator, no entry for the positive sign, and "-" for the representation of negative numbers.

Money Configure all currency-related settings that should differ from the default settings for the selected system language in this dialog. For example, on a US system, the currency symbol is "$", the decimal symbol is ".", thousands are separated with a ",", and the number of fraction digits is "2". The position of the currency symbol and the prefix for positive and negative amounts is arranged in such a way that the currency symbol precedes the prefix and the amount.

Time & Date Here, enter the time format, the date format, the short date format, and the first day of the week. A detailed explanation is displayed if you click the "?" symbol in the title bar then the respective menu item.

Other This tab features the setting for the default paper format and measurements. On a US system, the default paper format is "US Letter" and the imperial system is used for measurements.

Keyboard Shortcuts

This module comprises two tabs. Use the 'Shortcut Schemes' tab to select an existing layout or create new keyboard layout schemes. The 'Modifier Keys' tab provides an overview of the special keys available on your keyboard.

Your system offers a number of predefined shortcuts for specific tasks arranged in schemes. Use the 'Shortcut Schemes' tab to manage all shortcuts on your system. By default, the following schemes are available on your system:

- Windows Scheme (With Win Key)
- Mac Scheme
- KDE Default for 3 Modifier Keys
- KDE Default for 4 Modifier Keys
- Windows Scheme (Without Win Key)
- Unix Scheme

To change the scheme used on your system, select one of the listed schemes and adopt it globally ('Global Shortcuts', 'Shortcut Sequences', and 'Application Shortcuts') or assign shortcuts to individual actions and save them as a custom scheme.

To create a new shortcut for an action or modify an existing shortcut, select the tab for the respective area (e.g., 'Global Shortcuts') and click the action to assign (e.g., 'Show Taskmanager'). The section 'Shortcut for Selected Action' is then activated in the lower part of the dialog. Three radio buttons offer the basic configuration options none, default, and custom.

Existing schemes are write-protected, allowing restoration of the default values at any time. Save your own modifications by clicking 'Save...' at the top right and entering a name for your custom scheme. The new scheme is then listed in the selection menu.

Note

Under 'Application Shortcuts', you can only configure standard actions available in all applications. Program-specific shortcuts must be configured in the program itself via 'Settings' -> 'Configure Shortcuts'.

Note

Accessibility

The settings in this module facilitate the access to the system for users with hearing problems or motor disorders. This module contains the 'Bell' and 'Keyboard' tabs.

Audible bell System bells can be communicated to the user in a visible or in an audible form. The default setting is the audible variant with 'Use System bell'. To configure a specific sound, activate 'Use customized bell' and use 'Browse...' to select a suitable sound from the list.

Visible bell For system bells to be communicated visually, activate 'Use visible bell'. If no other modifications are performed, the screen is inverted when a system bell rings ('Invert screen' is activated by default). The duration of the visual bell can be adjusted with the slider. Instead of the inversion, the screen can be set flash. To do this, activate 'Flash screen' and select a suitable color in the color editor by clicking the color bar.

Sticky Keys Some shortcuts require a key to be held down (this is the case with Alt, Ctrl, and Shift) while the second part of the shortcut is entered. If sticky keys are used, the system considers these keys to be pressed continuously even if they are only pressed once.

Slow Keys Here, determine if and to what extent the system delays the output of characters on the screen when a key is pressed. The longer the interval adjusted with the slider is, the longer a key can be pressed without triggering a repeated output of the respective character on the screen.

Bounce Keys If you activate this option, pressing a key twice is only interpreted as two characters if the interval selected with the slider has elapsed. If a key is pressed twice inadvertently, this will be ignored.

5.3 Konqueror as a File Manager

Konqueror is a unified web browser, file manager, document viewer, and image viewer. The following paragraphs cover the use of Konqueror for file management. Start Konqueror by clicking the house icon in the panel. The contents of your home directory are then displayed.

The file manager window consists of the menu bar at the top, the toolbar, and the location bar. The lower part of the window is split vertically into the navigation panel and the main window, which displays the contents.

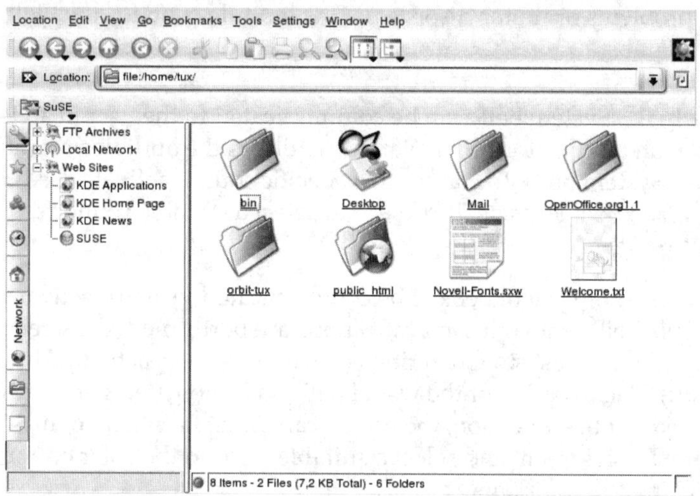

Figure 5.3: The File Manager Konqueror

5.3.1 The Konqueror Menu

Location Using the 'Location' menu, open additional Konqueror windows. If you click 'New Window', your home directory is displayed in a new window. 'Duplicate Window' produces a second window with the same content. You can also send a file or a link (using the browser function) by e-mail. If you click one of these menu items, the KMail composer opens. Specify the recipient and compose a text. Depending on the selected item, the file is already attached or the link is displayed in the e-mail body. You can also print directly from this menu.

Edit Most items under 'Edit' only become active if you select an object in the main window. Standard editing functions are available. The 'Shred' function destroys the data permanently. Create new directories and files or change file properties, such as the file permissions. Grant or deny the user, a group, or all users read, write, and execute permissions. In the main window, one or several files can be selected by moving the mouse pointer over them while keeping the left mouse button pressed or by using the selection functions in the 'Edit' menu.

View Use the 'View' menu to change views. If a directory is very full, the text view or the tree view may be more efficient. To view HTML pages, activate 'Use index.html'. With 'Lock to Current Location', stop animated images and, with 'Unlock View', resume the animation. 'Icon Size', 'Sort', 'Preview', 'Show Hidden Files', and 'Folder Icons Reflect Contents' control the icons shown in the main window. Also use this menu to choose a color or image for the background.

Go The 'Go' menu contains the navigation functions. However, you can access these functions more quickly in the toolbar. One interesting feature is available under this menu: the list of recently viewed directories, which can be selected and displayed.

Bookmarks Bookmarks can be Internet addresses (URL) or paths to specific files or directories on your host. If you select 'Add Bookmark', the current content of the location bar is saved as a bookmark. To access this location, simply click this bookmark. For practical reasons, arrange bookmarks in folders. The `SuSE` folder already exists. This folder contains bookmarks of important SUSE web pages. 'Edit Bookmarks' opens the bookmark editor in which to perform tasks like deleting obsolete bookmarks, renaming bookmarks, and moving bookmarks from one folder to another.

Settings Use the 'Settings' menu to configure the look and feel of Konqueror. Hide the menu bar by deactivating 'Display Menubar'. Press Ctrl + M to display it again. Under 'Toolbars', hide or display the main toolbar, an extra toolbar, the location bar, and the bookmark list. If you changed the view of a specific directory, save these changes under 'View Properties Saved in Directory' or 'Remove Directory Properties'. Using view profiles, change the view by means of predefined patterns. The default setting is 'File Management'. Under 'Load View Profile', switch to 'File Preview', 'Midnight Commander', or 'Web

Browsing'. For example, when you click the Konqueror icon in the panel, the web browser profile is displayed. Specify individual keyboard shortcuts with 'Configure Shortcuts', customize the toolbar with 'Configure Toolbars', and configure global settings for the file manager with 'Configure Konqueror'.

Window In the 'Window' menu, you can split the main window horizontally and vertically. With 'Remove Active View', remove the split. 'New Tab' creates an empty window in the Konqueror window. Switch between these windows with tabs. With 'Duplicate Current Tab', generate a second identical window that can be loaded to a separate Konqueror window with 'Detach Tab'. You can also close the active subwindow.

Help Under the 'Help' menu, access the Konqueror handbook or the 'What's This?' function. This function can also be accessed via the question mark symbol at the top right in the title bar. The mouse pointer is then displayed with a question mark. If you click an icon, a brief help text is displayed. The 'Help' menu also provides a short introduction to Konqueror and the possibility to report bugs and other concerns to the developers. 'About Konqueror' and 'About KDE' provide information about the version, license, authors, and translations of the project.

5.3.2 The Toolbar

The toolbar provides quick access to frequently-used functions that can also be accessed via the menu. If you let the mouse pointer rest above an icon, a short description is displayed. Right-click a free space in the toolbar to open a menu with which to change the position of the toolbar, switch from icons to text, change the icon size, and display or hide the individual bars. The configuration dialog can be started with 'Configure Toolbars'. To the right, the toolbar features the Konqueror icon, which is animated while a directory or web page is loaded.

5.3.3 The Location Bar

The location bar is preceded by a black symbol with a white X. If you click this icon, the contents of the line are deleted, allowing entry of a new location. Valid locations can be path specifications, like the one that appears when the home directory is displayed, or web page URLs. After entering an address, press Enter or click 'Go' to the right of the input line. Access directories or web pages visited recently via the black arrow to the right of the location bar. This function saves some typing if you need to access certain contents repeatedly. For even more convenience, create a bookmark.

5.3.4 The Main Window

The main window displays the content of the selected directory. If you click an icon, the respective file is displayed in Konqueror or loaded into the respective application for further processing. If you click an RPM package, the description is displayed. Install the package with 'Install package with YaST'.

If you right-click an icon, a menu opens. The kind of menu displayed depends on the file type and offers common actions, such as 'Cut', 'Copy', 'Copy', 'Paste', and 'Delete'. Use 'Open with' to select the application with which to open the file from a list of suitable programs. Files can be encrypted directly in Konqueror. However, to use this function, a key must be generated manually or in KGpg. Refer to Chapter 15 on page 249 to see how this is done.

The quickest way to perform many actions is the drag and drop method. For instance, easily move files from one Konqueror window to another by simply dragging them there while pressing the left mouse button. Subsequently, you will be asked whether the objects should be moved or copied.

5.3.5 Creating an Image Gallery

To facilitate the management of extensive image collections in a directory, Konqueror can generate an HTML file with thumbnails. Open the respective directory in Konqueror and select 'Tools' -> 'Create Image Gallery ...'. A dialog opens in which to specify the background and foreground colors, the page title, the location to which to save the gallery, and other settings. Click 'OK' to start the action. By default, a file called `index.html` is created. If you click this file in Konqueror, your images are displayed in a miniaturized, well-arranged view. Click an image to access the full-size view.

5.4 Important Utilities

The following pages introduce a number of small KDE utilities intended to assist in daily work. These applications perform various tasks, such as managing your keys for encrypting and signing files and e-mail messages, managing your clipboard, formatting floppy disks, compressing and decompressing diverse file archive types, and sharing your desktop with other users.

5.4.1 KInternet — Connecting to the Internet

To surf the Internet or send and receive e-mail messages, connect a modem or an ISDN or Ethernet card to your machine and configure it. This can be done with the help of the system assistant YaST. As soon as the respective device has been configured correctly, control the Internet dial-up with KInternet.

On start-up, KDE loads KInternet. The program checks whether an Internet connection can be established. If this is possible, the application icon, a plug, automatically appears in the right part of the KDE panel. The following is an overview of the icons and their meanings:

Currently there is no connection to the Internet.

The connection is just being established or terminated.

The connection has been established.

Data is transmitted to or from the Internet.

An error has occurred. If a connection has already been configured with YaST, use 'View Log ...' to identify the reason for the error. The menu can be accessed by right-clicking the KInternet icon.

The connection is not yet active, but will be established as soon as a request is made.

Right-click KInternet to access a menu for configuring KInternet. To configure your access, select 'Settings ...' -> 'Configure with YaST ...'. After entering the root password, YaST is started. Depending on the access type, start the modem, ISDN, network, or DSL configuration of YaST to select a provider from a list.

KInternet can do even more: if the option 'Channel Bundling' is activated in YaST, a second ISDN channel can be added to an existing connection with 'Add link'. This doubles the transfer rate (although at a higher price). Activate channel bundling if you need to download large files. The activated channel bundling is evident from the red plus symbol at the top left corner of the KInternet icon.

Users who want to establish Internet connections automatically can use *dial on demand* (DoD). If this mode is selected, KInternet automatically connects to your Internet service provider (ISP) as soon as a request is submitted. After a certain time-out, the connection is terminated. A DoD connection is evident from the blue D at the bottom right corner of the KInternet icon. DoD only makes sense if you have a flat rate Internet account. Otherwise the repeated establishment and termination of the connection can be quite costly.

5.4.2 The Download Manager KGet

KGet is the download manager for KDE, similar to GetRight or Golzilla. With

KGet, manage your transfers in a window. Stop, resume, delete, and queue transfers and add new transfers.

Adding Transfers

Start KGet by pressing Alt + F2 and entering the command `kget`. When the program is started for the first time, a dialog is displayed. Confirm this dialog to integrate KGet in Konqueror. When you close the dialog, KGet is integrated in the system tray of the panel as an icon with a downward arrow.

Click this arrow to open the dialog displaying your transfers. To add a transfer to the list, select the menu item 'File' -> 'Paste'. A dialog opens. Enter a URL in the input field and confirm with 'OK'. Then specify the location for saving the downloaded file. After all information has been entered, the entry for the transfer is added to the main window of KGet and started.

Another way to add a transfer is by means of drag and drop. Simply drag a file (e.g., from an FTP server) from Konqueror and drop it in the main window.

Timer-Controlled Transfers

You can also instruct KGet to perform your transfers at a specific time. Activate 'Options' -> 'Offline Mode'. All transfers inserted from this point are not started immediately but queued. To start the clock, double-click the respective entry. A dialog opens. Select 'Advanced'. The dialog is expanded by the settings needed for starting the transfer at a certain time. Enter the day, month, year, and time. Then close the window.

After making the desired settings for all your transfers, set KGet back to the online mode by deactivating 'Options' -> 'Offline Mode'. The transfers should start at the specified times.

Settings

In 'Settings' -> 'Configure KGet ...', set preferences for the connection, determine directories for specific file extensions, and specify other settings.

5.4.3 SuSEWatcher

SuSEWatcher is a program that is integrated in the system tray of the panel. It checks for new updates and new hardware. To be able to find any new updates, it requires an online connection. The program SuSEWatcher is located in the package `kdebase3-SuSE`. The status of SuSEWatcher is displayed by means of colorful icons in the panel.

When you click the icon in the panel, a window opens, informing you about the status of your online updates and the availability of any new updates. You can also launch the check manually by clicking 'Check for updates'. Start the online update by selecting 'Start online update' and entering the root password. The YaST Online Update window is displayed.

5.4.4 The Clipboard Klipper

The KDE program Klipper serves as a clipboard for selected text, normally marked by keeping the left mouse button pressed. This text can be transferred to another application by moving the mouse pointer to the target location then pressing the middle mouse button (on a two-button mouse, press both buttons simultaneously). The text is copied to the selected location from the clipboard.

By default, Klipper is started when KDE is loaded and appears as a clipboard icon in the panel. View the contents of the clipboard by clicking this icon. The Klipper context menu and the last seven entries, also referred to as the history, are displayed (see Figure 5.4). If an extensive text was copied to Klipper, only the first line of the text is displayed. The most recent entry is listed on top and is marked as active with a black check mark. To copy an older text fragment from Klipper to an application, select it by clicking it, move the mouse pointer to the target application, and then middle-click.

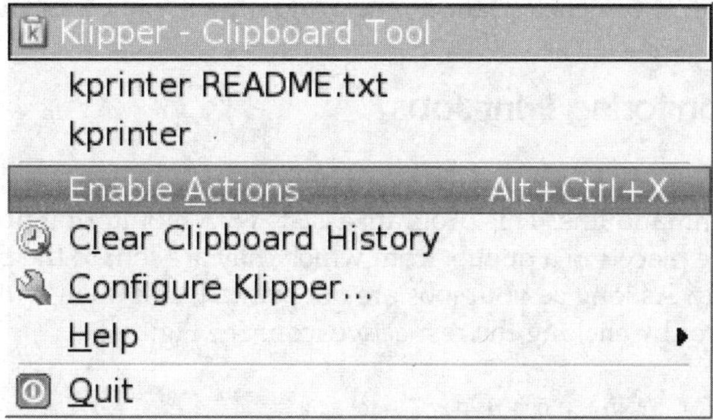

Figure 5.4: The Clipboard Klipper

As well as the contents of the clipboard, the context menu features the following menu items:

Enable Actions If you click this, a black check mark is displayed in front of it. For example, if you mark a URL with the mouse when actions are enabled, a window opens, enabling you to select a browser for displaying this URL. Click 'Actions Enabled' to disable this function.

Clear Clipboard History Deletes all entries from the clipboard.

Configure Klipper... This opens the Klipper configuration dialog. Klipper can be customized in many ways. Control the program with keyboard shortcuts or use regular expressions. Check the Klipper handbook for details. Former Windows users may appreciate the option for activating the keyboard shortcuts Ctrl + C and Ctrl + X for cutting and Ctrl + V for pasting under the 'General' tab. To use this feature, activate the entry 'Synchronize contents of the clipboard and the selection' in 'Clipboard/Selection Behavior'. Subsequently, use the mouse or the keyboard shortcuts to which you are accustomed.

Help This item opens a submenu from which to open the Klipper handbook, send a bug report to the developers, and view information about Klipper and KDE.

Quit If you click 'Quit', a dialog is displayed asking whether Klipper should be started automatically the next time you log in. If you click 'No', start the program from the main menu the next time you want to use it. If you click 'Cancel', the program will not be terminated.

5.4.5 Monitoring Print Jobs

Start KJobViewer from the main menu or with the command `kjobviewer` from the command line. This program assists with monitoring print jobs. Print jobs are placed in a queue, from which they are sent to the printer consecutively. As long as your jobs are not printed, edit them with the 'Jobs' menu or by clicking the respective icon. See Figure 5.5.

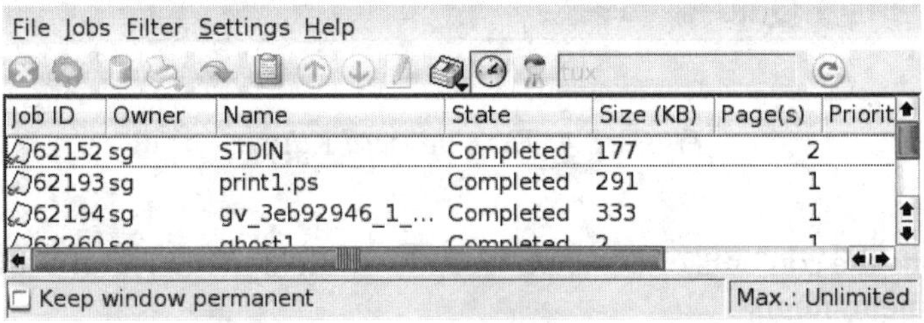

Figure 5.5: Monitoring Print Jobs with KJobViewer

If, for example, you want to check if you sent the correct document to the printer, you can stop the job and resume it if you decide to print it. Remove your own print jobs from the queue with 'Remove'. To change the printer, select a different printer with 'Move to Printer ...'.

With 'Restart', reprint a document. To do this, select 'Toggle Completed Jobs' from the 'Filter' menu, select the desired document, and click 'Restart' in the 'Jobs' menu. 'Job IPP Report ...' contains the technical details of a job. Use 'Increase Priority' and 'Decrease Priority' to set the priority, depending on how quickly you need the document.

'Filter' enables you to switch between various printers, toggle completed jobs, and limit the view to your own print jobs by selecting 'Show Only User Jobs'. The current user will be displayed in the top right field.

'Settings' -> 'Configure KJobViewer ...' opens a configuration dialog. Here, determine the maximum number of print jobs to display. Enter a number in the field or use the slider to the right to determine a value. Press 'OK' to save the setting or 'Cancel' to exit the dialog without saving.

The icons in the toolbar correspond to the functions you can access by way of the menu. A help text explaining the function is displayed when you move the mouse pointer over one of the icons.

The job list consists of eight columns. The job ID is automatically assigned by the print system to identify the various jobs. The next column contains the login of the user who sent the job followed by the file name of the document. The status column indicates whether a job is still in the queue, currently being printed, or already completed. Next, the size of the document is displayed in kilobytes and number of pages. The default priority of 50 can be increased or reduced if necessary. Billing information can be cost centers or other company-specific information. If you right-click a job in the list, the 'Jobs' menu opens under the mouse pointer, allowing you to select an action. Only a few functions are available for completed jobs. If you activate 'Keep window permanent', KJobViewer window opens automatically when you log in the next time. You can also start KJobViewer using the printer icon in the panel.

5.4.6 Formatting Floppy Disks with KFloppy

KFloppy is the floppy disk formatter of KDE. Start the program from the main menu or from the command line with the command `kfloppy`. KFloppy opens a dialog, shown in Figure 5.6 on the next page, in which to specify a number of settings. Under 'Floppy Drive', select the primary or the secondary drive, provided your machine has two floppy disk drives. The default setting for the size is '3.5" 1.44 MB', which is the most commonly used floppy disk type. The setting for the file system is very important. Choose between the Linux format ext2 and MS-DOS. If you select MS-DOS, you will be able to read and write the floppy disk on a Windows machine.

In the center, select 'Quick Format' or 'Full Format'. The quick format procedure merely rewrites the file system and deletes all data. The full format procedure rewrites all tracks and sectors and is able to detect and mark bad sectors. Sectors marked as bad are not used for writing data. Select 'Verify Integrity' to have the formatting checked and verified upon completion. If you activate 'Volume Label', designate a name for the floppy disk in the input field below.

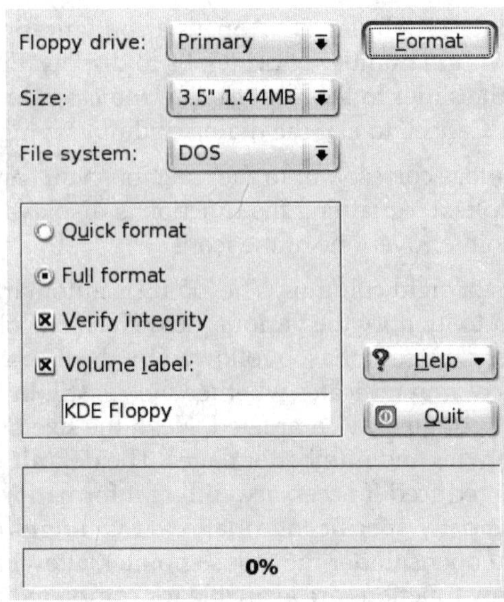

Figure 5.6: The Floppy Disk Formatter KFloppy

After making all settings, click 'Format'. You will be warned that all data on the disk will be lost and prompted to confirm. KFloppy informs you if any problems occur during the formatting procedure, including information about any bad sectors.

Click 'Help' to access a short menu that offers the KFloppy handbook. Additionally use it to send a bug report or other concerns to the developers of KFloppy. Selecting 'About KFloppy' accesses information about the version, authors, translation, and license. 'About KDE' provides information about KDE and web pages of the KDE developers. Exit KFloppy by clicking 'Quit'.

5.4.7 Ark: Displaying, Decompressing, and Creating Archives

To save space on the hard disk, use a packer that compresses files and directories to a fraction of their original size. The application Ark can be used to manage such archives. It supports common formats, such as `zip`, `tar.gz`, `tar.bz2`, `lha`, `rar`, and `zoo`.

Start Ark from the main menu or from the command line with the command `ark`. If you already have some compressed files, move these from an open Konqueror window to the Ark window to view the contents of the archive. To view an integrated preview of the archive in Konqueror, right-click the archive in Konqueror and select 'Preview in Archiver'. Alternatively, select 'File' -> 'Open' in Ark to open the file directly. See Figure 5.7.

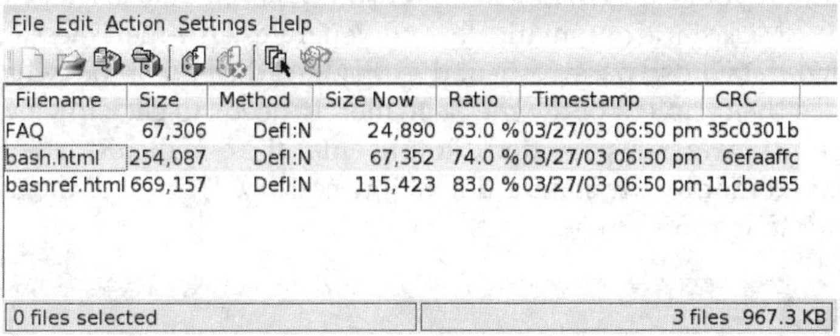

File Edit Action Settings Help

Filename	Size	Method	Size Now	Ratio	Timestamp	CRC
FAQ	67,306	Defl:N	24,890	63.0 %	03/27/03 06:50 pm	35c0301b
bash.html	254,087	Defl:N	67,352	74.0 %	03/27/03 06:50 pm	6efaaffc
bashref.html	669,157	Defl:N	115,423	83.0 %	03/27/03 06:50 pm	11cbad55

0 files selected 3 files 967.3 KB

Figure 5.7: Ark: File Archive Preview

Once you have opened an archive, perform various actions. 'Action' offers options such as 'Add File', 'Add Directory', 'Delete', 'Extract', 'View', 'Edit With', and 'Open With'.

To create a new archive, select 'File' -> 'New'. Enter the name of the new archive in the dialog that opens. If you enter a file extension, an archive with the specified format is generated. If you omit the extension, `.zip` is used as the default.

After you have entered the archive name, an empty window is displayed. Move files or directories into this window from Konqueror. Ark compresses and lists the files. For more information about Ark, go to 'Help' -> 'Ark Handbook'.

5.4.8 Desktop Sharing

You can share your desktop for use by other users on their hosts. Desktop sharing makes use of the RFB protocol, more commonly referred to as VNC. This feature enables a Linux desktop to be made available for clients using other operating systems, provided they support VNC.

To grant trustworthy users access to your desktop, send them a password. This can be done by means of an invitation. Start the Control Center from the main menu and select 'Desktop Sharing' in the 'Internet & Network' module.

Click 'Create & manage invitations' and choose between 'Create Personal Invitation...' and 'Invite via Email'. If you click 'Create Personal Invitation...', an invitation indicating the IP address of the host, password, and expiry of the invitation is generated. Send this data manually to the respective person. If you click 'Invite via Email', all required data is transmitted by e-mail. KMail starts automatically and generates an e-mail message with the needed data (host, password, and expiry). At the end of the e-mail, a link, which the recipient of the message merely needs to click to view your desktop in a browser, is provided. Simply enter the e-mail address of the recipient and modify the standard text, if necessary. Then send the message. Refer to Figure 5.8.

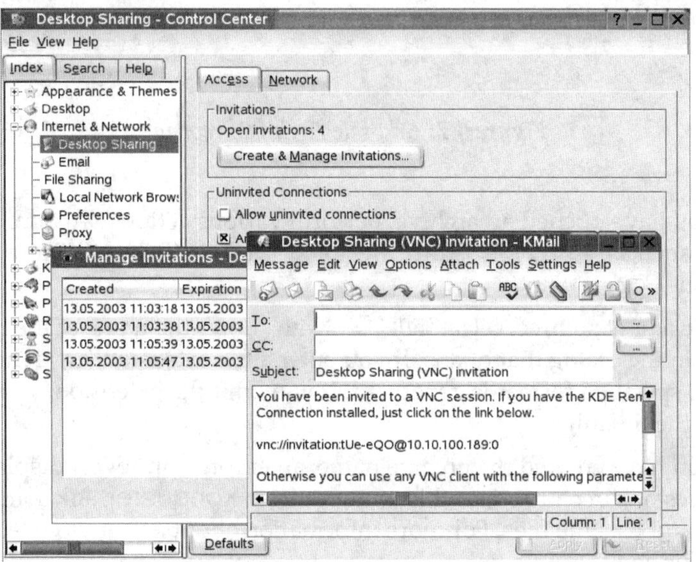

Figure 5.8: Desktop Sharing with Invitation by E-Mail

Use 'Delete All...' to revoke all invitations. To delete an individual invitation, select it then click 'Delete...'.

If an invited person requests a connection, KDE informs you about this request. Decide to accept or deny the connection. If you accept the connection, also use the check box to release the keyboard and mouse control. For security reasons, the maximum duration for a connection is one hour.

To change the default settings, start the 'Control Center' via 'Settings' in the main menu. In the left frame, select 'Internet & Network' -> 'Desktop Sharing'. Various configuration options are available in the lower part of the window. However, for security reasons you should not modify the default settings.

5.4.9 KSnapshot: Taking Screenshots

With KSnapshot, create snapshots of your screen or special applications. Start the program from the main menu or from the command line with the command `ksnapshot`. The dialog window of KSnapshot consists of two parts (see Figure 5.9). The upper area ('Current Snapshot') contains a preview of the current screen and three buttons for creating and saving the screenshots. In the lower part of the window, determine further options for the actual creation of the screenshot.

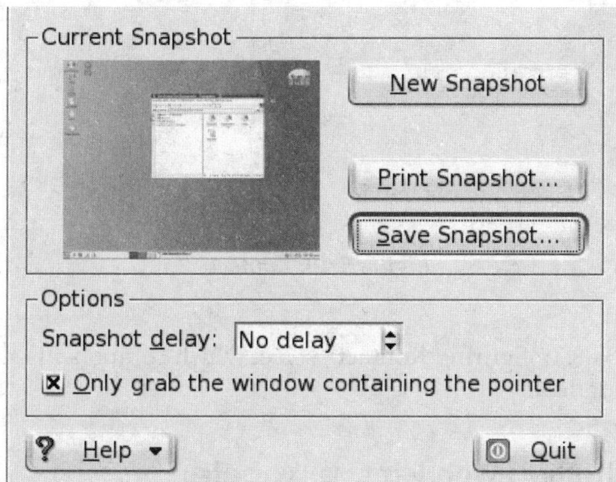

Figure 5.9: Taking Screenshots with KSnapshot

To take a screenshot, use 'Snapshot delay' to determine the period in seconds to wait between the click on 'New Snapshot' and the actual creation of the screenshot. If 'Only grab the window containing the pointer' is active, only the window containing the pointer is "photographed." To save the screenshot, click 'Save Snapshot...' and designate the directory and file name for the image in the following dialog. Use 'Print Snapshot...' to print the screenshot.

5.4.10 Kontact

The application Kontact bundles the display of e-mails, notes, contacts, news, weather, and a calendar into one window. Open it by pressing Alt-F2 and entering `kontact`. See Figure 5.10.

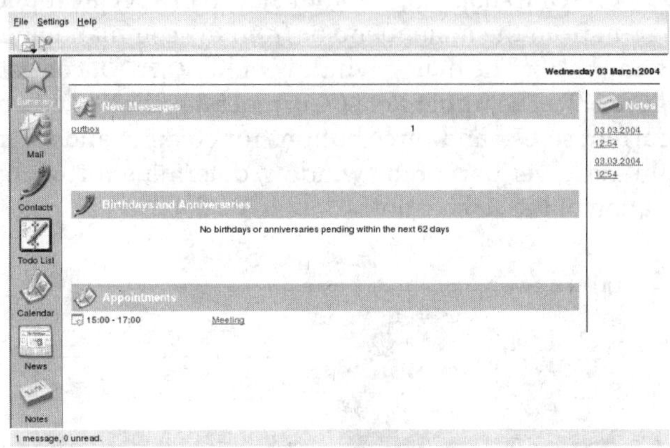

Figure 5.10: Kontact

In 'Settings' → 'Configuring Kontact', select which components should appear in the window.

5.4.11 Chatting With Friends: Kopete

Kopete is an online messenger application allowing multiple partners connected to the Internet to chat with each other. Kopete currently supports all common messenger protocols, such as ICQ, MSN, Yahoo, SMS, Jabber, and IRC.

Configuring Kopete

Configure Kopete by entering your personal user data. Click 'Settings' -> 'Configure Kopete'. 'Connections' shows all currently available protocols. Check the desired connection type to activate it.

With 'Accounts', enter your user data. You must register with a provider offering instant messaging services before using such service. Click 'New' to open a configuration assistant that can assist you in completing your user profile.

The next step lists the avilable messaging services. Select the service with which you have registered and click 'Continue'. In the next step, enter the user data received upon registration with the messaging service. This usually consists of the nickname or e-mail address and the password you chose. Complete the configuration of the messenger account by clicking 'Finish'.

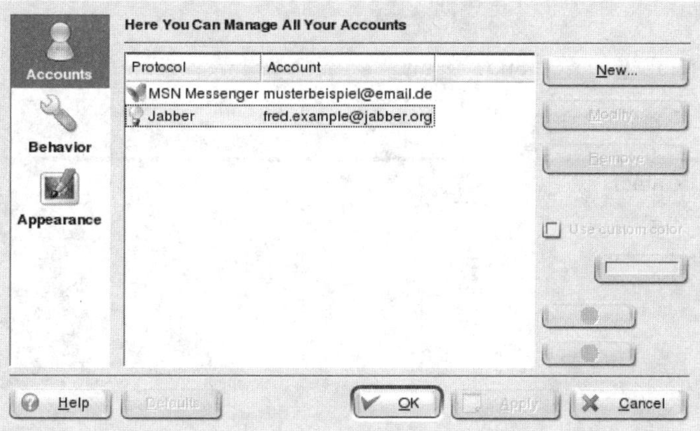

Figure 5.11: Kopete Configuration Panels

The next item in the configuration dialog is 'Appearance'. It influences how Kopete is displayed. The tab 'Emoticons' provides a selection of various types of smileys.

The tabs 'Chat window' and 'Colors & Fonts' offer the possibility to adjust the appearance of the chat windows for communication with other participants. Choose between the classic themes of the corresponding providers or to create a custom theme by adjusting the font or color to personal preference.

Adding Contacts

It is necessary to add contacts in order to chat with a participant. If you have already created an account on another PC, this data is readily imported and automatically added to your contact list. To create a contact entry manually, click 'File' -> 'Add contact'.

A new assistant appears automatically that will accompany you until completion. However, consider that must be online to add a contact to your list.

Adding Groups

Access this with 'File' → 'Create New Group'. Name the group and confirm this with 'OK'. A new folder appears in the contact list that can be used to store the desired contacts. You can drag and drop contacts into the desired folder. This allows grouping contacts for a better overview.

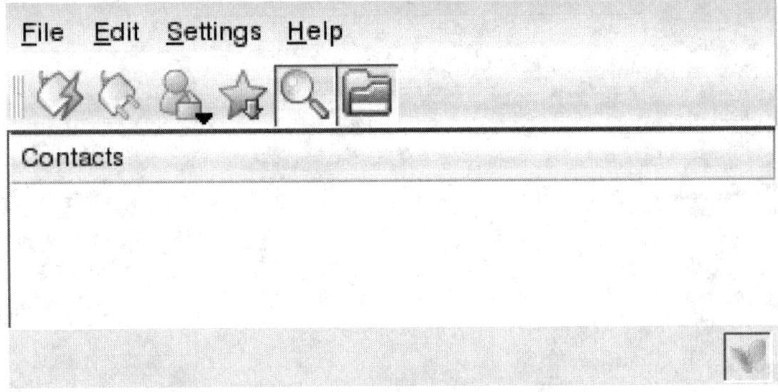

Figure 5.12: The Main Kopete Application

Using Kopete

It is necessary to establish a connection to the Internet to be able to chat with other participants. When this is done, clicking 'File' → 'Connection' → 'Connect All' then establish a connection between Kopete and the selected messaging service.

The main application windows features a list of contacts. When you right-click a contact marked as online, a menu opens with various options. Send that person a message or start a chatting session. A chat allows invitation of other participants for real-time discussion. The connection to all other participants is closed when the creator of the chat session leaves the room first.

Files can be transferred comfortably with an instant messenger by right-clicking a user and then clicking his name. Many options, like 'Delete Contact', 'Show User Information', 'Block User', and 'Send File', can be found here. Clicking 'Send File' opens a dialog for selecting the desired file. Confirming with 'OK' sends a dialog to the receiving user asking whether he wants to accept the file. If he accepts, the file transfer starts.

5.4.12 Font Administration with KFontinst

By default, SUSE LINUX provides various fonts commonly available in different file formats (Bitmap, TrueType, etc.). These are commonly known as *System Fonts*. Users can additionally install their own fonts from various collections on CD-ROM. Such user-installed fonts are, however, only visible and available to the corresponding user.

The KDE control center provides a comfortable tool for administering system and user fonts. It is shown in Figure 5.13.

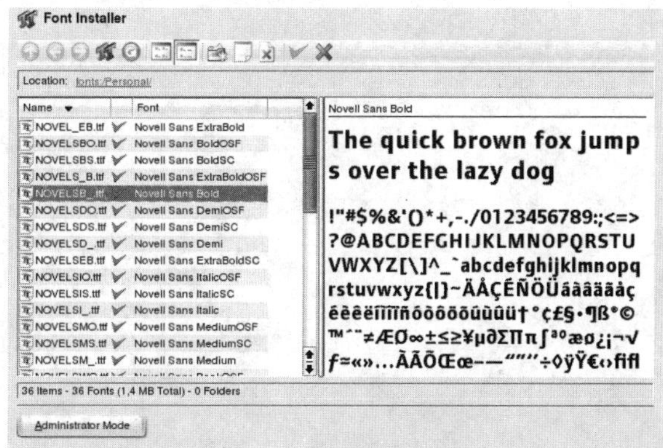

Figure 5.13: Font Administration from the Control Center

To check which fonts are currently available, type the URL `fonts:/` into the address field of a Konqueror session. This displays two windows: `Personal/` and `System/`. User-installed fonts are installed to the folder `Personal/`. Only root can install to the `System/` folder.

To install fonts as a user, follow these steps:

1. Start the Control Center and access the appropriate module with 'System Administration' → 'Font Installation'.

2. Choose 'Add Fonts' from the icon bar or from the menu available when right-clicking the list.

3. In the dialog that opens, select one or more fonts for installation.

4. The marked fonts are then installed to your personal font folder. Selecting a font shows a preview.

To update system fonts, first select 'System administration mode' and enter your root password then proceed as described for user font installation.

The feature for deactivating installed fonts is very useful. They are not removed but are made unavailable to the system. Select the 'deactivate' icon or its counterpart from the context menu. This makes the green checkmark disappear. The new settings become active after confirmation with 'Apply'. The deactivated fonts are then no longer available to applications. This reduces the size of font lists displayed in applications.

The GNOME Desktop

GNOME (GNU Network Object Model Environment) is a fast Linux desktop. The aim of its development was to make the user interface more uniform while streamlining the various aspects of the look and feel. The basic components for window management and other components enable data sharing among various applications and are based on a uniform operating concept and help system.

6.1 The Desktop

The most important elements of the GNOME desktop are the icons on the desktop, the panel at the lower border, and the desktop menu. The mouse is your most important tool.

6.1.1 The Icons

By default, the desktop features three symbols: your personal folder, the start dialog for the configuration of the desktop, and the trash can. If you double-click your personal folder, Nautilus starts and displays your home directory. More information about the use of Nautilus is available in Section 6.3 on page 177. All files deleted with Nautilus are sent to the trash can.

Right-clicking an icon displays a menu offering file operations, like copying, cutting, or renaming. Selecting 'Properties' from the menu displays a configuration dialog. The title of an icon as well as the icon itself can be changed with 'Use custom icon'. The 'Emblems' tab offers the possibility to add graphical descriptive symbols to the icon. The 'Permissions' tab provides access to the access, read, and write permission settings for this file for the user, the group, or others. The 'Notes' tab offers the management of comments. The menu for the trash can additionally features the 'Empty Trashcan' option. This deletes its contents.

To remove an icon from the desktop, simply move it into the trash can. However, be careful with this option — if you throw folder icons or file icons into the trash can, the actual data is deleted. If the icons only represent links to a file or to a directory, only the links are deleted.

To create a link on the desktop to a folder or a file, access the object in question with Nautilus. Right-click the object and select 'Make Link'. Drag the link from the Nautilus window and drop it on the desktop.

6.1.2 The Desktop Menu

Right-clicking a free spot on the desktop displays a menu with various options. Select 'New Folder' to create a new folder. Create a launcher icon for an application with 'New Launcher'. Provide the name of the application and the command for starting it then choose an icon to represent it. It is also possible to change the desktop background or to reset it to its default setting.

6.1.3 The Panel

The panel contains the window icons of all started applications in the taskbar. If you click the name of a window in the taskbar, it is moved to the foreground. If the program is already in the foreground, a mouse click minimizes it. Clicking a minimized application reopens the respective window.

Beside the taskbar, the 'Workspace Switcher' provides access to additional work areas. These virtual desktops provide extra space in which to arrange open applications and windows. For example, put an editor on one workspace, some shells on another, and your e-mail application and web browser on a third.

If you right-click an empty spot in the panel, a menu opens, offering help, information, and commands for GNOME and panels. Select 'Properties' to open a configuration dialog in which to change the position and background of the panel. If desired, create additional panels or add launchers, tools, and various applets to the existing panels with 'Add to Panel'. Use drawers to organize your favorite applications or important documents. The contents are only displayed when the drawer is opened with a single click. Right-click the drawer and select 'Properties' to modify its size and appearance. Click the icon to change it. Remove panel elements by right-clicking the respective icons and selecting 'Remove'.

6.1.4 The Main Menu

Open the main menu by means of the icon to the far left of the panel. Apart from the applications, which are organized in categories, find default functions, such as 'Log out' and 'Lock screen'. Use 'Open Recent' to gain quick access to recent files. Use 'Search for Files' to find files.

With 'Run Program ...', enter and run a command, for example, for starting a program instead of navigating through the various program menus. From the main menu, you can also start the 'GNOME Control Center' for configuring the desktop or YaST for installing additional software.

6.1.5 Handling Floppy Disks, CDs, or DVDs

To access floppy disks, CDs, or DVDs, insert the medium in the appropriate drive. Right-click an empty spot of the desktop and select the desired medium from the 'Drives' list. A floppy disk or CD icon appears. Double-clicking the icon launches Nautilus, which displays the contents of the medium. Copy files to your personal home directory by dragging and dropping. Copy files to a floppy disk in the same way.

Caution

Do not simply remove floppy disks from the drive after using them. Floppy disks, CDs, and DVDs must always be unmounted from the system first. Close all Nautilus sessions still accessing the medium then right-click the icon for the medium and select 'eject' from the menu. Then safely remove the floppy disk or CD (the tray opens automatically). The icon disappears from the desktop.

Caution

Floppy disks can also be formatted from the floppy disk menu. In the dialog, choose the format and density of the floppy disk. In 'file system type', choose between 'Linux native (ext2)', the file system for Linux, and 'DOS (FAT)', because Windows cannot access Linux file systems. Help provides some instructions for the tool.

6.2 Settings

The GNOME desktop can be customized according to your preferences and needs. Click the 'Start Here' icon on the desktop. If this icon is not visible, start Nautilus by right-clicking the desktop then selecting 'New Window'. Under 'Location:', enter `preferences://`. Open the various configuration dialogs by double-clicking the respective icons.

Note

In the individual modules, access specific help for the options with 'Help'. The system immediately adopts every change made in a configuration module.

Note

6.2.1 Keyboard

In the 'Keyboard' module, determine settings such as the repeat rate and sound events associated with your keyboard. The module consists of the 'Keyboard' and 'Audio' tabs. Use the 'Audio' tab to configure of an audio signal for your keyboard. For audible notification when a wrong key is pressed, activate the corresponding radio button. Exit the 'Keyboard' module with 'Close' or go the accessibility module with 'Accessibility'. The functionality of this module is described in Section 6.2.9 on page 175.

6.2.2 Mouse Configuration

The mouse configuration consists of three tabs: 'Buttons', 'Cursor', and 'Motion'. The configuration options of the 'Buttons' tab refer to the 'Mouse Orientation'. Left-handed users should activate 'Left-handed mouse' to swap the right and left mouse buttons. Use the slider to determine the maximum delay (in seconds) between two clicks that the system should interpret as a double-click.

The appearance and size of the cursor can be changed under the 'Cursor' tab. Four different settings are available. Changes are not activated until the next login. Under 'Locate Pointer', activate an option that causes the cursor to be highlighted when you press Ctrl, making it easier to find. Under 'Movement', set the 'Acceleration' and 'Sensitivity' of the screen cursor.

6.2.3 Menus and Toolbars

The settings in this module affect the menus and toolbars of all GNOME-compatible applications. Select for toolbar icons to be displayed as 'Text Only', 'Icons Only', 'Text Beside Icons', or 'Text Below Icons'. The default setting is 'Text Only'.

Activate 'Toolbars can be detached and moved around' to allow the detachment of the toolbar from all other window elements and allow its free positioning on the desktop. This makes a grabbing area appear on the left side of the toolbar. Clicking and holding this area relocates the toolbar.

Every menu entry in any application menu can be displayed with the corresponding icon. Activating 'Show icons in menus' tests the settings with the provided example menu.

6.2.4 Screensaver

The module for configuring the screensaver is subdivided into two tabs: 'Display Modes' and 'Advanced'. Select the screensaver in 'Display Modes'. The 'Advanced' tab contains a few special options that normally do not need to be modified.

Select the screen saver mode under the 'Display Modes' tab. Choose from 'Random Screen Saver' (random selection of screen savers from a custom-defined list), 'Only One Screen Saver', 'Blank Screen Only', or 'Disable Screen Saver'.

Select one or more screensavers from the list for the operating modes 'Only One Screen Saver' or 'Random Screen Saver'. The currently selected screensaver is displayed in the small preview window. The 'Preview' button launches a fullscreen preview of that screensaver, which can be aborted by pressing any key. Select the previous or following screensaver for preview by clicking the corresponding triangles below the selection list.

In the last step, determine after how long the screen should be made completely black ('Blank After'), the screensaver module should be changed ('Cycle After'), or the screen should be locked ('Lock Screen After'). All time references are given in minutes.

6.2.5 Windows

This module controls the behavior of application windows. Determine how the window should react to contact with the mouse pointer or to double-clicks on its title and define the key to hold for moving an application window.

When several application windows populate the desktop, the active one, by default, is the one last clicked. Change this behavior by activating 'Select windows when the mouse moves over them'. If desired, activate 'Raise selected window after an interval' and adjust the latency time with the slider. This activates a window only when the cursor was placed within the window for a time exceeding the set latency.

Application windows can be shaded by double-clicking the title bar, leaving only the title bar visible. This saves space on the desktop and is the default behavior. It is alternatively possible to set windows to maximize when the title bar is double-clicked.

With the radio buttons, select the modifier key to press for moving a window. The possible choices are Ctrl, Alt, and the Windows key.

6.2.6 Background

Determine a background for your desktop. By default, the changes made here are applied to all virtual desktop. If you do not want any background picture, click 'No Picture' and define a background style. The drop-down menu offers a horizontal gradient, a vertical gradient, or no gradient at all. Use 'Color' to define the desired colors in the color editor.

To use an image file as a background picture, drag it from the file manager and drop it in 'Select picture'. Alternatively, click 'Select picture' to open a dialog in which to select the desired image.

'Picture Options' determines what processing steps should be applied to the selected image to adapt it optimally to the current screen resolution. The options are 'Wallpaper', 'Centered', 'Scaled', and 'Stretched'.

6.2.7 Font

This module determines the font to use for the desktop. In a second step, enable optional effects for the improvement of the font quality. The upper part of the dialog window shows the fonts selected for 'Application font', 'Desktop font', 'Window title font', and 'Terminal font'. Click one of the buttons to open a selection dialog in which to set the font family, style, and size. The options for 'Font Rendering' and the additional configuration options accessible through 'Details' are set to optimal values by default.

6.2.8 Theme

The style for all control elements on the desktop and of GNOME applications is set here. Choose from various preinstalled themes. Selecting a style in the list overview applies it automatically. 'Details' opens another dialog in which to customize the style of single desktop elements, like window content, window borders, and icons. Making changes and leaving the dialog with 'Close' switches the theme to 'Custom theme'. Click 'Save theme' to save your modified theme under a custom name. The Internet and other sources provide many additional themes for GNOME as `.tar.gz` files. Install these with 'Install theme'.

6.2.9 Accessibility

The settings of this module facilitate the use of the keyboard for users with motion impairments. The module consists of the three tabs 'Basic', 'Filters', and 'Mouse'. Before modifying settings, activate 'Enable keyboard accessibility features'.

Features The keyboard accessibility functions can be deactivated automatically after a certain time. Set an appropriate time limit measured in seconds with the slider. The system can additionally provide audible feedback when the keyboard accessibility functions are activated and deactivated.

Enable Sticky Keys Some keyboard shortcuts require that one key is kept pressed constantly (this applies to Alt, Ctrl or Shift) while the rest of the shortcut is typed. When "sticky" keys are used, the system regards those keys as pressed after being hit once. For an audible feedback generated each time a modifier key (Ctrl or Alt) is pressed, activate 'Beep when modifier is pressed'. If 'Disable if two keys pressed together' is selected, the keys do not stick anymore once two keys are pressed simultaneously. The system then assumes that the keyboard shortcut has been completely entered.

Repeat Keys Activate 'Repeat Keys' to make settings with sliders for 'Delay' and 'Speed'. This determines how long a key must be pressed for the automatic keyboard repeat function to be activated and at what speed the characters are then typed.

Test the effect of the settings in the field at the bottom of the dialog window. Choose parameters that reflect your normal typing habits.

Enable Slow Keys To prevent accidental typing, set a minimum time limit that a key must be pressed and held before it is recognized as valid input by the system. Also determine whether audible feedback should be provided for keypress events, accepted keypresses, and the rejection of a keypress.

Enable Bounce Keys To prevent double typing, set a minimum time limit for accepting two subsequent keypress events of the same key as the input of two individual characters. If desired, activate audible feedback upon rejection of a keypress event.

Toggle Keys It is possible to request audible feedback from the system when a keycap modifier key is pressed.

Mouse Activates the keyboard mouse — the mouse pointer is controlled with the arrow keys of the number pad. Use the sliders to set the maximum speed of the mouse pointer, the acceleration time until the maximum speed is reached, and the latency between the pressing of a key and the cursor movement.

6.2.10 Keyboard Shortcuts

Use this module to manage global keyboard combinations. It is possible to determine the keyboard combinations to use during text input and those for objects on the desktop.

The list overview window displays a list of all currently available actions along with their keyboard shortcuts. Deactivate or change a keyboard shortcut by clicking the corresponding shortcut entry. Then enter a new shortcut or delete the current one with Delete. All changes take effect immediately. Restore the current keyboard shortcut by clicking its entry and leaving the dialog with 'Close'.

6.2.11 Sound (system alerts)

This module allows the association of certain system events and application alerts with characteristic audio signals. The dialog box consists of two tabs ('General' and 'Sound Events'). The two check boxes in the 'General' tab must be activated to use audio signals for certain desktop events.

In the second tab, determine which events and application alerts should be associated with which sounds. All sound associations already defined for applications are listed. Test a sound by first selecting the corresponding notice in the 'Event' column then clicking 'Play'. Change the sound by clicking 'Event' then 'Browse'. The dialog that appears provides a list of files from which to choose. Close it with 'OK'.

6.3 File Management with Nautilus

Nautilus is the file manager and viewer of GNOME. The following section provides an overview of the basic functions of Nautilus as well as a few tips on its configuration. More information can be found in the help pages for Nautilus.

6.3.1 Navigating in Nautilus

Nautilus has a navigation behavior similar to most web browsers. Open a new window by right-clicking a free area of the desktop then selecting 'new window'. Alternatively, double-click the personal folder.

The standard window is shown in Figure 6.1 on the next page. Use the icons in the toolbar to move forward and backward, to move one level up in the directory tree, to stop loading a document, to reload the document, or to go to the preferred starting page. 'Location' shows the path to the current directory or to the current file. A different path can be directly entered here.

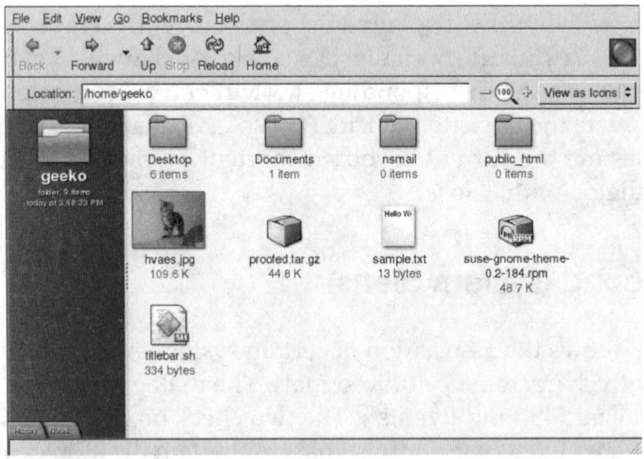

Figure 6.1: Nautilus Showing a Home Directory

The left sidebar contains the current object and some information about it. A drop-down menu is located right above the sidebar and is set by default to 'Information'. It is, however, possible to switch this to other display modes:

Tree The Tree view shows the complete directory tree of the system.

History The 'History' view lists objects that have been accessed previously.

Emblems The 'Emblems' view presents all available emblems. These are used for marking files, for instance, as art. To mark a file as art, drag the 'art' emblem to the file and drop the emblem on top of the file. Emblems are removed by dropping the Eraser emblem over a file.

Notes 'Notes' is useful for managing personal information about objects. These notes are saved along with the object.

Nautilus tries to select appropriate icons for objects according to their associated file information. Image and text files are shown as a thumbnail. Double-clicking shows the file in a viewer. The left sidebar in its 'Information' view shows a list of applications with which the file can be opened. The file cannot be processed directly with Nautilus.

Nautilus also manages bookmarks. Access the 'Bookmarks' menu to edit, access, or create your bookmarks.

6.3.2 File Management

Nautilus supports dragging and dropping for managing files. To move files from one directory to another, use 'New Window' from the context menu or the 'File' menu in Nautilus to open two windows. Access the path of the original location of the objects in one window and access the destination path for those files in the second window. To move the files, drag the files from one window to the other and drop them there. Copying files is a little more complicated. Right-click the object to copy and select 'Duplicate'. Then move the copy to the new directory. The context menu that appears when right-clicking an object provides functions for renaming files and other tasks.

6.3.3 Configuring Nautilus

Nautilus retrieves its default font and other preferences from the desktop configuration. To set Nautilus-specific preferences, select 'Edit' -> 'Preferences' in any Nautilus window. The configuration dialog offers four tabs: 'Views', 'Behavior', 'Icon Captions', and 'Preview'.

The 'Views' dialog allows switching the 'Default View' between 'Icon View' and 'List View'. A sorting order can be set for any of these options.

The 'Behavior' dialog allows choosing between single-click and double-click response and also sets the handling of executable files. These can either be started on activation or the content displayed. The operating mode of the trash is also set here. Activate a confimation dialog before deletion, if desired. 'Include a Delete command that bypasses trash' can also be set. The files are immediately deleted if this option is activated.

The 'Icon Captions' dialog features three options for determining what information should be displayed for icons and how it should be displayed. In the 'Preview' dialog, select whether to activate preview thumbnails for certain file types.

6.4 Important Utilities

GNOME features a wealth of applets and applications. This section provides an introduction to some of the most useful and interesting, all of which are compatible with the GNOME configuration scheme.

6.4.1 Dictionary

Dictionary is a useful applet for checking the spelling and the meaning of words. An Internet connection is required, as this applet accesses an online dictionary.

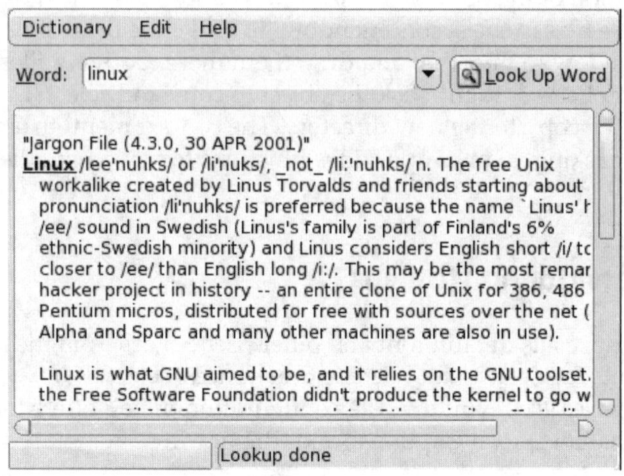

Figure 6.2: *GNOME Dictionary*

Enter the term to look up in 'Word'. The menu under 'Dictionary' gives a choice between 'Look Up Word' and 'Check Spelling'. By default, the query is sent to the dict.org server. To use a different server, select 'Edit' -> 'Preferences'. Refer to Figure 6.2. dict.org allows you to choose between various databases for special vocabularies, such as jargon or computer terminology. Under 'Default strategy', specify what to look for: the exact word, parts of the word, or the prefix or suffix. Under 'Help', access the online manual of the application with 'Contents' and information about the author and version of the application with 'About'.

6.4.2 Managing Archives with File Roller

In GNOME, manage file archives with File Roller. This application is able to handle archives of the following types: `.tar`, `.tar.gz`, `.tgz`, `.tar.bz`, `.tar.bz2`, `.tar.Z`, `.zip`, `.lha`, `.rar`, `.lzh`, `.ear`, `.jar`, and `.war`. Easily view archive contents from File Roller with other applications without having to decompress the archives. File Roller supports drag and drop, allowing you to drag file icons from the desktop or from the file manager (Nautilus) to the File Roller dialog and drop them there.

To create a new archive, select 'Archive' -> 'New'. In the next dialog, specify the directory in which to create the new archive in the left window. Enter the file name of the new archive in the input field below without the file extension. Then determine the archive type with the drop-down menu above the name field. Exit the dialog with 'OK' and return to the main view of File Roller. Now, add files to the archive by inserting files from the desktop or the file manager with drag and drop or by selecting 'Edit' -> Add Files. In the following dialog, select one or several files (keep Ctrl pressed to select multiple files) or directories. If necessary, determine the following advanced options for the archive:

Add only if newer If the archive already contains a file with the same name, the file is only added if it is newer than the one existing in the archive.

Include subfolders To compress an entire directory, activate this option to include all subdirectories.

Exclude backup files (*) Avoid unnecessary data trash by disabling the inclusion of backup copies when creating an archive.

Exclude hidden files (.*) Usually, hidden files do not contain any data that are relevant for the user. By default, they are not included in the archive to reduce the amount of data.

Exclude files This explicitly excludes certain files from the archive. This option is useful if you want to compress entire directories but exclude certain files from the archive. Instead of file names, you can also specify search patterns.

Ignore case File Roller ignores different spellings of file names and extensions, like `JPEG` or `jpeg`.

After completing the selection and configuration, exit the dialog. The archive created is available for further processing at the desired location. To decompress an archive, load it to File Roller, click 'Edit' -> 'Extract to', and specify the target directory.

Part III

Office Applications

7

The OpenOffice.org Office Suite

OpenOffice.org is a powerful Linux office suite that offers tools for all types of office tasks, such as writing texts, working with spreadsheets, or creating graphics and presentations. With OpenOffice.org, use the same data across different computing platforms. You can also open and edit files in Microsoft Office formats then save them back to this format, if needed. This chapter only covers the basic skills needed to get started with OpenOffice.org.

7.1 The Quickstarter

When started for the first time from the main menu ('Applications' -> 'Accessories' -> 'More' -> 'OpenOffice.org Quickstarter'), you will be asked whether the quickstart function of the program should be enabled. If you intend to use OpenOffice.org frequently and have enough RAM available, it can be useful.

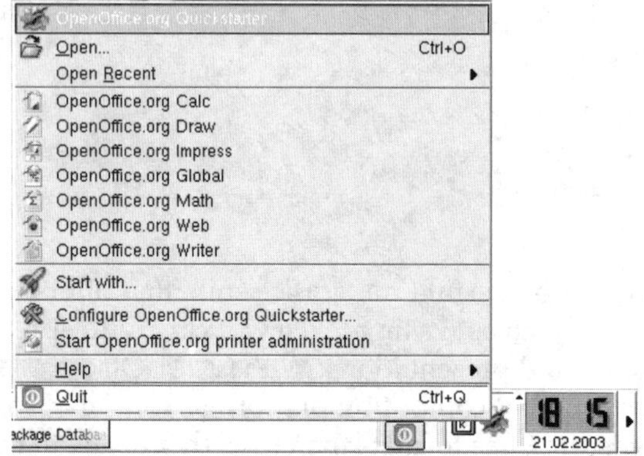

Figure 7.1: The OpenOffice.org Quickstarter

The Quickstarter icon then appears in the desktop panel at the lower right edge of the screen. Right-clicking it displays a menu like the one shown in Figure 7.1, which gives access to a number of possibilities: directly start the individual OpenOffice.org application modules, quickly reopen the recently used files, or create a new document from a template. Customize the Quickstarter settings by selecting 'Configure OpenOffice.org Quickstarter...'.

Once enabled, the Quickstarter is started automatically each time you log in to your desktop. To stop this from happening in the future, click 'Quit' in the Quickstarter menu, shown in Figure 7.1.

7.2 Overview of the Application Modules

OpenOffice.org comprises several application modules (subprograms), which are designed to interact with each other.

***Table 7.1:** The OpenOffice.org Application Modules*

Writer	Powerful word processor application
Calc	Spreadsheet application that includes a chart utility
Draw	Drawing application for creating vector graphics
Math	Application for generating mathematical formulas
Impress	Application for creating presentations

The discussion in this chapter is focused on Writer and Calc. The other modules are only explained briefly. A full description of each module is available in the online help, described in Section 7.3).

7.3 Getting Help

Get help for OpenOffice.org at any time from the 'Help' menu. Depending on your selection, the depth and type of help provided varies. To get thoroughly acquainted with a topic, select 'Help' -> 'Contents'. The help system provides information about each of the modules of OpenOffice.org (Writer, Calc, Impress, etc.).

If you find this information too broad or overwhelming, try the 'Help Agent' instead, which offers help and tips as you perform different actions with OpenOffice.org. Select 'Help' -> 'Help Agent' to enable this. If less information should be sufficient, try 'Tips' and 'Extended Tips'. They enable the program's tooltips — short information about the element to which the mouse is pointing. These items can easily be disabled later when you are more familiar with the program.

Note

If you are not sure whether the features are active, open the 'Help' menu. A checked menu item indicates that the corresponding help function is currently active.

Note

7.4 Converting Microsoft Office Documents

OpenOffice.org is able to work with Microsoft Office documents. To convert such documents, select 'File' -> 'AutoPilot' -> 'Document Converter. . . '. Choose the file format from which to convert. There are several StarOffice and Microsoft Office formats available. After selecting a format, click 'Next' then specify where OpenOffice.org should look for documents to convert and in which directory the converted files should be placed. Before continuing, make sure all other settings are appropriate.

Note

Documents from a Windows partition are usually in a subdirectory of `/windows/`.

Note

Click 'Next' to see a summary of the actions to perform, which gives another opportunity to check whether all settings are correct. Finally, start the conversion by clicking 'Convert'.

7.5 Changing the Global Settings

Global settings can be changed by selecting 'Tools' -> 'Options. . . '. This opens the window shown in Figure 7.2 on the facing page. A tree structure is used to display categories of settings.

'OpenOffice.org' This entry covers various basic settings. This includes your user data, like your address and e-mail, important paths, and settings for printers and external programs.

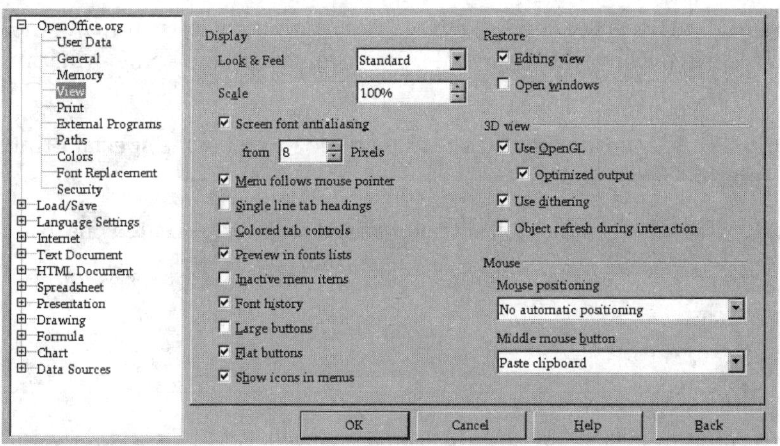

Figure 7.2: *The Options Dialog*

'Load/Save' This entry includes settings related to the opening and saving of several file types. There is a dialog for general settings and several special dialogs to define how external formats should be handled.

'Language Settings' This entry covers various settings related to languages and writing aids, namely your locale and spell checker settings. This is also the place to enable support for Asian languages.

'Internet' This entry includes dialogs to configure any proxies and to change settings related to search engines.

'Text Document' Under this entry, configure global word processing options, such as the basic fonts and layout Writer should use.

'HTML Document' Under this entry, change the settings related to the HTML authoring features of OpenOffice.org.

'Spreadsheet' Use this to change settings for Calc, such as those related to sort lists and grids.

'Presentation' Under this entry, change settings that should apply to all presentations. For instance, specify the measurement unit for the grid used to arrange elements.

'Drawing' This entry covers settings related to the vector drawing module, such as the drawing scale, grid properties, and some print options.

'Formula' This entry provides a single dialog to set some special print options for formulas.

'Chart' This defines the default colors used for newly created charts.

'Data Sources' Use this to define how external data sources should be accessed.

Note

All settings as listed above are applied *globally* — they are used as defaults for every new document you create.

Note

7.6 Word Processing with OpenOffice.org Writer

7.6.1 Creating Texts with the AutoPilot

To use a standard format and predefined elements for your own documents, try the AutoPilot. This is a small utility that lets you make some basic decisions then produces a ready-made document from a template. For instance, to create a business letter, select 'File' -> 'AutoPilot' then select 'Letter...'. This opens the dialog as shown in Figure 7.3 on the next page.

Click 'Next' in each page to proceed to the next one. To modify any previous entries, use 'Back'. When finished, click 'Create' to generate the letter according to your specifications. Exit the dialog with 'Cancel'. Access a help document with 'Help'.

When finished, click 'Create'. OpenOffice.org produces a letter according your specifications. Now, compose the text (body) of the letter itself. AutoPilot is not limited to letters, but can also assist in the creation of faxes, agendas, memos, and presentations.

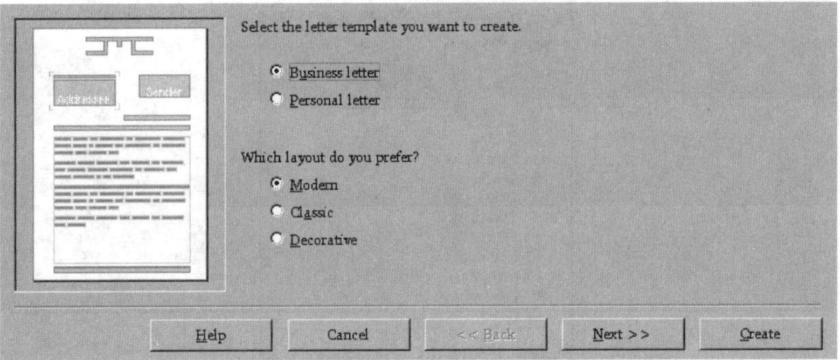

Figure 7.3: The OpenOffice.org AutoPilot

7.6.2 Creating Texts without the AutoPilot

Create a new text document by selecting 'File' -> 'New' -> 'Text Document'. When editing a text document, a second toolbar, called the object bar, is available just below the standard function bar. Move the mouse pointer over an icon to get a short help text. Documents can also be formatted with the Stylist, which is described in Section 7.6.4 on the following page.

7.6.3 Selecting Text

To select text, click the desired beginning of the selection and, keeping the mouse button pressed, move the cursor towards the end of the range (which can be characters, lines, or entire paragraphs). Release the button at the end of the desired selection. While selected, text is displayed in inverted colors. Open a context menu by right-clicking the selection. Use the context menu to change the font, the font style, and other text properties.

The Navigator displays information about the contents of a document. It also enables you to jump quickly to the different elements included. For example, use the Navigator to get a quick overview of all the chapters or to see a list of the images included in the document. Figure 7.4 on the next page shows the Navigator in action. The elements listed in the Navigator vary according to the document loaded in Writer. Open the Navigator by selecting 'Edit' -> 'Navigator'.

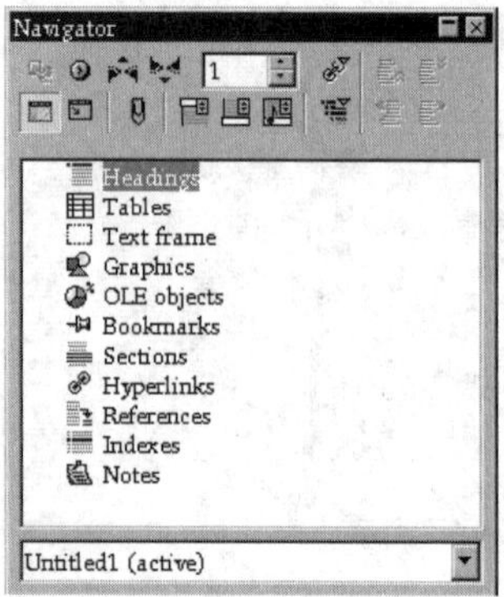

Figure 7.4: *The Navigator in Writer*

7.6.4 Working with the Stylist

The Stylist can help you format text in a number of ways. It can be opened or closed at any time by toggling 'Format' -> 'Stylist' or by pressing (F11). The dialog window of the Stylist is shown in Figure 7.5 on the facing page.

If you set the drop-down list at the lower edge of the Stylist to 'Automatic', OpenOffice.org tries to offer a selection of styles adapted to the task at hand. On the other hand, if you select 'All', the Stylist offers all styles from the currently active group. Groups are selected with the buttons at the top. Text can be *hard-formatted* or *soft-formatted*:

Hard Formatting Formatting properties are *directly* assigned to a text range and each property must be applied to each range by hand. The assignment is static and can only be changed manually. This is only recommended for short documents.

Soft Formatting With this method, text is not formatted directly. It has a style applied to it. The style itself can be modified quite easily. Modifying a style automatically results in a formatting change of all the text to which it is assigned.This approach has many advantages when creating larger documents (theses, books, and the like). Although not as intuitive, it is very efficient and fast if the formatting needs to be changed extensively and consistently. Using this method also makes it much easier to try different layouts with the document. Define the format of paragraphs, pages, and frames for a style and select fonts and numbering methods.

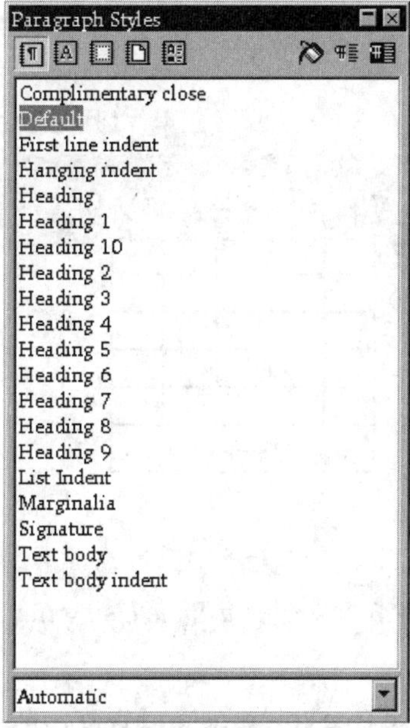

Figure 7.5: *The Stylist for Writer*

To assign a style to a paragraph select the style to use and click the paint-bucket icon in the Stylist. Click the paragraphs to which to assign the style. Pressing (Esc) or clicking the paintbucket icon again turns off the function.

Easily create your own styles by formatting a paragraph or a character as desired. Use the 'Character…' and 'Paragraph…' items in the 'Format' menu to achieve the desired results. In the Stylist, click 'New Style from Selection' (to the right of the bucket symbol). Enter a name for your style and click 'OK'.

Now, you can use the newly created style on other parts of the document. Change details of the style easily by selecting it in the list, right-clicking, and selecting 'Modify…' from the menu. This opens a dialog in which all the possible formatting properties are available for modification.

7.6.5 Inserting a Table

Create a table by clicking the 'Insert' icon in the main toolbar and keeping it pressed for a few seconds. This opens another toolbar in which to specify the object to insert. If you now move the mouse cursor to the third icon, see a grid open, as shown in Figure 7.6.

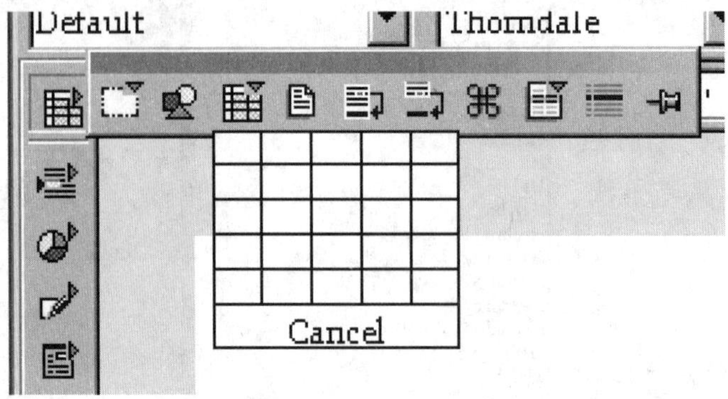

Figure 7.6: Inserting a Table Using the Toolbar

If your table should have two columns and two rows, for instance, just run the mouse over that range of columns and rows to select them from the grid. When you release the button, the table is inserted into the document at the current text cursor position.

Note

The 'Insert' icon changes depending on the last object selected for insertion. This also means that you can now insert a table again with just a short click, without any need to reopen the pop-up toolbar.

Note

7.6.6 Inserting Graphics

Graphics can be inserted with the same vertical pop-up toolbar as tables, only you need to select its second button. Alternatively, select 'Insert' -> 'Graphics' -> 'From File...'. This opens a dialog window in which to select the desired file. If you check 'Preview', the selected image is displayed in the right part of the dialog. Such a preview may take some time in the case of larger images. After confirming your choice, the inserted image is placed in the document at the cursor position.

In the document itself, select an image by clicking it. When selected, an image has little square handles on its edges. Then select 'Graphics...' from the context menu to open a dialog in which to change various image settings, such as the wrap type and border style.

To change the size of an image, first click it to activate it. Now click any of its handles, keep the button pressed, and drag the handle until the dashed frame reaches the desired size. When you release the button, the image is scaled according to your changes. To change the position of an image while leaving its size unchanged, click the image and keep the mouse button pressed. Drag the image to the desired position.

7.7 Spreadsheets with OpenOffice.org Calc

Calc is the spreadsheet module of OpenOffice.org. Use this application, for example, to handle your private or business accounting data. If Writer is already running, start Calc by selecting 'File' -> 'New' -> 'Spreadsheet'.

After starting, Calc presents an empty spreadsheet divided into rows and columns. Rows are numbered from top to bottom and columns are lettered from left to right. The intersection of a row and a column marks the location of a cell, so each cell has a unique address coordinate. For instance, the address `B3` refers to the cell located in the second column (`B`) and the third row. This address is also shown at the top to the left of the entry field.

A cell may be active or inactive. The currently active cell has a thick black frame around it. To activate another cell, move the frame with the cursor keys or click another cell with the mouse. You can edit a cell if it is currently active.

7.7.1 Changing Cell Attributes

To enter something in a cell, simply write in that cell. By default, texts are aligned to the left and numbers to the right. To confirm your entry, hit (Enter). To change the formatting of selected cells, right-click to open a context menu and select 'Format Cells...'. This opens a dialog in which to change the cell attributes. The dialog, as shown in Figure 7.7 on the following page, has the tabs 'Numbers', 'Font', 'Font Effects', 'Alignment', 'Borders', 'Background', and 'Cell Protection'. By enabling 'Protected' under 'Cell Protection', prevent a cell from being modified.

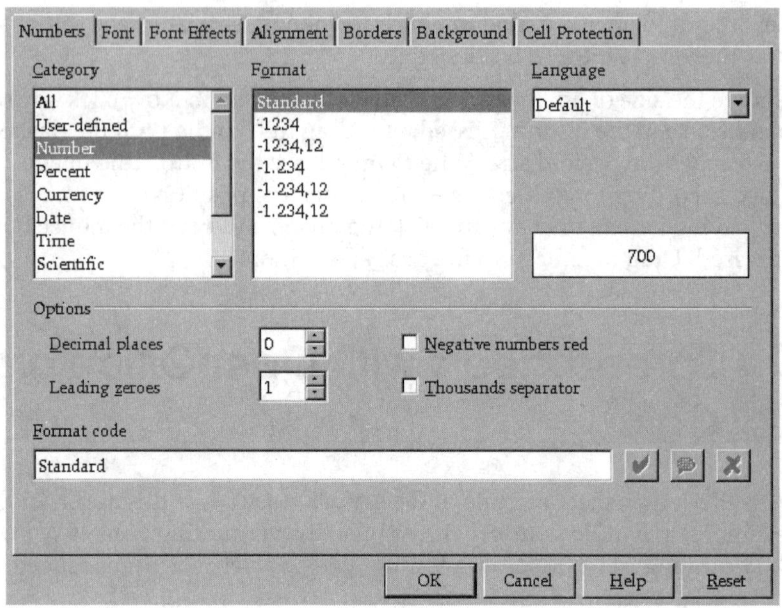

Figure 7.7: *The Cell Attributes Dialog*

7.7.2 A Practical Example: Monthly Expenses

Calculations can be done using formulas. Any numeric values entered in cells can be used in formulas by referring to the unique coordinates of each cell. For example, you may want to keep a record of your monthly expenses. This could be done by writing a few items into a very basic spreadsheet as in Figure 7.8 on the next page. The cell `B3` contains the phone bill for January and `B4` the fuel expenses. To add both amounts together, enter `= B3+B4` in cell `B5`. Now cell `B5` should display the corresponding result. If you have mistyped the numbers (or estimated your phone bill inaccurately), just reenter the amounts and Calc will automatically update the sum.

Calc offers many functions beyond the four fundamental arithmetic operations. A comprehensive list arranged in categories is available under 'Insert' -> 'Function…'. Any spreadsheet can be easily extended. For instance, to insert another row between `Fuel` and `Sum`, right-click the `5` button to the left and select 'Insert Row' from the context menu. A new row is inserted below the current one and can immediately be used for additional input.

	A	B
1		Month
2	**Expenses**	**January**
3	Telephone	500
4	Gas	200
5	***Sum***	700
6		

Figure 7.8: *A Spreadsheet Example for Calc*

Entering formulas in the above way is cumbersome when many cells are involved. For example, if you have several items in your `A` column and want to add them, try the `SUM` function. In the field `B6`, enter the formula `=SUM(B3:B5)`. An alternative possibility is to click the Sigma (Sigma) icon next to the input line and enter the range manually. This formula adds all numbers from `B3` to `B5`. You can also specify several ranges at once.

As shown in the above formula, a range is defined by two cell addresses separated by a colon. Separate ranges by semicolons. Accordingly, the formula = `SUM(B3:B5;D3:D5)` adds everything from `B3` to `B5` *and* from `D3` to `D5`. Basically, the formula is a short form of a longer one, which would read: `=B3+B4+B5+D3+D4+D5`.

7.7.3 Creating Charts

Now, add some more entries to the spreadsheet, for instance, by including some more months in row `2`. After doing so, the table could look like Figure 7.9 on the following page.

Select the range from `A2` to `E5`. The text appears white on black.
To create a chart, select 'Insert' -> 'Chart…'. This opens a dialog window. The first page in this dialog gives the option to modify the original cell selection and to specify whether to use the first row or column as chart labels. Usually, the settings on this page can be accepted without change. Continue by clicking 'Next'.

The dialog consists of four pages. The main page shows the available chart types. The types offered include line, area, column, and bar charts. To the left, the page displays a preview of your data according to the type

	A	B	C	D	E
1		Month			
2	**Expenses**	**January**	**February**	**March**	**April**
3	Telephone	500	300	430	350
4	Gas	200	80	200	470
5	*Sum*	***700***	***380***	***630***	***820***
6					

Figure 7.9: *Expanded Example Spreadsheet*

selected. The most suitable type for our example is the line chart. Click 'Next' to proceed to a page in which to choose from different variants of line charts: with or without symbols, stacked, percent, cubic spline, and so on. For the current example, select 'Symbols'. If you enable 'Show text elements in preview', the column headers (`January`, `February`, etc.) are displayed on the X axis and the numerical values on the Y axis. Also, a chart legend is added on the right-hand side.

On the next page, give the chart, as well as its X axis and Y axis, a title. In this case, use 'Monthly Expenses' as a chart title and 'Euro' on the Y axis. The X axis title is disabled by default. Finally, after clicking 'Create', the chart is inserted into your spreadsheet. Figure 7.10 on the next page shows the sample chart in its final form.

7.7.4 Importing Spreadsheet Tables

There is often a need to import data available as a table, so it can be presented as a spreadsheet. In Calc, there are two ways to achieve this.

Importing Data from the Clipboard

For instance, you may want to import stock exchange data. Display the desired table in your web browser. Then select the table with the mouse or using 'Copy', depending on the browser. This copies the selected data to the clipboard.After that, open a new OpenOffice.org document with 'File' -> 'New' -> 'Spreadsheet'. Select the cell in which the inserted table should start. Then select 'Edit' ->'Paste'. This inserts the table into the document with all the formatting specifications, hyperlinks, and other information included.

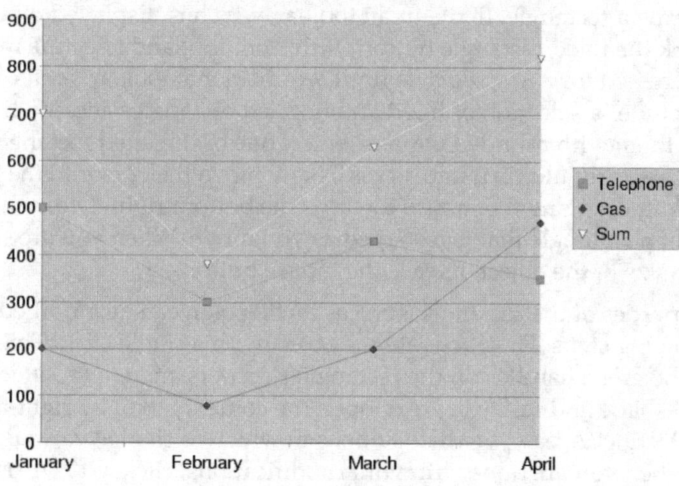

Figure 7.10: A Chart in Calc

Importing Data with a Filter Import a saved HTML file to Calc by selecting 'File' -> 'Open'. This opens a dialog window in which to select 'Web Page (OpenOffice.org Calc)' under 'File type'. Use the arrow keys to scroll the list of file types. Finally, select the file name then 'Open' to import the table.

7.8 Creating Graphics Using OpenOffice.org Draw

Draw can be used to create vector graphics. Vector graphics are images in which lines and curves are defined through certain parameters, such as the location of points and the curvature.

To create a new drawing, start Draw from the main menu: 'Applications' -> 'OpenOffice.org Draw'. If OpenOffice.org is already running, select 'File' ->

'New' -> 'Drawing'. The graphical objects available in Draw can be modified in various aspects, such as line thickness, line type, color, and fill.

Try to draw a rectangle. In the main toolbar, which is displayed on the left side, click the filled rectangle button (fifth from top) and keep the mouse button pressed for a few seconds until an additional toolbar opens. The latter includes a selection of filled and unfilled rectangles and squares, some of them with rounded corners. Select one of the filled rectangles. The mouse cursor should turn into a cross. Now move the cursor to the canvas and click it, dragging the mouse towards the bottom right. Draw shows the outline of a rectangle that is reshaped as you move. When you are satisfied with the size of the object, release the mouse button.

The properties of the rectangle, such as its fill color, can be modified with the following steps: First, activate the object with a single click. This should enable the green handles on the rectangle's corners and edges, which allow you to reshape and resize it. Next, open the context menu by right-clicking. After selecting 'Area...', a dialog opens in which to change various properties. When you are done with your modifications, click 'OK'. As an alternative method to change the fill color, select one directly in the object bar at the top (to the right of the paintbucket).

There are many more useful drawing objects available in the toolbar. Use it to create circles, ellipses, lines, and even 3D elements.

7.9 Creating Presentations with OpenOffice.org Impress

7.9.1 Creating Presentations with the AutoPilot

Less experienced users may prefer to use Autopilot to create presentations. Select 'File' -> 'AutoPilot' -> 'Presentation...'. With the AutoPilot, define the basic structure of a presentation in three brief steps. In doing so, set backgrounds, the output medium, and various effects. You can also import data from an existing presentation with the help of assistants.

After completing the procedure by clicking 'Create', Impress offers a number of templates for the page layout. Select one that suits your purposes and enter a name for the first slide. Then click 'OK' to generate the first slide of the new presentation.

To complete your presentation, enter a title and the text for each page. When finished, view the presentation by selecting 'Slide Show' -> 'Slide

Show'. To advance to the next page during the show, click. To exit from it, press Esc. Refer to the help system of OpenOffice.org to learn more.

7.9.2 Adding a Slide

To add another slide to your presentation, select 'Insert' -> 'Slide'. This opens the dialog window shown in Figure 7.11. Enter a name for the slide and determine which of the predefined layouts to use. Then click 'OK' to insert the slide or 'Cancel' to abort the procedure. To use templates, select 'File' -> 'New' -> 'From Template...'.

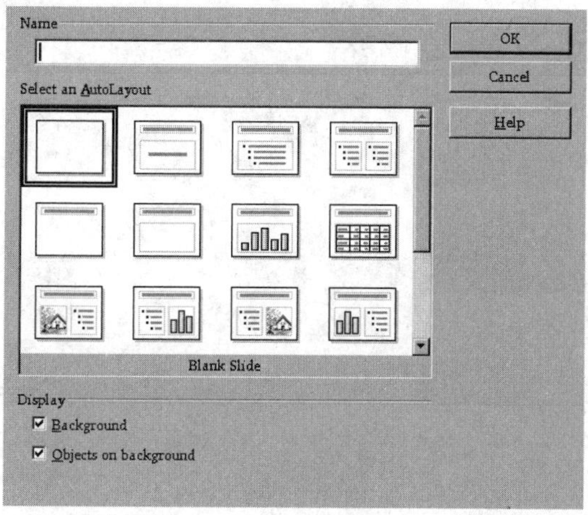

Figure 7.11: Inserting Slides in Impress

The KWrite Text Editor

KWrite can be used to write simple texts or lists. As well as text editing, KWrite can also be used to view and edit various different types of source code or HTML with syntax highlighting. This chapter provides a brief overview of the main features of KWrite, introducing the main menus and tools.

Start KWrite from the main menu or using the command `kwrite`. The command can be entered on the command line together with the name of the file to open. As well as using the menu bar, the toolbar, and a number of shortcuts, you can right-click the opened document to access a context menu providing basic editor functions.

KWrite supports the drag and drop functions of KDE, which means that you can simply drag documents with the mouse from one application into another or paste data from the clipboard (see Section 5.4.4 on page 156). To edit a text file for which you have put an icon on the desktop, click the icon with the left mouse button and hold the button while dragging it into the editor window. You can now edit the file as usual. Paste text from the clipboard by middle-clicking. To edit or view the source code of an HTML page, drag the URL into the editor window of KWrite, keeping the left mouse button pressed.

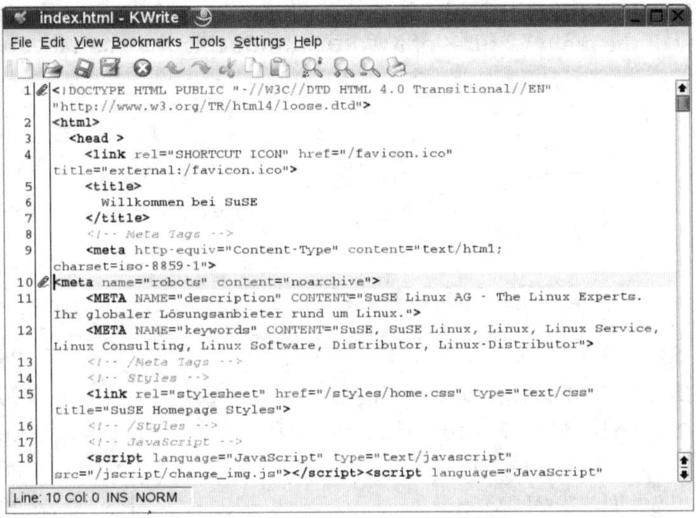

Figure 8.1: The KWrite Text Editor

8.1 The File Menu

'New' (Ctrl + N) This creates a new file and, at the same time, opens a new KWrite window in which to start typing your text.

'Open...' (Ctrl + O) Use this to open an existing file. It opens a file selection dialog that resembles a file manager. The left-hand area provides a number of quick navigation buttons to use to list the files in your home directory or on the floppy with just one click. Alternatively, use the entry field in the toolbar at the top or browse directories with the arrow buttons. As soon as a directory is selected, the files and subdirectories in it are listed in the right-hand part of the dialog. To speed things up, narrow down the list according to the file type by specifying the file extension (e.g., `*.txt`) under 'Filter'.To mark the current directory for quick return later, click the star button in the toolbar and create a bookmark for it. Any directory bookmarked in this way can subsequently be reached via the menu to avoid going through the entire file system again and again. Use the configuration menu accessible with the wrench button to customize the way in which the items in the dialog are sorted and viewed.

'Save' (Ctrl + S) This saves the document in its current form. If you have been editing a new document, the program display a dialog with which to specify the name of the file and its location (directory).

'Save As...' This opens a dialog in which to specify the name and the directory under which to save the document. The dialog is essentially the same as the one displayed after selecting 'File' -> 'Open...'.

'Print...' (Ctrl + P) This opens a simple dialog in which to define printing options for the document and start the print job.

'Close' (Ctrl + W) This closes the currently loaded document. If there are changes that have not yet been saved, a dialog opens to ask whether to do so.

'Quit' (Ctrl + Q) This exits the editor. If there are unsaved changes to a loaded document, KWrite shows a dialog asking whether to save before exiting.

8.2 The Edit Menu

This menu provides all the program's editing functions, such as selecting and searching or replacing text according to certain patterns.

'Undo/Redo' Use this to undo any unwanted changes and to restore the original text after an undo step. These functions are also available using the keyboard shortcuts Ctrl + Z and Ctrl + Shift + Z.

'Cut' This cuts the currently selected text region. The corresponding keyboard shortcut is (Ctrl) + (X).

'Copy' This copies the selected text region to the clipboard. The same can be achieved with the shortcut (Ctrl) + (C).

'Paste' Use this to insert text from the clipboard. The shortcut for this function is (Ctrl) + (V). You can also paste text by middle-clicking.

'Select All' This selects all the text in a document. The shortcut for this function is (Ctrl) + (A).

'Deselect' This menu option deselects a previously selected text area. The shortcut for this function is (Ctrl) + (Shift) + (A). You can do the same by clicking in the document window.

'Toggle Block Selection' KWrite not only supports marking and removing horizontal selections (lines or paragraphs), it also supports vertical selections (any desired text block). This toggles the block selection mode, which can also be done with the shortcut (Ctrl) + (Shift) + (B).

'Toggle Insert' This changes the program's input mode. By default, KWrite inserts new text at the current cursor position. Selecting this menu item switches the editing mode so any existing text is overwritten. Alternatively, switch between editing modes by pressing (Ins).

'Find... and Replace...' Selecting 'Find...' (or pressing (Ctrl) + (F)) displays a dialog in which to enter a search string or a regular expression. Also define the search direction, the starting point, and other details. To go from one match of the search term to the next, select 'Find Next' ((F3)). To go to a previous match of the search term, select 'Find Previous' ((Shift) + (F3)). To replace a search term with another string, use 'Replace...' ((Ctrl) + (R)).

'Go to Line...' To jump to a particular line in the document, select this menu item, enter the line number in the dialog that opens, then confirm with 'OK'.

8.3 The View Menu

From this menu, change several aspects of the text display in KWrite. Enable or disable the editor's word wrap feature and toggle the display of line numbers ((F11)). Also decide whether to display the icon border ((F6)) to see or hide the bookmarks. Finally, the menu has an item to set the encoding of the text document.

8.4 The Bookmarks Menu

In KWrite, bookmarks are references to specific positions in the document. They can be used to navigate quickly to a given line, which is especially useful with longer documents. To use bookmarks, first enable the icon border ('View' -> 'Show Icon Border'). Add a bookmark by clicking the icon border at the desired line. A paper clip should appear after this to indicate that the bookmark has been set. Remove a bookmark by clicking the corresponding clip.

To navigate between bookmarks, press Alt + Page down (next bookmark) and Alt + Page up (previous bookmark). Remove all bookmarks in one step by selecting 'Clear Bookmarks'.

8.5 The Tools Menu

This menu provides a number of actions that can be used to format the current document in a basic way.

'Highlight Mode' This is set to 'Normal' by default, but you can choose from numerous highlight modes for different document formats (such as HTML) and programming languages.

'End of Line' The end-of-line characters as stored by KWrite should always be set according to the operating environment in which the documents will be used and distributed. Use this menu to choose 'UNIX', 'Windows/DOS', or 'Macintosh'.

'Indent' Text blocks can be indented by a certain amount, as defined under 'Settings' -> 'Configure Editor. . . ' -> 'Editing'. To indent the current text, select 'Indent' or press Ctrl + I. To undo one level of indentation, select 'Unindent' or press Ctrl + Shift + I.

8.6 The Settings Menu

'Show Toolbar' Enable this to display a toolbar of the main editing functions.

'Show Statusbar' Enable this for KWrite to include a status bar at the lower edge of its window. The status bar would display the current line and column number, the input mode, and the save status of the document.

'Show Path' If this is enabled, KWrite displays the file name of the loaded document together with its complete path (rather than just the file name) in the window title bar.

'Configure Editor...' This opens a dialog with all the configuration options available for KWrite. This includes the color scheme and the fonts used, settings for indentation, text selection and word wrap, shortcuts and highlighting options, and some others. The dialog also allows you to define a default view profile and to integrate an external spell check module.

'Configure Shortcuts...' This opens a dialog in which to change the existing keyboard shortcuts or define custom shortcuts.

'Configure Toolbars...' This opens a dialog in which to add and remove toolbar buttons.

8.7 The Help Menu

This menu gives access to the KWrite handbook. Click 'What's This?' (or use the shortcut Shift + F1) to invoke all available context-sensitive tooltips.

8.8 Kate

The editor Kate provides further possibilities. It is based on the same editor component as KWrite, but supports concurrent editing of multiple files.

A useful feature is syntax highlighting. Both KWrite and Kateoffer this feature. It formats program code to make it more readable. This can be activated in 'Extras' -> 'syntax highlighting'.

Sychronizing a Handheld Computer with KPilot

Handheld computers are in widespread use nowadays among users who need to have their schedules, to-do lists, and notes with them everywhere they go. Often users want the same data to be available both on the desktop and on the portable device. This is where KPilot comes in — it is a tool to synchronize data on a handheld with that used by the KDE applications KAddressBook, KOrganizer, and KNotes.

The main purpose of KPilot is to allow the sharing of data between the applications of a handheld computer and their KDE counterparts. KPilot does come with its own built-in memo viewer, address viewer, and file installer, but these cannot be used outside the KPilot environment. Independent KDE applications are available for all these functions except the file installer.

For the communication between the handheld and the different desktop programs, KPilot relies on conduits. KPilot itself is the program that oversees any data exchange between the two computer devices. Using a particular function of the handheld on your desktop computer requires that the corresponding conduit is enabled and configured. For the most part, these conduits are designed to interact with specific KDE programs, so in general they cannot be used with other desktop applications.

The time synchronization conduit is special in that there is no user-visible program for it. It is activated in the background with each sync operation, but should only be enabled on computers that use a network time server to correct their own time drift.

When a synchronization is started, the conduits are activated one after another to carry out the data transfer. There are two different sync methods:

1. A HotSync operation only synchronizes the data for which any conduits have been enabled.

2. A backup operation performs a full backup of all data stored on the handheld.

Some conduits need to open certain files during a sync operation, which means the corresponding program should not be running at the given time. Specifically, KOrganizer should not be running during a sync operation.

9.1 Conduits Used by KPilot

The conduits used by KPilot can be enabled and configured after selecting 'Settings' -> 'Configure Conduits...'. The following conduits are available:

KDE Addressbook Conduit This conduit handles the data exchange with the handheld's address book. The KDE counterpart is KAddressBook. Start it from the main menu or with the command `kaddressbook`.

KPilot KNotes Conduit This conduit allows you to transfer notes created with KNotes to the handheld's memo application. Start the KDE application from the main menu or with the command `knotes`.

KPilot Expenses Conduit This conduits allows you to transfer data from the handheld's expenses program to the desktop computer. Data can be imported as a comma separated list (CSV format) or directly into a PostgreSQL or MySQL database table.

KOrganizer Todo Conduit, KOrganizer Calendar Conduit These two conduits are responsible for syncing with the to-do and calendar applications of the handheld. The desktop equivalent for these applications is KOrganizer. For more information, refer to Section 10 on page 217.

Time Synchronization Conduit Enabling this conduit adjusts the handheld's clock to that of the desktop computerduring each sync operation.This is only a good idea if the clock of the desktop computer itself is corrected by a time server at fairly frequent intervals.

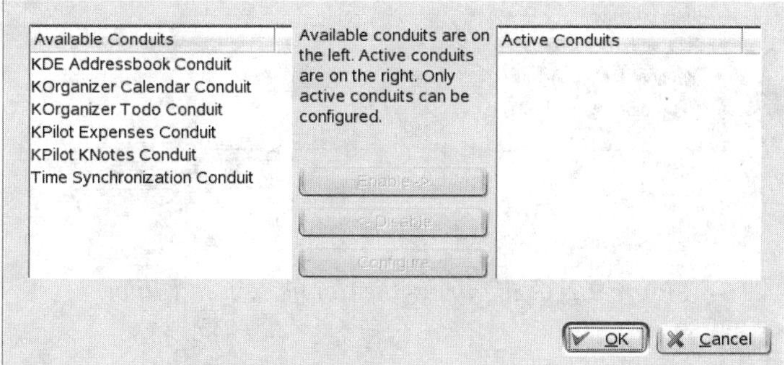

Figure 9.1: Configuration Dialog with the Available Conduits

9.1.1 Configuring the Handheld Connection

Apart from setting up the physical link, there is also some manual configuration necessary on the software side. The configuration depends on the type of cradle (docking unit) used with the handheld. There are basically two types of these: USB cradles and serial cradles. The connection can be configured either on a system-wide basis by the administrator (the `root` user) or by a regular user for his personal environment.

Configuring the Connection from within KPilot

To set up the connection with the handheld cradle, select 'Settings' -> 'Configure KPilot…'. First, specify the correct device file under 'Pilot device'. If you have a USB cradle, enter `/dev/ttyUSB0`. If you have a serial cradle connected to the first or second serial port, enter `/dev/ttyS0` or `/dev/ttyS1`, respectively. The connection speed should normally be set to `57600`. Also provide the user name set on the handheld in the corresponding field. The program checks that the name actually matches the user name on the handheld when you first sync with it. The configuration dialog is shown in Figure 9.2.

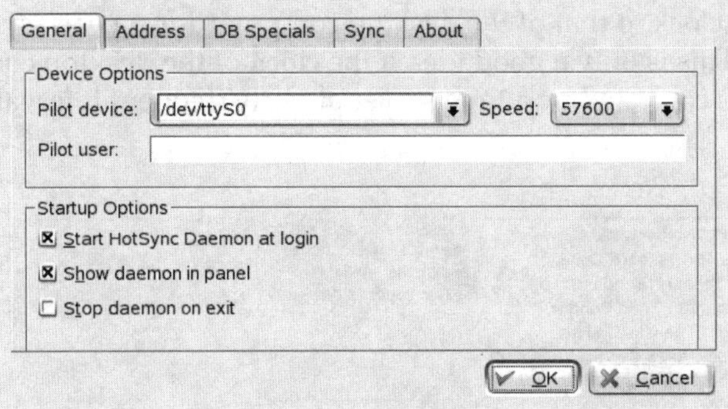

Figure 9.2: *Configuring the Connection in KPilot*

Creating a /dev/pilot Link

There should be no need to create a `/dev/pilot` link if you have configured the cradle connection as a regular user. As a handheld cradle is normally connected to one specific computer, possibly with several users on it, it may still be useful to configure the connection with administrator permissions.

Note

The following configuration steps require administrator permissions and cannot be performed from a regular user account. After completing the steps as described below, add users to the `uucp` group to allow them to use KPilot.

Note

USB Cradle To connect over a USB cradle, create a symbolic link from `/dev/ttyUSB?` to `/dev/pilot`. To to so, first check to which USB bus the cradle is connected. If you do not have any other USB devices on the same first USB bus, it can be safely assumed that this is `/dev/ttyUSB0`. In this case, the command to create the symbolic link would be as follows: `ln -s /dev/ttyUSB0 /dev/pilot`

Serial Cradle First, determine to which port the cradle is connected. The device files for serial ports are named `/dev/ttyS?` and, just as USB ports, the counting starts from zero for the first port. To create the link for a cradle connected to the first serial port, enter the command: `ln -s /dev/ttyS0 /dev/pilot`

9.1.2 Configuring the KAddressBook Conduit

Initially, it should be sufficient to enable the KAddressBook conduit without changing any of the defaults. After the data has been synchronized for the first time, configure the details: what to do in case of conflicts, the way in which backup databases are saved, and how certain fields as stored on the handheld should be assigned to the fields expected by KAddressBook.

9.1.3 Managing To-Do Items and Events

On the KDE desktop, to-dos (tasks) and events (appointments) are managed with KOrganizer. Start the application from the main menu or with the command `korganizer`. After enabling the calendar and the to-do conduit of KPilot, set some configuration options before using them.

KOrganizer stores its files in the directory `~/.kde/share/apps/korganizer`. However, given that the directory `.kde/` begins with a dot, it may not be shown by the file selection dialog. In this case enter the complete path manually or explicitly toggle the display of hidden files (dot files) in the file selection dialog. The default shortcut for this is (F8).

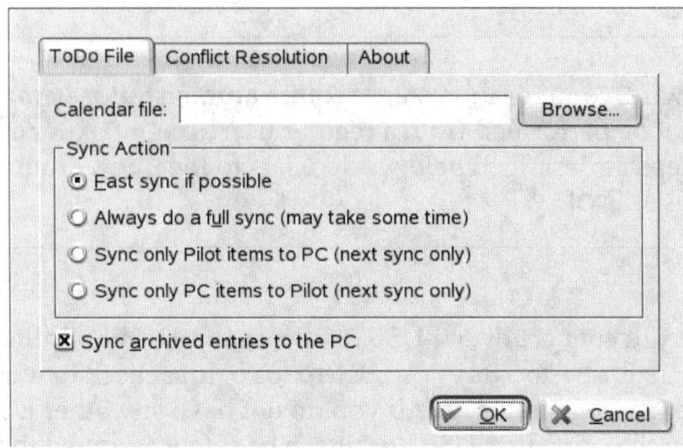

Figure 9.3: *KPilot Configuration*

Having opened the directory `~/.kde/share/apps/korganizer`, select a file that can be used as a calendar file by KOrganizer. In our example, this is the file `palm.ics`. In the case of a user called `tux`, the complete path and file name would be `/home/tux/.kde/share/apps/korganizer/palm.ics`, as shown in Figure 9.4.

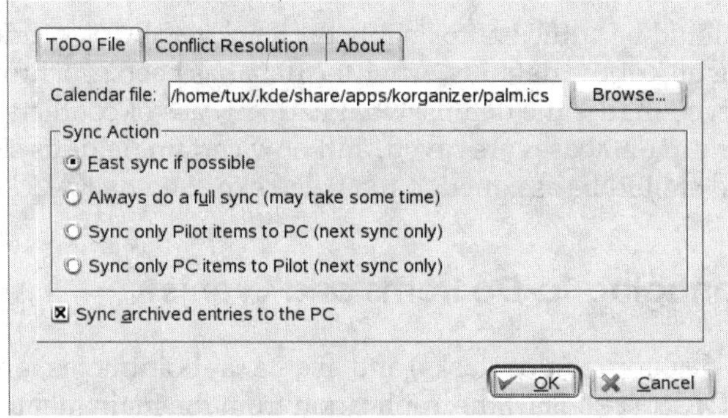

Figure 9.4: *Dialog Showing the Path to a KOrganizer Calendar File*

KOrganizer should not be running when data is being exchanged with the handheld. Otherwise KPilot will fail to carry out the sync operation.

9.2 Working with KPilot

Synchronizing the data of KDE applications with those of the handheld computer is quite easy. Simply start KPilot then press the "HotSync" button on the cradle to start the sync operation.

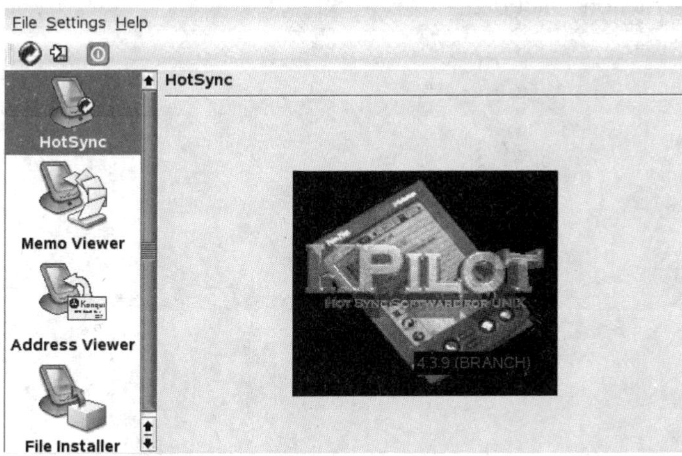

Figure 9.5: The Main Window of KPilot

9.2.1 Backing up Data from the Handheld

To do a full backup, select 'File' -> 'Backup'. The backup will be performed during the next sync operation. After that, switch back by selecting 'File' -> 'HotSync' from the menu. Otherwise, the time-consuming full backup will be performed again during the next sync operation.

After a full backup, all copies of the handheld's programs and databases are found in `~/.kde/share/apps/kpilot/DBBackup/<user>`, where <user> is the name of the actual user as registered on the handheld.

The two built-in KPilot viewers can be used for a quick lookup of addresses or memos, but they are not designed to actually manage this data. The KDE applications mentioned above are much more suited for these tasks.

9.2.2 Installing Programs on the Handheld

The 'File Installer' module is an interesting and useful tool for the installation of handheld programs. These programs normally have the extension `.prc` and they are ready to start immediately after uploading them to the handheld. Before using such add-on programs, read their licenses as well as the instructions included.

Scheduling with KOrganizer

KOrganizer is a KDE application for scheduling and managing events and tasks. Because of the variety of ways in which the program can present your schedule, it is a very helpful tool for keeping track of deadlines, outstanding tasks, and appointments. It can also remind you of birthdays and meetings, if you enable this function.

10.1 Starting KOrganizer

Start KOrganizer from the main menu or with `korganizer`. The main window has several toolbars, a menu bar, the date navigator with a month view of the calendar, the main part displaying the currently selected calendar view, and a list containing all the current to-do items. All the common program actions, such as saving, printing, and creating or deleting events, can be performed from the menus. See Figure 10.1.

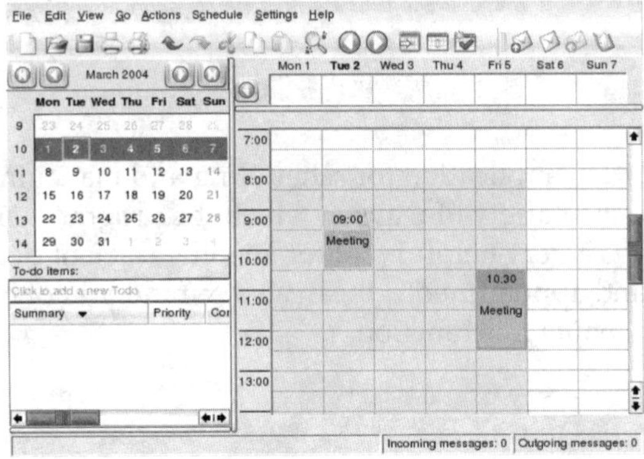

Figure 10.1: *The Main Window of KOrganizer*

KOrganizer can also be started in a windows containing other tools for office planning. More details are available in Section 5.4.10 on page 164.

10.2 Configuring KOrganizer

To configure KOrganizer, select 'Settings' -> 'Configure KOrganizer. . . '. This opens a dialog in which to enter your name and e-mail address. When working with the program, the name is used to indicate who is the owner of a given to-do item or event. The e-mail address is used to identify the owner of the calendar. A user who is not the owner can read the calendar, but not modify it. 'Send copy to owner when mailing events' should be enabled if you want to receive a copy of every e-mail sent out by the program (in your name) to the attendees of an event.

For KOrganizer to save your scheduling items automatically when exiting, check 'Enable automatic saving of calendar'. This also saves all changes automatically at a user-definable interval. To be prompted before any items are deleted, enable 'Confirm deletes'.

Under 'Time & Date', customize the defaults for working hours and appointments, define the default alarm time, and set your time zone. KOrganizer switches between winter and daylight savings time automatically.

Under 'Fonts', set your preferred font type and size for the different text fields of the program. Fonts can be selected for the time bar, the month view, and, under 'Agenda view', for the day view, week view, and work week view.

Under 'Colors', set the colors that should be used to highlight events, to-do items, and other elements. For instance, define that to-do items due on the current day should be dark red and that overdue to-do items should be light red.

The other items of the preferences dialog allow customization of the various views and the program's group features. Under 'Group Scheduling', provide additional e-mail addresses, which is useful if you are registered for a certain event under a different address.

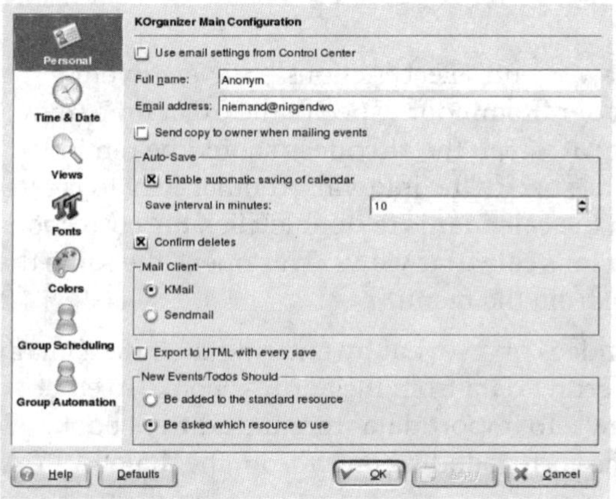

Figure 10.2: Configuring KOrganizer

10.3 Using the Calendar

The calendar of KOrganizer can be displayed in a number of different views to show a certain month, day, week, or work week. There is also a view of the next three days. Details of these views can be configured with 'Settings' -> 'Configure KOrganizer...' under the 'Views' item. Switch between the different views with the 'View' menu or by clicking the corresponding button in the toolbar.

Existing event items can easily be modified with the mouse. One possibility is to change the start and end date or time by clicking the item's upper or lower edge then dragging it to the desired position. In the day, week, and work week view, directly move an item to another time by clicking it then dragging it to the new position. You can also move events outside the time of the current view. For instance, an item can be dragged to the date navigator to the left. Even drag an item to the date navigator of another KOrganizer window.

10.3.1 Events

To schedule a new event, select 'Actions' -> 'New Event...'. Enter the desired details. Under 'Reminder', specify the exact time (minutes, hours, or days in advance) at which the attendees should be reminded of the event. If an event recurs, specify the interval. Another way to create an event at a specific point in the calendar is to double-click the corresponding field in one of the program's calendar views. This opens the same dialog window as that available from the menu.

Specify the attendees of an event by entering their data manually in the dialog or by inserting data from the address book. To enter such data manually, select 'New'. To import data from the address book, select 'Address Book...' then the corresponding entry from the dialog.

10.3.2 Attendees

Participants for a schedule item are listed under 'Attendees' in the item view. Sort the attendee list by clicking the column header of the value by which to sort.To add an attendee for an item, click 'New'. Then enter the name in 'Name' and the e-mail address in the field below. Use 'Address Book...' to query the address book and select entries from it. In 'Role', define the function of an attendee (observer, chair, participant), which can

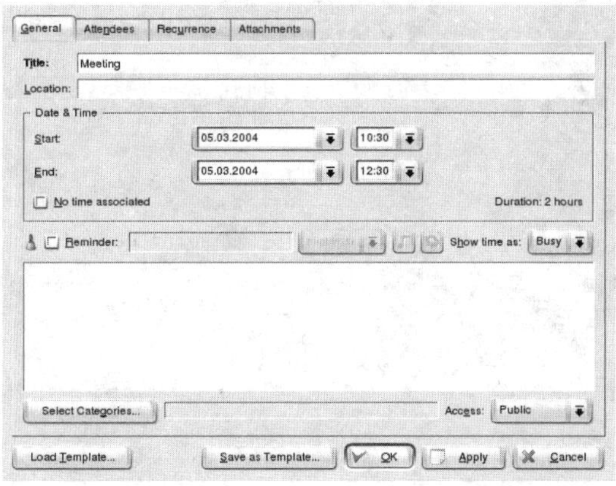

Figure 10.3: Scheduling with KOrganizer

also be used to sort the list of attendees later. With 'Status:', assign a status to an attendee, such as needs action, accepted, or completed. Change the status of an attendee at any time by selecting the attendee in the list then choosing another status from the drop-down list. If you check 'Request response', the attendees receive an e-mail with the relevant schedule item.

10.3.3 To-Do Items

Create a new to-do item by selecting 'Actions' -> 'New To-Do. . . '. In the dialog that opens, specify the exact start and due date and time for the new task, its progress in percent, and its priority. If other people are involved, specify their details under 'Attendees'. The created to-do item is then automatically included in the left list under 'To-do items'. The 'Summary' column in this list shows the description. 'Priority' shows the value selected.

10.3.4 Categories

To manage your schedule, group events and to-dos according to certain categories. Assign the scheduling items to one or several categories, for instance, if one of your items is related to job training, you could assign it to both 'Business' and 'Education'. Categories can be assigned in the dialogs for the creation of new events and to-dos after selecting 'Categories. . . '. Create additional categories with 'Edit Categories'.

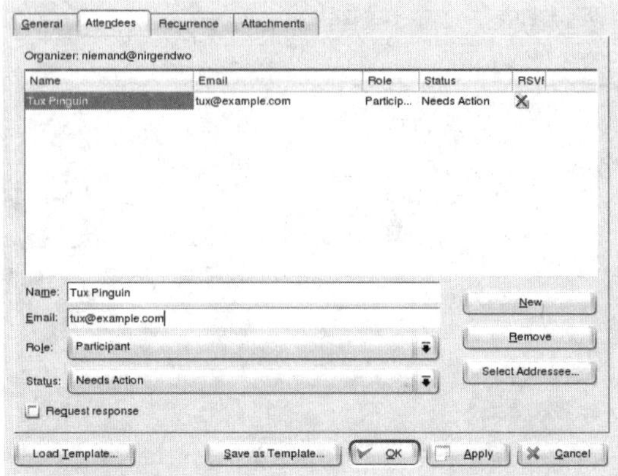

Figure 10.4: Entering Attendee Details

10.4 Printing

Selecting 'File' -> 'Print. . . ' opens a dialog in which to define the calendar period to print and the type of view to use. To specify the period, enter the dates by hand or use the calendar available from the drop-downs. To use the print preview function, you must have KGhostView installed. Alternatively, specify a different PostScript viewer, such as gv, after selecting 'File' -> 'Print. . . ' -> 'Print. . . ' -> 'System Options. . . ' then going to the 'Preview' item in the dialog.

10.5 Address Book

To store important contacts or to search for a contact, open the address book by selecting 'File' -> 'Addressbook'. In the address book window, make a new entry by selecting 'File' -> 'New Contact. . . '. The KDE address book application, although linked with KOrganizer, is an independent program. Learn more about it in Chapter 11 on page 225.

10.6 Help

For any problems or questions regarding KOrganizer, consult the detailed instructions for the program. Access them with 'Help' -> 'KOrganizer Handbook'.

Address Management with KAddressBook

KAddressBook provides quick and comfortable access to all address data of your contacts. As well as managing your local address data, KAddressBook can access, if available, a central LDAP server that hosts contact data for your entire department or your entire company. KAddressBook supports the import and export of vCard data, ensuring the smooth interaction with other programs.

KAddressBook can be started independently from the main menu, from the appointment scheduler KOrganizer, or the mail program KMail. On start-up, the KDE Address Book window consists of three frames, shown in Figure 11.1. The top frame contains the menu and toolbars. The two lower frames contain the current list of contacts and the address data of the currently selected contact.

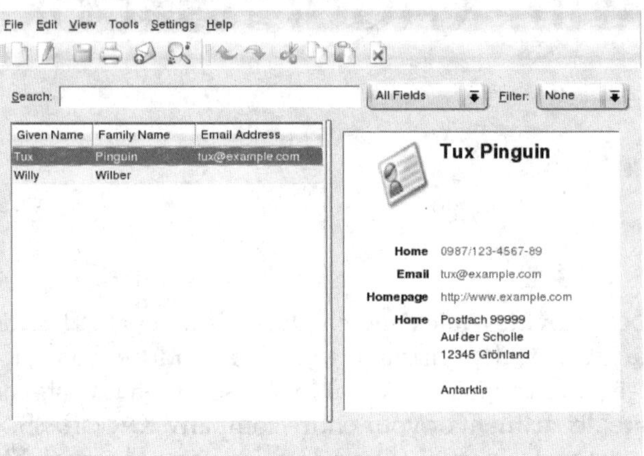

Figure 11.1: KAddressBook Main Window

11.1 Creating a New Contact

Open the contact editor with 'File' -> 'New Contact', the respective icon, or the entry in the toolbar. A dialog opens with two tabs in which to make your entries. Refer to Figure 11.2 on the next page.

Enter all important information, including name, title, private and business addresses, all phone numbers, e-mail addresses, and URLs, under the 'General' tab. If desired, assign the contact to a category that can later be used for filtering the address view. Select a standard category (Family, Friend, Business, Customer, or School) or create a new category.

The 'Details' tab contains some useful additional information, such as birthdays and anniversaries, and offers the possibility to add comments for this contact. As soon as all required fields under these tabs are completed, save the data with 'OK'. The new contact then appears in a list of current contacts in the left part of the window.

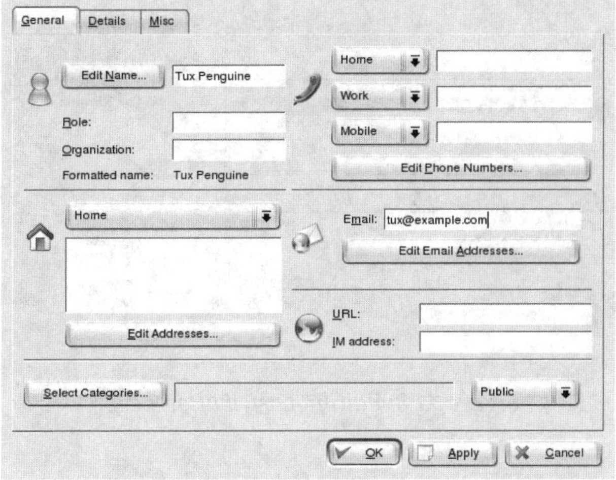

Figure 11.2: Recording New Contact Information

'Miscellaneous' allows adding a picture or logo to the selected contact. Other features, like the entering the longitude and latitude of a location, are possible.

11.2 Creating Address Lists

To generate lists from your address data, open the editor for distribution lists with 'Settings' -> 'Toolbars' -> 'Distribution Lists'. Use 'New List' to create one or several new lists under different names. The new entries appear in the drop-down menu at the top left corner of the editor. Select the desired list then drag and drop all desired contacts from the overview in the left part of the window to the list overview. Renaming and deleting lists is also possible here. See Figure 11.3 on the following page.

11.3 Searching Address Data

Basically, KAddressBook offers three options for searching address data:

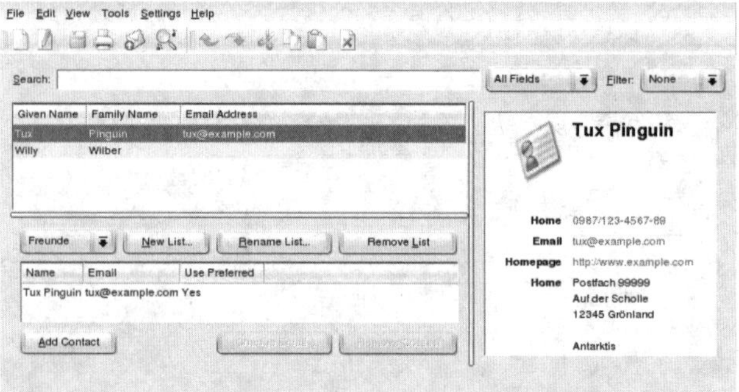

Figure 11.3: Editing Distribution Lists

Incremental search Use the drop-down menu to determine search details, such as the 'Given Name', 'Family Name', or 'Email Address'. As soon as you enter a character string in the adjacent input field, the data is searched by the selected criterion. The search result is displayed in the overview and in the detailed view.

Searching for initials or numbers (jump bar) Activate this toolbar with 'Settings' -> 'Show Jump Bar'. Depending on the activated search criterion in the 'Incremental search', clicking the respective letter or number produces the contact entries whose given name, family name, or e-mail address begins with this letter or number.

Search in a remote LDAP directory To use this function, first configure an LDAP server in your network. Go to 'Settings' -> 'Configure KAddressBook' -> 'LDAP' to access a list of various LDAP servers. If no selection is offered, ask your system administrator for the name of the server, the port number, and the base DN. Enter this data in the dialog opened with 'Add Host'. Activate your settings with 'Apply' and 'OK'.To start the actual search, click the magnifying glass icon in the upper toolbar. In the following dialog, select a suitable search criterion (phone number, name, e-mail) and enter the search string in the adjacent input field. The result of your search appears in an overview below the search options. To integrate the retrieved entries in your address book, click the respective buttons. You can also send an e-mail message to all addresses found.

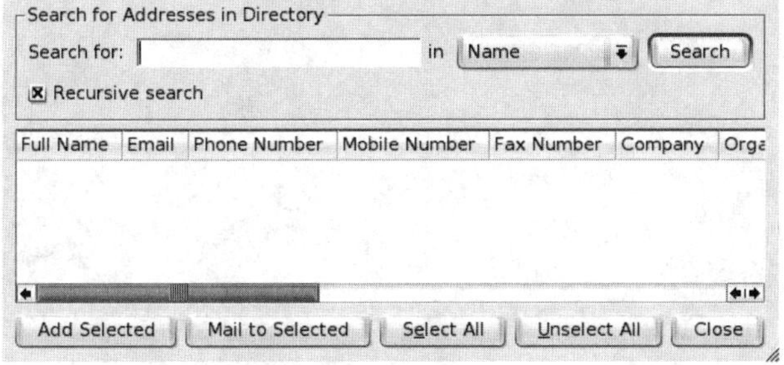

Figure 11.4: Searching an LDAP Directory

11.4 Importing and Exporting Address Data

'File' → 'Import' adds a contact present in another file or location. 'Export' exports a contact in a certain format. It is, for example, possible to transfer the addresses onto a mobile phone or to create a VCard and send it via e-mail.

Part IV

Internet

12

The Web Browser Konqueror

Konqueror is not only a versatile file manager. It is also a modern web browser. If you start the browser with the icon in the panel, Konqueror opens with the web browser profile.

12.1 Opening Web Pages

Simply enter a web address in the URL line, for example, `www.suse.de`. Konqueror displays the address. Writing the protocol (`http://`) at the beginning is optional, as it is recognized automatically by the program. This feature only works properly with web addresses, however. For FTP servers, enter `ftp://` at the beginning of the entry line.

Figure 12.1: The Browser Window of Konqueror

12.2 Saving Web Pages and Graphics

As in other browsers, you can save web pages. To do this, select 'Location' -> 'Save as …' and specify a name for your HTML file. However, images will not be saved. To archive an entire web page including the images, select 'Extras' -> 'Archive Web Page'. Konqueror suggests a file name that you can usually accept. The file name ends with `.war`, the extension for web archives. To view the saved web archive later, simply click the respective file and the web page is displayed in Konqueror along with its images.

12.3 Enhanced Web Browsing (Internet Keywords)

Searching the web using Konqueror is very practical. Konqueror defines a number of search engines for you, all with a specific shortcut. To search for a certain topic on the Internet, enter the shortcut and the keyword separated by a colon. The relevant page containing the search results is then displayed.

You can also define your own shortcuts. Simply select 'Settings' -> 'Configure Konqueror' -> 'Web Shortcuts'. A dialog appears in which to define your own abbreviations.

12.4 Bookmarks

If you frequently visit certain pages, it can be useful to save them as bookmarks. Use the 'Bookmark' menu to save all important locations of web pages or directory links on your local hard disk.

To create a new bookmark in Konqueror, click 'Bookmarks' -> 'Add Bookmark'. If you have already added some bookmarks, also see them in this menu. It is recommended to arrange your collection by subjects, grouped hierarchically. Create a new group for bookmarks with 'New Directory'. Open the bookmark editor by selecting 'Bookmarks' -> 'Edit Bookmarks …'. Use this program to organize, rearrange, add, and delete bookmarks.

If you are using Netscape or Mozilla as additional browsers, it is not necessary to recreate your bookmarks. 'File' -> 'Import Netscape Bookmarks' in the bookmark editor enables you to integrate your Netscape and Mozilla bookmarks into your most current collection. The reverse is also possible via 'Export as Netscape Bookmark'.

Change your bookmarks by right-clicking the entry. A pop-up menu appears in which to select the desired action (cut, copy, delete, etc.). When you achieve the desired results, save it with 'File' -> 'Save'.

To save your bookmark list and have instant access to it, make your bookmarks visible in Konqueror. Select 'Settings' -> 'Show Bookmark Toolbar'.

A bookmark panel is automatically displayed in the current Konqueror window.

12.5 Java and JavaScript

Do not confuse these two languages. Java is an object-oriented, platform-independent programming language from Sun Microsystems. It is frequently used for small programs (applets), which are executed over the Internet for things like online banking, chatting, and shopping. JavaScript is an interpreted scripting language mainly used for the dynamic structuring of web pages (e.g., for menus and other effects).

Konqueror allows you to enable or disable these two language. This can even be done in a domain-specific way, which means that you can permit access for some hosts and block access for others. Java and JavaScript are often disabled for security reasons. Unfortunately, some web pages require JavaScript for correct display.

The Web Browser Galeon

Recently, the widely-used web browser has been transformed into a real jack-of-all-trades. The fact that today's Internet applications feature such depth in integration and are heavily integrated into their corresponding desktop environments is almost taken for granted. Users of outdated machines soon feel the effects of this development. All-around browsers are often memory-eaters, sluggish in their operation, and occupy thirty megabytes on the hard disk.

That is why the idea behind Galeon is to devote itself just to one assignment: the web and only the web. Galeon implements the speedy Gecko engine of the Mozilla browser and integrates this into a functional user interface. The application loads quickly and is one of the fastest browsers available.

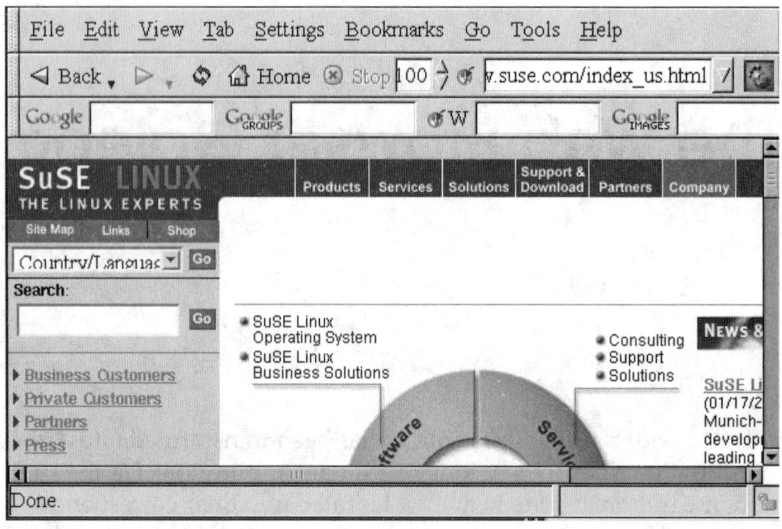

Figure 13.1: The Main Window in Galeon

Galeon's most essential navigation tools are available in the first toolbar. 'Next' and 'Back' flip through the history of visited Internet sites, as in other browsers. 'Reload' updates the contents of a site. 'Cancel' stops a connection or transfer from taking place. Zoom, the magnification level of a document, is usually scaled to 100% — a 1:1 display of the document. The up and the down arrows to its right set the zoom levels in intervals of ten. Enter Internet addresses (URLs) in the following entry box. The GNOME foot shows Galeon's progress. If the icon is animated, Galeon is working and transferring data.

13.1 Optimized for the Web

Galeon is primarily designed to make surfing the Internet as convenient as possible. In the default configuration, Galeon presents a second toolbar, enabling quick access to the popular Google search engine and its news and image search function. It can also offer access to an online dictionary and use the *bookmarklets*. This is made possible by small JavaScript functions built into Galeon, for example, find out how current a page is or allow the Internet site to slowly scroll down the screen.

13.2 Efficient Surfing with Tabs

Galeon can display multiple documents in a single application window. To open a link in a web site in the form of a new tab, right-click that link. Select 'Open in new tab' in the pop-up menu. Create a fresh Galeon tab by clicking 'File' -> 'Open New Tab'. Click the tabs to switch the display.

13.3 Smart Bookmarks

Smart bookmarks give access to a site's functions along with its address, for example, searching the Internet for terms with Google. Enter the word in the input field after the Google icon. The result is displayed after a few seconds.

To activate or create additional smart bookmarks, select 'Bookmarks' -> 'Smart Bookmarks Toolbar' -> 'Folder actions' -> 'Edit ...'. A window opens in which to edit the bookmarks. To create a new bookmark, mark 'Smart Bookmarks Toolbar' and select 'File' -> 'New item'. Enter a name in 'Name' and the web address in 'URL'. The 'Smart URL' field is a URL that additionally contains a wild card for the entered string. For example, the smart URL for Google is `http://www.google.com/search?q=%s`. %s is the wild card. Save your bookmark settings with 'File' -> 'Save'.

13.4 Settings and Controls

Modify the configuration of the browser with 'Settings' -> 'Preferences'. This dialog provides access to settings controlling both appearance and functionality.

Galeon features built-in password management and cookie controls. It also has options that specify the web sites from which images may be downloaded. All these options can be accessed through a single dialog via 'Tools' -> 'Cookies' -> 'View Cookies'.

13.5 For More Information

For more information about Galeon, see `http://galeon.sourceforge.net`. The GNOME home page `http://www.gnome.org` can also be helpful.

The Mozilla Web Browser

Mozilla is a web browser developed as an Open Source program with the aim of providing an Internet application that is fast, compliant with standards, and portable across different computing platforms. In addition to the basic browser, Mozilla includes a number of extra components, such as a mail component and a web page design component. This chapter focuses on the web browser component.

14.1 The Initial Browser Window

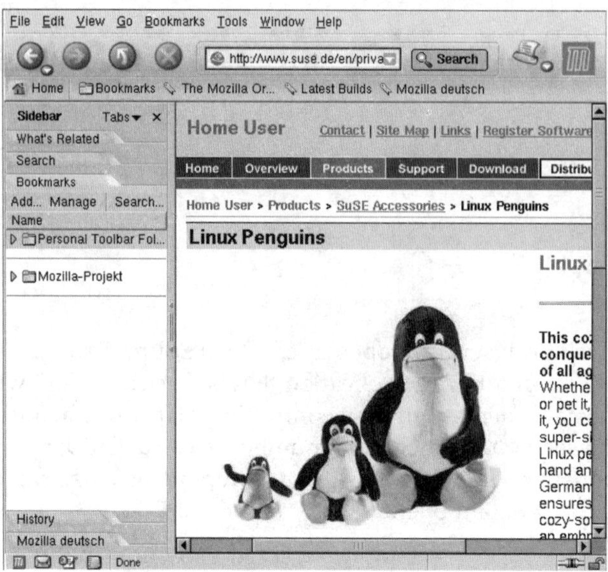

Figure 14.1: *The Initial Browser Window*

In its default configuration, the window presented by the browser includes these elements: the actual document window, occupying the majority of the window, used to display web pages (although it may be empty at the outset), the menu bar, the navigation toolbar, and the personal toolbar. There is also a combined status and component bar at the bottom of the window. Finally, to the left of the document window, Mozilla provides a sidebar that contains a number of different tabs, each of them giving access to a particular task.

When you right-click in the document window, Mozilla opens a context menu with a number of entries. Use this menu, for example, to add the current page to your bookmarks ('Bookmark This Page') or to view its source code ('View Page Source').

14.1.1 The Menu Bar

The menu bar includes the following menus:

File This menu provides the common entries to open, save, and print files or web pages. It also allows you to send an entire web page or only the link to a page as an e-mail. Selecting 'Edit Page' loads the current page into the Mozilla Composer, which allows you to edit web pages and to create your own from scratch. Mozilla's online help documents include an introduction to creating web pages, which you may want to read as a primer on the topic. The 'File' menu also includes the 'Work Offline' item, which tells the browser to use only locally stored or cached web pages.

Edit 'Edit' includes the common editing operations, such as 'Undo', 'Cut', 'Copy', 'Paste', and 'Delete'. There is also an item to search for words or text strings in web pages. 'Find Previous' repeats the previous search action. 'Preferences' opens a dialog in which to change the browser's configuration options. The details of this are described in Section 14.3 on page 246.

View The 'View' menu includes items to display or hide the different elements of the browser and also to stop loading a web page or reload it. There are also items to change the text zoom for the pages displayed and to change the character coding. Another item in this menu lets you view the source of a web page.

Go This is the navigation menu with items to go 'Back' or 'Forward' in the page history or to jump to the 'Home' page. Selecting 'History' opens a window thats lists the addresses of all the web pages recently visited with the browser.

Bookmarks Use 'Bookmarks' to create and edit bookmarks. Bookmarks can be arranged in folders. Any previously created bookmarks can be selected from the menu.

Tools A number of useful browser functions can be accessed via the 'Tools' menu. For example, access a search engine to find certain contents on the Internet. The Cookie Manager gives control over the cookies the browser has stored on your computer and lists each cookie together with the address of the site from which it originated. Use it to reverse previous decisions on whether to accept or reject cookies. The Image Manager allows you to block images and advertising banners from web sites, which improves speed. The Password Manager can make things easier for you if you frequently log in to sites via web interfaces (both in internal networks and on the Internet). Mozilla can remember the passwords for you. However, this feature also poses a certain security risk, so you may not want use it for sites with high privacy requirements, such as online banking sites.

Window This menu lets you switch to other browser windows and to those of other Mozilla components (if installed) — to the mail client, the composer, and the address book.

Help Mozilla is a multipurpose tool, so you may want to use this menu to access the online help, which provides information and hints about the features of the program.

14.1.2 The Navigation Toolbar

The buttons of the navigation toolbar give quick access to the basic functions of the browser. Use 'Forward' and 'Back' to jump one step ahead or back in the history of pages viewed previously. 'Reload' updates the contents of a page. Usually, web sites are stored in the cache for a certain time, in case they are called again. Reload always loads the current page from the Internet. 'Stop' aborts the loading of a page, so no further data is transferred from the corresponding site.

The next element to the right is the location bar in which to enter Internet addresses (URLs) or search terms. If you enter a search term then press 'Search', Mozilla searches the web for that term using the search engine set in the preferences. After having visited a number of sites, directly select their addresses again by clicking the down arrow, which opens a dropdown list. Mozilla stores the contents of this list so it is available in your next browser session. Start typing a previous address then hit (Tab) to complete it automatically.

'Print' prints the current page. The downward arrow to its right also gives access to a print preview of the document. To the very right, the navigation toolbar displays the Mozilla logo, which is animated as long as the browser is transferring data.

14.1.3 The Personal Toolbar

The personal toolbar is a customizable toolbar that is preconfigured to include the following elements:

Home This points to a web address configured to be displayed as Mozilla's start page.

Bookmarks This button lets you access the bookmarks collected from intranet or Internet sites.

The Mozilla Organization This points to the home page of the Mozilla project.

SuSE — The Linux Experts This points to the home page of SUSE LINUX.

14.1.4 Sidebar

The sidebar is located to the left in a separate subwindow.

What's Related Under this tab, Mozilla can list a number of sites whose topic is related to the current one.

Search This is an interface to several well-known search engines.

Bookmarks This tab is an additional entry point to your bookmarks, which are presented here in a tree structure.

History This tab provides a list of the recently visited web pages.

14.2 Working with Tabs

Mozilla can display several web pages at a time in one window by using tabbed browsing. This is often more convenient than opening a new browser window for each new document. To display a document (open a link) under a new tab, right-click the corresponding link then select 'Open Link in New Tab' from the context menu. The different documents are now directly available by clicking the different tabs arranged at the top of the main window.

As soon as you start using tabs, an extra button appears to the left of the tab bar, which allows you to open a new empty tab. Press Ctrl + T to achieve the same. To close the currently active tab, click the button with the X to the very right of the tab bar. Right-click a tab to open context menu that offers several related actions, such as closing the tab or closing all other tabs.

14.3 Preferences

Many often-needed browser settings are available in the dialog that opens when you select 'Edit' -> 'Preferences'.

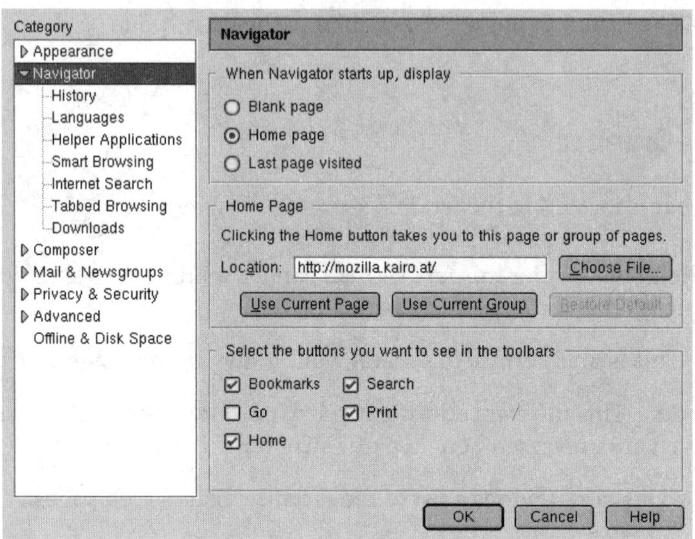

Figure 14.2: Preferences

Appearance Under this entry, set the fonts and colors the browser should use, select a theme, and switch between the German and the English language version.

Navigator The first thing that can be changed under this entry is the start page for the browser. Configure Mozilla to start with a blank page, the home page as defined below (which may be your organization's intranet portal, for instance), or the last page visited. In the 'History' dialog, define the number of days for which the addresses of visited pages should be stored. 'Languages' lets you define a list of preferred languages, which is useful for pages that are available in several languages. Under 'Internet Search', tell Mozilla which search engine to use.If you do not want Mozilla to show matching Internet addresses from the history automatically as soon as you start typing, disable this feature under 'Smart Browsing' -> 'Automatically complete text typed into Location bar'. Alternatively, configure Mozilla to autocomplete addresses in the entry field itself. To do so, select the 'Advanced...' button then, in the dialog, 'Autocomplete best match as you type'. One of the options available in the 'Tabbed Browsing' dialog is to have Mozilla open a new tab for a web page whenever you middle-click a link. Under 'Downloads', specify how the progress of file downloads should be monitored. Enabling 'Open the download manager' causes the browser to open the full-featured download manager dialog. 'Open a progress dialog' limits the dialog to a progress bar displayed during download. Turn off all download feedback by enabling 'Don't open anything'.

Privacy & Security This is one of the most important parts of the preferences, with a number of settings related to cookie handling and the built-in password management. In addition to that, there is an entry in which to specify from which web sites Mozilla should accept images.To maintain a degree of privacy, it is often a good idea to accept cookies only from the server from which the requested document is received. To achieve this, enable 'Enable cookies for the originating web site only'. Enabling 'Disable cookies' may cause some web pages not to function in the intended way. With 'Manage Stored Cookies', inspect the properties of any cookies that have been accepted.Use the 'Images' dialog to define similar settings for the handling of graphics. This is especially useful if you do not want to clog an already slow connection (modems) with the download of large images. The dialog also allows you to suppress the animation of any images. To achieve this, just select 'Never' under the 'Animated images should loop' header.In the 'Passwords' dialog, decide whether Mozilla should store any passwords entered. Consider both convenience and security. However, if you use the browser for online banking, you should definitely not have the corresponding password stored by Mozilla.

Advanced Often, web pages are not only written in plain HTML. Many sites also use JavaScript or Java to produce some special effects. As a general rule, it is recommended to turn off Java. Under 'Scripts & Plugins', you should also turn off JavaScript at least for 'Mail & Newsgroups'. Other dialogs available under this entry are related to the browser's 'Cache' and to the 'Proxies' used by it. The settings in the 'Cache' dialog depend on the specific circumstances with which the browser needs to cope, but the default 4096 kB size of the 'Memory Cache' is often too small. A cache is a temporary storage area used for the files fetched from the network so they can be reused.

Encryption with KGpg

KGpg is an important component of the encryption infrastructure on your system. With the help of this program, generate and manage all needed keys, use its editor function for the quick creation and encryption of files, or use the applet in your panel to encrypt or decrypt by dragging and dropping. The generation and management of keys is required for other applications, such as KMail or Konqueror, to handle encrypted files or e-mail messages correctly. This chapter covers the basic functions needed for daily work with encrypted files.

15.1 Key Management

This section covers operations needed for handling your digital key ring. Other programs, such as your mail program (KMail or Evolution), access the managed key data to process signed or encrypted contents.

15.1.1 Generating a New Key Pair

To be able to exchange encrypted messages with other users, first generate your own key pair. One part of it — the *public key* — is distributed to your communication partners, who can use it to encrypt the files or e-mail messages they send. The other part of the key pair — the *secret key* — is used to decrypt the encrypted contents.

Note

The public key is intended for the public and is distributed to all of your communication partners. However, only you should have access to the secret key. Do not grant other users access to this data.

Note

Start KGpg from the main menu or with the command `kgpg` from the command line. A padlock icon for KGpg appears in your panel. Click the icon to open the function menu. Select 'Open key manager'. Refer to Figure 15.1. Under 'Key', access all options related to the generation or management of keys. To generate a new key pair for yourself, click 'Generate Key Pair' (Ctrl + N).

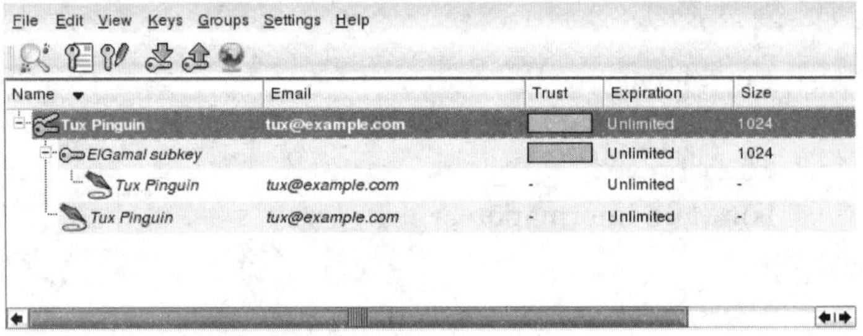

Figure 15.1: The Key Manager

In the following dialog, shown in Figure 15.2, enter your user name, your e-mail address, and an optional comment. The default setting for 'Expiration' (`Never` — key pair is valid for an indefinite period) can be accepted unless you want your keys to expire after a certain time. The default settings for 'Key size' and 'Algorithm' can be accepted as they are. Now, start the key generation with 'OK'. After this process is completed, the newly generated key appears in the overview window of the key manager.

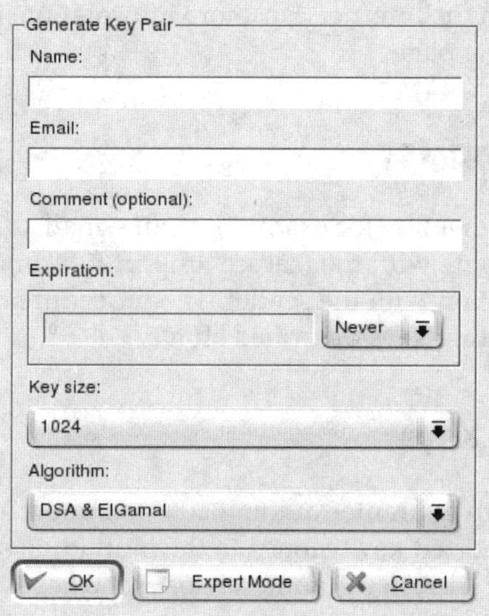

Figure 15.2: Generating Keys

15.1.2 Exporting the Public Key

After generating your key pair, make the public key available to other users. This enables them to use it to encrypt or sign the messages or files they send you. To make the public key available for others, select 'Keys' -> 'Export Public Key'. The dialog that opens offers three options:

Export Public Key To Email Your public key is sent to a recipient of your choice by e-mail. If you activate this option and confirm with 'OK', the dialog for creating a new e-mail message with KMail appears. Enter the recipient and click 'Send'. The recipient will receive your key and can then send you encrypted contents.

Export Public Key To Clipboard You can place your public key here before you continue to process it.

Export Public Key To File If you prefer to distribute your key as a file on a data medium instead of sending it by e-mail, click this option, confirm or change the file path and name, and click 'OK'.

To make your public key available to a wide audience, export it to one of the key servers on the Internet. For more information, refer to Section 15.2 on the facing page.

15.1.3 Importing Keys

If you receive a key in a file (for example, as an e-mail attachment), integrate it in your key ring with the feature 'Import Key' and use it for encrypted communication with the sender. The procedure is similar to the procedure for exporting keys described above.

15.1.4 Signing Keys

Keys can be signed to guarantee authenticity and integrity. If you are absolutely sure an imported key belongs to the individual specified as the owner, express your trust in the authenticity of the key by means of your signature.

Note

Encrypted communication is only secure to the extent that you can positively associate public keys in circulation with the specified user. By cross-checking and signing these keys, you contribute to the establishment of a web of trust.

Note

Select the key to sign in the key list. Select 'Keys' -> 'Sign Key'. In the following dialog, designate the secret key to use for the signature. An alert reminds you to check the authenticity of this key before you sign it. If you have performed this check, click 'Yes' and enter the password for the selected secret key in the next step. Other users can now check the signature by means of your public key.

15.2 The Key Server Dialog

Several Internet-based key servers offer the public keys of many users. To engage in encrypted communication with a large number of users, use these servers to distribute your public key. For this purpose, export your public key to one of these server. Similarly, KGpg enables you to search one of these servers for the keys of certain people and import their public keys from the server.

15.2.1 Importing a Key from a Key Server

By means of the 'Import' tab in the key server dialog, import public keys from one of the Internet-based key servers. Use the drop-down menu to select one of the preconfigured key servers and enter a search string (e-mail address of the communication partner) or the ID of the key to find. When you click 'Search', your system connects to the Internet and searches the specified key server for a key that matches your specifications. Refer to Figure 15.3.

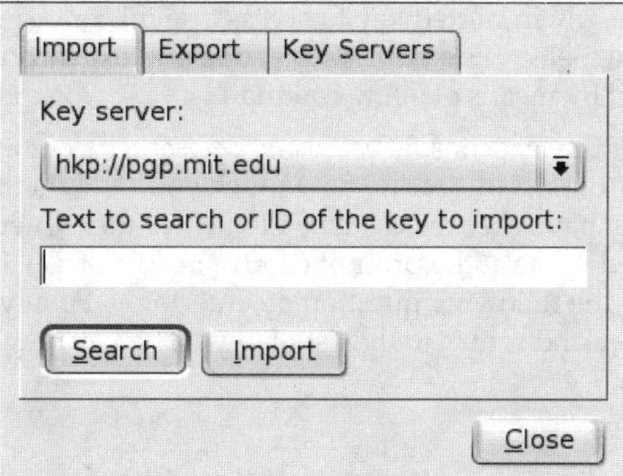

Figure 15.3: *Search Screen for Importing a Key*

If your search on the key server is successful, a list of all retrieved server entries is displayed in a new window. Select the key to include in your key ring and click 'Import'. See Figure 15.4 on the following page. Confirm the following message with 'OK' then exit the key server dialog with 'Close'.

The imported key then appears in the main overview of the key manager and is ready for use.

Figure 15.4: *Hits and Import*

To avoid being asked repeatedly about whether you trust the key and assume that this key is really used by its authorized owner, edit the trust level of the newly imported key. By default, a newly imported key always appears with a "?" instead of a setting regarding the trust level.

Right-click the newly imported key to access a small context menu for the key management. Select 'Edit Key'. KGpg opens a text console in which to set the trust level by means of a few commands.

At the prompt of the text console (`Command >`), enter `trust`. Now assign a value between 1 and 5 indicating how much you trust that the signers of the imported key have checked the true identity of the owner of this key. Enter the selected value at the prompt (`Your decision?`). If you are sure, enter `5`. Answer the following question by entering `y`. Finally, enter `quit` to exit the console and return to the list of keys. The key now has the trust level `Ultimate`.

15.2.2 Exporting Your Keys to a Key Server

To export your key to one of the freely accessible key servers on the Internet, select 'Export' in the key server dialog. Designate the target server and the key to export by means of two drop-down menus. Then start the export with 'Export'.

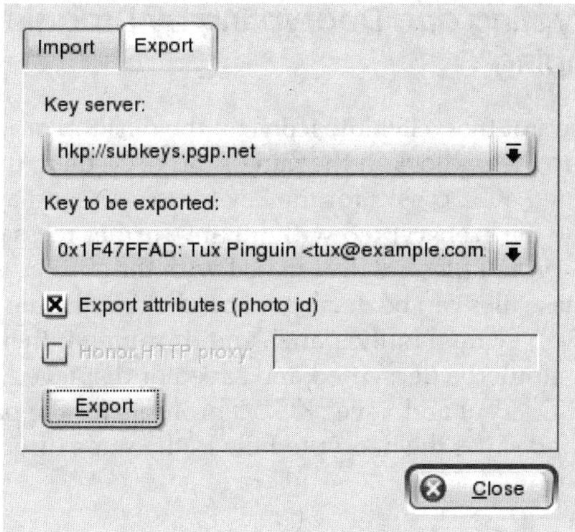

Figure 15.5: Exporting a Key to a Key Server

15.3 The Applet

On start-up, KGpg is available as an applet in the panel. Click the padlock icon with the left or middle mouse button to open a menu with all available functions. Apart from the options introduced above ('Open key manager', 'Key server dialog'), find the options 'Encrypt clipboard' and 'Decrypt clipboard' as well as the option for opening the integrated editor. Right-click to open a menu for configuring and closing KGpg.

15.3.1 Encrypting and Decrypting the Clipboard

Files copied to the clipboard can easily be encrypted with a few clicks. Open the function overview by clicking the KGpg icon. Select 'Encrypt clipboard' and designate the key to use. A status message about the encryption procedure is displayed on the desktop. The encrypted contents can now be processed from the clipboard as needed. The decryption of clipboard contents is just as easy. Simply open the function overview, select 'Decrypt clipboard', and enter the password associated with your secret key. The decrypted version is now available for processing in the clipboard and in the KGpg editor.

15.3.2 Encrypting and Decrypting by Dragging and Dropping

To encrypt or decrypt files, click the icons on the desktop or in the file manager, drag them to the padlock in the panel, and drop them there. If the file is not encrypted, KGpg asks for the key to use. As soon as you have selected a key, the file is encrypted without any further messages. In the file manager, encrypted files are designated with the suffix `.asc` and the padlock icon. These files can be decrypted by clicking the file icon, dragging it to the KGpg symbol in the panel, and dropping it there. Then select whether the file should be decrypted and saved or displayed in the editor. If you select 'Decrypt and Save', KGpg prompts for the password of your secret key and saves the decrypted file in the same directory as the encrypted file.

15.3.3 The KGpg Editor

Instead of creating contents for encryption in an external editor then encrypting the respective file with one of the methods described above, you can use the integrated editor of KGpg to create the file. Open the editor (context menu -> 'Open Editor'), enter the desired text, and click 'Encrypt'. Then select the key to use and complete the encryption procedure. To decrypt files, use 'Decrypt' and enter the password associated with the key.

Generating and checking signatures is just as easy as encrypting directly from the editor. Go to 'Signature' ->'Generate Signature' and select the file to sign from the file dialog. Then designate the secret key to use and enter the associated password. KGpg informs you about the successful generation of the signature. Files can also be signed from the editor by simply clicking 'Sign/verify'. To check a signed file, go to 'Signature' -> 'Verify Signature' and select the file to check in the following dialog. As soon as you confirm the selection, KGpg checks the signature and reports the result of the operation. Another possibility is to load the signed file into the editor and click 'Sign/verify'.

15.4 For More Information

For theoretical background information about the encryption method, refer to the brief and clear introduction on the GnuPG project pages at `http://www.gnupg.org/documentation/howtos.html.en`. This document also provides a list of further information sources.

16

KMail — The KDE Mail Application

KMail — The KDE Mail Application

KMail is the KDE mail application. In addition to sending and receiving e-mail and using multiple mail protocols, it offers the possibility to configure several user-defined filters for sorting e-mail messages in individual folders. The encryption, decryption, and signing of e-mail messages can also be handled conveniently in KMail.

16.1 KMail and Kontact

KMail can be displayed along with other applications in one window. This is done with the `Kontact` utility. Refer to 5.4.10 on page 164 for more details about this.

16.2 Mail Formats

KMail can save messages in the following formats:

mbox This traditional UNIX format (the oldest) saves all messages in a single file. Directories are also simulated by means of individual files. The individual mails can only be distinguished by the From line.

MailDir In contrast to the mbox format, the MailDir format has a unique file name for every message. The messages are stored in the respective directories and can easily be identified and further processed. KMail uses the MailDir format (as the more convenient alternative) by default, but MailDir is not supported by many other e-mail programs. This can be a disadvantage if you want to switch to a different e-mail program later and still access your old e-mails. Processing old mails in mbox format is no problem, however, if you select MailDir. Just copy or move the files to the MailDir folder.

16.3 Access Types

KMail allows you to access your electronic mail in various ways. The access type largely depends on your Internet Service Provider (ISP) or mail server. The main access types are POP3 and IMAP.

POP3 (Post Office Protocol Version 3)
POP3 is a standardized procedure for receiving e-mail. A POP3 server stores the messages until the user retrieves them with a POP3 client (in this case, KMail). This method is used frequently by Internet Service Providers (ISPs).

IMAP (Internet Message Access Protocol)
With IMAP, e-mail messages can be received and administered on

the server without downloading them to the hard disk. This is often used in internal networks as it allows access to mail from different computers.

16.4 Configuring KMail

When KMail is started for the first time, a `Mail` folder is added to your home directory. This folder contains some basic mail directories (inbox, outbox, drafts, sent, and trash). Go to 'Settings' -> 'Configure KMail...' to enter the information needed for sending and receiving messages. All configuration options can be accessed under 'Configure KMail' (wrench icon).

16.4.1 Defining Your User Identity

You can manage several e-mail addresses (e.g., your private e-mail address and your business address) with KMail. Select from the defined identities when writing e-mail. To create a new identity profile, select 'New...' and enter a name for the profile, such as "Private" or "Office".

Click 'OK' to proceed to a dialog in which to enter some additional information. Under 'General', enter your name, organization, and e-mail address. Under 'Advanced', enter your OpenPGP key, specify a default BCC field or reply-to address, and determine the folder in which your messages should be stored. Under 'Signature', define a signature footer to use for every message. To use this feature, select 'Enable signature'. Insert the signature from a file, an input field, or a command output. Confirm your profile settings with 'OK'.

16.4.2 Setting up Network Connections

The settings under 'Network' (in the 'Configure KMail' menu) instruct KMail how to receive and send e-mail. There are two tabs, one each for sending and for receiving mail. Many of these settings vary depending on the system and network in which your mail server is located. If you are not sure about the settings or items to select, consult your Internet service provider or system administrator.

Sending Create outgoing mail boxes under the 'Send' tab. 'Add' gives the choice of either SMTP or sendmail. For most purposes, select SMTP here. After making this selection, a window appears in which to enter SMTP server data, such as 'Name', 'Server', and, if needed, the required authorization. A preprocessing command to run before sending each message can be entered in the corresponding field.Security settings are under the 'Security' tab. Specify your preferred encryption method here. If uncertain about which one to choose, click 'Test server capacity'. The respective settings are then tested and applied. If necessary, consult your system administrator.

Receiving Make settings for receiving e-mail under the 'Receiving' tab. Use 'Add' to create a new account. Choose between different methods for fetching mail, such as local (Mbox or Maildir format), POP3, or IMAP. Usually POP3 is suitable. After making your selection, a window appears in which to enter the POP3 server data. Enter the name of the server in the field at the top. In the other fields, enter the values provided by your Internet service provider or your system administrator. The fields 'User', 'Server', and 'Password' are required.The 'Extras' tab offers several methods for encryption and authorization. If you are uncertain about which options your server provides, try 'Test server capabilities'.

16.4.3 Configuring the Appearance of KMail

Under 'Appearance', customize KMail according to your preferences. Use the 'Fonts' tab to configure the fonts for the various displays, such as the message text and first-level quoted text. To do this, activate 'Use custom fonts'.

To customize the colors, activate 'Use custom colors' in the 'Colors' tab. Double-click an entry to access a dialog in which to select the colors. The 'Layout' tab offers options for splitting the KMail window and for displaying a MIME tree. A MIME tree shows all the attachments to a message.

The 'Header' tab provides options for general settings, like displaying the file size or encryption symbols. Also, customize the date display and message grouping. 'Profiles' is responsible for the administration of default appearance presets. Some standard profiles are provided already, like those for users who prefer high contrast. Selecting a profile overwrites the current layout settings.

16.5 Using KMail

When KMail starts, the main window opens. By default, the main window consists of the following three sections:

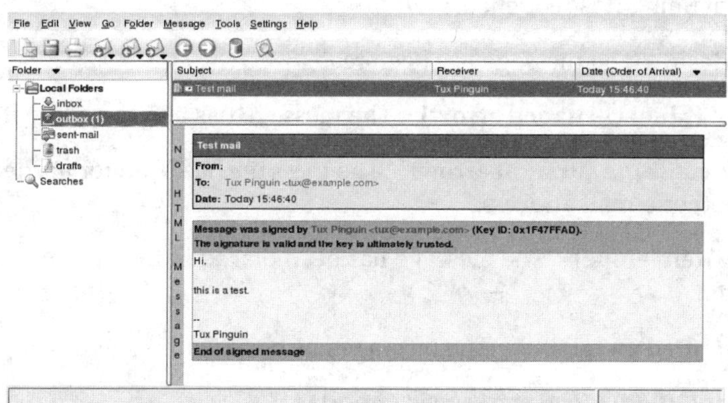

Figure 16.1: Main Window of KMail after Start-Up

Folder Area (left) This section contains a list of your mail folders (mail boxes) indicating the total number of messages and how many are still unread. To select a folder, simply click it. The messages it contains appear in the top right frame. The number of messages is also displayed in the status bar at the bottom of the application window.

Header Area (right) The subject, sender, and time of reception of received messages are listed in this area. Click a message to select it and display it in the message window. Sort the messages by clicking one of the columns (subject, sender, date, etc.).

Message Area (below) The contents of the currently selected message are displayed in this frame. Attachments are depicted as icons at the end of the message, based on the MIME type of the attachment. Use (PgUp) and (PgDn) to scroll through the pages of the message or use (↑) and (↓) to scroll line by line. The shortcuts are indicated after the respective menu items in the main menu.

Messages can be marked with different status flags. Change the status with 'Message' -> 'Highlight as'. The available flags are:

'New' (red dot, header in red) The message is new and has not yet been read.

'Unread' (green dot, header in blue) A message changes its status from 'New' to 'Unread' after the folder containing it is reopened.

'Read' (dash) The message has been read.

'Replied' (blue, U-shaped arrow) The message has been answered.

'Forwarded' (blue, straight arrow) The message has been forwarded to another e-mail address.

'Waiting' (envelope) The message has been placed in the outbox to send later.

'Sent' (slanted envelope) The message has been read.

'Important' (flag) The message is important.

16.6 Creating a New Message

To compose new messages, select 'Message' -> 'New Message ...' or press Ctrl + N. Alternatively, click the envelope and paper icon in the toolbar to start the mail editor.

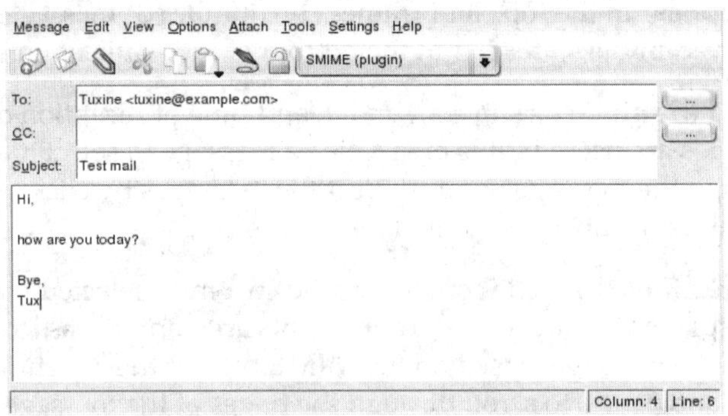

Figure 16.2: Composing a Message

To compose a message, fill in the respective fields in the 'New Message' window. To send messages from different e-mail accounts, select one of the identities configured as described in Section 16.4.1 on page 259. The buttons next to 'To:' and 'CC:' (and possibly 'blind copy (Bcc):') open the address book, allowing you to select an address. After entering the first few characters of an address, press Ctrl + T to see a list of possible completions. When the message is completed, click 'Send'. Under 'View' -> 'Headers', select various header types with more or fewer entries.

To attach files to your message, click the paper clip icon and select the file to attach. Alternatively, drag a file from the desktop or another folder to the 'New Message' window or select one of the options in the 'Attach' menu.

Normally, the MIME type (encoding) of a file is recognized correctly. If this is not the case, select the type from a list. Enter a short description in the 'Description' field. Then select an encoding from the list of encoding options (the default values usually work). When a file is attached to your message, it appears in the list of attachments in the lower part of the window. Attachments can be saved, removed, or opened by selecting the name of the attachment and subsequently clicking the desired item in the 'Attach' menu. You can also attach PGP keys to your messages by means of this menu. PGP keys are treated like file attachments. Their MIME type is application/pgp-keys.

16.7 Message Folders

Message folders serve as an organizing tool for your messages. By default, all message folders are stored in the `Mail` folder in your home directory. The `inbox`, `outbox`, `sent-mail`, and `trash` folders are created when KMail is started for the first time. These folders have the following functions:

- inbox: KMail stores new messages here (unless a filter has been defined).
- outbox: Messages to send are stored here.
- sent-mail: Copies of all e-mails sent are stored here.
- trash: Stores deleted e-mails.

Using 'Folder' -> 'New Folder', create additional folders for organizing your e-mail messages. Enter the name of the new folder in the dialog that opens, shown in Figure 16.3 on page 271. To create a subfolder, select the parent folder from 'Belongs to:'. Specify the folder type, any mailing list associated with it, and an expiration date after which the messages are marked for deletion. Additionally, you can select an identity or display a certain sender or recipient.

To move messages from one folder to another, highlight the message to move then press (M) or click 'Message' -> 'Move to…'. In the list of folders that appears, select the folder to which to move your messages. Messages can also be moved by dragging the message from the upper window and dropping it into the appropriate folder in the left window.

To remove all the messages from a folder, click 'Folder' -> 'Empty'. All messages located in the folder are then moved to the trash.

Note

Messages are not deleted permanently until you empty the trash.

Note

16.8 Importing Mail

KMail assists in importing e-mail messages from previously-used applications. Select 'Extras' → 'Import messages'. KMail currently features import filters for Outlook Express 4, 5 and 6, the mbox format, simple e-mail texts, and Pegasus Mail folders. The import utility can also be started separately by pressing (Alt)-(F2) and entering the command `kmailcvt`.

Select the corresponding application from the pop-up menu and confirm with 'Continue'. A file or a folder must be provided, depending on the selected type. KMail then completes the process.

16.9 The Address Book

Save frequently-used addresses and contacts in the address book. Access it from the 'Tools' menu, with the respective icon in the main window, or from the 'Composer' window. Create a new entry with 'File' -> 'New Contact'. A window opens in which to enter the data of the person under the 'General' tab.

The 'View' menu allows creation of custom views of the contacts. The table view is the default setting. 'Add view' opens a dialog in which to name the view. 'View type' has options for whether the contacts should be displayed as icons, in a table, or as cards. 'OK' continues to the next dialog box in which to select the fields to include in the custom view. Filters and preferences can be set in the corresponding items. 'OK' activates the newly created view.

16.10 Filters

Filters enable automatic processing of incoming messages and manual processing of selected messages in a folder. To filter selected messages to a specific folder, highlight the messages and enter Ctrl + J to activate existing filter rules or select 'Message' -> 'Create Filter' to create a new one. In doing so, all existing filter rules are applied to this message. There is no way to use only certain filters.

16.10.1 Filter Rules

A filter consists of one or several filter rules and filter actions. A filter rule can select messages according to criteria, such as the sender, content, or recipient. The respective filter action can perform tasks like moving, deleting, marking, or forwarding these messages.

16.10.2 Examples of Filters

Assume, for instance, to be subscribed to the KDE user list (`kde-user@kde.org`). Whenever a message from the mailing list arrives, the message is moved into another folder. The following steps are necessary for creating this filter.

1. Add a new folder as described in Section 16.7 on page 263. A name like `kde-user/` can be assigned.
2. First, find a way of identifying messages to filter. The messages of the KDE user list described in our example can be identified by the `kde-user@kde.org` address, found in the 'To': or 'Cc': field.
3. Click 'Settings' -> 'Configure Filters'. The left side of the window that opens displays the existing filters. The right side is composed of two panels: filter rules and filter actions.

4. Click the 'New' icon to create an empty filter. It appears as `unknown`.
5. Select 'To:' or 'Cc:' from the first drop-down menu and 'contains' from the second drop-down menu. Enter `kde-user@kde.org` in the text field.
6. In 'Filter actions', select 'Move to Folder' from the first drop-down menu. A second drop-down menu with the list of folders appears. Choose the folder to which the filtered messages should be moved if they meet the desired criteria. In this case, choose `kde-user` from the drop-down menu.
7. Confirm the changes with 'OK'.

More complex filters are also possible. For example, you may want to save only the messages written by Fred Johnson to the KDE user list (`fj@anywhere.com`). Here, the remaining filter criteria come into play:

1. Click 'Settings' -> 'Configure Filters' and mark the newly created filter.
2. To filter all messages containing `kde-user@kde.org` in the 'To:' or 'Cc:' fields *and* originating from Fred, define a second filter under 'Filter Criteria' using the second row of drop-down menus. Select 'From' in the first menu and 'contains' in the second. Then enter the e-mail address to filter. Activate 'Applies to all'.
3. Select the action to execute (move, delete, etc.).

You have now created a filter that transfers all mails from Fred Johnson on the KDE user list as specified.

16.10.3 Spam Filters

While electronic mail has many advantages, it has a significant disadvantage: spam. Unsolicited mass mailings, also known as spam, sent by the advertisement industry, clog your electronic inbox and cause long transfer times. Filtering tools can separate the annoying ballast from important messages. SpamAssassin is such a tool that can be embedded into KMail. It relies on various built-in rules and has the ability to learn from its experience with spam. The configuration of this useful application for KMail is described here.

Preparations

The actual software needs to be present before spam messages can be filtered. Run YaST as user `root` and install the package `spamassassin` with the package manager ('Software' → 'Software').

Then configure the system to activate the SpamAssassin service on system start-up by opening the RunLevel editor in YaST (located under 'System'). Search the list of services for `spamd` and select 'activate'. Confirm the choice with 'Finish'. This completes the SpamAssassin installation process.

Create an additional folder in KMail (naming it `spam`, for instance) in which to store the messages classified as spam. If you already have collected some spam messages, move as many of them as possible into this folder. This folder can be later used as a *training stock* and allows the tool to decide which of your incoming messages should be classified as spam.

Spam Filtering

KMail requires two filters for spam processing:

1. The first filter examines the size of a message. Select 'Settings' → 'Configure filters. . . '. In the dialog that appears, create a new filter entry and name it `SpamAssassin` (modify the name, if desired). Select '<Size in bytes>' as the filtering property and 'is less than' as the qualifier. Set the threshold to '300000'.

   Select 'pipe through application' for 'filtering actions' and enter `spamc` in the field next to it. The option 'abort processing here upon matching filter condition' must be *deactivated*. Confirm the first filter with 'Apply'.

   This filtering rule specifies that KMail passes only messages to `spamc` whose size is less than 300 KB. It is possible to adjust other threshold values. The processing time for messages rises, however, with an increasing size threshold. SpamAssassin then tests all messages for characteristics of spam and alters the message header by adding the line `X-Spam-Status: YES`. The second filter relies on this.

2. Add a second filter to the list and name it `SPAMFilter`. This filter moves the messages marked by SpamAssassin to the spam folder.

   Select '<header field>' as the property and 'contains' as the qualifier. Enter 'X-Spam-Status: YES' in the corresponding text entry field. Set 'filtering action' to 'file in folder' and select `spam`. Confirm with 'Apply'.

These two filters should be placed in the described order at the top of the list. Any other filters can be placed below them.

Distinguishing Wanted and Unwanted Messages

SpamAssassin ships with predefined rules that control the recognition of spam messages. It is possible for the tool to miss a message occasionally. This is where the rate of false negatives can be lowered by training SpamAssassin.

The utility `sa-learn` is included for this purpose. If your messages are stored in the MailDir format (refer to Section 16.2 on page 258) run the following command:

```
sa-learn --spam --dir ~/Mail/spam/cur/
```

If your messages are stored in the mbox format, run the following command:

```
sa-learn --mbox --spam ~/Mail/.spam.directory/*
```

SpamAssassin returns the following message upon a successful spam recognition event:

```
Learned from 15 message(s)
```

Visit the site `http://www.spamassassin.org` or read the corresponding man page to discover more about this tool.

16.11 Encrypting Mail with PGP or GnuPG

You can encrypt outgoing e-mail with KMail. To encrypt your e-mail, first generate a key pair as described in Chapter 15 on page 249. Then log out and log in again.

With 'Settings' -> 'Configure KMail. . . ' -> 'Security' -> 'Crypto plugins' -> 'Configure', determine in what cases and with which process your e-mail messages should be encrypted. The corresponding module (usually openpgp) must be activated first. In 'path', enter the file name of the crypto library. In the case of OpenPGP, this is `/usr/lib/cryptplug/gpgme-openpgp.so`. `/usr/lib/cryptplug/gpgme-smime.so` is valid for smime. An asterisk in the displayed table marks the active module. If desired, select to be alerted when attempting to send an unencrypted e-mail. To encrypt any attachments as well, check 'Encrypt all message parts' in 'Settings' -> 'Configure KMail. . . ' -> 'Security' -> 'Crypto Plugins' -> 'Configure'.

After setting the preferences, click 'Identities' (under 'Configure KMail'). Select the identity with which encrypted or signed messages should be sent and choose 'Change'. Select the 'Advanced' tab in the dialog that opens. Click 'Change' for 'OpenPGP key' to display a selection box from which to choose the keys. Confirm with 'OK'. The encryption system is now ready.

The public key must be made available to recipients of a signed message so they can verify its authenticity. It also needs to be accessible to enable others to send encrypted messages to the owner of the key. Public keys can be stored on a public PGP key server, such as `http://www.pgp.net`.

16.11.1 Signing Messages

Create your messages as usual. Before sending the message, click the corresponding icon (second to last) in the toolbar of the window or choose 'Options' -> 'sign message'. The message can then be sent. To sign it, KMail must know your PGP password. However, if you have already provided the password, KMail signs the message without requesting any further information. The results of the PGP signing process can be reviewed in the `SentMessages` folder (or in the outbox if you did not use 'Send now'). There, your e-mail should be marked with the notice that it was signed by you.

16.11.2 Checking the Signature of a Received Message

If KMail is able to verify the signature of an e-mail, a green frame with the key ID is displayed. If the signature cannot be verified, a yellow frame with an alert is displayed. This means that you do not have a suitable public key for the signature.

16.11.3 Sending Public Keys

Create a message for the person who should receive your public key. Choose 'Attach' -> 'Attach Public Key'. The mail can then be sent. There is no guarantee that the recipient of a signed message receives the correct key. It is possible for the mail to be intercepted on the way to the recipient and signed with another key. Therefore, the recipient should check the attached key by comparing the finger print with a previously received value. Further information about this can be found in the PGP and GnuPG documentation.

16.11.4 Decoding Encrypted Messages

In KMail, select the message to decrypt. Enter your password when prompted. KMail attempts to decrypt the message. If it was encrypted with your public key, KMail displays it in clear text. If not, you cannot read the e-mail message. KMail saves these e-mail messages encrypted to prevent anyone from reading them without your password.

16.11.5 Encrypting Messages

To send an encrypted message to a recipient for whom you have the public key, simply write the message in the 'Create Message' window. Before sending the message, click the red key icon in the window's toolbar. Now, the message can be sent. If KMail cannot find a key for the recipient, a list with all available keys is shown. Select the appropriate one from the list or abort the process. KMail also informs you if errors occur during the encryption process. You cannot read encrypted messages if you did not click 'Always encrypt to self' in the 'Security' tab.

16.12 For More Information

More information is available on the KMail home page at `http://kmail.kde.org`.

Figure 16.3: *Creating New Folders*

17

Evolution: An E-Mail and Calendar Program

Evolution is a groupware suite created by Ximian. It offers regular e-mail features along with extended features, like task lists and a calendar. The application also provides a complete address book, including the ability to send contact information to others in vCard format.

17.1 Starting Evolution

Start Evolution from the main menu or with `evolution`. When started for the first time, Evolution offers a configuration assistant. If it is not opened automatically, select 'Tools' -> 'Settings' -> 'Mail Accounts' and click 'Add'. Click 'Next' to access the assistant. Enter your name and your e-mail address in the respective fields. Additional addresses can be configured later. Click 'Next'.

Select the appropriate incoming e-mail format for this address in 'Server Type'. 'POP' is the most common format for downloading mail from a remote server. 'IMAP' works with mail folders on a special server. Obtain this information from your ISP or server administrator. Complete the other relevant fields displayed when the server type is selected. Click 'Next' when finished.

The next set of information to enter is about mail delivery. This is used for all configured e-mail addresses. To submit outgoing e-mail on the local system, select 'Sendmail'. For a remote server, select 'SMTP'. Get the details from your ISP or server administrator. For SMTP, complete the other fields displayed after selection. Click 'Next' when finished.

By default, the e-mail address is used as the name to identify the account. Enter another name if desired. The field 'Make this my default account' determines whether the account should be used as the default. The default account is the e-mail address initially selected for sending e-mail. Another account can be selected in the message composition window if desired. Click 'Next'.

The time zone information from the next window is used for the calendar functions. It is important to select the correct time zone for using the appointment scheduling functions. Click the dot on the map for a city in your time zone. Selection zooms the display to that area and a change can be made if desired. When the correct time zone is displayed under 'Selection', click 'Next'. In the next window, click 'Finish' to save the data entered. Use 'Back' to make changes.

17.2 Importing E-Mail from Other Mail Programs

Evolution can import e-mail from other e-mail programs, such as Netscape or KMail. To do so, select 'File' -> 'Import...'. For KMail or mutt, select 'Import a single file'. For Netscape, select 'Import data and settings from older programs'. Get more information with 'Help'.

17.3 Evolution Overview

The default window view is shown in Figure 17.1. The available menus, menu items, and the icons in the toolbar vary from window to window. Use the 'Shortcuts' panel to the left to select the information to display in the right panel. Adjust the size of any panels by dragging the dividing bars.

Use 'View' to remove the 'Shortcuts Bar' or add a 'Folder Bar' at any time. The different items listed in 'Shortcuts' are described in the following.

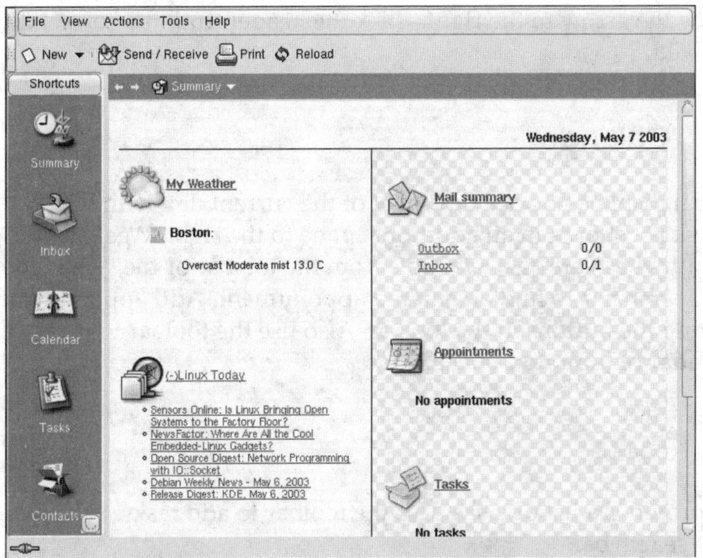

Figure 17.1: The Evolution Window with Shortcuts and Summary

17.3.1 Summary

The 'Summary' provides some basic information about e-mail, appointments, and tasks along with personally configurable weather and news sources. This window is shown in Figure 17.1 on the preceding page. Use 'Tools' -> 'Settings' -> 'Summary Preferences' to configure the information displayed.

17.3.2 Inbox

In this view, the upper half of the window shows the contents of the folder Inbox. The lower half is a preview pane used to display the selected mail message. Disable the preview pane with 'View' -> 'Preview Pane'.

To change the folder displayed, click the down arrow next to 'Inbox' and select another folder from the list. Use the search bar to search the messages in a folder. If desired, click a table header for the message list to sort the messages by that header. The sort can be either ascending or descending as shown by the arrow to the right. Click the header until the correct direction is displayed.

17.3.3 Calendar

The initial display shows a day view of the current day with the month and a task list shown in an additional pane to the right. Week, work week, and month views are also available from the toolbar or the 'View' menu. Use the search bar to find an entered appointment. Add appointments and tasks using the buttons in the toolbar. Also use the toolbar to page through the calendar or jump to a specific date.

17.3.4 Tasks

'Tasks' provides a list of tasks. Use the toolbar to add tasks. Search the tasks with the search bar.

17.3.5 Contacts

This view shows all the addresses in your address book. To locate a particular address, use the search bar or click the button to the right displaying the first letter of the contact's last name. Add contacts or lists with the toolbar.

17.4 E-Mail

To configure the mail settings in Evolution, go to 'Shortcuts' -> 'Inbox'. Then activate 'Tools' -> 'Settings'.

17.4.1 Configuring Accounts

Evolution is capable of fetching e-mail from multiple mail accounts. The account from which to send e-mail can be selected when composing a message. To edit a current account, select the account in 'Settings' -> 'Mail Accounts' and click 'Edit'. To add a new account, click 'Add'. The configuration assistant described in Section 17.1 on page 274 opens. To delete an account, select it and click 'Delete'.

To make an account the default account for sending e-mail, select the desired account then press 'Default'. To disable fetching e-mail from an account, select the account then click 'Disable'. A disabled account can still be used as the address for sending, but that account is not checked for incoming e-mail. If necessary, reactivate the account with 'Enable'.

17.4.2 Mail Preferences

Use 'Mail Preferences' to select or disable the quote highlight color or how long after opening a message is marked as read. Also make settings regarding how images in HTML mail messages are handled.

17.4.3 Creating Messages

To compose a new message, click 'New' -> 'Mail Message'. Replying to or forwarding a message opens the same message editor. Next to 'From', select from which account to send the message. In the recipient fields, enter an e-mail address or part of a name or address in your address book. If Evolution can match what you enter to something in the address book, a selection list is displayed. Click the desired contact or complete your input if none match. To select directly from the address book, click 'To' or 'CC'.

Evolution can send e-mail as plain text or HTML. To format HTML mail, select 'Format' in the toolbar. To send attachments, select 'Attach' or 'Insert' -> 'Attachment...'.

To send your message, click 'Send'. If not ready to send it immediately, make another selection under 'File'. For example, save the message as a draft or send it later.

17.4.4 Encrypted E-Mail and Signatures

Evolution supports e-mail encryption with PGP. It can sign e-mail and check signed e-mail messages. To use these features, generate and manage keys with an external application, such as gpg or KGpg.

To sign an e-mail message before sending it, select 'Security' -> 'PGP sign'. When you click 'Send', a dialog prompts for the password of your secret key. Enter the password and exit the dialog with 'OK' to send the signed e-mail. To sign other e-mail messages in the course of this session without needing to "unlock" the secret key repeatedly, activate 'Remember this password for the remainder of this session'.

When you receive signed e-mail from other users, a small padlock icon appears at the end of the message. If you click this symbol, Evolution starts an external program (gpg) to check the signature. If the signature is valid, a green check mark appears next to the padlock symbol. If the signature is invalid, a broken padlock appears.

The encryption and decryption of e-mail is just as easy. After composing the e-mail message, go to 'Security' -> 'PGP encrypt' and send the e-mail message. When you receive encrypted messages, a dialog opens to ask for the password of your secret key. Enter the passphrase to decrypt the e-mail message.

17.4.5 Folders

It is often convenient to sort e-mail messages into a variety of folders. To view your folder tree, select 'View' -> 'Folder Bar'. If accessing mail over IMAP, the IMAP folders are also shown in this folder bar. For POP and most other formats, your folders are stored locally, sorted under 'Local Folders'. Your 'Contacts', 'Calendar', and 'Tasks' are also treated as folders in this view, but should not be used for storing e-mail.

Several folders are included by default. 'Inbox' is where new messages fetched from a server are initially placed. 'Sent' is used for saving copies of sent e-mail messages. 'Outbox' is temporary storage for e-mail that has not yet been sent. It is useful if working offline or if the outgoing mail server is temporarily unreachable. 'Drafts' is used for saving unfinished e-mail messages. The 'Trash' folder is intended for temporary storage of deleted items. The folder can be emptied automatically by activating the respective option under 'Tools' -> 'Settings' -> 'Mail Preferences'.

New folders can be created under 'Local Folders' or as subfolders of existing folders. Create as complex a folder hierarchy as desired. To create a new folder while in the 'Inbox' view, select 'File' -> 'Folder' -> 'New Folder'. In the following dialog, enter a name for the new folder. Leave the 'Folder Type' as 'Mail' for a new mail storage folder. Use the mouse to determine the parent folder under which to place the new folder. Exit the dialog with 'OK'.

To move a message into a folder, select the message to move. Right-click to open the context menu. Select 'Move to Folder...' and, in the dialog that opens, the destination folder. Click 'OK' to move the message. The message header in the original folder is shown with a line through it, meaning it is marked for deletion in that folder. The message is stored in the new folder. Messages can be copied in a similar manner.

Manually moving a number of messages into different folders can be time-consuming. Filters can be used to automate this procedure.

17.4.6 Filters

Evolution offers a number of options for filtering e-mail. Filters can be used to move a message into a specific folder or to delete a message. Messages can also be moved directly to the trash with a filter. There are two options for creating a new filter: creating a filter from scratch or creating a filter based on a message to filter. The latter is extremely useful for filtering messages sent to a mailing list.

Setting up a Filter

Select 'Tools' -> 'Filters'. This dialog lists your existing filters, which can be edited or deleted. Click 'Add' to create a new filter.

Enter a name for the new filter in 'Rule Name'. Select the criteria to use for the filter. Options include sender, recipients, source account, subject, date, and status. The drop-box showing 'Contains' provides a variety of options, such as contains, is, and is not. Select the appropriate condition. Enter the text for which to search. Click 'Add criterion' to add more filter criteria. Use 'Execute actions' to determine if all or only some of the criteria must be met to apply the filter.

In the lower part of the window, determine the action to take when the filter criteria are met. Messages can, for example, be moved or copied to a folder or assigned a special color. When moving or copying, select the destination folder by clicking. In the folder list that appears, select the folder. Use 'New' to create a new folder. Click 'OK' when the correct folder is selected. When finished creating the filter, click 'OK'.

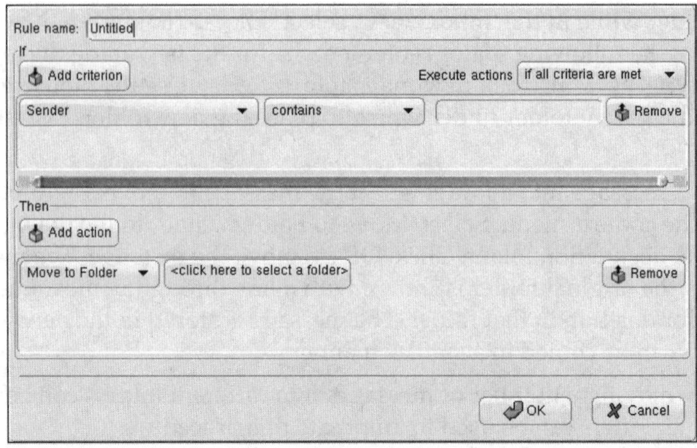

Figure 17.2: Setting up a Filter

Creating a Filter from a Message

Select the message on which to base the filter. Right-click and select 'Create Rule From Message'. Select the desired filter option. This opens the filter creation dialog with the correct criteria already selected. Add additional criteria if desired. Select the appropriate filter action. Click 'OK' when finished.

Applying Filters

Filters are applied in the order listed in the dialog accessed with 'Tools' -> 'Filters'. Change the order by highlighting a filter and clicking 'Up' or 'Down'. Click 'OK' to close the filter dialog when finished.

Filters are applied to all new mail messages. They are not applied to mail already in your folders. To apply filters to messages already received, select the desired messages then select 'Actions' -> 'Apply Filters'.

17.4.7 Virtual Folders

VFolders are a unique feature of Evolution. A VFolder is a virtual folder that displays messages based on search or filter criteria. Rather than moving the messages into a folder, messages shown in a virtual folder remain in their original folder. Actions are applied to the message in the original folder.

VFolders are a useful means of reading new mail in one place after it has been sorted into a number of different folders with filters. For example, a VFolder could be created to search all your folders for unread e-mail.

To create a new virtual folder, select 'Tools' -> 'Virtual Folder Editor...'. In the dialog, click 'Add'. Like filters, virtual folders can also be created from e-mail messages. Right-click the e-mail message, select 'Create Rule from Message', and define the desired criteria.

Enter a 'Rule Name'. For the new mail example mentioned above, set the criterion to 'Status' 'is not' 'Read'. Set the sources as desired. Other VFolder searches can be set similarly. Click 'OK' when finished. This returns to the virtual folder list. The order can be changed if desired. Click 'OK' to close it.

The new VFolder is in the folder list under 'VFolders'. You can read, answer, and delete e-mail with the VFolder. However, deleting the message deletes it from the real folder in which it is stored, not just the VFolder.

17.5 Calendar

17.5.1 Adding Appointments

To add a new appointment to your calendar, click 'New Appointment'. Under the 'Appointment' tab, enter the details for the appointment. Select a category, if desired, to ease searching and sorting later. Optionally set for Evolution to provide a reminder before your appointment under the 'Reminder' tab. If the appointment occurs regularly, set that under 'Recurrence'. Click 'Save and Close' after all settings are made. The new appointment is then shown in your calendar.

17.5.2 Scheduling a Meeting

To schedule a meeting with other people, click 'New Appointment' then select 'Actions' -> 'Schedule Meeting'. Enter information as for an appointment. Under 'Meeting', add attendees. For those in your 'Contacts', click 'Invite Others...' and select attendees from the dialog. When finished, click 'Save and Close'. The attendees will be sent an e-mail about the scheduled meeting.

This system can also be used to schedule a time that fits all attendees or to reserve resources. For more information about the scheduling functions, refer to the internal help.

17.5.3 Adding Tasks

Evolution helps to keep track of your tasks. To add a new task to your list, click 'New Task'. Enter summary information, due and start dates, and a description. Enter task status and other information under 'Details'. Click 'Save and Close' to add the task to your list. Double-click the task to reopen the dialog and make changes or mark it as completed.

17.6 Contacts

17.6.1 Adding Contacts

Along with the name and e-mail address, Evolution can store other address and contact information about a person. The e-mail address of a sender can quickly be added by right-clicking the marked address in the message preview. Select 'Add to Contacts' and confirm the inclusion in the following pop-up. To enter more information, click 'Edit Full' to open the contact editor. Otherwise, click 'OK'. If you have selected 'Edit Full', click 'Save and Close' to exit the contact editor when you are finished.

To enter a completely new contact, click 'New Contact' in the 'Contacts' view. Enter all desired contact information. Click 'Save and Close' when finished.

17.6.2 Making a List

If you frequently send e-mail messages to a group of people, make this easier by creating a list. Click 'New' -> 'Contact List' in the 'Contacts' view. The contact list editor opens. Enter a name for the list. Add addresses by typing the address in the box and clicking 'Add' or by dragging contacts from the 'Contacts' view and dropping them in the box. Toggle 'Hide addresses' to select whether the recipients can see who else has received the mail. Click 'Save and Close' when finished. The list is now one of your contacts and appears in the composition window after the first few letters are typed.

17.6.3 Sharing Contacts

To send contact information from your address book to another Evolution user, right-click the contact to share. Select 'Forward Contact'. This sends the contact card as an attachment in an e-mail. Compose and send this message as usual. To add a contact you have been sent, go to the contact in the e-mail message and click 'Save in addressbook' to add the complete contact card to your address book.

17.7 Public Address Books in Evolution

By means of the LDAP protocol, Evolution can access public address books, such as those used by SUSE LINUX Openexchange Server or Microsoft Exchange. Evolution offers full access to these address books — it can read them and add new entries. If you use SUSE LINUX in a large network (e.g., in your company), do not hesitate to make use of this possibility.

Note

Some specific information about your network is required for configuring LDAP access. Obtain this information from the responsible system administrator.

Note

To configure access to an LDAP server from your workstation, select 'Tools' -> 'Settings' -> 'Directory Servers'. All previously configured LDAP accesses are listed in the overview. Click 'Add' to add a new LDAP access. A configuration assistant starts, helping configure the LDAP access in a few steps. Exit the welcome screen of the assistant with 'Next' and specify the following settings in the dialogs:

Server Information Enter the server name and the login method for the LDAP server. The default method is anonymous access.

Connecting to the Server Enter the port number and the security protocols (SSL or TLS) to use.

Searching the Directory Enter the search base, the search range, the search duration, and, possibly, a limitation of the displayed hits.

Display Name In this last step, enter the name under which the selected server should appear in the list. Close the assistant with 'Next' and 'Finish'.

Upon completion of the configuration, the new LDAP server appears in your contact list under 'Other Contacts' and can be browsed for any entries.

17.8 For More Information

Evolution offers extensive internal help pages. Use the 'Help' menu to access this information. For more information about Evolution, refer to Ximian's web site at `http://www.ximian.com`.

ISDN Telecommunication

Even in this age of the Internet and e-mail, traditional communication means like phone and fax are still important. The communication package CapiSuite offers an ISDN-based solution for a computer-supported answering machine and fax.

The following chapter explains how CapiSuite works. This is followed by a description of its configuration with YaST and a brief introduction to the usage of the system.

CapiSuite is a daemon (a program that runs in the background) that provides basic telecommunication functions. The current version mainly offers functions for telephone and fax connections.

For example, the system supports the establishment and termination of incoming and outgoing fax and voice connections. Fax and audio files can then be sent and received over these connections. Some special functions, like the switching of a phone connection to a fax connection and the processing of DTMF (Dual Tone Multi Frequency — common touchtone phone tones), are supported.

However, the system does not constitute a complete application suite for certain tasks, such as an answering machine application. The actual application was written in the Python scripting language (a language especially suitable for beginners) and can thus be freely adjusted to the your requirements. CapiSuite merely processes the provided scripts and executes the specified commands. This allows the creation of flexible solutions from a simple answering machine or fax program to a small call center (for which the system is still lacking some basic features).

The CapiSuite package includes some ready-made scripts that enable a comfortable multiuser answering machine and fax solution. The following pages refer to the use of these scripts. Following the installation, details on the system as well as instructions for writing custom scripts are available in `/usr/share/doc/packages/capisuite/manual/index.html` and on the project page `http://www.capisuite.de`.

18.1 Configuration

CapiSuite makes use of the CAPI programming interface for ISDN hardware. Because this interface has only been available for Linux for a short time, suitable drivers are not yet available for all ISDN adapters. However, drivers are already available for ISDN adapters from AVM and can easily be installed and configured with YaST. Refer to the chapter on the ISDN configuration and the help texts of the

YaST module for more information.

Test the functionality of the CAPI driver by executing the command `capiinfo` as the user `root`. If detailed information about the capabilities of the ISDN adapter is returned, the driver is installed correctly and CapiSuite can be installed and used.

The CapiSuite package must be installed with YaST to be able to configure CapiSuite. More information about installing software is provided in the relevant section of the YaST chapter.

Caution

CAPISuite might not be included in the Personal Edition. This package is, in any case, available for download on the SUSE Internet servers. If needed, installation instructions are published on the web site of the CAPISuite project at `http://www.capisuite.de`.

Caution

Following the installation, YaST contains two modules for configuring the fax and answering machine functionality. These modules are described below.

18.1.1 Configuring Fax Services

The YaST module 'Fax' from the 'Network Devices' group contains a form with a user list and buttons for the processing of list entries. The list contains all the users already configured for the fax system. The CapiSuite scripts used here are multiuser and allow each user to send and receive faxes individually. The target number of an incoming call determines which user receives the fax. The list of this module is empty when it is started for the first time.

If various users want to receive faxes with CapiSuite, it must be ensured that the associated phone numbers are all different and that all these numbers are also associated with the line to which the ISDN adapter is connected. This is of importance if you concurrently use an ISDN PBX.

Note

Use only the answering machine module if you intend to receive both fax messages and regular calls under one number, as this module includes the functionality for recognizing and receiving fax messages. See Section 18.1.2 on page 289. To be able to send fax messages, configure a suitable entry in the fax module, but leave the field for incoming phone numbers empty.

Note

Use the buttons under the list to edit or delete existing entries or create new entries. When editing or creating, a dialog opens in which to enter or modify the following data:

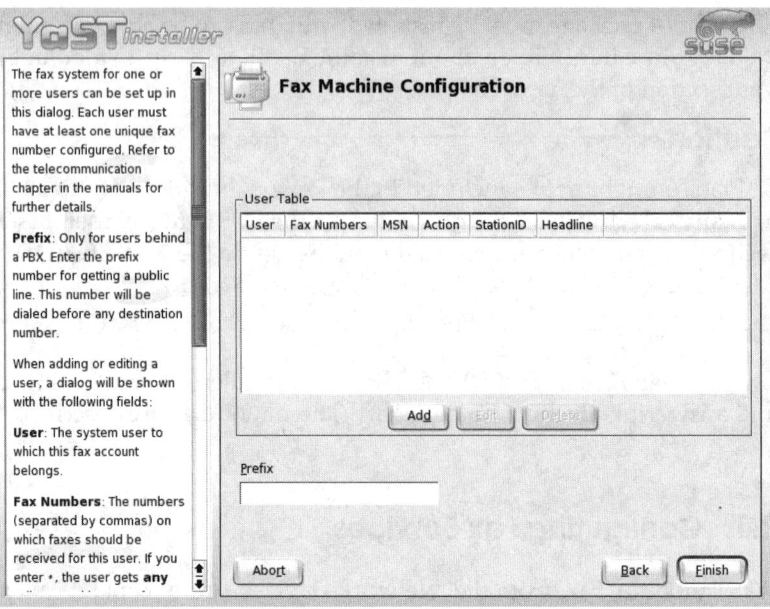

Figure 18.1: YaST Module for the Configuration of the Fax Function

'User' Here, select the user for whom to activate the fax functionality. Incoming fax messages and status reports will be sent to this user account.

'Fax Numbers' Phone numbers assigned to the user for incoming fax messages are entered in this field. Separate multiple phone numbers with commas. All faxes sent to these numbers will be forwarded to the user by e-mail. Leave this field empty if you only want the user to be able to send fax messages.

'StationID' For identification purposes, the fax protocol uses a special ID that should normally contain the external phone number of the fax device in international notation. An example for a valid station ID is `+49 89 123456` for the fax number 123456 in Munich, Germany. The maximum length of this entry is twenty digits. Valid characters are numbers, spaces, and the + symbol as prefix to the international country code.

'Header' This field can contain an arbitrary text to use as a header for sent

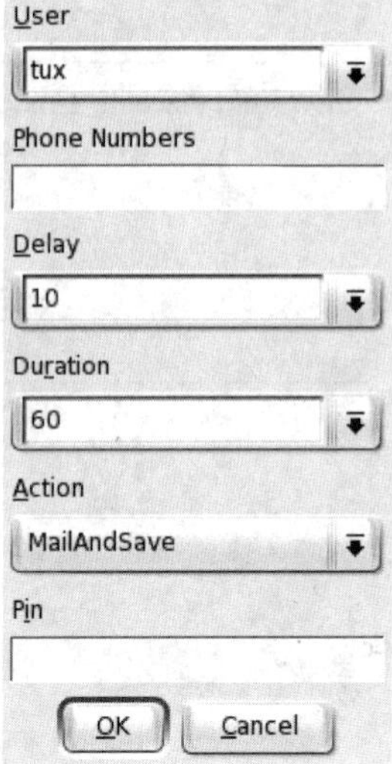

Figure 18.2: *Fax Functionality: User Preferences*

faxes. Whether and how this text is featured on the sent document depends on the ISDN driver used.

'Action' The default setting `MailAndSave` causes a received fax message to be saved in the system and forwarded to the user by e-mail. The `SaveOnly` option merely causes the fax to be saved to the hard disk. This option is recommended for expert users only.

Click 'OK' to accept the changes. Click 'Cancel' to drop the changes and close the form.

18.1.2 Configuring the Answering Machine

The provided standard scripts also offer a comfortable multiuser answering machine. This can be be configured with the YaST 'Answering Machine' module in the 'Network Devices' group.

Similar to the fax configuration, there is a list with the already configured users (which is empty when the module is started for the first time). The recorded incoming call is sent to the user associated with the phone number. This shows the importance of assigning unique phone numbers to the

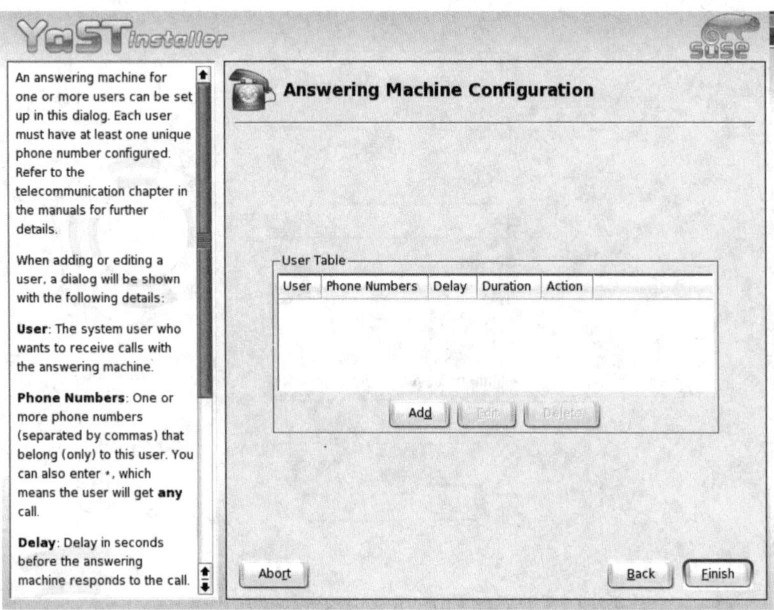

Figure 18.3: *YaST Module for Configuring the Answering Machine*

users. The individual user welcome message cannot be set at this point. The recording can be made later with the remote access function of the configured answering machine. The answering machine has an automatic silence recognition routine that terminates the recording session after five seconds without noises.

Note

Incoming fax calls are also automatically recognized and received in most cases. This automatic routine can, however, fail with older fax machines, which is why a separate fax number is to preferred wherever possible.

Note

Use 'Add', 'Edit', and 'Delete' to administer the entries. The entry form for creating a new entry or for modifying an existing one contains the following fields:

'User' Select the system user for whom the answering machine should be

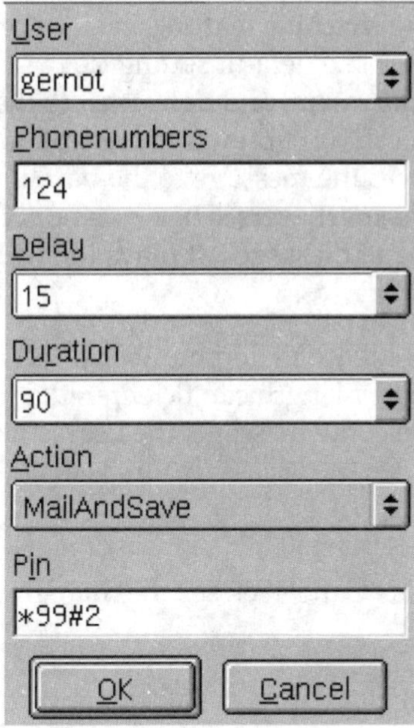

Figure 18.4: Answering Machine: User Preferences

configured. One or more fax numbers are assigned to each registered user. Incoming calls to these numbers are then sent to the user as e-mails.

'Phone Numbers' Set the phone numbers for which messages should be recorded for the user. Faxes can also be sent to the declared phone numbers as the answering machine has an automatic fax recognition feature. Separate multiple numbers with commas.

'Response Time' This value defined in seconds determines after how much time the answering machine should answer an incoming call. A value can be selected from the list or entered.

'Duration' Determines the maximum recording time for the answering machine — the maximum duration of a recorded incoming call in seconds. This value is usually of secondary importance, as the recording is usually terminated when the caller hangs up. However, to avoid extensive recordings, this value should be set to a reasonable time, such as two minutes (120 seconds).

'Action' The answering machine features various processing options for incoming messages. The default setting `MailAndSave` records a message, saves it in the system, and delivers it to the user by e-mail. The `SaveOnly` option can be chosen if the reception of e-mails is not desired. It merely saves the message to the hard disk. This option is only recommended for expert users. The `None` option completely deactivates the recording of messages. It plays the welcome message then hangs up.

'PIN' Enter a personal identification number (PIN) for remote access. A numerical code of any length can be entered. If it is entered during playback of the welcome message, the user is taken to the remote access menu. The remote access feature is disabled if the field is left empty.

'OK' accepts the changes. 'Cancel' closes the dialog without applying any changes.

18.2 Usage

The following section briefly describes the use of the system. Following a short introduction to the reception of messages with the Linux mail system, a description is provided for the operation of the fax functionality and the answering machine.

18.2.1 General Notes about Reception

The development of CapiSuite heavily relied on using already existing capabilities of Linux. This is why the delivery of incoming faxes and voice messages is handled by the internal Linux mail system instead of proprietary applications and protocols.

This requires the configuration of a mail client for receiving local messages for each user of CapiSuite. For details, read the chapter about the mail program or the documentation provided with the application.

Follow these steps to activate reception of local e-mail messages in KMail:

- Start KMail as usual.
- Select 'Settings' -> 'Configure KMail'.

- Click the network icon in the list to the left.
- Select the 'Receiving' tab.
- Reception is already configured if an entry with the type `local` is already present in the list. The dialog can be closed with 'Cancel' in that case. If not, click 'Add...'.
- Select 'Local mailbox' from the list and confirm with 'OK'.
- Name the new account (for example, "local inbox") by entering the name in the upper input field. All the other settings can be left at their default values.
- Then complete the configuration by clicking 'OK'.

If you have not disabled the sending of mail in the CapiSuite configuration, you will receive all incoming voice and fax messages in your e-mail program, where you can view them or listen to them as usual.

18.2.2 Fax Operation

No further instructions are necessary for receiving fax messages. As soon as a fax is received for a number assigned to a user, the message is stored in the system and delivered to the user as an e-mail with a PDF attachment (PDF is a common exchange format for documents and can be read in virtually all operating systems with Acrobat Reader from Adobe). The user can open, read, and print the document as in his mail program.

For backup purposes, every received document is also stored on the hard disk in `/var/spool/capisuite/users/<username>/received/`. This directory can be accessed if anything goes wrong during the e-mail transmission of if an e-mail message was accidentally deleted. More information can be found in the CapiSuite documentation in `/usr/share/doc/packages/capisuite/manual/index.html`.

The command line tool `capisuitefax` is available for sending faxes. It accepts one or more target fax numbers and one or more documents in the PostScript format. This format is generated by most Linux applications when printing to a file.

`capisuitefax` supports parameters such as the following:

`-h` **or** `-help` Returns a short summary of valid parameters.

`-d <number>` **or** `-dialstring=<number>`
This parameter declares the target number to which the fax should be sent.

`-q` **or** `-quiet` `capisuitefax` usually generates a few informative messages. This option suppresses this and only allows the display of possible error messages.

The following command would send the two documents `document1.ps` and `document2.ps` to the target number 089123456:

```
capisuitefax -d 089123456 document1.ps document2.ps
```

`capisuitefax` converts the documents to the correct format and stores them together with a description file in a special folder from which they are then fetched and sent by CapiSuite. There can be a short delay between the execution of the command and the actual sending. The user is notified by e-mail when a fax message has been successfully sent or after the failure of a set number of attempts.

In the standard desktop KDE, fax messages can easily be sent from any KDE application with the help of the KDEPrintFax utility. Configure KDEPrintFax as follows:

- Start KDEPrintFax. This can be done by pressing Alt + F2 and entering `kdeprintfax`.
- Select 'Settings' -> 'Configure KDEPrintFax'.
- Click the 'System' icon in the left pane.
- As `capisuitefax` is largely compatible with the HylaFAX suite, select HylaFAX under 'Fax system'.
- Set 'Command' to `/usr/bin/capisuitefax -d %number %files`.
- Finish the configuration by clicking 'OK' and closing KDEPrintFax.

'Send to Fax' is then available in the 'Print' menu of any KDE application. Selecting it starts KDEPrintFax, which requests the target phone number and sends the fax.

Non-KDE applications can also use this function if their print command can be set manually. In this case, replace `lpr` with `kprinter`. When you print a document, the KDE print menu will be displayed along with the possibility to transmit fax messages.

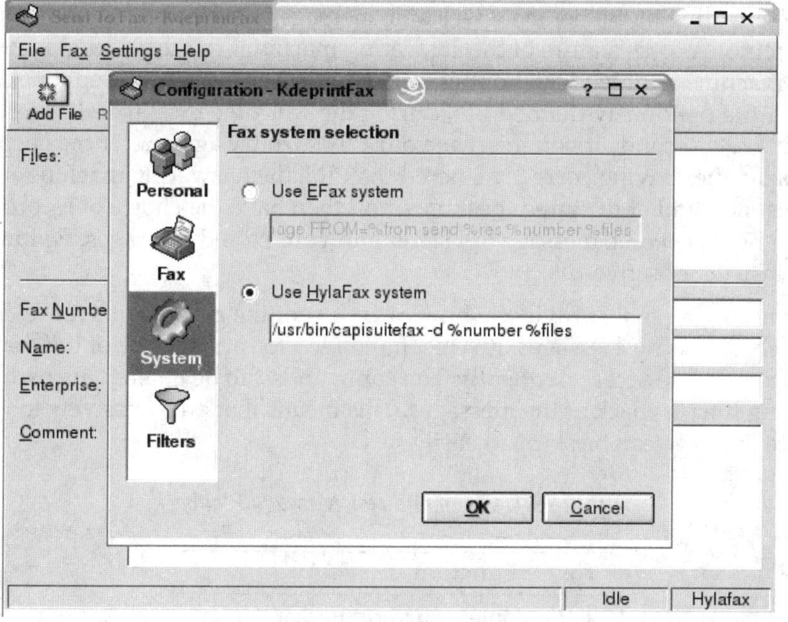

Figure 18.5: Configuring CapiSuite in KDEPrintFax

Caution

To date, `capisuitefax` does not support the full range of HylaFAX features. Thus, features such as the resolution settings are currently ignored.

Caution

18.2.3 Operation of the Answering Machine

If e-mail transmission was not deactivated, voice messages left on the answering machine are sent by e-mail to the recipient associated with the dialed phone number. Thus, the operation of the answering machine does not require any additional description. All incoming messages can be received and opened in the e-mail client. For backup purposes, the incoming messages are also stored in `/var/spool/capisuite/users/<username>/received/`.

The recording of the personal welcome message is performed directly over the remote access feature of the answering machine. To access your answering machine remotely, call your associated number from any telephone. Enter the previously-defined PIN during the welcome message playback. Wait a few seconds if you mistype your PIN then try again after the beep. Shortly after having correctly entered the PIN, the answering machine gives the number of stored messages. You then have the choice of recording a new welcome message or listening to your stored messages. Follow the instructions given.

The following table provides a brief overview of the menu items for remotely accessing messages. It is recommended to carry a copy of it if you use the remote access frequently. The commands can be entered at any time during the playback of the messages. This means that an excessively long voice message can be skipped easily.

Table 18.1: *Commands for Message Playback*

Key	Function
1	delete current message
4	skip to the next message
5	skip to the previous message
6	replay current message

Part V

Multimedia

Sound in Linux

Linux offers a wide range of sound applications in various stages of development. This chapter provides an overview of a wide range of applications for various multimedia tasks together with some technical background information. Applications that are not part of the standard installation can be installed with YaST.

19.1 The ALSA PCM Types

As of version 0.9 of the Advanced Linux Sound Architecture (ALSA), the concept for PCM devices was fundamentally modified and expanded. PCM is an acronym for "Pulse Code Modulation" and designates the digital output interfaces when relating to sound cards. The user can influence the way ALSA addresses the sound card by selecting a specific PCM type. The main PCM types are `hw` and `plughw`.

To understand the difference between the two types, consider how a PCM device is opened. It must be opened with specific settings for at least the following parameters: sample format, sample frequency, number of channels, number of periods (previously referred to as fragments), and size of a period. For example, an application may attempt to play a WAV file with a sample frequency of 44.1 kHz although the sound card does not support this frequency. In this case, ALSA can automatically convert the data in the plug-in layer to a format supported by the sound card. The conversion affects the following parameters: sample format, sample frequency, and number of channels.

Activate the plug-in layer by selecting the PCM type `plughw`. If the PCM type `hw` is selected, ALSA tries to open the PCM devices directly with the parameters required by the application. The complete designator for a PCM device consists of the PCM type followed by a colon, the card number, and the device number, for example, `plughw:0,0`.

The `dmix` output plug-in is a recent addition to the PCM types. It allows applications to share access to a PCM device on sound cards that do not support this natively. The complete identifier in this case is `plug:dmix`. More information about `dmix` can be found at `http://alsa.opensrc.org/index.php?page=DmixPlugin`.

19.2 Mixers

Mixers provide a convenient means of controlling the volume and balance of the sound output and input of computers. The main difference between the various mixers consists in the outer appearance of the user interface. Select one that best suits your needs.

> **Note**
>
> Generally, it is advisable to open a mixer application prior to opening other sound applications. Use the mixer to test and adjust the control settings for the input and output of the sound card. Some sound cards may not allow simultaneous access from multiple applications. If a sound application freezes, this might be the cause.
>
> **Note**

19.2.1 gamix

If you have multiple sound cards, gamix provides a set of controllers for each card. Slide the control sliders to set the levels as desired.

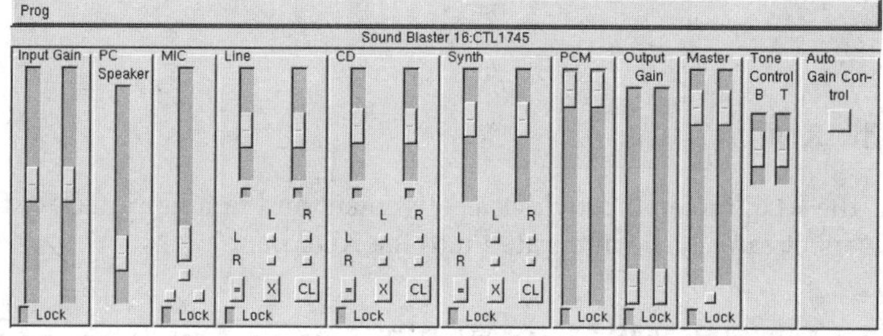

Figure 19.1: The Mixer gamix

19.2.2 qamix

QAMix is a mixer with a QT interface. If necessary, the application interface can be configured in a flexible way in an XML file. All parameters can be controlled via MIDI. On start-up, the application first searches the directory `~/.qamix` for an XML file corresponding to the name of the ALSA driver of your sound card. If such a file does not exist, it searches the same directory for the file `default.xml`. If this file does not exist either, the program continues its search in the directory `/usr/share/qamix`.

If you have several sound cards, select the desired card with the parameter `-c`. `hw:0` stands for the first sound card, `hw:1` for the second, and so on.

The parameter `-g` can be used to specify a file for the XML description of the application interface explicitly. Detailed information about the XML format is available in the directory `/usr/share/doc/packages/qamix`.

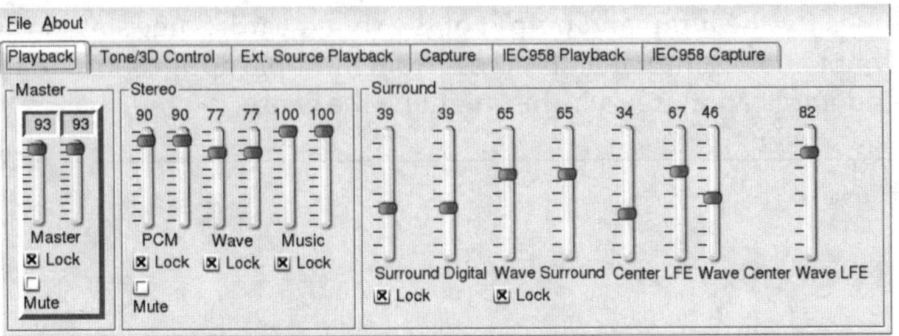

Figure 19.2: The Mixer QAmix

19.2.3 KMix

KMix is the KDE mixer. It provides a convenient and familiar interface for KDE users. It can also be integrated into the KDE panel.

19.2.4 The GNOME Mixer Applet

If you use GNOME, the GNOME Mixer appler can added to the panel for convenient volume control. Simply right-click the panel then select 'Add to Panel' -> 'Multimedia' -> 'Volume Control'. Right-click the volume control applet then select 'Run Volume Control' to access the more advanced mixer functions.

19.2.5 alsamixer

alsamixer can be run from the command line without the X environment. The application is operated with the cursor keys. Use Q, W, E, Y, X, and C to set different levels for the left and right channels. M mutes single channels. In this case, 'MM' appears above the muted controller. To terminate alsamixer, press Esc.

The basic controls for sound output are 'Master', 'PCM', and 'CD'. 'Master' sets the master volume. 'PCM' and 'CD' control the respective weighting of the PCM and audio CD channels.

Determine the recording source by pressing Space. The 'capture' controller regulates the input amplifier. Whether the 'Line' controller or the 'MIC' controller is used depends on the recording source.

For more information, enter `man alsamixer`. alsamixergui is a mouse-operated variant of alsamixer with a graphical interface.

Note

The look and feel of alsamixer depends on the type of sound card used. The description referred to the AC97 standard for mixer functionality. If your sound card does not comply with this standard, some features may not be supported. The mixer Envy24 should be used for sound cards equipped with the Envy24 (ice1712) chip (see Section 19.2.7).

Note

19.2.6 Mixer Parameters of Soundblaster Live! and Audigy

Apart from the parameters of the 'AC97' standard, there are many additional options for Soundblaster Live! and Audigy cards. The controls 'AC97', 'Wave', and 'Music' are used for playback. 'AC97' can be used to adjust the level of the 'AC97' mix. This mix also receives input from the 'line', 'mic', and 'CD' signals. 'Wave' adjusts the level of the PCM channels. 'Music' controls the volume of the internal wavetable synthesis of MIDI data.

Apart from the 'Capture' parameter for recordings, the 'AC97 Capture' control is used to control the level of the 'AC97' recording sources. Furthermore, 'Wave' and 'Music' can be selected as recording source. This internal loopback capture can be activatedin the 'AC97' standard by selecting the 'Mix' control as recording source.

19.2.7 The Mixer for the Sound Chip Envy24

envy24control is a mixer application for sound cards using the Envy24 (ice1712) chip. Start this mixer with 'SUSE' -> 'Multimedia' -> 'Sound' or from the command line with `envy24control &`. The flexibility of the Envy24 chip can result in varying functionalities in different sound cards. The latest details on this sound chip are available in `/usr/share/doc/packages/alsa/alsa-tools/envy24control`.

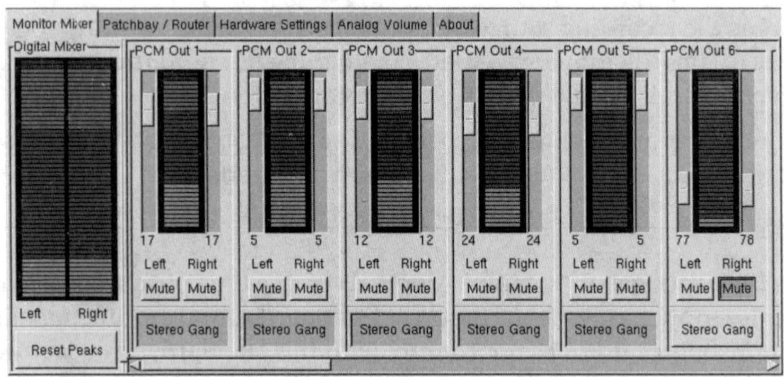

Figure 19.3: *Monitor and Digital Mixer of envy24control*

Monitor and Patchbay of envy24control

The 'Monitor Mixer' of envy24control shows the signal levels that can be mixed digitally in the sound card. The signals designated as 'PCM Out' are generated by applications that send PCM data to the sound card. The signals of the analog inputs are shown under 'H/W In'. The 'S/PDIF' inputs are shown to the right. The input and output levels of the analog channels must be set under 'Analog Volume'.

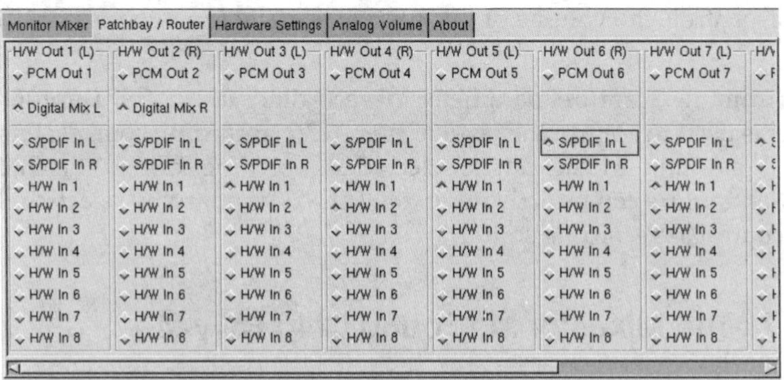

Figure 19.4: *The Patchbay*

Use the 'Monitor Mixer' sliders for digital mixing. The respective levels are displayed in the 'Digital Mixer'. For each output channel, the 'Patchbay' contains a row of radio buttons for selecting the desired channel source.

Analog Inputs and Outputs

Adjust the amplification for the analog-to-digital and digital-to-analog converters under 'Analog Volume'. The 'DAC' sliders are used for the output channels and the 'ADC' sliders are used for the input channels. Use the radio buttons to switch the levels between +4 dBu and -10 dBV. The first setting is intended for audio professionals. The latter is for private purposes.

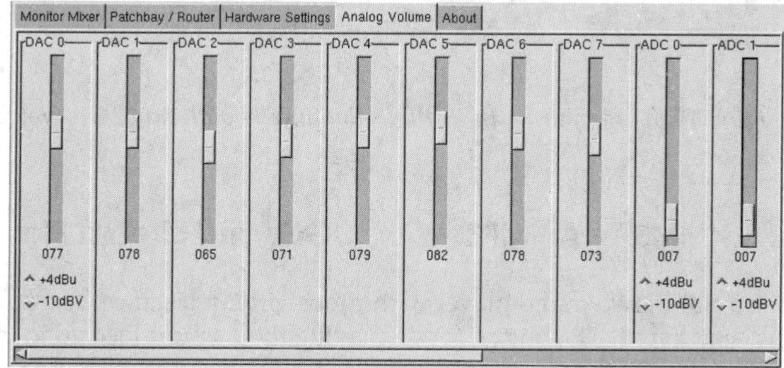

Figure 19.5: Mixer for Analog Inputs and Outputs

Configuration of the S/PDIF Channels

The S/PDIF channel settings are made under 'Hardware Settings'. The Envy24 chip reacts to volume changes with a delay that can be configured with 'Volume Change'.

19.3 Players

Linux offers a variety of programs for playing audio CDs and various music formats such as MP3, OGG, and WAV files. Where possible, the supported formats of the players are listed.

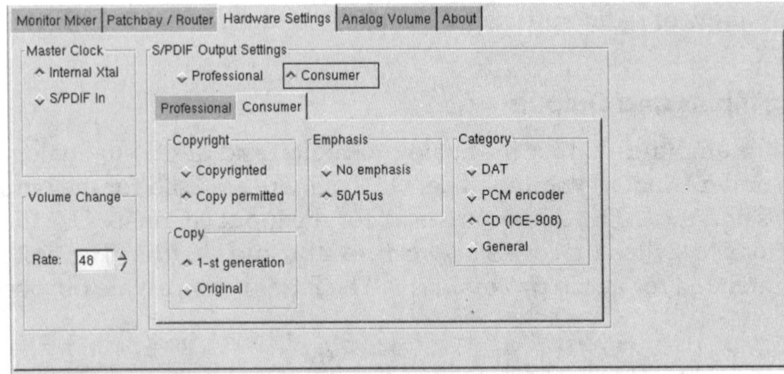

Figure 19.6: *Configuring the S/PDIF Parameters with envy24control*

19.3.1 XMMS — An MP3, WAV, OGG, and Stream Player

XMMS is a full-blown audio player with robust jitter resistance. The application is easy to use. The button for displaying the menu is located in the upper left corner of the program window.

Select the output plug-in module with 'Options' -> 'Preferences' -> 'Audio I/O Plugins'. If the `xmms-kde` package is installed, the aRts sound server can be configured here.

Note

XMMS automatically redirects its output to the 'Disk Writer Plugin' if it is not able to find a configured sound card. In this case, the played files are written to the hard disk as WAV files. The time display then runs faster than when playing the output through a sound card.

Note

Various visualization plug-ins can be started through 'Options' -> 'Preferences' -> 'Visualization Plugins'. If you have a graphics card with 3D acceleration, select an application such as the OpenGL spectrum analyzer. If the `xmms-plugins` package is installed, try the Infinity plug-in.

To the left under the menu button, there are five buttons with different letters on them. These buttons allow quick access to additional menus, dialog boxes, and configurations. The playlist can be opened with the 'PL' button and the equalizer can be activated with the 'EQ' button.

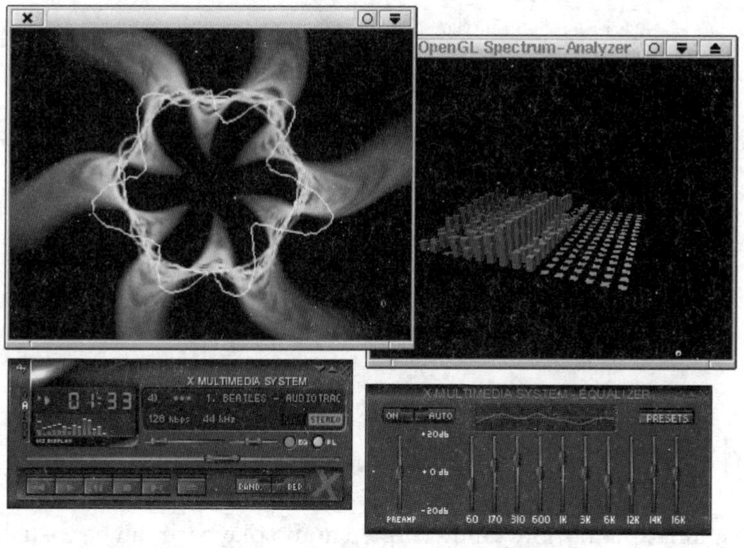

Figure 19.7: *XMMS with Equalizer, OpenGL Spectrum Analyzer, and Infinity Plug-Ins*

19.3.2 kscd — Audio CD Player

kscd is an easy-to-use audio CD player. It can be accessed from the 'SUSE' menu under 'Multimedia' -> 'CD' -> 'KsCD'. To access the configuration menu, click the tool icon. kscd can be configured to search an online CDDB server for the name and track names of a CD.

19.3.3 The Audio CD Player WorkMan

WorkMan offers a simple user interface with an abundance of functions. It is ideal for those who prefer a CD player without the KDE look and feel.

19.3.4 GNOME CD Player Applet

This is a simple applet that can be added to a GNOME panel. Add it by right-clicking the panel and selecting 'Add to Panel' -> 'Multimedia' -> 'CD Player'.

Figure 19.8: The kscd User Interface

19.4 Buffering and Latencies

This section explains how uninterrupted audio playback can be ensured. This problem is by no means limited to Linux, but is inherent in all multitasking operating systems. In a multitasking operating system, several processes usually run concurrently. As the processor can only handle one process at a time, each process is assigned a certain amount of time by the operating system's scheduler. The switching action between processes normally happens so quickly that the user does not notice it.

However, during audio playback, even brief interruptions are noticeable in the form of clicks. Therefore, audio programs use a buffer for the playback, enabling the audio data in the buffer to be emitted continuously by the sound card even when the audio program is interrupted by the scheduler. Accordingly, the playback is click-free if the buffer is large enough to bridge the longest possible interruption.

However, the buffer size also determines the reaction time (latency) of the program. Therefore, the buffer size is kept as small as possible especially for interactive applications, such as real-time synthesizers and DJ mixer consoles. Basically, the length of the interruptions depends on the system load and the priority of the process. Consequently, the size of the buffer required for click-free playback can be reduced by increasing the priority of the audio program or by switching to a real-time scheduler. For this reason, many audio programs attempt to switch their processes to a real-time scheduler, but switching a process to another scheduler is only possible with `root` privileges. The application setpriority in the `rtstools` package is required for this task.

For example, proceed as follows to run the application timidity with the

FIFO scheduler:

1. Start timidity
2. Open a `root` console session.
3. Use `pidof timidity` to find the process ID of timidity.
4. Change the scheduler with the command `setpriority <processID> fifo 10`.

You can use the following command in a `root` shell to speed up this procedure:

```
for i in 'pidof timidity'; do setpriority $i fifo 10; done
```

Running a program in `root` mode is always risky, as the program is permitted to do anything. If the computer is connected to the Internet, the security risk would be unacceptable. Security bugs in the program could be exploited for the purpose of gaining access to the system.

Caution

The commands described in the following paragraphs should *never* be executed on machines that can be accessed from the Internet or if a system crash or data loss would have serious consequences.

Caution

The `sudo` mechanism should be used for running a program in `root mode`. This mechanism is demonstrated by means of the timidity++ application. To enable all users on your system to execute timidity++ with `root` privileges, modify the file `/etc/sudoers`. See and for the procedure. If you are not familiar with vi, select a different editor, such as joe, by exporting the desired editor, for example, with the command `export EDITOR=joe`. Then execute `visudo` as `root` and append the following line at the end of the file `/etc/sudoers`:

```
ALL ALL=(ALL) /usr/bin/timidity
```

Now all system users are permitted to run timidity++ in `root` mode with the command `sudo timidity`. The password of the respective user is requested if more than five minutes passed since the last `sudo` command.

19.5 The JACK Audio Connection Kit

Using the JACK Audio Connection Kit (packages named `jack` and `qjackconnect`), applications can exchange audio data with each other and with the sound card. This is only possible if the respective application has a JACK interface. JACK support has become a standard feature, so there are many applications that have the needed interface.

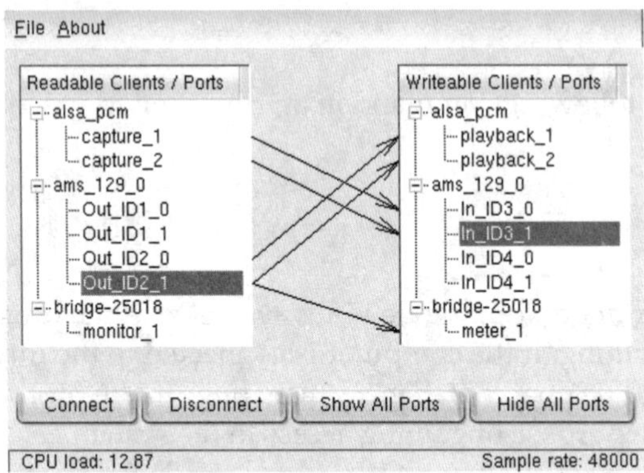

Figure 19.9: *QJackConnect — a Patchbay for Jack*

To use JACK, first start the engine with `jackd -d alsa -d hw:0`. JACK was designed to achieve a low latency. Therefore, the engine should run with real-time priority. For more information, read the file `/usr/share/doc/packages/jack/README.SuSE`.

The patchbay QJackConnect assists in tracking the JACK clients running in your system. Following the program launch with `qjackconnect`, the clients with readable ports are listed on the left side and the clients with writable ports are listed on the right side. If no JACK clients were started, the lists initially only display the inputs and outputs of the sound card. The lists are updated automatically as the port configuration changes. The ports are displayed in a tree view under the client. Connect individual ports by selecting them from the lists and clicking 'Connect'. Connect multiple ports simultaneously by selecting clients.

19.6 Hard Disk Recording with Audacity

With audacity (package `audacity`), record and edit audio files. This is called hard disk recording. When you start the program for the first time, select a language. At other times, change the language setting under 'File' -> 'Preferences' -> 'Interface'. The language change is then effective the next time you start the program.

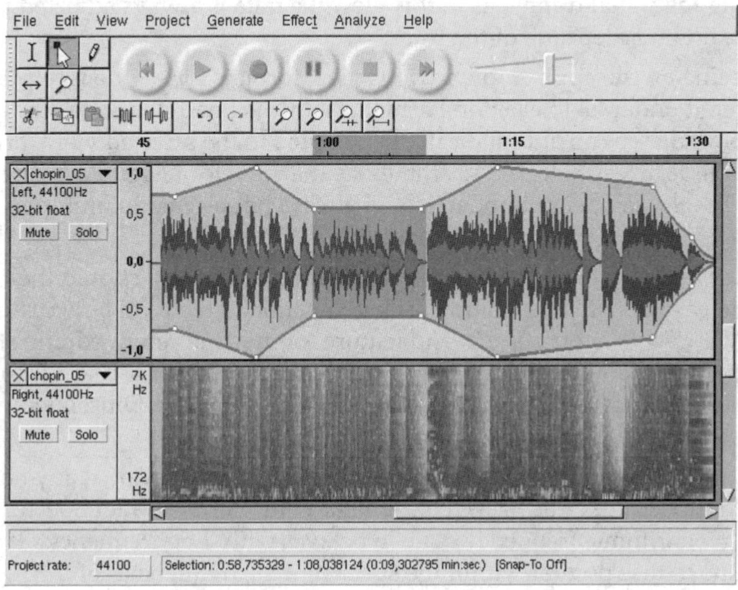

Figure 19.10: Spectral View of the Audio Data

19.6.1 Recording WAV Files and Importing Files

Click the red recording button to generate an empty stereo track and start the recording. To change the standard parameters, specify the settings under 'File' -> 'Preferences'. 'Audio I/O' and 'Quality' are important for the recording. Even if tracks already exist, pressing the recording button creates new tracks. Initially, this may be confusing, as these tracks cannot be seen in the standard-size program window.

To import audio files, select 'Project' -> 'Import Audio'. The program supports the WAV format as well as the compressed MP3 and Ogg Vorbis formats. See Section 19.8 on page 314 for more information about these formats.

19.6.2 Editing Audio Files

The 'AudioTrack' menu can be opened to the left of each track and offers various views. One of them is 'Waveform dB', which is not suitable for checking the signal tuning, as in this view the data is always adjusted to the maximum amplitude of the track.

Depending on the application, various view formats for segment selections are offered under 'Set Selection Format'. With 'Set Snap-To Mode', the segment boundaries can automatically be adapted to the selected view format. For example, if you select 'PAL frames' as the view format and activate 'Snap-To', the segment boundaries will always be selected in multiples of frames.

The many editing tools are all equipped with tool tips and should therefore be quite easy to use. The 'Undo History' function, which can be accessed with 'View' -> 'History', is a useful feature for viewing recent editing steps and undoing them by clicking the respective item in the list. Use 'Discard' with caution, because it deletes editing steps from the list. Subsequently, these steps can no longer be undone.

The built-in spectrum analyzer assists in quickly tracking down any noises. View the spectrum of the selected segment with 'View' -> 'Plot Spectrum'. Select a logarithmic frequency scale in octaves with 'Log frequency'. If you move the mouse pointer within the spectrum, the frequencies of the peaks are automatically displayed together with the respective notes.

Unwanted frequencies are best removed with 'Effect' -> 'FFT Filter'. In connection with the filtering process, it may be necessary to readjust the signal amplitude with 'Amplify'. Additionally, 'Amplify' can be used to check the amplitude. By default, the 'New Peak Amplitude' is set to 0.0 dB. This value represents the highest possible amplitude in the selected audio format. 'Amplification' shows the value needed to amplify the selected segment to this peak amplitude. A negative value indicates overamplification.

19.6.3 Saving and Exporting

To save the entire project, select 'File' -> 'Save Project' or 'Save Project As'. This generates an XML file with the extension `.aup`, which describes

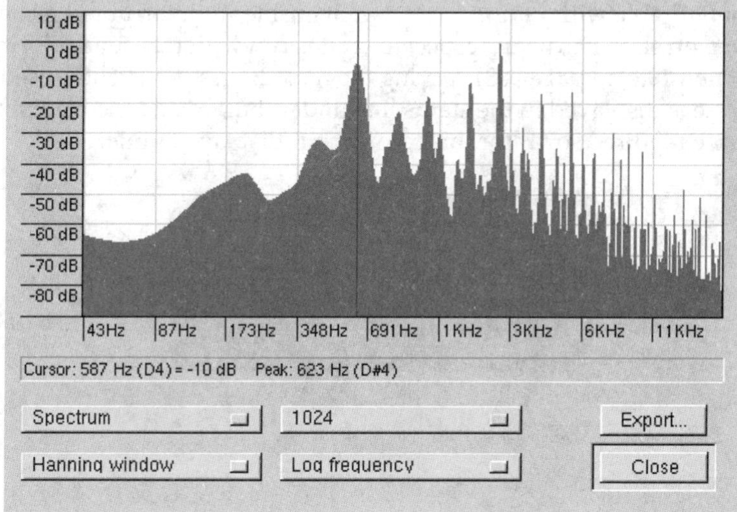

Figure 19.11: The Spectrum

the project. The actual audio data is saved in a directory named after the project with `_data` appended.

The entire project or the currently selected segment can also be exported as a stereo WAV file. To export the project in MP3 format, refer to the information in Section 19.8 on the next page.

19.7 Direct Recording and Playback of WAV Files

`arecord` and `aplay` from the `kalsatools` package provide a simple and flexible interface to the PCM devices. `arecord` and `aplay` can be used to record and play audio data in the WAV format among other formats. The command `arecord -d 10 -f cd -t wav mysong.wav` records a WAV file of ten seconds in CD quality (16 bit, 44.1 kHz). List all options of `arecord` and `aplay` by running them with the `--help` option.

qaRecord is a simple recording program with a graphical interface and level display. As this program makes use of an internal buffer of about 1

MB (configurable with `--buffersize`), it enables uninterrupted recordings even on slow hardware, especially if it is run with real-time priority (see Section 19.4 on page 308). During the recording, the currently-used buffer size is displayed in the status line under 'Buffer' and the maximum buffer size required so far for this recording is displayed under 'Peak'.

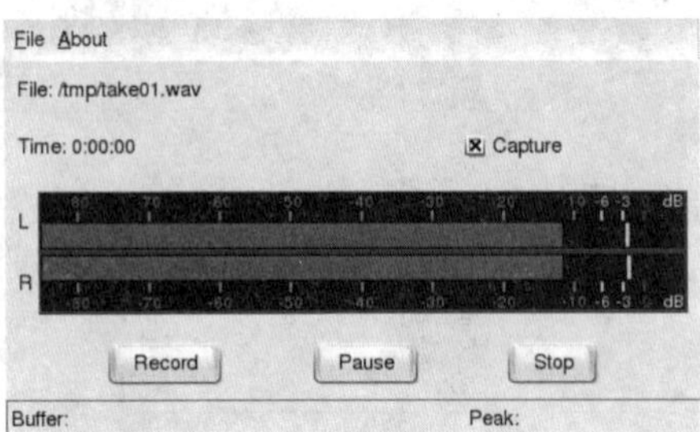

Figure 19.12: *QARecord — A Simple Hard Disk Recording Application*

19.8 Compressing Audio Data

Uncompressed audio data in CD quality consumes almost ten MB per minute. The MP3 procedure was developed by Fraunhofer IIS for the purpose of drastically compressing this data. Unfortunately, this procedure is patented. Therefore, companies that distribute MP3 encoders are required to pay license fees. The powerful MP3 encoder Lame was developed for Linux. Although the source code of Lame is under the GPL, SUSE is not allowed to include this encoder in our distribution. For more information about the legal situation, visit the project web page at `http://lame.sourceforge.net`. In some countries (including Germany and the USA), the use of Lame is permitted for research purposes only.

Ogg Vorbis (package name `vorbis-tools`) is a free audio compression format that is now supported by the majority of audio players. The web page of the project is `http://www.xiph.org/ogg/vorbis`. The vorbis-tools package includes an encoder and a simple player. The encoder is started from the command line with `oggenc`. The only parameter needed is the WAV file to compress. The option `-h` displays an overview of the other parameters. The latest version of the Ogg encoder even supports encoding with a variable bit rate. In this way, an even higher degree of compression can be achieved. Instead of the bit rate, specify the desired quality with the parameter -q. The parameter -b determines the average bit rate. -m and -M can be used to specify the minimum and maximum bit rate.

ogg123 is a command-line Ogg player. The program requires the specification of a playback device. Start it with a command like ogg123 -d alsa09 mysong.ogg.

19.9 ALSA and MIDI

Apart from the possibility to play PCM data, many sound cards also offer MIDI functionality. The ALSA MIDI sequencer implements an efficient architecture for routing MIDI data. You need the packages pmidi, aseqview, vkeybd, awesfx, snd_sf2, and kalsatools.

Many sound cards have an external MIDI port for connecting MIDI devices, such as synthesizers, keyboards, and sound modules. If the MIDI port of the card is supported by ALSA, use a sequencer application, such as jazz, to record and play MIDI files. An overview of the MIDI devices provided by your card is available in the KDE Control Center under 'Sound & Multimedia' -> 'Sound System' -> 'MIDI'. Here, also determine the devices to use for playing MIDI files. On the command line, list the available MIDI devices and their internal ALSA port numbers with the command pmidi -l. For a Soundblaster Live! card, the listing would appear as in Example 19.1.

***Example 19.1:** MIDI Devices of a Soundblaster Live! Card*

```
Port     Client name              Port name
72:0     External MIDI 0          MIDI 0-0
73:0     Emu10k1 WaveTable        Emu10k1 Port 0
73:1     Emu10k1 WaveTable        Emu10k1 Port 1
73:2     Emu10k1 WaveTable        Emu10k1 Port 2
73:3     Emu10k1 WaveTable        Emu10k1 Port 3
```

The first column lists the internal port numbers by which the device is addressed by the ALSA driver. The other columns show the designation and port name of the device. Apart from the external MIDI port, several WaveTable ports are listed. Use a command like pmidi -p 73:0 mysong.mid to play a MIDI file over one of the listed ports.

Note

If a MIDI player is interrupted during playback, a continuous sound may persist. If this happens, run the `all_notes_off` script or restart ALSA as `root` with `rcalsasound restart`.

Note

Many sound cards (like Soundblaster AWE and Live!) have an internal WaveTable synthesizer that converts MIDI events into audible sounds. These MIDI events can be sent to the WaveTable synthesizer by an external MIDI keyboard or by a program, such as a MIDI player or sequencer. For Soundblaster AWE and Live! cards, the WaveTable synthesizer must be initialized with a sound font before any sound can be heard.

19.9.1 Loading Sound Fonts: SB Live! and AWE

The package `awesfx` contains the `sfxload` command for loading sound fonts in Soundblaster AWE and Live! cards. Suitable sound font files are available on the driver CD of your sound card. The start-up script of ALSA can automatically load the sound fonts required for the WaveTable synthesis, provided the respective files were installed from the Creative driver CD using YaST. Currently, the script only works for one sound card. However, ALSA can easily manage up to eight sound cards.

Sound fonts can be loaded with a command like `sfxload -D <n> /usr/share/sfbank/creative/8MBGMSFX.SF2`. ⟨*n*⟩ stands for the number of the sound card (0, 1, etc.). This may not be the number under which the sound card was configured. This number is instead determined by the order in which the individual sound drivers are loaded.

You can also load one of the sound fonts installed in `/usr/share/sounds/sf2`. The sound font `Vintage_Dreams_Waves_v2.sf2` by IAN WILSON contains 128 analog synthesizer sounds and eight drum sets. It is suitable for SB AWE as well as for SB Live! cards. The ROM sound font `gu11-rom.sf2` by SAMUEL COLLINS is *only* suitable for SB AWE cards. It provides an extended general MIDI bank for these cards. Review the copyright files and the documentation in `/usr/share/doc/packages/snd_sf2`. More sound fonts are available at URLs such as `http://www.hammersound.net`.

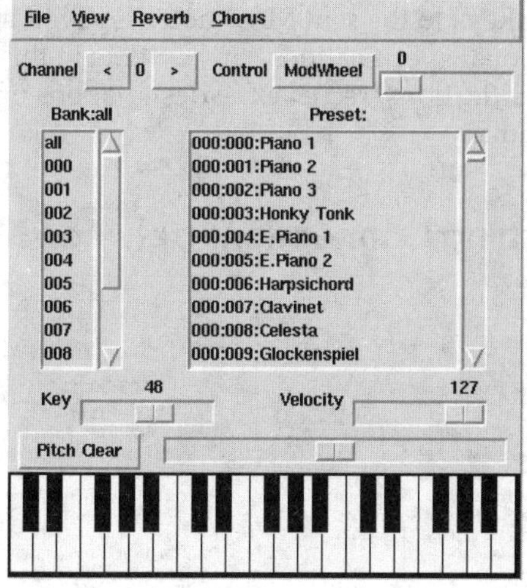

Figure 19.13: vkeybd — Virtual MIDI Keyboard

19.9.2 vkeybd — Virtual MIDI Keyboard

If you do not have an external MIDI keyboard connected to your sound card, use the virtual keyboard vkeybd. For this purpose, the internal port numbers listed with `pmidi -l` as described above are important. To start the program from the command line, enter `vkeybd --addr 73:0 &`. The port address must be adapted to your system. Specify the first WaveTable port from the list. If an external sound generator is connected, alternatively specify the port number of the external MIDI port.

vkeybd supports a number of additional options. For example, enter `vkeybd --addr 73:0 --octave 5 &` to increase the number of displayed octaves to five. An overview of the command line options can be accessed with `vkeybd --help` or in .

The instrument designation in the preset list can be configured by specifying a preset file with the `--preset` option. Extract the instrument names of a sound font file with the command `sftovkb`. Change to the respective directory with `cd /usr/share/sounds/sf2` and enter the command `sftovkb Vintage_Dreams_Waves_v2.sf2 > /vintage.vkb` to save the names in your home directory in `vintage.vkb`. The vkeybd interface can be configured with the 'view' menu.

The mapping of the keys to the sent MIDI notes is saved in the file ~/ .vkeybdrc. Additional specifications can be made in this file. To implement your own modifications, retrieve the designations of keyboard events with the xev program.

19.9.3 Establishing Connections between MIDI Ports

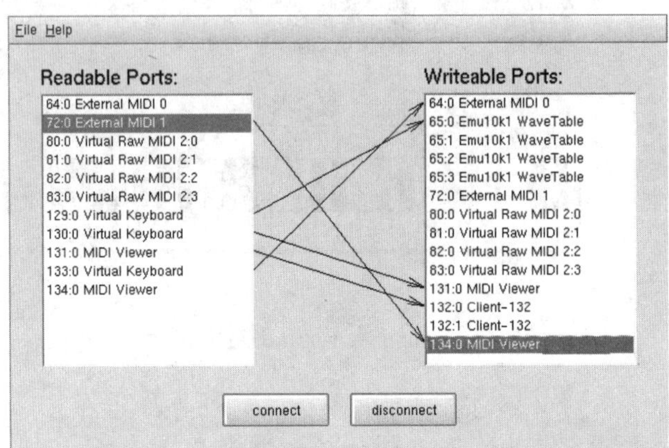

***Figure 19.14:** Connecting MIDI Ports and Status Display with kaconnect*

ALSA provides an efficient infrastructure for the connection of several MIDI ports. Sound cards and MIDI programs (provided these support the ALSA sequencer structure) have one or several MIDI ports for communicating with each other. These ports can be connected with the KDE program kaconnect or the command aconnect. On start-up, kaconnect shows the readable and writable MIDI ports available on your system and the connection status. To test the procedure, start two MIDI programs with the commands vkeybd and aseqview. For the connection between MIDI ports, specify the port address of the program after the program name. For example, assign port number 128:0 to the first program and 129:0 to the second. The ports of the programs are also displayed by kaconnect.

As vkeybd was executed without the --addr parameter, the connection between the program port and the WaveTable port (or the external MIDI) port can now be established manually. To do this, select the respective ports and click 'connect'. To use the command-line tool aconnect, enter `aconnect 128:0 73:0` (or the respective ports) to establish a unidirectional connection between the sender port `128:0` and the receiver port `73:0`.

You can now establish a connection between the MIDI port of the keyboard and the MIDI port of the ALSA sequencer viewer. If you modify keyboard settings, such as the panning or the pitch wheel (which must first be activated under 'View'), these changes are promptly reflected in aseqview.

List the ports available for sending and receiving as well as their connection status with `aconnect -il` or `aconnect -ol`. Terminate connections established with `aconnect` with the option `-d`, for example, `aconnect -d 128:0 129:0`. To terminate all connections, enter `aconnect -x`. Get information about other options with `man aconnect`.

Note

`aseqnet` can be used to establish MIDI connections over a network.

Note

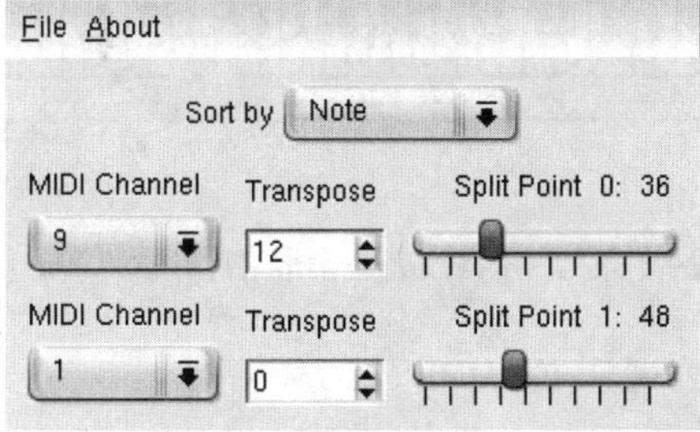

Figure 19.15: Configuring Split Zones with QMidiRoute

The program QMidiRoute enables flexible MIDI routing. It sorts the MIDI events received on the writable port according to pitch, velocity, or channel and immediately forwards them to the readable ports. Using the parameters 'Channel' and 'Transpose', change the channel and pitch of the lower split zone.

19.9.4 kmid — The KDE MIDI Player

If the `kdemultimedia` is installed, find 'Midi/Karaoke Player' in the KDE start menu under 'Multimedia'. Some demo files for kmid are available in

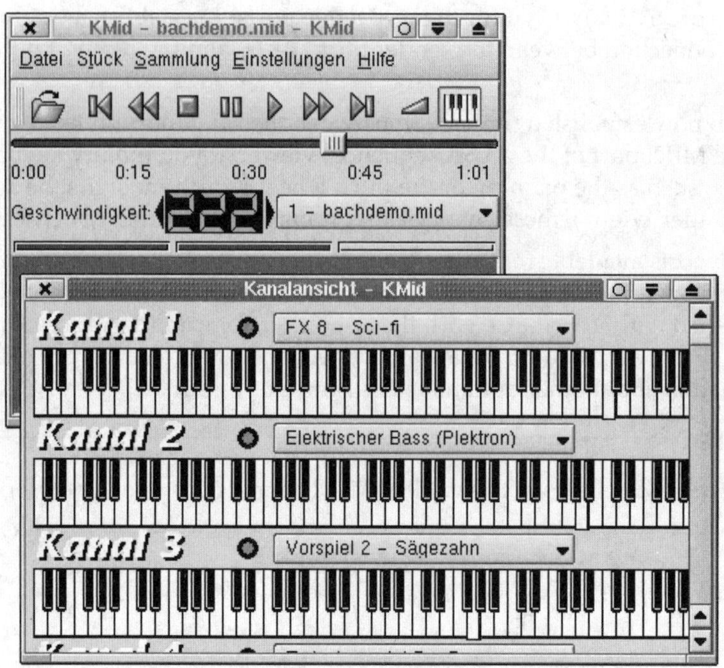

Figure 19.16: Main Window and Channel View of kmid

`.kar` format in the directory `/opt/kde3/share/apps/kmid`. These files also contain the lyrics, which are scrolled and highlighted in sync with the playback.

Access the detailed online help of kmid with F1. The MIDI ports must be set correctly under 'Settings' -> 'MIDI Settings'.

The channel view presented when you click the keyboard button in the tool bar is especially noteworthy. Enlarge the window accordingly to see each channel represented as a piano keyboard. For each channel, select the preferred instrument.

Note

If kmid is started by clicking a MIDI file in the KDE file manager Konqueror, the MIDI settings specified in the KDE Control Center are applied. If the program is started separately, the settings specified in the program itself are applied.

Note

19.10 MIDI Playback without a WaveTable Card

Some sound cards do not have a WaveTable synthesizer for playing MIDI files with the loaded sound font (or instrument patch). In this case, use a software WaveTable synthesizer like fluidsynth or timidity++.

19.10.1 The Sound Font Synthesizer fluidsynth

After the program is started with a command like `fluidsynth -a alsa -m alsa_seq gm.sf2`, fluidsynth appears in the list of writable MIDI ports and can be used as sound source. In this example, `gm.sf2` is a file in the widely-used SoundFont format. Suitable files are available on the Internet. fluidsynth has numerous command-line options that can be displayed with `fluidsynth -h`.

19.10.2 Configuration of timidity++

timidity++ is configured by means of the configuration file `/usr/share/timidity/timidity.cfg`. View documentation for the configuration with `man timidity.cfg`. Also refer to the documentation in `/usr/share/doc/packages/timidity`.

Suitable instrument patches are available at `http://www.stardate.bc.ca/eawpatches/html/default.htm`. From this URL, you can download the file `eawpats12_full.rar`. Although the size of this file is 22 MB, the download is worthwile, as it equips you with a full set of GM, GS, and XG instruments. To use these patches with timidity++, proceed as follows. First, assume the `root` user identity. Then create the directory `/usr/share/timidity/eawpats`, copy eawpats12_full.rar there, and change to this directory. The command unrar x eawpats12_full.rar decompresses the archive.

Now edit the file timidity.cfg in the directory /usr/share/timidity/. It should only contain the two lines shown in File 19.2.

Example 19.2: *timidity.cfg*

```
dir /usr/share/timidity/eawpats
source timidity.cfg
```

eawpats12_full.rar also contains a file called timidity.cfg, which is placed in the directory eawpats following the decompression. The file is included with the source command. In this file, only the four lines shown in Example 19.3 are relevant. All other lines can be deleted.

Example 19.3: *timidity.cfg of eawpats12_full.rar*

```
source gravis.cfg
source gsdrums.cfg
source gssfx.cfg
source xgmap2.cfg
```

Then the file permissions must be updated. To do this, enter the command chmod -R a+r /usr/share/timidity/eawpats. To use sound fonts instead of the Gravis instrument patches, modify the file /usr/share/timidity/timidity.cfg. For example, to use the Vintage Dreams sound font with timidity++, create a timidity.cfg consisting of a single line: soundfont /usr/share/sounds/sf2/Vintage_-Dreams_Waves_v2.sf2. More information about this subject is available in /usr/share/doc/packages/timidity/C/README.sf.

19.10.3 Starting timidity++ with the Graphical Interface

There are few programs that offer as many program interfaces as timidity++. For an overview, enter man timidity. The *Athena Widget Interface* is a mature interface that is started with /usr/bin/timidity -iatv &.

Note

You should not be in the directory /usr/share/timidity when you start timidity++.

Note

19.10.4 The ALSA Server Mode of timidity++

To start timidity++ in the ALSA server mode, enter `/usr/bin/timidity -iA -B2,8 -Os &`. A message, such as `Opening sequencer port: 128:0 128:1`, will be displayed, showing the MIDI port by means of which the synthesizer can be addressed (e.g., with `vkeybd --addr 128:0`). To terminate timidity++, enter `killall timidity` to kill all timidity++ processes.

19.11 AlsaModularSynth — Synthesizer and Effect Processor

AlsaModularSynth (from the package `alsamodular`) is a digital replica of an analog modular synthesizer. The program has a JACK interface and can load all kinds of LADSPA effect plug-ins. Thus, it can also be used as a versatile effect processor.

Enter `ams` to start AlsaModularSynth from the command line. The parameter `-j` activates the JACK mode, provided the JACK engine `jackd` is running (see Section 19.5 on page 310). The required port connections can be established with QJackConnect. Individual ports are generated for each PCM module in the JACK mode. AlsaModularSynth only appears in the list of QJackConnect if at least one PCM module exists.

The directory `usr/share/doc/packages/alsamodular` contains numerous example patches that demonstrate the various possibilities. Detailed documentation is available in the subdirectory `html`.

19.11.1 Synthesizer Patch Examples

The application package for AlsaModularSynth provides a selection of patch examples to allow the user to start working with the application right away. The folder `demos` is located in the directory `/usr/share/doc/packages/alsamodular`. A few autonomous patches are contained there that generate interesting random sound loops. The files concerned begin with `example_ams_demo`. Patches containing `scope` and `spectrum` in their name feature corresponding modules whose visualization can be opened by right-clicking the module title. Experiment a little, for example, and experience how the character of the music changes when

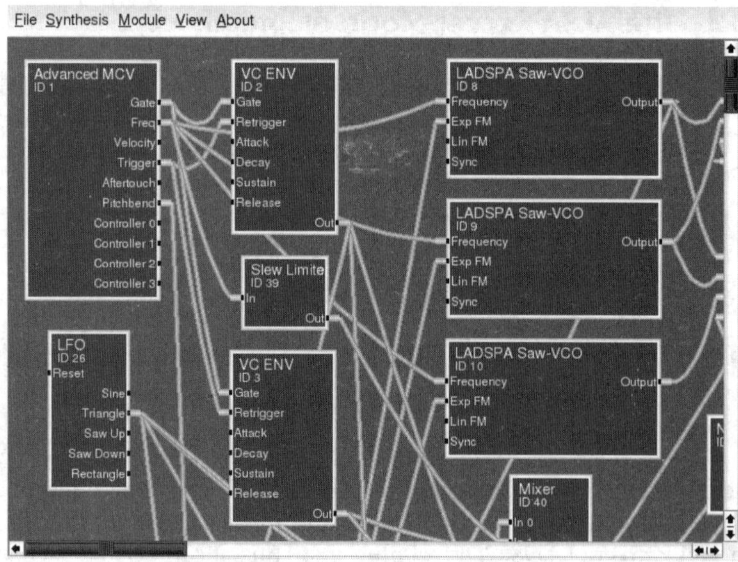

Figure 19.17: *The AlsaModularSynth Main Panel*

the quantization of the Quantizer module (ID 7) is changed from pentatonic to 1/6 (full range scale). Complete instruments can be found in the folder `instruments`. The patches `miniams.ams` as well as `phaser_instrument.ams` are actually quite versatile. These patches are supplied with a number of presets that can be called with MIDI program changes. A few of the presets are defined with the 'Parameter View' dialog available from 'View'. A systematic guide to the creation of custom patches is provided in the `tutorial` folder.

19.11.2 AlsaModularSynth as an Effect Processor

Especially in the JACK mode, AlsaModularSynth can be used as a versatile effect processor. One example for this is `example_capture.ams`. If you connect an external sound source to your sound card and use alsamixer to specify the correct settings for the capture, the example will work even without JACK. With the 'Ladspa Browser', started with 'Module' -> 'Show Ladspa Browser', generate modules for LADSPA effects. Plug-ins should always be created with 'Create Plugin', unless you use AlsaModularSynth

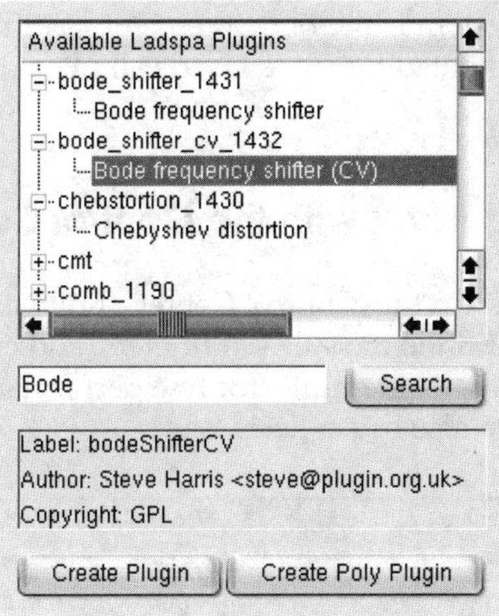

Figure 19.18: *The Ladspa Browser*

as a polyphonic synthesizer. 'Create Poly Plugin' generates a separate plug-in instance for each part.

19.11.3 AlsaModularSynth as a Synthesizer

After having used the MIDI patchbay kaconnect to connect AlsaModularSynth with a master keyboard (vkeybd or an external keyboard), you can use the program as a synthesizer. If polyphony is not explicitly activated with the parameter `--poly`, AlsaModularSynth will be monophonic, just like its classical model. The envelope modules are single-triggered, as is often the case with analog synthesizers. This means that they are not restarted during legato play. This allows interesting phrasing. Multitriggering is activated by connecting the trigger output signal of the MCV module to the retrigger input port of the envelope module.

A few LADSPA plug-ins greatly enhance the virtual analog sound of AlsaModularSynth. The plug-ins "Saw-VCO", "Mvclpf-3", "Mvclpf-4", and "Phaser1" by Fons Andersen deserve special attention. "Saw-VCO" is designed to resemble an analog saw-toothed wave generator. "Mvclpf-3" and "Mvclpf-4" are very realistic reproductions of the filter cascade invented by R. A. Moog. These plug-ins represent a milestone in the digital reproduction of this legendary low-pass filter. An effect module frequently featured in a classic modular system is the Bode Frequency Shifter. The plug-in of the same name implemented by Steve Harris allows experimenting with frequency shifting.

19.11.4 Keeping Track with the Control Center

Select the MIDI channel in the 'Control Center', build connections between the MIDI controllers and the module parameters, and create individually operable user interfaces, for example, for live performances. Range limitations for the sliders can also be set here.

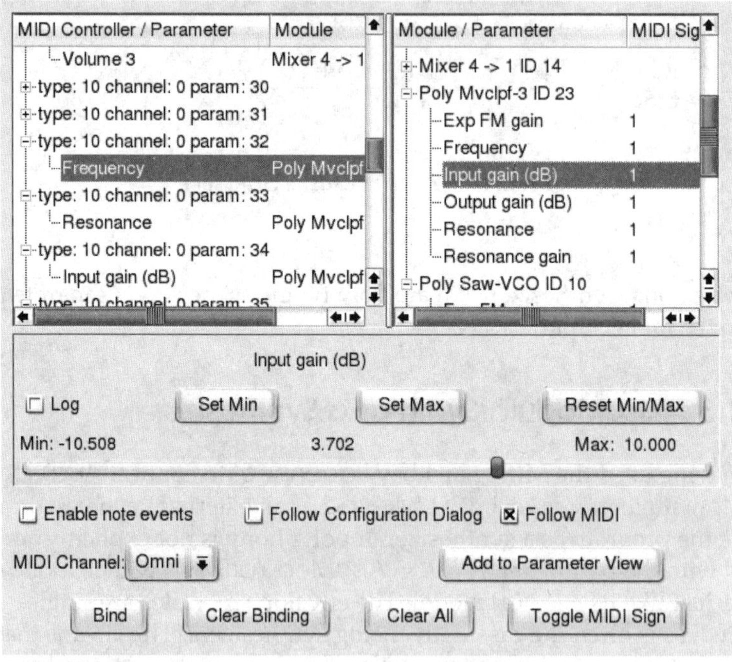

Figure 19.19: *MIDI Controllers and Module Parameters in the Control Center*

The list to the left displays the MIDI controllers used in a patch. In this tree view, the parameters associated with a controller are shown under the respective controller. As soon as a controller event that does not exist in the list is received via MIDI, it is added to the list. The list to the right shows the modules and their parameters. If you select a parameter here, the respective control appears, enabling modification of the parameter and range limits.

To create a MIDI binding, select a controller in the list to the left and a parameter in the list to the right. Then click 'Bind'. To clear a MIDI binding, simply select the respective parameter in the list to the left under the controller and click 'Clear Binding'. 'Clear All' clears the entire list of MIDI controllers and bindings. With 'Toggle MIDI Sign', determine whether a parameter should increase or decrease with rising controller values. The settings of these MIDI controllers become effective only when the current parameter value has been attained. This prevents sudden parameter jolts.

'Add to Parameter View' adds the currently marked module parameter to the 'Parameter View' dialog. The parameters can be easily arranged into tabulators and labeled frames.

19.11.5 The MIDI Out Module

The output of the MIDI events generated by a MIDI Out module is realized by way of the two readable MIDI ports of AlsaModularSynth in the left list of kaconnect. If several MIDI Out modules are used simultaneously, the MIDI events are merged accordingly. As both notation and controller events can be sent, the module can also be used to control all kinds of parameters via control voltage. To do this, the readable MIDI ports must be connected with the writable MIDI port. The example `example_midiout_controller.ams` shows the change in an envelope with autogenerated controller events. Easily follow the movement of the envelope by opening the configuration dialog of the ENV module (ID 5) with the right mouse button. The option 'Follow MIDI' in the 'Control Center' should be deactivated while this patch is running.

If you connect the readable MIDI ports of AlsaModularSynth with a MIDI sound generator, `example_midiout_note.ams` plays scales controlled by an LFO. `example_midiout_note_velocity.ams` shows that the velocity data can also be autogenerated. `example_midiout_random.ams` generates random music with drums.

19.11.6 Writing WAV Files with the WAV Out Module

Using the WAV Out module, directly record the signals generated or processed by AlsaModularSynth as a WAV file in CD quality. In the configuration dialog of the module, select 'New File' to open a file browser. If the file displayed under 'File' is successfully generated, the buttons under 'Record' are activated and can be used.

19.12 NoteEdit and MIDI Sequencers

NoteEdit is one of the most comprehensive Linux applications for editing scores with a graphical interface. As the entered notes are sounded immediately by the selected MIDI device, even newcomers can easily prepare scores with NoteEdit. This program offers the entire range of music symbols for writing scores. With NoteEdit, even play and record MIDI files. The scores can be exported in several formats, including MusicTeX and LilyPond.

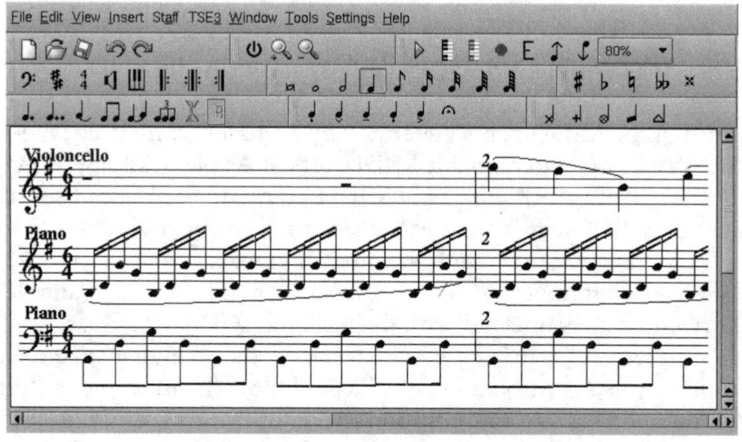

Figure 19.20: The Composition Editor NoteEdit

Start the application with `noteedit`. A few examples can be found in `/usr/share/doc/packages/noteedit/examples/`, which can be opened with 'File' -> 'Open'. Use 'TSE3' -> 'TSE3 Midi In' to import MIDI files. These are loaded into the editor with 'TSE3' -> 'Score'. Set various options for the conversion in the 'Filter' dialog box.

'Midi' -> 'Devices' allows selection of one of the ALSA MIDI devices configured in the system. This device is then used for playback as well as for recording. The instrument, the MIDI channel, and many other parameters, such as the stereo panorama, can be set under 'Staff' -> 'Staff Properties'.

Notes can easily be entered with the help of the mouse. First, choose the length of the note and any required accidental in the toolbar. Click to insert a note or right-click to insert a rest. The 'Insert' menu provides objects like clef, meter, and key. More information about NoteEdit is available in the directory `/usr/share/doc/packages/noteedit`.

In Linux, there are several MIDI sequencers, some of which are very mature. For example, Jazz is a proven, stable program. The development of Rosegarden, the classic among sequencer programs and notation editors for Linux, has been resumed. Therefore, this program may also be of interest to you. MusE is also a very active project. Meanwhile, the program can be used as a sequencer.

TV, Video, Radio, and Webcam

The configuration of TV cards is integrated in the configuration tool YaST. If your card has been correctly identified, it can be automatically configured. Otherwise, enter the card settings manually.

The following sections focus on the motv application, created by the author of the BTTV driver. Another TV application is KWinTV. If you prefer KWinTV, it should be easy to use after reading this chapter.

20.1 Watching TV with motv

motv is an improved successor to xawtv. It incorporates all essential functions into the user interface. Start the application with 'SUSE' -> 'Multimedia' -> 'Video'. Start it at the command line with `motv`. Initially, only a TV window appears after the application starts. Open a menu window by right-clicking it.

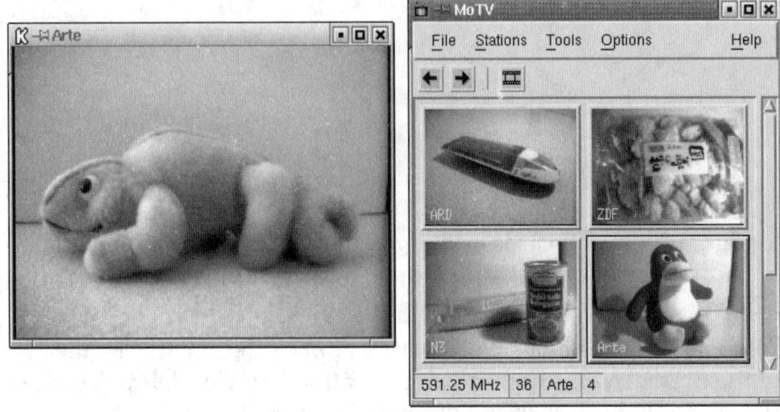

Figure 20.1: The TV Application motv

20.1.1 Video Source and Network Search

In 'Settings' -> 'Input', select the video source. If you select 'Television' here, set up the broadcasting network before starting the application. This automatically takes place with the network search, also found under the 'Settings' menu. If you click 'Save settings', the network found is entered into the `.xawtv` file in your home directory and will be available the next time you start the application.

Note

If you do not want to browse for all available channels, find the next channel with Ctrl + ↑. If needed, subsequently adjust the broadcast frequency with ← or →.

Note

20.1.2 From Silent Film to Sound Film

The audio output of the TV card is connected to the line input of your sound card, to the speakers, or to an amplifier. Some TV cards can change the volume of the audio output. The volume can then be set with the sliders that appear after selecting 'Settings' -> 'Slider'. This window also provides the sliders for brightness, contrast, and color.

To use your sound card for audio playback, check the mixer settings using gamix, described in Section 19.2 on page 300. For sound cards meeting the AC97 specifications, set 'Input-MUX' to 'Line'. The volume can then be adjusted with the 'Master' and 'Line' sliders.

20.1.3 Screen Proportions and Full-Screen Mode

Most television images have a height and width ratio of 4:3. These proportions can be set with 'Tools' -> 'Screen Dimensions'. If '4:3' is selected here (this is the default setting), the screen dimensions are retained automatically, even when the display size is changed.

With Ⓕ or 'Tools' -> 'Fullscreen', switch to full-screen mode. If the TV image in full-screen mode is not scaled to the full monitor size, some fine-tuning is required. Many graphics cards can scale the full-screen mode television image to the full monitor size without changing the graphical mode. If your card does not support this function, the graphics mode must be switched to 640x480 for the full-screen mode. Create the related configuration in 'Settings' -> 'Configuration'. After restarting motv, the monitor mode is also changed if you have switched to full-screen mode.

Note

The `.xawtv` file is created automatically and updated by clicking 'Settings' -> 'Save settings'. Here, the broadcasters are saved along with the configuration. More information about the configuration file can be found in the man page for `xawtvrc`.

Note

20.1.4 The Launcher Menu

Use the launcher menu to start other applications to use with motv. Start the audio mixer gamix and the video text application alevt, for example, using a keyboard shortcut. Applications to launch from motv must be entered in the `.xawtv` file. The entries should look like this:

```
[launch] Gamix = Ctrl+G, gamix AleVT = Ctrl+A, alevt
```

The shortcut then the command used to start the application should follow the application name itself. Start the applications entered under [launch] via the 'Tool' menu.

20.2 Video Text with alevt

Use alevt to browse video text pages. Start the application via 'SUSE' -> 'Multimedia' -> 'Video' -> 'alevt' or at the command line with `alevt`.

The application saves all the pages of the selected station just activated with motv. Browse pages by entering the desired page number or by clicking a page number. Move forward or backward through the pages by clicking '«' or '»', located in the lower window margin.

20.3 Webcams and motv

If your webcam is already supported by Linux, access it with motv. Find a summary of the supported USB devices at `http://www.linux-usb.org`. If you have already used motv to access the TV card prior to accessing the webcam, the bttv driver is loaded. The webcam driver is loaded automatically when your webcam is connected to the USB. Start motv at the command line with the parameter `-c /dev/video1` to access the webcam. Access the TV card with `motv -c /dev/video0`.

When connecting the webcam to the USB before the bttv driver has been automatically loaded (for example, by starting a TV application), `/dev/video0` is reserved for the webcam. In this case, if you start motv with the `-c /dev/video1` parameter to access the TV card, you might get an error message, because the bttv driver was not automatically loaded. Solve this problem by loading the driver separately with `modprobe bttv` as the user `root`. Access an overview of the configurable video devices on your system with `motv -hwscan`.

20.4 nxtvepg — The TV Magazine for Your PC

From some broadcasters, an EPG signal (Electronic Program Guide) is transmitted along with the video text signal. Easily view this electronic guide using the program nxtvepg. To do this, however, you must have a TV card supported by the bttv driver and be able to receive one of the channels broadcast with an EPG.

With nxtvepg, the broadcasts are sorted according to channel and topic, such as 'movie' and 'sport', and filtered according to criteria, such as Live, Stereo, or Subtitle. Start the application via the 'SUSE' -> 'Multimedia' -> 'Video' menu or at the command line with `nxtvepg`.

20.4.1 Importing the EPG Database

To set up and update the program database via the EPG signal, set the tuner of your TV card to a station that broadcasts EPG. This can be done using a TV application, such as motv or nxtvepg. Only one application at a time can access the tuner.

If you set an EPG broadcaster in motv, nxtvepg immediately begins importing the current list of TV programs. The progress will be displayed.

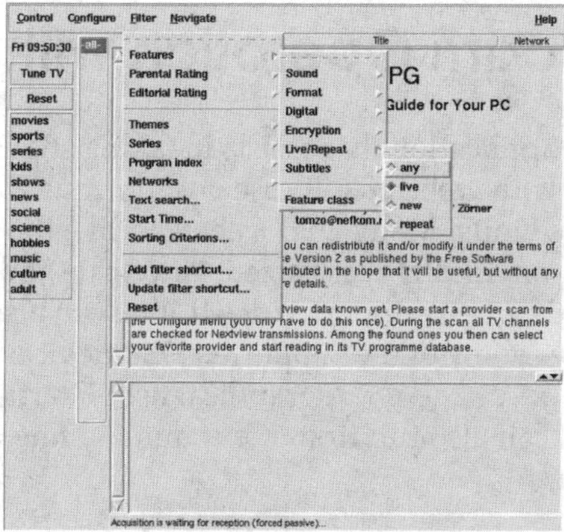

Figure 20.2: The Electronic TV Magazine nxtvepg

If you have not started a TV application, let nxtvepg search for EPG broadcasters. To do this, use 'Configure' -> 'Provider scan'. 'Use .xatv' is activated by default. This indicates that nxtvepg is accessing the broadcasters saved in this file.

Note

If there are problems, check to see if the proper video source has been chosen under 'TV card input'.

Note

Select from the EPG providers found in 'Configure' -> 'Select Provider'. 'Configure' -> 'Merge Providers' even creates flexible associations between the various provider databases.

20.4.2 Sorting the Programs

nxtvepg provides a convenient filter function for managing even the most extensive program offerings. Activate a network selection list with 'Configure' -> 'Show networks'. The 'Filter' menu offers plenty of filter functions. Right-click the program list to open a special filter menu in which to activate contextual filter functions.

Of particular interest is the 'Navigate' menu. This is built directly from the EPG data. It will appear in the language provided by the network.

20.5 Webcam Operation with gqcam

gqcam is a webcam application that assists in taking snapshots or automatic picture series with webcams. To use gqcam, your webcam must be supported by Video4Linux. Many USB webcams, like the Logitech Quickcam Express, are automatically recognized. Grayscale and color cameras can be used. TV cards wthat support Video4Linux can also be used as an image source. An overview of the supported USB devices is maintained at `http://www.linux-usb.org`. A graphical user interface is not compulsory because gqcam can also run from the command line.

20.5.1 Operation

Connect your camera to the USB port of your computer before starting gqcam. Then run gqcam. The current picture of your webcam is automatically shown in the upper part of the application window. The lower part has sliders for adjusting the brightness, white balance, contrast, tint, and color saturation according to your liking. The brightness is automatically preset. This feature can be set in 'General' in 'File' → 'Preferences'. 'Filters' features false color correction switches because some cameras swap the red and blue channels in transmission.

If you operate more than one webcam, use 'File' → 'Open New Camera' to switch to another camera. Select the new device from the dialog that opens. The first camera is attached to the device `/dev/video0`, the second is attached to `/dev/video1`, and so on.

20.5.2 Snapshots

To take a snapshot with a camera, click 'Snap Picture'. Select a file name and picture format in the dialog that opens. Create a picture series with 'Camera' → 'Set Timer...'. Set the capturing frequency in seconds or minutes along with the properties of the images in 'Set image information'. An optional script to run after every capture event can be chosen with 'Run command after snap:'. This could, for example, be used to upload the captured image onto an FTP server.

20.5.3 Command Line

gqcam can also be run without its graphical user interface. This may be interesting, for instance, for automatic surveillance controlled by a cron job. This requires that all the necessary settings be passed to the application as parameters. Running `gqcam -t JPEG -s -d webcam.jpg` saves the current image captured by the camera with the file name `webcam.jpg`. The option `-t` defines the file format. Possible values are JPEG, PNG, and PPM. The command line switch `-s` activates the color correction. The file name for saving is passed with the option `-d`. If more than one webcam is operated, the name of the device must be passed. If no device is given, the default device `/dev/video0` is used. To capture an image from the second camera, the option `-v /dev/video1` must be added. List all options with `gqcam --help`.

K3b — The KDE Burning Application

K3b is a comprehensive program for writing data and audio CDs. Along with the usual features, the program offers some additional options that facilitate work, especially in the field of multimedia. Start the program from the main menu or by entering the command `k3b`. The main program features are described in the following sections.

21.1 Creating a Data CD

Creating a data CD is easy. Go to 'File' -> 'New Project' -> 'New Data Project'. The project view appears in the lower part of the window, as shown in Figure 21.1. Drag the desired directories or individual files from your home directory to the project folder and drop them there. Save the project under a name of your choice with 'File' -> 'Save as'.

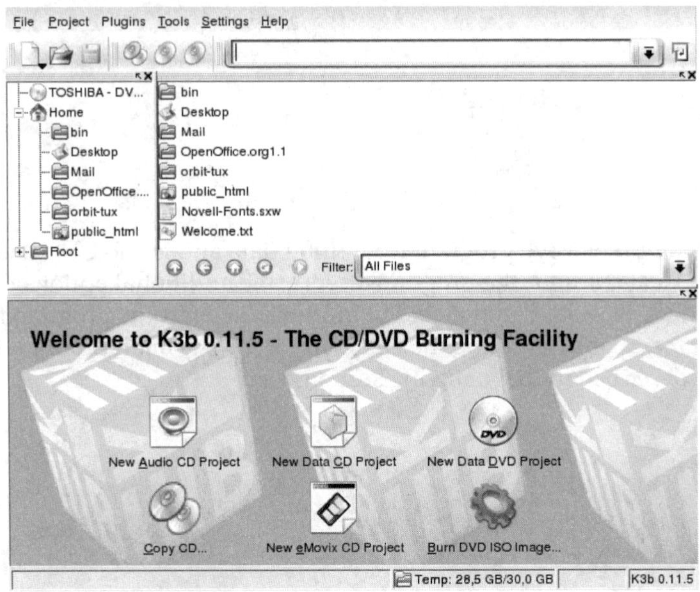

Figure 21.1: Creating a New Data CD

Then select 'Burn' from the toolbar. A dialog with five tabs offering various options for writing the CD opens. See Figure 21.2 on page 342.

21.2 Burning CDs

The detected writer is displayed under 'Device' in the burning dialog. Set the burning speed in 'Burning Speed'. The following options are offered here:

'Mode' This option determines how the laser writes a CD. In the DAO (disk at once) mode, the laser is not deactivated while the CD is written. This mode is recommended for the creation of audio CDs. However, it is not supported by all CD writers. In the TAO mode (track at one), a separate write process is applied for every individual track. The RAW mode is not used very often, as the writer does not perform any data corrections. The best setting is 'automatic', as it allows K3b to use the most suitable settings.

'Simulate' This function can be used to check if your system supports the selected writing speed. The writing is performed with the laser deactivated to test the system.

'On the fly' Burns the desired data without first creating an image file (do not use this feature on low-performance machines). An image file — also known as an ISO image — is a file containing the entire CD content that is subsequently written to the CD exactly as it is.

'Burnfree' This option was formerly known as burn-proof. It helps to avoid buffer underruns of a CD writer. If burnfree is selected, the CD writer will mark the current position and can return here in the event of a buffer underrun. However, this causes small data gaps that are audible in audio CDs. It is preferable to select a suitable burning speed that avoids buffer underruns.

'Create Image File only' This option creates an image file. Set the path for this file under 'Temporary File'. The image file can be written to CD at a later time. To do this, use 'Tools' -> 'Write ISO Image'. If this option is used, all other options in this section are deactivated.

The 'Settings' tab features options needed for the creation of CDs with multiple data or audio tracks (multisession CDs). In the 'Name of Media' tab, specify a name, description, publisher, and other details for the CD.

Under 'File system', specify settings for the file system on the CD (Rock-Ridge, Joliet, UDF). Also determine how symbolic links, file permissions, and blanks are treated. In the 'Advanced' tab, experienced users can specify additional settings.

21.3 Creating an Audio CD

Basically, there are no significant differences between creating an audio CD and creating a data CD. Select 'File' -> 'New Audio Project'. Drag and drop

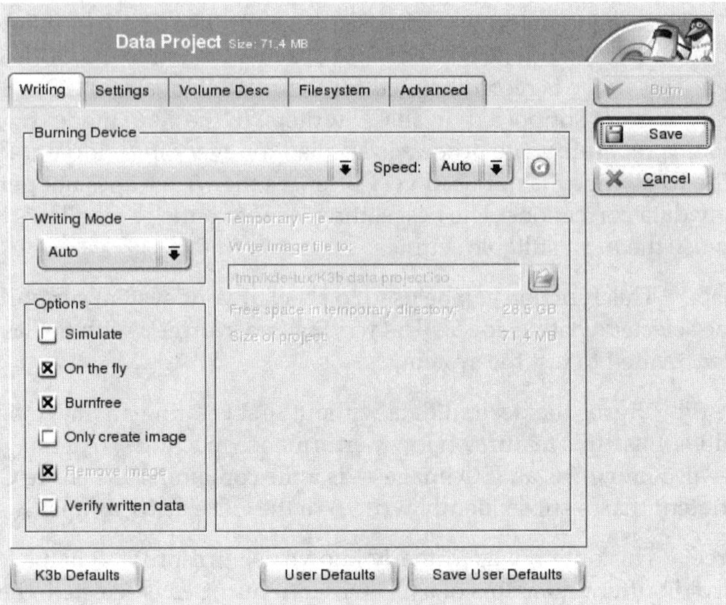

Figure 21.2: Burning CDs with K3b

the individual audio tracks to the project folder. The audio data must be in MP3, WAV, or Ogg Vorbis format. The sequence of the tracks can be determined by moving them up or down in the project folder.

The dialog for burning an audio CD is not very different from the dialog for burning a data CD. However, the option 'Disc at once' and the 'Track at once' mode bear greater importance. The 'Track at once' mode inserts an intermission of two seconds after each track.

21.4 Copying a CD

Select 'Copy CD' from the toolbar. In the following dialog, make the settings for the reading and writing device as shown in Figure 21.3 on the facing page. The options introduced above are also available here. An additional function enables the creation of several copies of the CD.

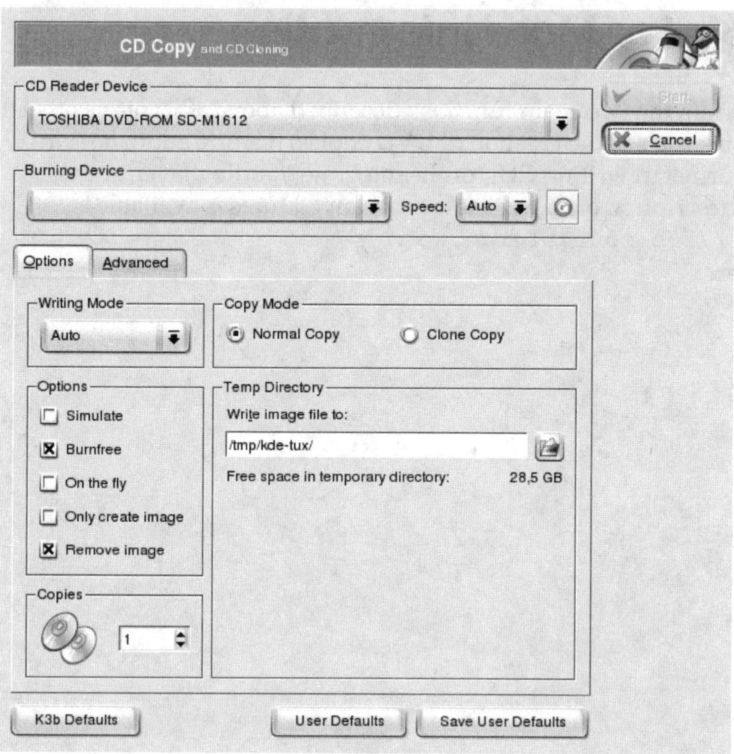

Figure 21.3: *Copying a CD*

21.5 Writing ISO Images

If you already have an ISO image, go to 'Tools' -> 'Write ISO Image' A window opens in which to enter the location of the 'Image to Write'. K3b calculates a check sum and displays it in 'MD5 Sum'. If the ISO file was downloaded from the Internet, this sum shows if the download was successful.

Use the 'Options' and 'Advanced' tabs to set your preferences. To burn the CD, click 'Write'.

21.6 For More Information

Apart from the two main functions described above, K3b offers other functions such as the creation of DVD copies, reading audio data in WAV format, rewriting CDs, or the integrated audio player. A detailed description of all available program features is available at `http://k3b.sourceforge.net`.

Digital Cameras and Linux

gPhoto 2.0 is a command-line program for communicating between the computer and a digital camera. It is compatible with several graphical interfaces (front-ends), including gtKam, Konqueror, Kamera, and GnoCam. This chapter covers the use of gtKam, Konqueror, and Digikam.

A comprehensive list of supported cameras is available at `http://www.gphoto.org/cameras.html`. If gphoto2 is installed, retrieve the list with the command `gphoto2 --list-cameras`. `gphoto2 --help` provides information about the available commands in the command-line interface.

22.1 Connecting to the Camera

The fastest and most convenient way to connect digital cameras to the computer is USB, provided the kernel, the camera, and the computer support USB. The standard SUSE kernel provides this support. A suitable cable is also required.

Note

Using the USB connection can quickly drain your camera's batteries. Consider using a power adapter.

Note

Simply connect the camera to the USB port and turn on the camera. You may need to switch your camera to a special data transfer mode. For this procedure, consult the manual of your digital camera.

22.2 Installating the Programs

Use YaST to install the gtkam package. The other required packages are selected automatically. Digikam is included in the default installation. If it is not installed, use YaST to install it, if desired. For more information about installing packages with YaST, refer to Section 4.3.4 on page 59.

22.3 Using Konqueror

KDE users can easily access digital cameras by means of the familiar Konqueror interface. Connect your camera to the USB port. A camera icon should appear on the desktop. Click this icon to open the camera in Konqueror. The camera can also be accessed by entering the URL `camera:/` in Konqueror. Navigate through the camera's directory structure until the files are shown. Use the usual Konqueror file management features to copy the files as desired. More information about using Konqueror is available in Chapter 12 on page 233.

22.4 Using gtKam

gtKam is a graphical interface for downloading and deleting pictures from the digital camera. To adjust or edit your pictures, use The GIMP as described in Chapter 24 on page 357.

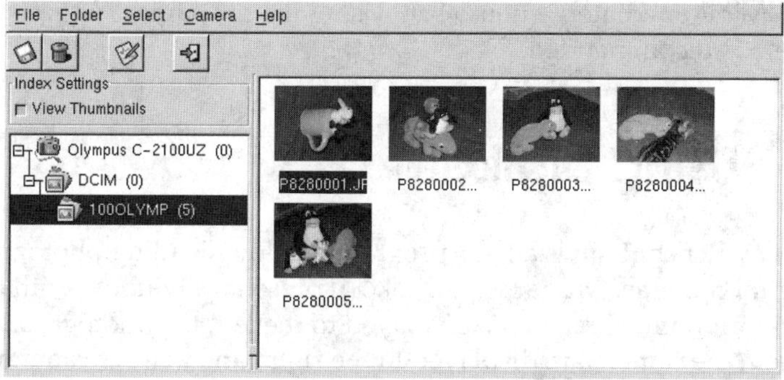

Figure 22.1: The Main Window of gtKam

Connect your camera to the appropriate port and turn on the camera. Start gtKam with the command `gtkam &`. From the menu, select 'Camera' -> 'Select Camera...'. In the dialog that opens, select the camera model or use 'Detect'. Select the appropriate port if the detection fails.

The main gtKam window is divided into three sections — the menu and toolbars, the left pane with index settings and camera and directory selection, and the right pane for displaying an index listing with or without thumbnails. The icons in the toolbar provide the main functions needed. The disk icon saves the selected images. The trash icon deletes them. The icon with the arrows loads the image index displayed in the right pane. The icon with the paper and pencil opens the camera configuration options. The door icon exits the program.

Your camera should be listed in the left pane. Use the plus sign (+) to the left to expand the tree display of the directory structure. Your exact directory structure depends on the camera type and model. Continue expanding until you reach the entries that cannot be expanded. These are the index listings of the pictures. Click an item to select it. If 'View Thumbnails' is activated, the picture names and thumbnails are displayed in the right window pane. Otherwise, the names and an icon are displayed.

Images in the right pane can be selected or deselected by clicking them. Select all images with 'Select' -> 'All' or (Shift) + (A). To save the selected images, use the disk icon in the toolbar, select 'File' -> 'Save Selected Photos...', or use the shortcut (Ctrl) + (S). The 'Save' dialog, shown in Figure 22.2 on page 350, has a number of options. Under 'What to Save', select whether to save the thumbnails, the images, or both. With 'Open image(s) with:', save the image and open it in another program. To open the images in The GIMP immediately, enter `gimp`. Using the file names suggested by the camera is recommended.

22.5 Using Digikam

Digikam by Renchi Raju is a KDE program for downloading photographs from digital cameras. On start-up, Digikam presents a window with three sections: your home directory is displayed to the left, the photographs available in the camera are displayed to the right, and a list of cameras is displayed below.

To set up a camera in Digikam, select 'Configure' -> 'Setup'. A window displaying a list of supported cameras opens. First, try to autodetect the camera with 'Auto-Detect'. If this fails, browse the list for your model. If your camera model is not included in the list, try an older model. Normally, this should work.

The path to your image folders (the location where your photographs are saved) can be specified in the same dialog under the 'General Settings' tab. You can also determine the size of the thumbnails, the way file names are displayed, and some other settings.

After your camera has been detected correctly and you have configured the program as desired, confirm with 'OK'. The name of your camera is then displayed at the bottom left in the main window. Double-click it or select 'Camera' -> 'Connect' to connect Digikam to your camera. The thumbnails are displayed to the right. Right-click the image to open a pop-up menu with which to view, save, or delete the image or view its properties.

Select all photographs to download from the camera by pressing the left mouse button or clicking individual photographs with (Shift) pressed. Selected photographs appear with inverted colors. Drag the selected photographs to the desired directory. Digikam then downloads the photographs and saves them in the selected directory.

More information about Digikam is available in theDigikam help ('Help' -> 'Digikam Handbook'). Information is also available on the Internet at `http://digikam.sourceforge.net/`.

22.6 For More Information

For more information about using digital cameras with Linux, refer to the following web sites.

- `http://www.gphoto.org` Information about gPhoto, gPhoto2, and gPhoto2-compatible GUIs
- `http://www.thekompany.com/projects/gphoto/` Information about Kamera, a KDE front-end for gPhoto2
- `http://www.stud.uni-karlsruhe.de/~urc8/GnoCam/` Information about GnoCam

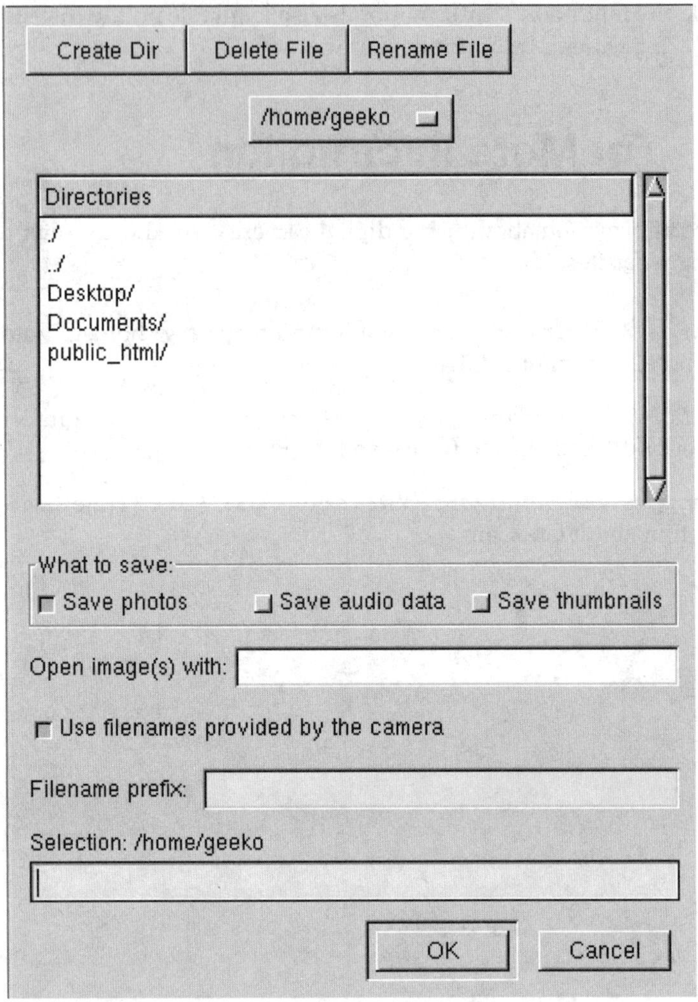

Figure 22.2: *Saving Images*

Kooka — A Scanning Application

Kooka is a KDE application for scanning. This chapter explains the user interface and the functionality of the application.

23.1 The Kooka Window

Start Kooka from the main menu or enter the command `kooka`. When started, Kooka opens a three-frame window with a menu bar to the upper left and a toolbar directly below it. All windows can be freely readjusted or rearranged with the mouse. It is also possible to completely detach single frames from the Kooka window for deliberate placement on the desktop. To move the frames, click and drag the thin double line right above the frame. Any frame, except the main window, can be placed within any other frame aligned to the left, right, top, bottom or centered. Centered windows have the same size, are stacked, and can be brought to the foreground with tabs.

The 'Image Viewer' and the 'Scan Preview' frames share a window by default. Tabs allow switching between them. The left frame provides the gallery. This is a small file browser for accessing the scanned images. The frame to the lower right is shared by the OCR (optical character recognition) and the thumbnails, which can be loaded into the image viewer with a simple click of the mouse. See Figure 23.1 on the next page.

Selecting 'Show Scan Parameters' in the 'Tool Views' subentry of the 'Settings' menu creates a third tab labeled 'Scan Parameter' next to the already existing 'Image Viewer' and 'Scan Preview' tabs in the main window. This is where the actual scanning parameters are set.

23.2 The Preview

A preview should always be created when the object to scan is smaller than the total scanning area. Set a few parameters to the left of the preview frame. Select the scanning size with 'Custom' or one of the standard formats. See Figure 23.2 on page 354. The 'Custom' setting is the most flexible, because it allows selection of the desired area with the mouse. Once the settings have been made, request the preview of the image to scan by clicking 'Preview Scan' on 'Scan Parameter'.

23.3 The Final Scan

If you selected 'Custom' for the scanning size, use the mouse to select the rectangular area to scan. The selected area is confined by a dotted border.

Figure 23.1: The Kooka Main Window

Click 'Scan Parameter' again. Choose between color and black-and-white scanning and set the resolution with the slider. See Figure 23.3 on page 355. The higher the resolution, the better the quality of the scanned image is. However, this also results in a correspondingly larger file and the scanning process can take a very long time at high resolutions. Activate 'Use custom gamma table' and click 'Edit' to change the settings for brightness, contrast, and gamma.

Once all settings have been made, click 'Final Scan' to scan the image. The scanned image is then displayed in the image viewer and as a thumbnail. When prompted, select the format in which to save the image. To save all the future images in that same format, check the corresponding box. Confirm with 'OK'.

23.4 The Menus

Some of the functions of the toolbar are also available in the 'File' and 'Image' menus. Modify preference settings for Kooka in 'Settings'.

File Use this menu to start the KPrinter printing assistant, to create a new folder for your images, and to save, delete, and close files. The OCR

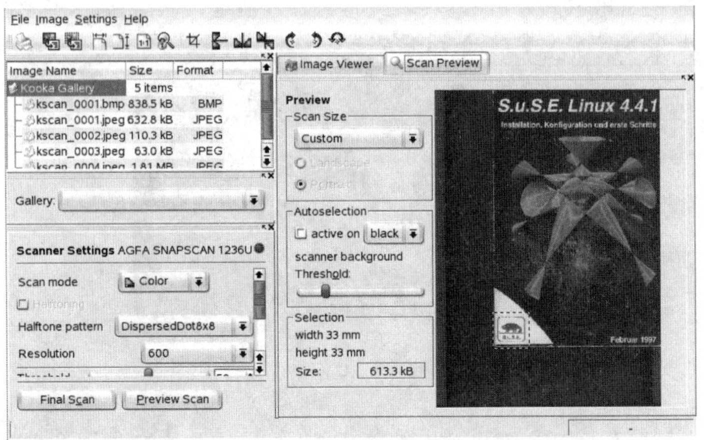

Figure 23.2: The Kooka Preview Window

results of a scanned text document can be saved here. Also use this menu to close Kooka.

Image The 'Image' menu allows starting a graphics application for post-processing or optical character recognition of an image. The recognized text from an OCR operation is displayed in its own frame. Various tools for scaling, rotating, and flipping an image are available. These functions can also be accessed from the toolbar. The submenu 'Create From Selection' allows saving an area of an image previously marked with the mouse.

Settings 'Settings' adjusts of the look and feel of Kooka. The toolbar and status bar can be switched on and off and keyboard shortcuts for menu entries can be defined. 'Configure Toolbars' provides a list of all the functions available to the toolbar. 'Configure Kooka' opens a configuration dialog in which to modify the look and feel of Kooka. Normally, however, the defaults are sufficient. In 'Tool Views', enable and disable the thumbnail viewer, the preview, the gallery, the scanning parameters, and the OCR result window.

Help The 'Help' menu provides access to the online help manual for Kooka. Also use it to access a feedback channel for problems and wishes. It also provides information about the version, authors, and license of Kooka and KDE.

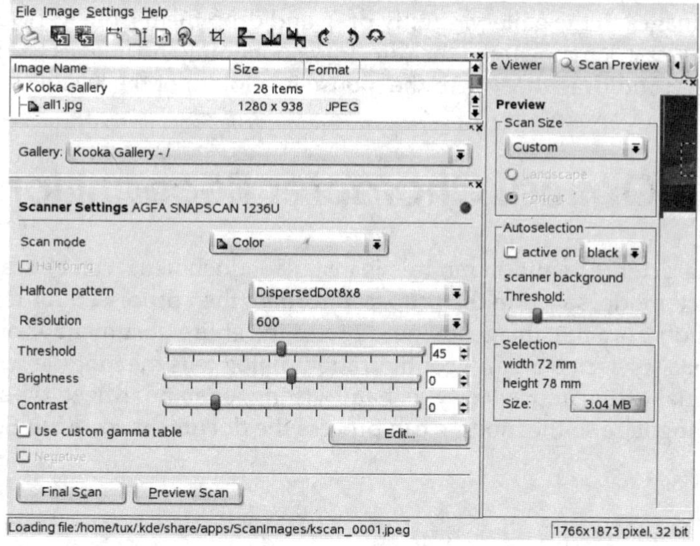

Figure 23.3: The Kooka Scanning Parameters

23.5 The Gallery

The gallery window shows the default folder where Kooka stores all its image files. An example is shown in Figure 23.4. To save an image to your personal home directory, click the thumbnail to select it then select 'File' -> 'Save Image'. Then enter your personal home directory and give the file a descriptive name.

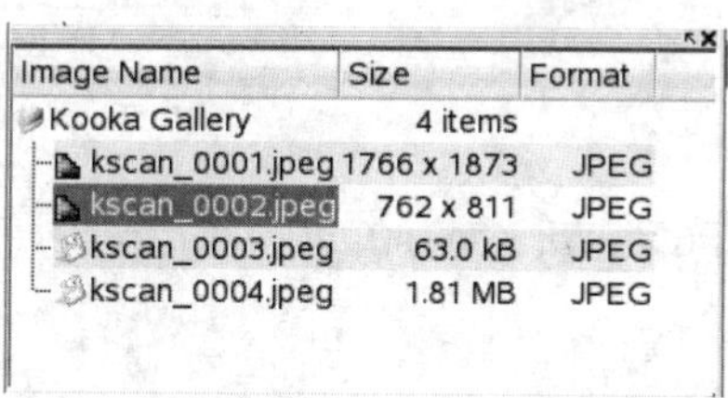

Figure 23.4: The Kooka Gallery

To add images to the gallery, simply drag and drop them from Konqueror. Start Konqueror, navigate to the directory containing the images to add to the gallery, and drag them with the mouse to a folder of the Kooka gallery.

23.6 Optical Character Recognition

If the character recognition module is installed, documents can be scanned in 'lineart' mode, saved in the proposed format, then processed for text recognition from the 'Image' menu. Process the entire document or only a previously selected area. A configuration dialog tells the module whether the original text is in printed type, handwriting, or standardized type. Also set the language so the module can process the document correctly. See Figure 23.5.

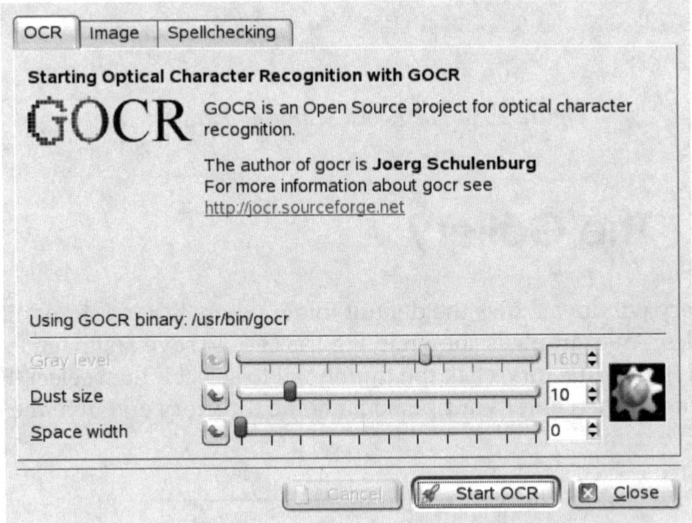

Figure 23.5: OCR with Kooka (Optical Character Recognition)

Switch to the 'OCR Result Text' window and check the text, which may need to be proofread. To do this, save the text with 'File' -> 'Save OCR Result Text'. The text can then be processed with OpenOffice or KWrite.

Manipulating Graphics with The GIMP

The GIMP (*The GNU Image Manipulation Program*) is a program for creating and editing pixel graphics. In most aspects, its features are comparable to those of Adobe Photoshop and other commercial programs. Use it to resize and retouch photographs, design graphics for web pages, make covers for your custom CDs, or almost any other graphics project. It meets the needs of both amateurs and professionals.

Like many other Linux programs, The GIMP is developed as a cooperative effort of developers worldwide who volunteer their time and code to the project. The program is under constant development, so the version included in your SUSE LINUX may vary slightly from the version discussed here. The layout of the individual windows and window sections is especially likely to vary.

The new 2.0 version offers many new features and an updated user interface. As many of these features and aspects of the user interface are mentioned here, both new and experienced GIMP users can benefit from this chapter.

The GIMP is an extremely complex program. Only a small range of features, tools, and menu items are discussed in this chapter. See Section 24.9 on page 373 for ideas of where to find more information about the program.

24.1 Graphics Formats

There are two main formats for graphics — pixel and vector. The GIMP works only with pixel graphics, which is the normal format for photographs and scanned images. Pixel graphics consist of small blocks of color that together create the entire image. The files can easily become quite large because of this. It is also not possible to increase the size of a pixel image without losing quality.

Unlike pixel graphics, vector graphics do not store information for all individual pixels. Instead, they store information about how image points, lines, or areas are grouped together. Vector images can also be scaled very easily. The drawing application of OpenOffice.org, for example, uses this format.

24.2 Starting The GIMP

Start GIMP from the main menu. Alternatively, enter `gimp &` in a command line.

24.2.1 Initial Configuration

When starting GIMP for the first time or the 2.0 version for the first time, a configuration wizard opens for preparatory configuration. The default settings are acceptable for most purposes. Press 'Continue' in each dialog unless you are familiar with the settings and prefer another setup.

24.2.2 The Default Windows

Three windows appear by default. They can be arranged on the screen and, except the toolbox, closed if no longer needed. Closing the toolbox closes the application. In the default configuration, The GIMP saves your window layout when you exit. Dialogs left open reappear when you next start the program.

GIMP Tip of the Day

This small window opens with useful tips and tricks each time the program starts. Reading the tips is recommended for new users. Uncheck 'Show tip next time GIMP starts' to disable it. This setting can also be changed in the preferences. Press 'Close' to close the window.

The Toolbox

The main window of The GIMP, shown in Figure 24.1 on the next page, contains the main controls of the application. Closing it exits the application. At the very top, the menu bar offers access to file functions, extensions, and help. Below that, find icons for the various tools. Hover the mouse over an icon to display information about it.

The current foreground and background color are shown in two overlapping boxes. The default colors are black for the foreground and white for the background. Click the box to open a color selection dialog. Swap the foreground and background color with the bent arrow symbol to the upper right of the boxes. Use the black and white symbol to the lower left to reset the colors to the default.

To the right, the current brush, pattern, and gradient are shown. Click the displayed one to access the selection dialog. The lower portion of the window contains the 'Tool Options' dialog. It allows configuration of various options for the current tool.

Layers, Channels, Paths, Undo

In the first section, use the drop-down box to select the image to which the tabs refer. By clicking 'Auto', control whether the active image is chosen automatically. By default, 'Auto' is enabled.

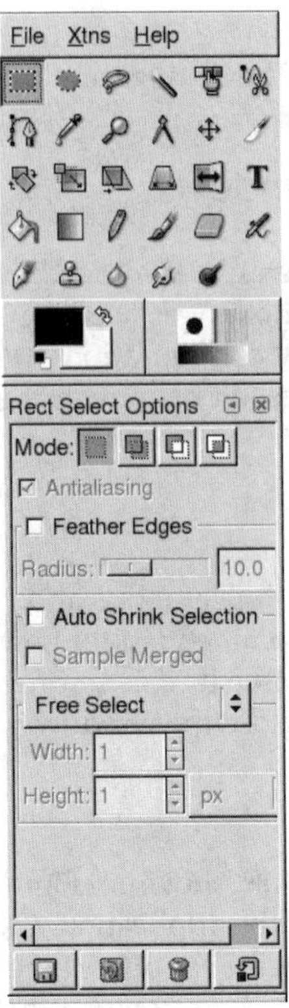

Figure 24.1: *The Main Window*

'Layers' shows the different layers in the current images and can be used to manipulate the layers. Information is available in Section 24.6.1 on page 370. 'Channels' shows and can manipulate the color channels of the image.

Paths are an advanced method of selecting parts of an image. They can also be used for drawing. 'Paths' shows the paths available for an image and provides access to path functions. 'Undo' shows a limited history of modifications made to the current image. Its use is described in Section 24.5.5 on page 370.

The bottom portion of the window contains three tabs. With them, select the current brush, gradient, and pattern.

24.3 Getting Started in GIMP

24.3.1 Creating a New Image

To create a new image, select 'File' -> 'New' or press Ctrl-N . This opens a dialog in which to make settings for the new image. If desired, use 'From Template' to select a template on which to base the new image. The GIMP includes a number of templates, ranging from an A4 sheet of paper to a CD cover, from which to choose. To create a custom template, select 'File' -> 'Dialogs' -> 'Templates...' and use the controls offered by the window that opens.

In the 'Image Size' section, set the size of the image to create in pixels or another unit. GIMP defaults use inches as the other unit. Click the unit to select another unit from the list of available units. Changing the pixel size modifies the other unit size and vice versa. The ratio between pixels and a unit is set in 'Resolution'. A resolution of 72 pixels per inch corresponds to screen display. It is sufficient for web page graphics. A higher resolution should be used for images to print. For most printers, a resolution of 300 pixels per inch results in an acceptable quality.

In 'Image Type', select whether the image should be in color ('RGB') or 'grayscale'. For detailed information about image types, see Section 24.6.2 on page 371. Select the 'Fill Type' for the new image. 'Foreground' and 'Background' use the colors selected in the toolbox. 'White' uses a white background in the image. 'Transparent' creates a clear image. Transparency is represented by a gray checkerboard pattern. Enter a comment for the new image in 'Image Comment'.

When the settings meet your needs, press 'OK'. To restore the default settings, press 'Reset'. Pressing 'Cancel' aborts creation of a new image.

24.3.2 Opening an Existing Image

To open an existing image, select 'File' -> 'Open' or press Ctrl + O. In the dialog that opens, the current directory is listed above the center column. Available directories are listed in the left column. Double-click the directory to make it the current one. ../ moves up a level in the hierarchy.

The center column shows the files available in the current directory. Click a file name to select it. If available, a preview of the selected file is shown in the right column. Alternatively, enter a file name in the field towards the bottom. Pressing Tab while entering a name in the field attempts to complete the name. Available completions are then listed in the 'Folders' and 'Files' columns. Select one or enter enough of the name to identify the file uniquely then press (Tab) again. Click 'OK' to open the selected image. Press 'Cancel' to skip opening an image.

24.3.3 The Image Window

The new or opened image appears in its own window. The menu bar in the top of the window provides access to all image functions. Alternatively, access the menu by right-clicking the image or clicking the small arrow button in the left corner of the rulers.

'File' offers the standard file options, such as 'Save' and 'Print'. 'Close' closes the current image. 'Quit' closes the entire application.

With the items in the 'View' menu, control the display of the image and the image window. 'New View' opens a second display window of the current image. Changes made in one view are reflected in all other views of that image. Alternate views are useful for magnifying a part of an image for manipulation while seeing the complete image in another view. Adjust the magnification level of the current window with 'Zoom'. When 'Shrink Wrap' is selected, the image window is resized to fit the current image display exactly.

24.4 Saving Images

No image function is as important as 'File' -> 'Save'. It is better to save too often than too rarely. Use 'File' -> 'Save as' to save the image with a new file name. It is a good idea to save image stages under different names or make backups in another directory so you can easily restore a previous state.

When saving for the first time or using 'Save as', a dialog opens in which to specify the file name and type. The current directory in shown in a box centered above the two columns. Select another directory by double-clicking it in 'Folders'. To save the image as an existing file, select it in 'Files'. Otherwise, enter a new name in the field at the bottom. It is recommended to leave 'Determine File Type' set to 'By Extension'. With that setting, GIMP determines the file type based on the extension appended to the file name. The following file types are frequently useful:

XCF This is the native format of The GIMP. It saves all layer and path information along with the image itself. Even if you need an image in another format, it is usually a good idea to save a copy as XCF to simplify future modifications. Information about layers is available in Section 24.6.1 on page 370.

PAT This is the format used for GIMP patterns. Saving an image in this format enables using the image as a fill pattern in GIMP.

JPG JPG or JPEG is a common format for photographs and web page graphics without transparency. Its compression method enables reduction of file sizes, but information is lost when compressing. It may be a good idea to use the preview option when adjusting the compression level. Levels of 85 percent to 75 percent often result in an acceptable image quality with reasonable compression. Saving a backup in a lossless format, like XCF, is also recommended. If editing an image, save only the finished image as JPG. Repeatedly loading a JPG then saving can quickly result in poor image quality.

GIF Although very popular in the past for graphics with transparency, GIF is less often used now because of license issues. GIF is also used for animated images. The format can only save *indexed* images. See Section 24.6.2 on page 371 for information about indexed images. The file size can often be quite small if only a few colors are used.

PNG With its support for transparency, lossless compression, free availability, and increasing browser support, PNG is replacing GIF as the preferred format for web graphics with transparency. An added advantage is that PNG offers partial transparency, which is not offered by GIF. This enables smoother transitions from colored areas to transparent areas (*antialiasing*).

To save the image in the chosen format, press 'OK'. To abort, press 'Cancel'. If the image has features that cannot be saved in the chosen format, a dialog appears with choices for resolving the situation. Choosing 'Export', if offered, normally gives the desired results. A window then opens with the options of the format. Reasonable default values are provided.

24.5 Editing Images: Basics

24.5.1 Changing the Image Size

Once an image is scanned or a digital photograph is loaded from the camera, it is often necessary to modify the size for display on a web page or for printing. Images can easily be made smaller either by scaling them down or by cutting off parts of them. Making an image larger is much more problematic. Because of the nature of pixel graphics, quality is lost when an image is made larger. It is recommended to keep a copy of your original image before scaling or cropping.

Cropping an Image

Cropping an image works like cutting the edges off a piece of paper. Select the crop tool from the toolbox (it resembles a scalpel) or with 'Tools' -> 'Transform Tools' -> 'Crop & Resize'. Click a starting corner and drag to outline the area to keep.

A small window opens with information about the starting point and the size of the selected area. Adjust these values by clicking and dragging a corner of the crop box or by adjusting the values in the window. 'From Selection' adjusts the crop to fit the current selection (selections are explained in Section 24.5.2 on the next page). 'Auto Shrink' makes the crop smaller based on color changes in the image.

Press 'Cancel' to abort the crop. Press 'Crop' to crop the image. The results of 'Resize' are identical to those of 'Change Canvas Size', described in Section 24.5.1 on the facing page.

Scaling an Image

Select 'Image' -> 'Scale Image' to change the overall size of an image. Select the new size by entering it in 'New Width' or 'New Height' or by adjusting the 'Ratio'. To change the proportions of the image when scaling (this distorts the image), click the chain icon to the right of the ratio fields to break the link between them. When those fields are linked, all values are changed proportionately when the value in one of the four fields is changed. When the link is broken, width and height can be adjusted independently of each other or the X and Y ratios can be adjusted individually.

The values in the 'Print Size' are independent of the pixel size. In that section, modify the image resolution by modifying the resulting image size when printed or modifying the resolution itself. Use the unit drop-down boxes to change the measuring unit.

'Interpolation' is an expert option that controls the scale method. When finished adjusting the size, press 'OK' to scale the image. 'Reset' restores the original values. 'Cancel' aborts the procedure.

Changing the Canvas Size

Changing the canvas size is like putting a mat around an image. Even if the mat is smaller, the rest of the image is there, but you can only see part of it. If the mat is larger, you see the original image with extra space around it. To do this, select 'Image' -> 'Canvas Size'.

In the dialog that opens, enter the new size. By default, the width and height maintain the same proportions as the current image. To change this, click the chain icon to the right of 'Ratio'. Enter the desired size in the height and width fields or adjust the ratios.

After adjusting the size, determine how the existing image should be positioned in comparison to the new size. Use the offset values or drag the box inside the frame at the bottom. When satisfied with the changes, click 'OK' to change the canvas size. Click 'Reset' to restore the original values or 'Cancel' to cancel the canvas resize.

Note

The same results can be achieved using the 'Resize' option of the crop tool.

Note

24.5.2 Selecting Parts of Images

It is often useful to perform an image operation on only part of an image. To do this, the part of the image with which to work must be selected. Areas can be selected using the select tools available in the toolbox, using the quick mask, or combining different options. Selections can also be modified with the items under 'Select'. The selection is outlined with a dashed line, called *marching ants*.

Using the Select Tools

The main select tools are rather easy to use. The paths tool, which can also be used for more than selecting, is more complicated so is not described here. In the tool options for the other select tools, determine whether the selection should replace, be added to, be subtracted from, or intersect with an existing selection.

Rectangular Select This tool can be used to select rectangular or square areas. In the tool options, select among 'Free Select', 'Fixed Size', and 'Fixed Aspect Ratio' to control the shape and size of the selection.

Elliptical Select Use this to select elliptical or circular areas. The same options are available as with rectangular selection.

Lasso Draw a selection area freehand with this tool by dragging the mouse over the image with the left mouse button pressed. The end points will be connected with a straight line when you release the tool. The area inside is then selected.

Magic Wand This tools selects a region based on color similarities.

By Color With this, select all the pixels in the image with the same color as the clicked pixel.

Intelligent Scissors Click a series of points in the image. As you click, the points are connected based on color differences.

Using the Quick Mask

The quick mask is a way of selecting parts of an image using the paint tools. A good way to use it is to make a rough selection using the intelligent scissors or the lasso (freehand selection tool). Then activate the quick mask by pressing the small icon with the dashed box in the lower left corner.

The quick mask displays the selection using an overlay of red. Areas shaded with red are not selected. Areas appearing as they did before the mask was activated are selected. To modify the selection, use the paint tools. Painting with white selects the painted pixels. Painting with black unselects pixels. Shades of gray (colors are treated as shades of gray) are a partial selection. Partial selection allows smooth transitions between selected and unselected areas.

Note

To use a different color for displaying the quick mask, right-click the quick mask button then select 'Configure Color and Opacity' from the menu. Click the colored box in the dialog that opens to select a new color.

Note

After using the paint tools to adjust the selection as desired, convert from the quick mask view back to the normal selection view by clicking the icon in the lower left corner of the image window (currently displaying a red box). The selection is again displayed with the marching ants.

24.5.3 Applying and Removing Color

Most image editing involves applying or removing color. By selecting a part of the image, limit where color can be applied or removed. When you select a tool and move the cursor onto an image, the cursor's appearance changes to reflect the chosen tool. With many tools, an icon of the current tool is shown along with the arrow. For paint tools, an outline of the current brush is shown, allowing you to see exactly where you will be painting in the image and how large an area will be painted.

Selecting Colors

By default, paint tools use the foreground color. However, this can be changed in the tool options of fill tools. To select the color, first click the display box of the foreground or background color, as desired.

A dialog with four tabs opens. These tabs provide different color selection methods. Only the first tab, shown in Figure 24.2 on the next page, is described here. The new color is shown in 'Current'. The previous color is shown in 'Old'.

The easiest way to select a color is using the colored areas in the boxes to the left. In the narrow vertical bar, click a color similar to the desired color. The larger box to the left then shows available nuances. Click the desired color. It is then shown in 'Current'. If that color is not what you want, try again.

The arrow button to the right of 'Current' enables saving a number of possible colors. Click the arrow to copy the current color to the history. A color can then be selected by clicking it in the history. A color can also be selected by directly entering its hexadecimal color code in 'Hex Triplet'.

The color selector defaults to selecting a color by hue, which is usually easiest for a new user. To select by saturation, value, red, green, or blue, select the corresponding radio button to the right. The sliders and number fields can also be used to modify the currently selected color. Experiment a bit to find out what works best for you.

When the desired color is shown in 'Current', click 'OK'. To restore the original values shown when the dialog was opened, click 'Reset'. To abort changing the color, click 'Cancel'.

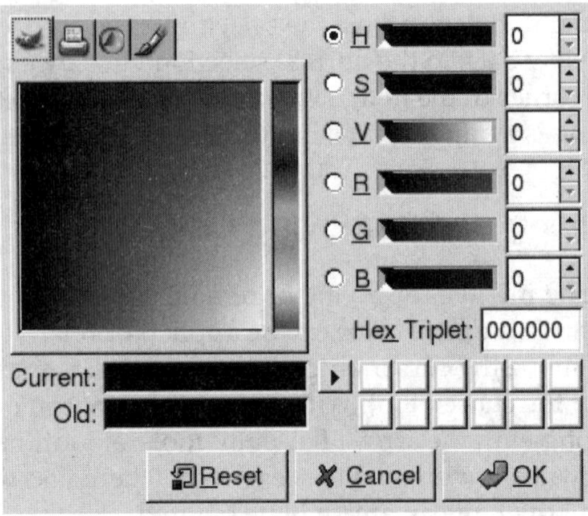

Figure 24.2: The Basic Color Selector Dialog

To select a color that already exists in your image, use the color picker tool, the icon for which resembles an eye dropper. With the tool options, set whether the foreground or background color should be selected. Then click a point in the image that shows the desired color. When the color is right, click 'Close' to close the tool's dialog.

Painting and Erasing

To paint and erase, use the tools from the toolbox. There are a number of options available to fine-tune each tool. Pressure sensitivity options apply only when a pressure-sensitive graphics tablet is used.

The pencil, brush, airbrush, and eraser work much like their real-life equivalents. The ink tool works like a calligraphy pen. Paint by clicking and dragging. The bucket fill is a method of coloring areas of an image. It fills based on color boundaries in the image. Adjusting the threshold modifies its sensitivity to color changes.

Adding Text

With the text tool, easily add text to an image. With the tool options, select the desired font, font size, color, justification, indent, and line spacing. Then click a starting point in the image. A small dialog opens in which to enter your text. Enter single or multiple lines of text then press 'Close'.

The text tool creates text on a special layer. To work with the image after adding text, read Section 24.6.1 on the following page. When the text layer is active, it is possible to modify the text by clicking in the image to reopen the entry dialog. Change the settings by modifying the tool options.

Retouching Images — The Clone Tool

The clone tool is ideal for retouching images. It enables you to paint in an image using information from another part of the image. If desired, it can instead take information from a pattern.

When retouching, it is usually a good idea to use a small brush with soft edges. In this way, the modifications can blend better with the original image.

To select the source point in the image, press and hold Ctrl while clicking the desired source point. Then paint with the tool as usual. When you move the cursor while painting, the source point, marked by a cross, moves as well. If the 'Alignment' is set to 'Non Aligned' (the default setting), the source resets to the original when you release the left mouse button.

24.5.4 Adjusting Color Levels

Images often need a little adjusting to get ideal print or display results. In many programs designed for inexperienced users, the brightness and contrast levels are modified. This can work and is also available in The GIMP, but better results can be obtained by adjusting the color levels.

To do this, select 'Layer' -> 'Colors' -> 'Levels'. A dialog opens for controlling the levels in the image. Good results can usually be obtained by clicking 'Auto'. To make manual adjustments to all channels, use the dropper tools in 'All Channels' to pick black, gray, and white points from the image itself.

To modify a channel individually, select the desired channel in 'Modify Levels for Channel'. Then drag the black, white, and middle markers in the slider in 'Input Levels'. Alternatively, use the dropper tools to select points in the image that should serve as the white, black, and gray points for that channel.

If 'Preview' is checked, the image window shows a preview of how the image would look with the modifications applied. When the desired result is achieved, press 'OK' to apply the changes. With 'Resest', restore the original settings. 'Cancel' aborts level adjustment.

24.5.5 Undoing Mistakes

Most modifications made in The GIMP can be undone. To view a history of modifications, use the undo dialog included in the default window layout or open one from the toolbox menu with 'File' -> 'Dialogs' -> 'Undo History'.

The dialog shows a base image and a series of editing changes that can be undone. Use the yellow arrow at the bottom left to undo changes. Use the green arrow at the right to redo an undone change. In this way, you can work back to the base image. If you undo a modification then make a new one, the undone modification cannot be redone.

Changes can also be undone and redone with the 'Edit' menu. Alternatively, use the shortcuts Ctrl + Z and Ctrl + Y.

24.6 Editing Images: Advanced Features

24.6.1 Layers

Layers are a very important aspect of The GIMP. By drawing parts of your image on separate layers, change, move, or delete those parts without damaging the rest of the image. To understand how layers work, imagine an image created from a stack of transparent sheets. Different parts of the image are drawn on different sheets. The stack can be rearranged, changing which parts are on top. Individual layers or groups of layers can shift position, moving sections of the image to other locations. New sheets can be added and others set aside.

Use the 'Layers' dialog to view the available layers of an image. The text tool automatically creates special text layers when used. The active layer is highlighted. The buttons at the bottom of the dialog offer a number of functions. More are available in the menu opened when a layer is right-clicked in the dialog. The two icon spaces before the image name are used for toggling image visibility (eye icon when visible) and for linking layers. Linked layers are marked with the chain icon and moved as a group.

Only layers with transparency (an alpha channel) can be placed above other layers in a stack. To add this to a layer, right-click and select it from the menu.

24.6.2 Image Modes

GIMP has three image modes — RGB, Grayscale, and Indexed. RGB is a normal color mode and is the best mode for editing most images. Grayscale is used for black-and-white images. Indexed limits the colors in the image to a set number. It is mainly used for GIF images. If you need an indexed image, it is normally best to edit the image in RGB then convert to indexed right before saving. If you save to a format that requires an indexed image, GIMP offers to index the image when saving.

24.6.3 Special Effects

The GIMP includes a wide range of filters and scripts for adding special effects to an image or making artistic manipulations. They are available in 'Filters' and 'Script-fu'. Experimenting is the best way to find out what is available. 'Xtns' in the toolbox includes a number of items for creating buttons, logos, and other things.

24.7 Printing Images

To print an image, select 'File' -> 'Print' from the image menu. If your printer is configured in SUSE, it should appear in the list. In some cases, it may be necessary to select an appropriate driver with 'Setup Printer'. Select the appropriate paper size with 'Media Size' and the type in 'Media Type'. Other settings are available in the 'Image / Output Settings' tab.

In the bottom portion of the window, adjust the image size. Press 'Use Original Image Size' to take these settings from the image itself. This is recommended if you set an appropriate print size and resolution in the image. Adjust the image's position on the page with the fields in 'Position' or by dragging the image in 'Preview'.

When satisfied with the settings, press 'Print'. To save the settings for future use, instead use 'Print and Save Settings'. 'Cancel' aborts printing.

24.8 Configuring GIMP

24.8.1 Customizing Windows

It is possible to customize your window layout extensively. Dialogs can be combined as multiple items in one window or with tabs. Do this by drag-

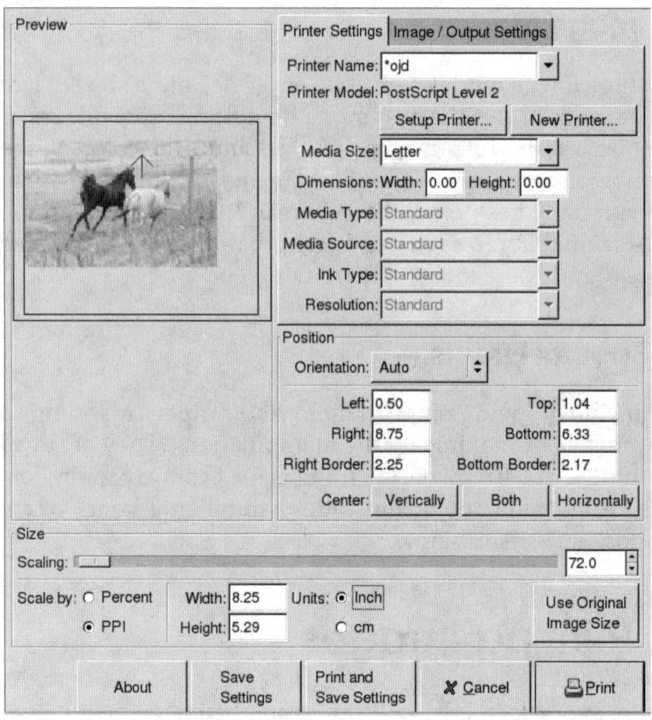

Figure 24.3: The Print Dialog

ging and dropping a dockable window into a dock bar or existing tab. New dialogs can be opened with 'File' -> 'Dialogs' from the toolbox.

24.8.2 Setting Preferences

A number of configuration options are available in 'File' -> 'Preferences'. The default settings should meet the needs of the average user. It may be useful, however, to review the options under 'Environment' -> 'Resource Levels' and 'Interface' -> 'Image Windows'.

24.9 For More Information

The following are some resources that may be useful for the GIMP user. Unfortunately, the newness of this version means that many resources may be outdated.

- 'Help' provides access to the internal help system.
- The GIMP User Group offers an informative and interesting web site at `http://gug.sunsite.dk`.
- `http://www.gimp.org` is the official home page of The GIMP.
- *Grokking the GIMP* by Carey Bunks is an excellent book based on an older GIMP version. Although some aspects of the program have changed, it can provide excellent guidance for image manipulation.
- `http://gimp-print.sourceforge.net` is the web page for the GIMP print plug-in. The user manual available from the site provides detailed information about configuring and using the program.

Part VI

Excursions

Working with the Shell

Graphical user interfaces are increasingly becoming important for Linux, but using the mouse is not always the best way to perform daily tasks. The command line provides high flexibility and efficiency. The first part of this chapter provides an introduction to the Bash shell. It is followed by an explanation of the user permissions concept in Linux and a list of the most important commands. The chapter closes with a description of the vi text editor.

Text-based applications are especially important for controlling older Linux computers that do not have the resources for demanding display systems. Virtual consoles are used in this case. Six of them are available in text mode. Press Alt + F1 through Alt + F6. The seventh console is reserved for X.

25.1 Introduction to Bash

In the KDE taskbar, there is an icon depicting a monitor with a seashell. When you click this icon, a console window opens in which to enter commands. The console normally runs Bash (Bourne again shell), a program developed as part of the GNU project. It is, by far, the most widely used derivative of the Bourne shell (sh). Once you have opened the shell, see the prompt on the first line. The prompt usually consists of the user name, host name, and current path, but it can be customized. When the cursor is behind this prompt, you can send commands directly to your computer system: `tux $ >`.

25.1.1 Commands

A command consists of several elements. The first element is always the actual command, followed by parameters or options. Commands are executed when you press Enter. Before doing so, easily edit the command line, add options, or correct typing errors. One of the most frequently used commands is `ls`, which can be used with or without arguments. Entering the plain `ls` command in the console shows the contents of the current directory.

Options are prefixed with a hyphen. The command `ls -l`, for instance, shows the contents of the same directory in full detail. Next to each file name, see the date when the file was created, the file size in bytes, and further details, which are covered later. One very important option that exists for many commands is the `--help` option. By entering `ls --help`, display all the options for the `ls` command.

Also use the `ls` command to view the contents of other directories. To do so, the directory must be specified as a parameter. For example, to see the contents of `Desktop`, enter `ls -l Desktop`.

25.1.2 Files and Directories

To use the shell efficiently, it is really useful to have some knowledge about the file and directory structures of a Linux system. You can think of directories as electronic folders in which files, programs, and subdirectories are stored. The top level directory in the hierarchy is the root directory, referred to as /. This is the place from which all other directories can be accessed.

The /home directory contains the directories in which the individual users can store their personal files. Figure 25.1 shows the standard directory tree in Linux, with the home directories of the example users xyz, linux, and tux. The directory tree of a Linux system has a functional structure that follows the File System Standard.

The following list provides a brief description of the standard directories in Linux.

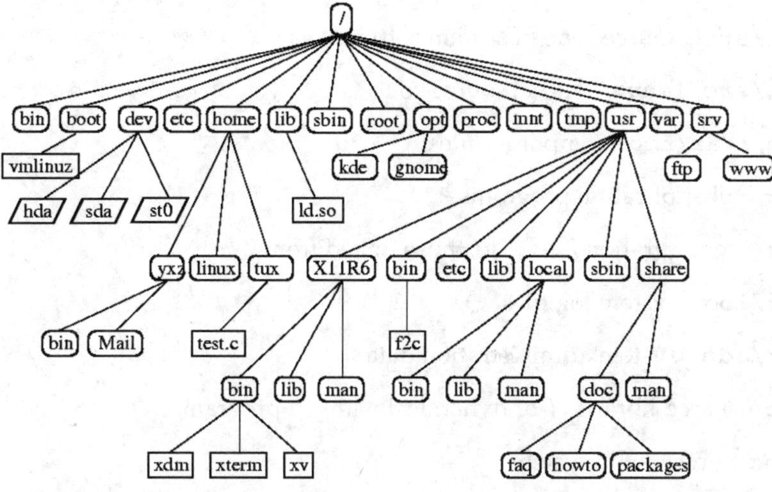

Figure 25.1: Excerpt from a Standard Directory Tree

/ root directory, starting point of the directory tree

/home (private) directories of users

/dev device files that represent hardware components

/etc important files for system configuration

/etc/init.d boot scripts

/usr/bin generally accessible programs

/bin programs needed early in the boot process

/usr/sbin programs reserved for the system administrator

/sbin programs reserved for the system administrator and needed for booting

/usr/include header files for the C compiler

/usr/include/g++ header files for the C++ compiler

/usr/share/doc various documentation files

/usr/share/man system manual pages (man pages)

/usr/src source code of system software

/usr/src/linux kernel source code

/tmp, **/var/tmp** temporary files

/usr all application programs

/var configuration files (e.g., those linked from `/usr`)

/var/log system log files

/var/adm system administration data

/lib shared libraries (for dynamically linked programs)

/proc process file system

/usr/local local, distribution-independent extensions

/opt optional software, larger add-on program packages (such as KDE, GNOME, Netscape)

25.1.3 Bash Functions

There are two important functions of the shell that can make your work a lot easier:

- The history function — To repeat a command that has been entered before, press ↑ until the previous command appears at the prompt. Move forward through the list of previously entered commands by pressing ↓. To edit the command line, just move the cursor to the desired position using the arrow keys and start typing. Use Ctrl + R to search in the history.
- The expansion function — Expand a file name to its full length after typing its first letters until it can be uniquely identified. To do so, type the first letters then hit Tab. If there are several file names starting with the same letters, obtain a list of them by hitting Tab twice.

First Example: Managing Files

Now that you know what a command looks like, which directories exist in SUSE LINUX, and how to speed up things when using Bash, put this knowledge into practice with a small exercise.

1. Open a console from the KDE desktop by clicking the shell icon.
2. Enter the `ls` command to see the contents of your home directory.
3. Use the command `mkdir` (which stands for make directory) to create a new subdirectory called `test` by entering `mkdir test`.
4. Now launch the KEdit editor by pressing Alt + F2 and entering kedit in the input field. Type a few letters in the editor then save the file as `Testfile` in your home directory. Linux distinguishes between uppercase and lowercase. For this example, use an uppercase T.
5. View the contents of your home directory again. Instead of typing `ls` again, just press ↑ twice and the `ls` command should reappear at the prompt. To execute the command, hit Enter. The newly created directory `test` should appear in blue letters and `Testfile` in black. This is how directories and files can be distinguished in a console.
6. Move `Testfile` into the subdirectory `test` with the command `mv`. To speed this up, use the expansion function: just enter `mv T` and press Tab. As long as there is no other file beginning with this letter

in the directory, the shell expands the file name and adds the string estfile. Otherwise, add a letter or two yourself and test (Tab) each time to see whether the shell can now expand the name. Finally, type a space then `test` after the expanded file name and press (Enter) to execute the command.

7. At this point, `Testfile` should no longer be in the directory. Check this by entering `ls` again.

8. To see whether the file has been successfully moved, change into the directory `test` with the command `cd test`. Now enter `ls` again. You should see `Testfile` in the listing. Change back to your home directory at any point by entering only `cd`.

9. To make a copy of a file, use `cp`. For instance, enter `cp Testfile Testbackup` to copy `Testfile` to `Testbackup`. Once again, the command `ls` can be used to see whether both files are in the directory.

25.1.4 Specifying Paths

When working with files or directories, it is important specify the correct path. However, you do not need to enter the entire (absolute) path from the root directory to the respective file. Rather, you can start from the current directory. Address your home directory directly with ~. Accordingly, there are two ways to list the file `Testfile` in the directory `test`: by entering the relative path with `ls test/*` or by specifying the absolute path with `ls /test/*`.

To list the contents of home directories of other users, enter `ls username`. In the above-mentioned directory tree, one of the sample users is `tux`. In this case, `ls tux` would list the contents of the home directory of `tux`.

Refer to the current directory with a dot. The next higher level in the tree is represented by two dots. By entering `ls ..`, see the contents of the parent directory of the current directory. The command `ls ../..` shows the contents of the directory two levels higher in the hierarchy.

Second Example: Working with Paths

Here is another example to illustrate how to move around in the directories of your SUSE LINUX system.

- Change into your home directory with the command `cd`. Then create a directory in it with the name `test2` by entering `mkdir test2`.
- Change into the new directory with `cd test2` and create a subdirectory in it with the name `subdirectory`. To change into it, use the expansion function: enter `cd su` then press Tab. The shell will expand the rest of the directory name.
- Now try to move the previously created file `Testbackup` into the current directory (`subdirectory`) without changing the directory again. To achieve this, specify the relative path to that file: `mv ../../test/Testbackup .`. The dot at the end of this command is required to tell the shell that the current directory is the destination to which to move the file. `../../`, in this example, refers to your home directory.

25.1.5 Wild Cards

Another convenience offered by the shell is wild cards. There are four different types of these in Bash:

? Matches exactly one arbitrary character

***** Matches any number of characters

[set] Matches one of the characters from the group specified inside the square brackets, which is represented here by the string set

[!set] Matches one character other than those identified by set

Assuming that your `test` directory contains the files `Testfile`, `Testfile1`, `Testfile2`, and `datafile`, the command `ls Testfile?` lists the files `Testfile1` and `Testfile2`. With `ls Test*`, the list will also include `Testfile`. The command `ls *fil*` shows all the sample files. Finally, you can use the `set` wild card to address all sample files whose last character is a number: `ls Testfile[1-9]`.

Of the four types of wild cards, the most inclusive one is the asterisk. It could be used to copy all files contained in one directory to another one or to delete all files with one command. The command `rm *fil*`, for instance, would delete all files in the current directory whose name includes the string fil.

25.1.6 More or Less

Linux includes two small programs for viewing text files directly in the shell. Rather than starting an editor to read a file like `Readme.txt`, simply enter `less Readme.txt` to display the text in the console window. Use (Space) to scroll down one page. Use (Page Up) and (Page Down) to move forward or backward in the text. To exit less, press (Q).

The program less got its name from the the precept that less is more and can also be used to view the output of commands in a convenient way. To see how this works, read Section 25.1.7.

Instead of less, you can also use the older program more. However, it is less convenient because it does not allow you to scroll backwards.

25.1.7 Pipes

Normally, the standard output in the shell is your screen or the console window and the standard input is the keyboard. To forward the output of a command to an application such as less, use a *pipeline*.

To view the files in the `test` directory, enter the command `ls test | less`. The contents of the `test` directory will be displayed with less. This only makes sense if the normal output with `ls` would be too lengthy. For instance, if you view the contents of the `dev` directory with `ls /dev`, you will only see a small portion in the window. View the entire list with `ls /dev | less`.

It is also possible to save the output of commands to a file. For example, `ls test > Content` generates a new file called `Content` that contains a list of the files and directories in `test`. View the file with `less Content`.

You can also use a file as the input for a command. For example, sort the text lines in `Testfile` with `sort < Testfile`. The output of the command `sort` is sent to the screen. The text is sorted by the first letters of the individual lines.

If you need a new file containing the sorted list, pipe the output of the command `sort` to a file. To test this, create an unsorted name list in an editor and save it under `list` in the `test` directory. Then change into `test` and enter the command `sort < unsortedlist > sortedlist`. Finally, view the sorted list with `less`.

Just like the standard output, the standard error output is sent to the console as well. However, to redirect the standard error output to a file named errors, append 2> errors to the corresponding command. Both standard output and standard error are saved to one file named alloutput if you append >& alloutput. Finally, to append the output of a command to an already existing file, the command must be followed by » instead of a single >.

25.1.8 Archives and Data Compression

Now that you have already created a number of files and directories, consider the subject of archives and data compression. Suppose you want to have the entire test directory packed in one file that you can save on a floppy disk as a backup copy or send by e-mail. To do so, use the command tar (for tape archiver). With tar --help, view all the options for the tar command. The most important of these options are explained here:

-c (for create) Create a new archive.

-t (for table) Display the contents of an archive.

-x (for extract) Unpack the archive.

-v (for verbose) Show all files on screen while creating the archive.

-f (for file) Choose a file name for the archive file. When creating an archive, this option must always be given as the last one.

To pack the test directory with all its files and subdirectories into an archive named testarchive.tar, use the options -c and -f. For the testing purposes of this example, also add -v to follow the progress of the archiving, although this option is not mandatory. After using cd to change to your home directory where the test directory is located, enter tar -cvf testarchive.tar test. After that, view the contents of the archive file with tar -tf testarchive.tar. The test directory with all its files and directories has remained unchanged on your hard disk. To unpack the archive, enter tar -xvf testarchive.tar, but do not try this yet.

For file compression, the obvious choice on Linux is the popular gzip program. Just enter gzip testarchive.tar. With ls, now see that the file testarchive.tar is no longer there and that the file testarchive.tar.gz has been created instead. This file is much smaller and therefore much better suited for transfer via e-mail or storage on a floppy.

Now, unpack this file in the `test2` directory created earlier. To do so, enter `cp testarchive.tar.gz test2` to copy the file to that directory. Change to the directory with `cd test2`. A compressed archive with the `.tar.gz` extension can be unzipped with the `gunzip` command. Enter `gunzip testarchive.tar.gz`, which results in the file `testarchive.tar`, which then needs to be extracted or untarred with `tar -xvf testarchive.tar`. You can also unzip and extract a compressed archive in one step by adding the `-z` option. The complete command would be `tar -xzvf testarchive.tar.gz`. With `ls`, you can see that a new `test` directory has been created with the same contents as your `test` directory in your home directory.

25.1.9 mtools

`mtools` are a set of commands for working with MS-DOS file systems. The commands included in `mtools` allow you to address the first floppy drive as `a:`, just like under MS-DOS, and the commands are like MS-DOS commands except they are prefixed with an `m`:

`mdir a:` displays the contents of the floppy disk in drive `a:`

`mcopy Testfile a:` copies the file `Testfile` to the floppy disk

`mdel a:Testfile` deletes `Testfile` in `a:`

`mformat a:` formats the floppy disk in MS-DOS format (using the `fdformat` command)

`mcd a:` makes `a:` your current directory

`mmd a:test` creates the subdirectory `test` on the floppy disk

`mrd a:test` deletes the subdirectory `test` from the floppy disk

25.1.10 Cleaning Up

After this crash course, you should be familiar with the basics of the Linux shell or command line. You may want to clean up your home directory by deleting the various test files and directories using the `rm` and `rmdir` commands. At the end of this chapter, find a list of the most important commands and a brief description of their functions.

25.2 Users and Access Permissions

Since its inception in the early 1990s, Linux has been developed as a multiuser system. Any number of users can work on it simultaneously. This resulted in some notable distinctions from the Microsoft end-user Windows operating systems.

The most important distinguishing feature is the necessity for users to log in to the system before starting a session at their workstation. Each user has a user name with a corresponding password. This differentiation of users guarantees that unauthorized users cannot see files for which they do not have permission. Larger changes to the system, such as installing new programs, are also usually impossible or restricted for normal users. Only the ☞*root* user, or *super user*, has the unrestricted capacity to make changes to the system and has unlimited access to all files. Those who use this concept wisely, only logging in with full `root` access when necessary, can cut back the risk of unintentional loss of data. Because under normal circumstances only root can delete system files or format hard disks, the threat from the Trojan horse effect or from accidentally entering destructive commands can be significantly reduced.

25.2.1 File System Permissions

Basically, every file in a Linux file system belongs to a user and a group. Both of these proprietary groups and all others can be authorized to write, read, or execute these files.

A group, in this case, can be defined as a set of connected users with certain collective rights. For example, call a group working on a certain project `project3`. Every user in a Linux system is a member of at least one proprietary group, normally `users`. There can be as many groups in a system as needed, but only `root` is able to add groups. Every user can find out, with the command `groups`, of which groups he is a member.

File Access The organization of permissions in the file system differs for files and directories. File permission information can be displayed with the command `ls -l`. The output could appear as in Output 25.1.

Example 25.1: *Sample Output Showing File Permissions*

```
-rw-r----- 1 tux project3 14197 Jun 21  15:03 Roadmap
```

As shown in the third column, this file belongs to user tux. It is assigned to the group project3. To discover the user permissions of the Roadmap file, the first column must be examined more closely.

-	rw-	r--	—
Type	Users Permissions	Group Permissions	Permissions for Other Users

This column is comprised of one leading character followed by nine characters grouped in threes. The first of the ten letters stands for the type of file system component. The dash (–) shows that this is a file. A directory (d), a link (l), a block device (b), or a character device could also be indicated.

The next three blocks follow a standard pattern. The first three characters refer to whether the file is readable (r) or not (–). A w in the middle portion symbolizes that the corresponding object can be edited and a dash (–) means it is not possible to write to the file. An x in the third position denotes that the object can be executed. Because the file in this example is a text file and not one that is executable, executable access for this particular file is not needed.

In this example, tux has, as owner of the file Roadmap, read (r) and write access (w) to it, but cannot execute it (x). The members of the group project3 can read the file, but they cannot modify it or execute it. Other users do not have any access to this file. Other permissions can be assigned by means of ACLs (Access Control Lists). See Section 25.2.6 on page 392 for details and refer to the chapter in the *Administration Guide* for further background information.

Directory Permissions Access permissions for directories have the type d. For directories, the individual permissions have a slightly different meaning.

Example 25.2: *Sample Output Showing Directory Permissions*

```
drwxrwxr-x 1 tux project3 35 Jun 21 15:15
      ProjectData
```

In Output 25.2, the owner (tux) and the owning group (project3) of the directory ProjectData are easy to recognize. In contrast to the file access permissions from Section 25.2.1, the set reading permission (r) means that the contents of the directory can be shown. The write permission (w) means new files can be created. The executable permission (x) means the user can change to this directory. In the above example, this means the user tux as well as the members of the group project3 can change to the ProjectData directory (x), view the contents (r), and add new files to it (w). The rest of the users, on the other hand, are given less access. They may enter the directory (x) and browse through it (r), but not insert any new files (w).

25.2.2 Modifying File Permissions

Changing Access Permissions The access permissions of a file or directory can be changed by the owner and, of course, by root with the command chmod, which must be entered together with the parameters specifying the changes to perform and the names of the respective files.Both parameters are comprised of

1. the categories concerned
   - u (*user*) — owner of the file
   - g (*group*) — group that owns the file
   - o (*others*) — additional users (if no parameter is given, the changes apply to all categories)
2. a character for deletion (–), setting (=), or insertion (+)
3. the abbreviations
   - r — *read*
   - w — *write*
   - x — *execute*
4. file name or names separated by spaces

If, for example, the user tux in Example 25.2 on the facing page also wants to grant other users write (w) access to the directory ProjectData, he can do this using the command chmod o+w ProjectData.If, however, he wants to deny all users other than himself write permissions, he can do this by entering the command chmod go-w ProjectData. To prohibit all users from adding a new file to the folder ProjectData, enter chmod -w ProjectData. Now, not even the owner can write to the file without first reestablishing write permissions.

Changing Ownership Permissions

Other important commands to control the ownership and permissions of the file system components are `chown` (change owner) and `chgrp` (change group). The command `chown` can be used to transfer ownership of a file to another user. However, only `root` is permitted to perform this change.Suppose the file `Roadmap` from Example 25.2 on page 388 should no longer belong to `tux`, but to the user `geeko`. `root` should then enter `chown geeko Roadmap`.`chgrp` changes the group ownership of the file. However, the owner of the file must be a member of the new group. In this way, the user `tux` from Output 25.1 on page 387 can switch the group owning the file `ProjectData` to `project4` with the command `chgrp project4 ProjectData`, as long as he is a member of this new group.

25.2.3 The setuid Bit

In certain situations, the access permissions may be too restrictive. Therefore, Linux has additional settings that enable the temporary change of the current user and group identity for a specific action.

For example, the `cdrecord` program normally requires root permissions to access the writer for burning CDs (or DVDSs). Thus, a normal user would not be able to create CDs, as it would be too dangerous to grant all users direct access to all devices. A possible solution to this problem is the setuid mechanism. setuid (set user ID) is a special file attribute that instructs the system to execute programs marked accordingly under a specific user ID. Consider the `/usr/bin/cdrecord` command:

```
-rwxr-x---   1 root root  281356 2004-03-12 21:30 cdrecord
```

Set the setuid bit with the command `chmod u+s /usr/bin/cdrecord`. Then, assign the `cdrecord` program to the group `users` with the command `chgrp users /usr/bin/cdrecord`. The following access permissions are granted:

```
-rws--x---   1 root users  281356 2004-03-12 21:30 cdrecord
```

By means of the setuid bit, all users belonging to the group `users` can use the program. In effect, this means that the program is executed as `root`.

Caution

Setting the setuid bit for a program makes your computer more vulnerable to attacks. Only do this in exceptional cases when you know the program well and are aware of the potential risks.

Caution

25.2.4 The setgid Bit

The setuid attribute applies to users. However, there is also an equivalent property for groups — the setgid attribute. A program for which this attribute was set runs under the group ID under which it was saved, no matter which user starts it. Therefore, in a directory with the setgid bit, all newly created files and subdirectories are assigned to the group to which the directory belongs. Consider the following example directory:

```
drwxrwxr--   2 root archive   48 Nov 19 17:12 backup
```

Set the setuid bit with the command `chmod g+s /test`. Subsequently, the access permissions appear as follows:

```
drwxrwxr--   2 root archive   48 Nov 19 17:12 backup
```

25.2.5 The Sticky Bit

There is also the *sticky bit*. It makes a difference whether it belongs to an executable program or a directory. If it belongs to a program, a file marked in this way will be loaded to the RAM to avoid needing to get it from the hard disk each time it is used. This attribute is used rarely, as modern hard disks are fast enough. If this attribute is assigned to a directory, it prevents users from deleting each other's files. Typical examples include the `/tmp` and `/var/tmp` directories:

```
drwxrwxrwt   2 root  root   1160 2002-11-19 17:15 /tmp
```

25.2.6 Access Control Lists

The traditional permission concept for Linux file system objects, such as files or directories, can be expanded by means of ACLs (access control lists). They allow the assignment of permissions to individual users or groups other than the original owner or owning group of a file system object.

Files or directories bearing extended access permissions can be detected wit a simple `ls -l` command:

```
-rw-r----- 1 tux project3 14197 Jun 21  15:03 Roadmap
```

The output of `ls` does not reveal much of a change compared to an `ls` on a file without an ACL. `Roadmap` is owned by `tux` who belongs to the group `project3`. `tux` holds both write and read access to this file and his group as well as all other users have read access. The only difference that distinguishes this file from a file without an ACL is the additional + in the first column holding the permission bits.

Get details about the ACL by executing `getfacl Roadmap`:

```
# file: Roadmap
# owner: tux
# group: project3
user::rw-
user:jane:rw-        effective: r--
group::r--
group:djungle:rw-    effective: r--
mask::r--
other::---
```

The first three lines of the output do not hold any information not available with `ls -l`. These lines only state file name, owner, and owning group. Lines 4 to 9 hold the ACL entries. Conventional access permissions represent a subset of those possible when using ACLs. Our example ACL grants read and write access to the owner of the file as well as to a user `jane` (lines 4 and 5). The conventional concept has been expanded allowing access to an extra user. The same applies to the handling of group access. The owning group holds read permissions (line 6) and the group `djungle` holds read and write permissions. The `mask` entry in line 8 reduces the effective permissions for the user `jane` and the group `djungle` to read access. Other users and groups do not get any kind of access to the file (line 9).

Only very basic information has been provided here. Find further background information about ACLs in the *Administration Guide*.

25.3 Important Linux Commands

This section gives insight into the most important commands of your SUSE LINUX system. Along with the individual commands, parameters are listed and, where appropriate, a typical sample application is introduced. To learn more about the various commands, use the ☞*manual pages*, accessed with `man` followed by the name of the command, for example, `man ls`.

In the man pages, move up and down with PgUp and PgDn. Move between the beginning and the end of a document with Home and End. End this viewing mode by pressing Q. Learn more about the `man` command itself with `man man`.

There are many more commands than listed in this chapter. For information about other commands or more detailed information, the O'Reilly publication *Linux in a Nutshell* is recommended. In the following overview, the individual command elements are written in different typefaces.

- The actual command is always printed as `command`. Without this, nothing can function.
- Options without which the respective program cannot function are printed in `italics`.
- Further details, like file names, which must be passed to a command for correct functioning, are written in the *Courier* font.
- Specifications or parameters that are not required are placed in `[square brackets]`.

Adjust the settings to your needs. It makes no sense to write `ls file(s)`, if no file named `file(s)` actually exists. You can usually combine several parameters, for example, by writing `ls -la` instead of `ls -l -a`.

25.3.1 File Commands

File Administration

ls `[option(s)] [file(s)]` If you run `ls` without any additional parameters, the program lists the contents of the current directory in short form.

-l Detailed list

-a Displays hidden files

cp [option(s)] sourcefile targetfile
Copies `sourcefile` to `targetfile`.

-i Waits for confirmation, if necessary, before an existing `targetfile` is overwritten

-r Copies recursively (includes subdirectories)

mv [option(s)] sourcefile targetfile
Copies `sourcefile` to `targetfile` then deletes the original `sourcefile`.

-b Creates a backup copy of the `sourcefile` before moving

-i Waits for confirmation, if necessary, before an existing `targetfile` is overwritten

rm [option(s)] file(s) Removes the specified files from the file system. Directories are not removed by `rm` unless the option `-r` is used.

-r Deletes any existing subdirectories

-i Waits for confirmation before deleting each file.

ln [option(s)] sourcefile targetfile
Creates an internal ☞*link* from the `sourcefile` to the `targetfile`. Normally, such a link points directly to the `sourcefile` on the same file system. However, if `ln` is executed with the `-s` option, it creates a symbolic link that only points to the directory in which the `sourcefile` is located, enabling linking across file systems.

-s Creates a symbolic link

cd [options(s)] **[directory]**
Changes the current directory. `cd` without any parameters changes to the user's home directory.

mkdir [option(s)] directoryname
Creates a new directory.

rmdir [option(s)] directoryname
Deletes the specified directory, if it is already empty.

chown [option(s)] username.group **file(s)**
Transfers ownership of a file to the user with the specified user name.

-R Changes files and directories in all subdirectories.

chgrp `[option(s)] groupname` **`file(s)`**
Transfers the group ownership of a given `file` to the group with the specified group name. The file owner can only change group ownership if a member of both the current and the new group.

chmod `[options] mode file(s)`
Changes the access permissions.The `mode` parameter has three parts: `group`, `access`, and `access type`. `group` accepts the following characters:

u user

g group

o others

For `access`, grant access with + and deny it with –. The `access type` is controlled by the following options:

r read

w write

x eXecute — executing files or changing to the directory.

s Set uid bit — the application or program is started as if it were started by the owner of the file.

As an alternative, a numeric code can be used. The four digits of this code are composed of the sum of the values 4, 2 and 1 — the decimal result of a binary mask. The first digit sets the set user ID (SUID) (4), the set group ID (2), and the sticky (1) flags. The second digit defines the permissions of the owner of the file. The third digit defines the permissions of the group members and the last digit sets the permissions for all other users. The read permission is set with 4, the write permission with 2, and the permission for executing a file is set with 1. The owner of a file would usually receive a 7 — the sum of all permissions.

gzip `[parameters]` **`file(s)`** This program compresses the contents of files using complex mathematical algorithms. Files compressed in this way are given the extension `.gz` and need to be uncompressed before they can be used. To compress several files or even entire directories, use the `tar` command.

-d Decompresses the packed gzip files so they return to their original size and can be processed normally (like the command `gunzip`)

tar `options archive file(s)` `tar` puts one or more files into an archive. Compression is optional. `tar` is a quite complex command with a number of options available. The most frequently used options are:

-f Writes the output to a file and not to the screen as is usually the case

-c Creates a new tar archive

-r Adds files to an existing archive

-t Outputs the contents of an archive

-u Adds files, but only if they are newer than the files already contained in the archive

-x Unpacks files from an archive (*extraction*)

-z Packs the resulting archive with `gzip`

-j Compresses the resulting archive with `bzip2`

-v Lists files processed

The archive files created by `tar` end with `.tar`. If the tar archive was also compressed using `gzip`, the ending is `.tgz` or `.tar.gz`. If it was compressed using `bzip2`, the ending is `.tar.bz2`. Application examples can be found in Section 25.1.8 on page 385.

locate `pattern(s)` The `locate` command can find in which directory a specified file is located. If desired, use ☞*wild cards* to specify file names. The program is very speedy, as it uses a database specifically created for the purpose (rather than searching through the entire file system). This very fact, however, also results in a major drawback: locate is unable to find any files created after the latest update of its database. The database can be generated by `root` with `updatedb`.

updatedb `[options(s)]` This command performs an update of the database used by `locate`. To include files in all existing directories, run the program as `root`. It also makes sense to place it in the background by appending an ampersand (`&`), so you can immediately continue working on the same command line (`updatedb &`).

find `[option(s)]` With `find`, search for a file in a given directory. The first argument specifies the directory in which to start the search. The option `-name` must be followed by a search string, which may also include wild cards. Unlike `locate`, which uses a database, `find` scans the actual directory.

Commands to Access File Contents

cat [option(s)] **file(s)** The cat command displays the contents of a file, printing the entire contents to the screen without interruption.

-n Numbers the output on the left margin

less [option(s)] **file(s)** This command can be used to browse the contents of the specified file. Scroll half a screen page up or down with (PgUp) and (PgDn) or a full screen page down with (Space). Jump to the beginning or end of a file using (Home) and (End). Press (Q) to exit the program.

grep [option(s)] searchstring **filenames**
The grep command finds a specific search string in the specified file(s). If the search string is found, the command displays the line in which the searchstring was found along with the file name.

-i Ignores case

-l Only displays the names of the respective files, but not the text lines

-n Additionally displays the numbers of the lines in which it found a hit

-l Only lists the files in which searchstring does not occur

diff [option(s)] **file1file2**
The diff command compares the contents of any two files. The output produced by the program lists all lines that do not match. This is frequently used by programmers who need only send their program alterations and not the entire source code.

-q Only reports whether the two files differ

File Systems

mount [option(s)] [device] **mountpoint**
This command can be used to mount any data media, such as hard disks, CD-ROM drives, and other drives, to a directory of the Linux file system.

-r mount read-only

-t filesystem Specifies the file system. The most common are ext2 for Linux hard disks, msdos for MS-DOS media, vfat for the Windows file system, and iso9660 for CDs.

For hard disks not defined in the file `/etc/fstab`, the device type must also be specified. In this case, only `root` can mount it. If the file system should also be mounted by other users, enter the option `user` in the appropriate line in the `/etc/fstab` file (separated by commas) and save this change. Further information is available in .

`umount` `[option(s)]` **`mountpoint`**
This command unmounts a mounted drive from the file system. To prevent data loss, run this command before taking a removable data medium from its drive. Normally, only `root` is allowed to run the commands `mount` and `umount`. To enable other users to run these commands, edit the `/etc/fstab` file to specify the option `user` for the respective drive.

25.3.2 System Commands

System Information

`df` `[option(s)]` **`[directory]`** The `df` (disk free) command, when used without any options, displays information about the total disk space, the disk space currently in use, and the free space on all the mounted drives. If a directory is specified, the information is limited to the drive on which that directory is located.

-H Shows the number of occupied blocks in gigabytes, megabytes, or kilobytes — in human-readable format

-t Type of file system (ext2, nfs, etc.)

`du` `[option(s)]` **`[path]`** This command, when executed without any parameters, shows the total disk space occupied by files and subdirectories in the current directory.

-a Displays the size of each individual file

-h Output in human-readable form

-s Displays only the calculated total size

`free` `[option(s)]` The command `free` displays information about RAM and swap space usage, showing the total and the used amount in both categories.

-b Output in bytes

-k Output in kilobytes

-m Output in megabytes

date [option(s)] This simple program displays the current system time. If run as root, it can also be used to change the system time. Details about the program are available in .

Processes

top [options(s)] top provides a quick overview of the currently running ☞*processes*. Press (H) to access a page that briefly explains the main options to customize the program.

ps [option(s)] [process ID]
If run without any options, this command displays a table of all your own programs or processes — those you started. The options for this command are not preceded by hyphen.

aux Displays a detailed list of all processes, independent of the owner

kill [option(s)] process ID
Unfortunately, sometimes a program cannot be terminated in the normal way. In most cases, you should still be able to stop such a runaway program by executing the kill command, specifying the respective process ID (see top and ps). kill sends a TERM signal that instructs the program to shut itself down. If this does not help, the following parameter can be used:

-9 Sends a KILL signal instead of a TERM signal. This brings the specified process to an end in almost all cases.

killall [option(s)] processname
This command is similar to kill, but uses the process name (instead of the process ID) as an argument, killing all processes with that name.

Network

ping [option(s)] host name|IP address
The ping command is the standard tool for testing the basic functionality of TCP/IP networks. It sends a small data packet to the destination host, requesting an immediate reply. If this works, ping displays a message to that effect, which indicates that the network link is basically functioning.

-c `number` Determines the total number of packages to send and ends after they have been dispatched. By default, there is no limitation set.

-f *flood ping*: sends as many data packages as possible. A popular means, reserved for `root`, to test networks.

-i `value` Specifies the interval between two data packages in seconds. Default: one second

`nslookup` The domain name system resolves domain names to IP addresses. With this tool, send queries to information servers (DNS servers).

`telnet` `[option(s)] host name or IP address`
Telnet is actually an Internet protocol that enables you to work on remote hosts across a network. telnet is also the name of a Linux program that uses this protocol to enable operations on remote computers.

Caution

Do not use telnet over a network on which third parties can eavesdrop. Particularly on the Internet, use encrypted transfer methods, such as `ssh`, to avoid the risk of malicious misuse of a password (see the man page for `ssh`).

Caution

Miscellaneous

`passwd` `[option(s)] [username]`
Users may change their own passwords at any time using this command. The administrator `root` can use the command to change the password of any user on the system.

`su` `[option(s)] [username]` The `su` command makes it possible to log in under a different user name from a running session. When using the command without specifying a user name, you will be prompted for the `root` password. Specify a user name and the corresponding password to use the environment of the respective user. The password is not required from `root`, as `root` is authorized to assume the identity of any user.

`halt` `[option(s)]` To avoid loss of data, you should always use this program to shut down your system.

reboot [option(s)] Does the same as halt except the system performs an immediate reboot.

clear This command cleans up the visible area of the console. It has no options.

25.4 The vi Editor

Operating the vi editor takes some practice. For many, it is the preferred editor, partly because it is available on any UNIX-like operating system and is included in default Linux installations. Also, if nothing else works, vi will. The short instructions that follow should enable you to edit various configuration files and other types of files with vi.

vi provides three operating modes. In command mode keys are interpreted as command elements. Insert mode interprets all keys as text entries. Last line mode is used for more complex commands, which are entered in the last line.

The most important commands in command mode are:

Table 25.2: Simple Commands of the vi Editor

ESC	Changes to last line mode.
i	Changes to insert mode (characters appear at the current cursor position).
a	Changes to insert mode (characters appear after the current cursor position).
A	Changes to insert mode (characters are added at the end of the line).
R	Changes to command mode (overwrites the old text).
r	Changes to insert mode and overwrites each character.
s	Changes to insert mode (the character where the cursor is positioned is replaced by the next entry you make).
C	Changes to insert mode (the rest of the line is replaced by the new text).

`o`	Changes to insert mode (a new line is inserted after the current one).
`O`	Changes to insert mode (a new line is inserted before the current one).
`x`	Deletes the current character.
`dd`	Deletes the current line.
`dw`	Deletes up to the end of the current word.
`cw`	Changes to insert mode (the rest of the current word is overwritten by the next entries you make).
`u`	Undoes the last command.
`J`	Joins the following line with the current one.
`.`	Repeats the last command.
`:`	Changes to last line mode.

Each command can be preceded by a number specifying on how many objects the following command should operate. Delete three words at once by entering `3dw`. The command `10x` deletes ten characters after the cursor position and `20dd` deletes twenty lines.

The most important commands in last line mode are:

Table 25.3: *Complex Commands of the vi Editor*

`:q!`	exits vi without saving any changes
`:w filename`	saves as `filename`
`:x`	saves the modified file and exits the editor
`:e filename`	edits (loads) `filename`
`:u`	undoes the last edit command

Ergonomics in the Workplace

This chapter is a short discussion of the ergonomic issues involved in the layout of computer workplaces. This text should not be seen as a substitute for studying the respective standards. No citations from these are included here and footnotes with references to other literature are completely omitted to preserve readability. The items referred to in each section are mostly gathered from German literature and are almost always based on regulations and policies in the Federal Republic of Germany. This information is still useful in designing an ergonomic work area.

26.1 The Working Environment

If ergonomics specialists examined the home workstations of computer users systematically, they would find many problems. Unfortunately, no standard has yet prevented individual users from buying so-called "special computer tables". The low-priced metal-tube frames with "practical rollers" (little stability), "ergonomically retractable keyboard tray" (no wrist pad), "integrated PC case holder and printer stand with paper shelf" (little stacking space and sometimes little legroom), "swiveling mouse pad" (unstable and insufficient working space), and "good view of the screen" (too close, too high) allow you to use a computer for a short time only. They should not be used at professional terminal workstations as they hardly meet any criteria of the corresponding standards. You will not find much of this kind of computer furniture in professional computer equipment catalogs, because manufacturers indirectly keep an eye on the employees' health by observing the minimum standards of computer workstations. Even these minimum standards should be improved.

26.1.1 The Right Desk

A table at the wrong height strains arm and back muscles. The resulting cramped posture especially strains the spine. Too little leg room can force an unnatural body posture and cause disorders to the blood supply.

Choosing the right table is very easy. It should be as wide and deep as possible. An individual adjustment of the table height would be optimal. Working tables at which you can change between sitting and standing by turning the table into a writing stand, often just at the push of a button, are a luxury, but changing between a sitting and standing position brings relief.

- The flexible arrangement of working materials requires a table top of at least 160 x 80 cm.
- Workstations made of several interlinked boards are recommended.
- Tables that cannot be vertically adjusted must be 72 cm high. Tables that are vertically adjustable must be between 68 and 76 cm high.
- Even more width is needed for certain working tasks, such as CAD workstations. When changing between screen work and other kinds of work, at least 200 cm is required.

- There should be at least 60 cm leg room. Previous experience has shown, however, that this leg room is often too little.
- When using large screens, tables should be 100 or even 120 cm deep.
- The table surface should not be in bright colors and should have minimal reflection. A lot of office furniture is available in a subdued grey only.

26.1.2 Sitting Correctly on the Right Working Chair

Sitting in a working chair makes you sit in the same posture for a long time, unlike in an easy chair where you can move around easily. Constant sitting in the wrong position, such as bending forward or twisting to the side, can harm the respiratory and digestive organs. This leads to premature fatigue, circulatory disturbances, and backache resulting from overstraining the spine and the vertebrate disks. In extreme cases, years of sitting in the wrong position can lead to muscular and skeletal illnesses.

Correct sitting means a frequent change of posture. Different parts of the body are then constantly being used. Basically, it is a question of the correct adjustment. The height of your working chair is best when your forearms lying on the table are at right angles to your upper arms. You should be able to place your feet completely on the floor and your thighs and lower legs should also be at right angles. Gymnastic balls and balancing chairs offer an alternative to conventional seating arrangements.

Unfortunately, a good chair, constructed according to ergonomic criteria, is relatively expensive, but the investment in your health is worth it. Important features of a good chair include:

- a backrest reaching to the shoulder blades and with an adjustable kinetic resistance
- support for the lumbar spinal column
- a seat that is also adjustable and can be tilted forwards or backwards
- automatic regulation of backrest and seat to retain an ideal angle
- springs that softly cushion the weight when sitting down
- stability and rollers that are restrained when you stand
- adjustable height of the seat (according to standards, 42 to 53 cm) and backrest

- individual adjustment of arm rests, if there are any (luxury)
- a footrest if your feet do not reach the floor

26.1.3 Good Lighting for Productive Work

Generally speaking, workplace lighting does not come close to the intensity of light outdoors. This difference is unnoticed because the human faculty of perception is very flexible. The influence of lighting conditions on our own efficiency is often underestimated. If the light is too bright, you cannot see what is on the screen. If it is too dark, sharpness of vision decreases. The wrong lighting overstrains the visual system and, eventually, causes symptoms of fatigue and stress.

It is assumed that a combination of general lighting and individual workstation lighting is best. For the workstation at home, the combination of a high-powered ceiling lamp (500 watts, preferably with a dimmer) and one or two workplace lamps is recommended. The fluorescent lamps usually found in offices for general lighting should be supplemented by individual workstation lamps. The lighting should, however, not be too intense and be individually adjustable. Stark contrasts should be avoided. Be careful with strong desk lamps. Good illumination is, unfortunately, very expensive and the minimum requirements of lighting can also be fulfilled with cheaper illumination layouts.

- It is important that you are exposed to daylight. A view outside is preferable.
- General lighting is considered pleasant if it is not below 250 lx (usually 500 lx is required, 1000 lx for an open plan office).
- 500–750 lx should be emitted by the individual workstation lighting. However, individual lamps are often problematic. If they are too strong, the contrast to the general lighting is too great. Harmonic, soft transitions are considered more pleasant.
- The lighting should not flicker. In the case of worn-out fluorescent lamps, a flickering can sometimes be noticed from the corner of the eye.
- Avoid dark shadows.
- Ceiling lights should emit light diagonally from above. Lighting strips should be set perpendicular to the screen table. The line of sight at the screen table should run parallel to the lighting strips.

- Whether the lighting is considered to be pleasant depends on the color temperature and light color of the lamp type. Warm white or neutral white is recommended.
- The light requirement depends not only on the working task, but also on age: older people need more light. The fact that older people often have only a small lamp in their homes has nothing to do with their light requirement, but rather with the fact that they want to save electricity.
- A screen workstation near daylight requires optimum shielding against direct and reflex glare, especially when the line of sight is directly out the window or at a 45 degree angle to it. The built-in antiglare facilities should be variable. Under no circumstances should artificial illumination cause reflex glare on the screen.

26.1.4 Optimum Climate

The room climate determines our well-being to a great extent. Problems arise more often if it is too cold, too warm, too drafty, or too dry. Low relative humidity can lead to burning eyes, dry mucous membranes, skin irritations, and increased susceptibility to colds. Things get complicated when people who work in the same room are accustomed to different base temperatures. For your well-being, it is important to observe the recommended basic values for temperature and humidity and to avoid strong air movement. The working material itself should not contribute to the increase of temperature.

- For activities in a sitting position or simple work, a room temperature of 20 to 22 °C is recommended. In summer, the temperature should be 26 °C at the most. This value should only be exceeded for a short time when the outdoor temperature is higher.
- A lot of equipment, as well as people, emit heat and influence room air conditions. This should be reduced as much as possible.
- The air humidity should be between 40 (sometimes 50) and 65 percent and should be checked. This value is especially affected by heating systems.
- Draft (possibly from open windows and doors or air conditioning) should not exceed 0.1 to 0.15 m/s. Draft on individual parts of the body should be avoided.

- An air conditioner should be individually adjustable. It should be serviced regularly.
- The windows should be able to be opened and have sunshades to avoid glare effects. Sunlight can increase the room temperature considerably. Sunshades attached to the outside of the building provide the best protection.
- Plants can improve room conditions and are therefore recommended in all cases. They increase the relative humidity and filter pollutants from the air.

26.1.5 Noise Levels

Noise is a physically powerful stress factor. Although it is often played down, too much noise makes you ill. Apart from health impairments, such as defective hearing, vegetative disorders, and psychic changes, noise affects our efficiency by impairing our ability to concentrate. Furthermore, discontent can reduce working motivation. The fact that proper noise abatement can possibly cost a lot of money is also problematic.

A calm working environment improves efficiency. Work at terminal workstations is often characterized as "mental activity". Therefore the maximum load value for scientific work or programming is 55 dB (A). The dB (A) represent a weighted evaluation of the acoustic pressure. The A-filter curve most resembles human perception. An increase of the sound level by 10 dB (A) is normally perceived as a duplication of volume.

- Because mainly mental work is done at terminal workstations, quiet working materials should be used from the start.
- The maximum limiting value for office work is 55 dB (A). With especially high mental demands or necessary communication of language, as low as 35–45 dB (A) is required. This is the case, for instance, for specialized work, scientific work, or programming.
- Furthermore, the evaluation level of a maximum of 55 dB (A) is important. If 70 dB (A) is measured for a quarter of an hour, the noise in the remaining time should be less than or equal to 55 dB (A).
- Workstations can be equipped with partitions, sound-absorbing floors, appropriately wallpapered walls, curtains, and other sound-reducing features.

- Loud working equipment, such as matrix printers, should be installed in sound-absorbing cases. The permissible noise levels for office equipment are determined in the DIN standards.
- An air conditioner should not increase the normal noise level.
- Strain caused by excessive noise can also be reduced by an organizational restructuring of work.

26.2 Office Equipment

26.2.1 Buying a Screen

If you already have poor sharpness of vision, low-quality screens can make things even worse. Apart from eye problems, tenseness, fatigue, and many other disorders can be caused.

The latest technological developments are triniton, or black-matrix, screens and TFT flat screens. Unfortunately, flat screens are still relatively expensive. There are extensive standards that regulate the readability of the depicted information. When buying a screen, it is recommended to study the extensive standards to avoid a wrong purchase. One thing is certain: a good screen is usually expensive. The normal tube screens do not last forever. They only retain their focus and contrast for a few years.

- All depicted characters should be sharply defined and clearly legible up to the edges of the screen. A positive representation (dark characters on a light background, as in a book) is recommended.
- As the depicted characters must be large enough, a 17-inch monitor is recommended, at least for graphical user interfaces (like KDE). For the processing of CAD, layout, and graphics, it should be 21 inches.
- It is especially important that the screen does not flicker. In concrete terms, the minimum sync frequency with 15-inch monitors should be at least 73 Hz. However, 85 Hz is recommended. For larger screens, such as 21-inch, 100 Hz is a good value.
- Luminosity and contrast should be variable. The focus of the characters should not differ with adjustments of brightness or contrast.
- The image should be free from distortion and show no color errors.

- To avoid reflex glare, a good antireflective coating of the screen surface is recommended.
- The screen should be rotatable and inclinable. A vertical adjustment is recommended.
- Colors make the displayed information easier to comprehend. However, the display of colors can also be straining for the eyes because different colors are refracted differently by the lenses. For red colors, people are farsighted, but for blue colors people are nearsighted. Older screens often have convergence errors — the three beams of the screen tube are no longer aligned precisely, so colored borders appear around letters, for example.
- Electromagnetic radiation emitting from the screen should be kept to a minimum.

26.2.2 Screen Location

A screen put in the wrong place leads to a cramped posture at work, which can cause illnesses. A work table that has insufficient depth often prevents the screen from being placed reasonably. The natural position of the head and arms is designed for work that lies in front of the body.

Ergonomics specialists have developed their own guidelines for the "vision and gripping area." These reject placing the screen to the side. An exception is only when the screen is rarely used. A reason for this placement is the fact that even the required minimum 80 cm worktable depth is insufficient with a large screen and the use of working documents. Often the screen is placed — as shown in many PC manual pictures — on top of the computer case. This also leads to an unnatural posture. Observe yourself while you are reading. Are you looking straight ahead or slightly down?

- Shoulder, keyboard, and screen should be in one line so you always look directly at the screen. This rule does not necessarily need to be observed all the time.
- Ultimately, the workstation should be individually adapted to the person and the working task. Flexibility is the key. Easily movable, rotatable, and, ideally, screens that retract into the table are encouraged.
- A comfortable visual distance varies individually. At least 50 cm is required. Some people need considerably more.

- It is a good idea for users to look away from the screen from time to time. In this way, their eyes can adapt to a different distance.
- If a document is being copied, it should be at the same distance as the screen to avoid frequent changes of focus.
- The difference in luminance between the direct working area, the screen, and the immediately surrounding areas, such as the screen case, should not be more than three to one. For this reason, computer cases in offices are not black. The difference between the working area and the surroundings should not be more than ten to one.
- Shiny areas create large differences of luminance. This is why office furniture is not available in bright colors and has a matt surface.
- To minimize the reflex glare on the screen, the screen and the keyboard should be arranged so the line of vision is parallel to window panes. The further the screen is away from the window, the better.
- The screen should not be directly under a lighting strip, but to the side of it. The line of vision should be parallel to the lighting strip.

26.2.3 The Keyboard and the Wrists

It is well-known that the keyboard arrangement derived from the typewriter is not necessarily ergonomic. During typing, the fingers, hands, arms, and shoulders are strained. This leads to tense muscles. The strain caused by a keyboard of inferior quality adds up over time. Unfortunately, the tiny movements produced while typing are very difficult to measure. Risk factors include the RSI syndrome.

The keyboard is, without doubt, the most frequently-used computer input device. Therefore, it must be especially well-designed. Ergonomic specialists often criticize the fact that the Shift and Enter keys are too small. Another basic problem is the cable, which is often too short, preventing a comfortable individual placement. Consider buying a wireless keyboard or an extension for the cable.

- The keyboard should be separate from the screen. It should also be inclinable, but set in a stable position (sufficiently large, rubber-coated feet).
- The middle key row should not be more than 30 mm above the surface of the table.

- There should be room to rest your hands in front of the keyboard. If there is no built-in wrist pad, get one.
- The marking must contrast with the color of the plastic and be easy to read. The keyboard should have no intense color and a satin-matt finish.
- For the keyboard legend, a dark script on a light background is recommended. Black keys are not ergonomic.
- The form of the keys should enable light and accurate typing. The lift of key should be 2–4 mm and the working point should be distinctly felt. Here 50–80 g is recommended as the force of the key depression stroke.
- Those who type a lot should take regular breaks.
- Learning the touch system helps because the workload is distributed across all fingers.
- Split or individually separable keyboards are something to which you have to get accustomed, but nevertheless are an alternative worth considering. They have been constructed according to the latest ergonomic findings and are already recommended in some standards. They prevent wrist strain to the side.
- The keyboard of a notebook or laptop cannot correspond to the standards because of the crowded keys. A notebook should therefore not be used as workstation equipment unless it is linked to an external keyboard and mouse.

26.2.4 The Mouse

Due to the advance of graphical user interfaces, users are practically forced to use a mouse. The intensive use of the mouse can cause not only fatigue, but also disorders in the hands, arms, and shoulders. An example of this is RSI. The danger increases when a "bad" mouse is used. So far, there are no commonly accepted standards for an ergonomic mouse. Often a PC is sold with the standard mouse. This mouse should certainly be examined closely. Is the mouse really suitable or should it be replaced by a better one? Have the dealer unpack several mice for you to try. The cable is probably too short. Ask the dealer to give you an extension. Evaluate your own mouse use. Can you reduce the use of the mouse? Many professional programs with a lot of interaction do without any mouse clicks. Learn how to use shortcuts to operate programs. It takes time to learn, but you can work up to four times as fast. Often a combination of mouse and keyboard operation is recommended.

- The ergonomic mouse feels good in your hand. The keys should not be too close or too small. There are even mice for children's hands.
- Your fingers should be able to rest on the keys in a relaxed position.
- The mouse should be next to the keyboard. Left-handed users have an advantage because the keyboard has several function keys and the numerical key block between letter keys and a mouse on the right side. These extend the gripping distance. If you are left-handed, get a mouse for left-handers.
- The cable should be long enough. If necessary, purchase an extension. A wireless mouse is a luxury.
- The mouse needs a proper base to function well. Get a good mouse pad.
- Pay attention to the mouse driver. Good mice have mouse drivers with a multitude of functions. You can, for example, adjust the cursor movement exactly according to your requirements or assign special instructions to the different mouse buttons. The double-click might be placed on the middle button with the mouse driver.
- Make sure you adjust the acceleration and double-click adjustment of the mouse to your own preferences. Some people work with the mouse from the hand joint. Others prefer moving their complete fore-arm.
- An alternative to the mouse is a trackball. Here, you move a ball inside a stationary casing to control the mouse pointer. In contrast to the mouse, the trackball reduces the movements in the hand and arm area.

26.3 Links and Literature

A great manual for staff members and superiors with many checklists and questionnaires that also take the mental strain into account: Burmester, M., Görner, C., Hacker, W., Kärcher, M. and others (1997). The SANUS Manual.

EU-compliant Screen Work (- research - FB 760). Berlin: Series of the Federal Office for Work Protection and Work Medicine. [SANUS: Safety and health protection for terminal work on the basis of international standards]

A clear and well-structured guide for analysis and work protection tasks around the terminal workstation:

Richenhagen, G., Prümper, J. & Wagner, J. (1998, 2nd edition). Handbuch der Bildschirmarbeit (trans: Manual of terminal work). Neuwied: Luchterhand.

Information Network of the European Agency for Safety and Health at Work. Available in many languages, comprehensive information: `http://europe.osha.eu.int/`

Help and Documentation

The SUSE Help Center provides central access to the most important documentation resources on your system in searchable form. These resources include all manuals enclosed with your product, online help for the installed applications, and databases on hardware and software issues in connection with SUSE LINUX.

Using the SUSE Help Center

When you start the SUSE Help Center for the first time from the main menu ('SuSE Help'), the view as shown in Figure A.1 on the following page is displayed. The dialog window consists of three main areas:

Menu Bar and Toolbar The menu bar provides the main editing, navigation, and configuration options. 'File' contains the option for printing the currently displayed content. Under 'Edit', access the search function. 'Go' contains all navigation possibilities: 'Home' (home page of the Help Center), 'Back', 'Forward', and 'Last Search Result'. With 'Settings' -> 'Configure KDE Help Center' -> 'Create Search Index', generate a search index for all selected information sources. The toolbar contains three navigation icons (forward, back, home) and a printer icon for printing the current contents.

Navigation Area with Tabs The navigation area in the left part of the window provides an input field for a quick search in selected information sources. Details regarding the search and the configuration of the search function in the 'Search' tab are presented in Section A on page 417. The 'Contents' tab presents a tree view of all available and currently installed information sources. Click the book icons to open and browse the individual categories.

View Window The view window always displays the currently selected contents, such as online manuals, search results, or web pages.

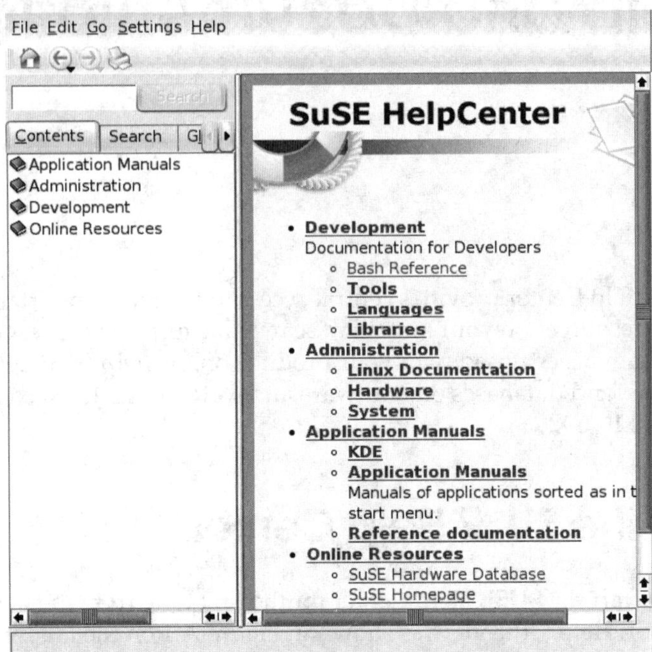

Figure A.1: The Main Window of the SUSE Help Center

Contents of the SUSE Help Center

The SUSE Help Center bundles useful information from various sources. It contains special documentation for SUSE LINUX (User Guide and Administration Guide), all available information sources for your workstation environment, online help for the installed programs, and help texts for other applications. Furthermore, the SUSE Help Center provides access to SUSE's online databases that cover special hardware and software issues in connection with SUSE LINUX. All these sources can be searched comfortably once a search index has been generated.

The Search Function of the SUSE Help Center

To search all installed information sources of SUSE LINUX, generate a search index and set a number of search parameters. To do this, open the 'Search' tab. See Figure A.2.

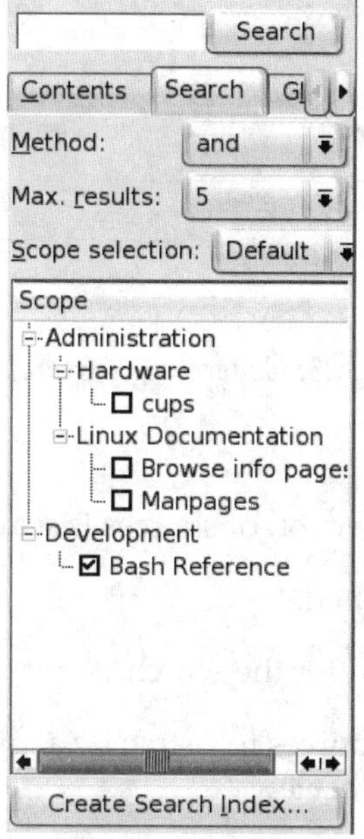

Figure A.2: Configuring the Search Function

If no search index was generated previously, the system automatically prompts you to do so when you click the 'Search' tab or enter a search string and click 'Search'. In the dialog window for generating the search index (Figure A.3 on the next page), use the check boxes to determine the information sources to index. The index is generated when you exit the dialog with 'OK'.

To limit the search base and the hit list as precisely as possible, use the three drop-down menus to determine the number of displayed hits and the selection area of sources to search. The following options are available for determining the selection area:

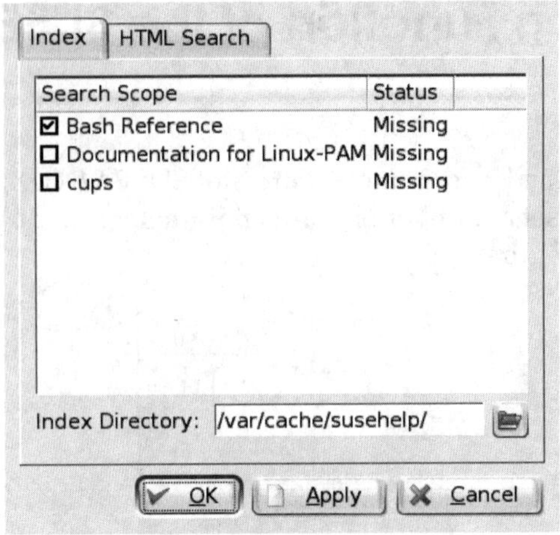

Figure A.3: Generating a Search Index

Default A predefined selection of sources is searched.

All All sources are searched.

None No sources selected for the search.

Custom Determine the sources to search by activating the respective check boxes in the overview.

Upon completion of the search configuration, click 'Search'. The relevant items are then displayed in the view window and can easily be navigated with mouse clicks.

SUSE LINUX FAQ

This section provides answers to frequently asked questions.

1. **I am the only person using my computer. Why do I always need to log in?**

   Linux is a multiuser system. A user name and a password are necessary so Linux knows who is working with it. Only log in as `root` to make changes to your system (installing software or changing configuration). For everyday use, create a regular user. This prevents accidental damage to the installation.

2. **Where can I find the SUSE manuals in PDF or HTML format?**

   Our manuals are also available on our CDs. The PDF files or HTML versions are available in the packages `suselinux-adminguide_en` and `suselinux-userguide_en`. In the installed system, go to the directory `/usr/share/doc/packages/suselinux-adminguide_en/` or `/usr/share/doc/packages/suselinux-userguide_en/`.

3. **Where can I get more information about SUSE LINUX?**

   Most of the information about the installation and features of SUSE LINUX is provided in the manuals. Documentation for applications is available in `/usr/share/doc/packages/` and the HowTos are located in `/usr/share/doc/howto/en/`. Read these files with a command like:

   ```
   less /usr/share/doc/howto/en/DOS-to-Linux-HOWTO.txt.gz
   ```

   Terminate the command by pressing Q.

4. **Where can I get special tips or help?**

   In Konqueror, enter the path `/usr/share/doc/sdb/en/html/index.html` to view our Support Database, which contains useful information. If this path does not exist, install the packages `sdb` and `sdb_en`. On the Internet, find the most recent version at `http://sdb.suse.de/en/sdb/html/`.

5. **How can I enter commands in KDE?**

   Click the screen with shell icon in the panel to start the Bash shell. Select alternative terminals from the main menu. To run a single command, press Alt + F2 then enter the command.

6. **I cannot find many programs in KDE.**

   You can start all programs from a terminal window by entering the program name and pressing Enter.

7. **What is a mirror? Why should I not get these things from `ftp.suse.com`?**

   As there are many users who need to retrieve things from the server at the same time, its capacity limit would be reached very quickly. For this reason, there are a number of other FTP servers that contain a duplicate of the SUSE server. These servers are referred to as mirrors. Select a mirror in your vicinity (same country) to speed up the download. A list of mirror is available at `http://www.suse.de/en/support/download/ftp/`.

8. **I cannot find any `.exe` files. Where are all the applications?**

   In Linux, executable files normally do not have file extensions. Most programs are located in `/usr/bin` and `/usr/X11R6/bin`.

9. **How can I recognize executable files?**

   The command `ls -l` returns all executable files in the directory `/usr/bin/` in green. Also recognize them by the `x` in the first column.

   ```
   -rwxr-xr-x  1 root root  64412  Jul 23 15:23 /usr/bin/ftp
   ```

10. **I want to remove Linux. How does this work?**

    With `fdisk`, delete the Linux partitions. You might need to run `fdisk` in Linux. Afterwards, boot from the MS-DOS disk and run `fdisk /MBR` in DOS or Windows.

11. **How can I access my CD?**

    First mount the CD with the `mount` command. Information about this command can be found in Section 25.3.1 on page 397.

12. **I cannot get my CD out of the drive. What should I do now?**

    First, unmount the CD with the `umount` command. More information about this can be found in Section 25.3.1 on page 398. In KDE, just right-click the CD-ROM icon and select 'Unmount Drive'. If YaST is running on your computer, exit it.

13. **How can I find out how much space is available in Linux?**

    With the `df -hT` command. See Section 25.3.2 on page 398.

14. **Can I copy and paste in Linux?**

    Yes, this is possible. To copy and paste in the text mode, you must have gpm running. In the X Window System and in the text mode, highlight the text block by clicking and dragging with the left mouse button then insert by clicking with the middle mouse button. The right mouse button has a special function in most programs and applications.

15. **Do I need to be afraid of a virus in Linux?**

    In Linux, there have been no serious viruses found. Also, viruses cannot cause any serious damage if they are not activated by root. The only virus scanners available in Linux search e-mails for Windows viruses (if Linux is used as a router or server). Nevertheless, you should back up important data and configurations.

16. **Do I need to compile a kernel myself?**

    No, this is usually unnecessary. The kernel has become so large that there are about eight hundred options to consider during the configuration. Because it is almost impossible to master all possible configurations and their effects, it is strongly discouraged for inexperienced users to recompile the kernel. Do so only at your own risk. In cases of custom compiled kernels, SUSE cannot provide any installation support.

17. **Where can I see the system messages?**

    In a terminal window, enter `tail -f /var/log/messages` as `root`. Additional interesting programs relating to this one are `top`, `procinfo`, and `xosview`. Use the command `less /var/log/boot.msg` to view the boot messages.

18. **I cannot log in to my computer with `telnet`. I always get the answer Login incorrect.**

    You are probably trying to log in as `root`. For security reasons, this is not possible via telnet by default. With YaST, set up a normal user account. Log in with this user name. Then change to the user `root` with `su`. It is much better and safer, however, to use the program `ssh` instead of `telnet`. The `ssh` program uses encrypted, secure connections.

19. **How do I connect to the Internet in Linux?**

    Section 5.4.1 on page 154 provides information about this.

20. **I found a bug in SUSE LINUX. Where should I report it?**

    First, ascertain whether it is actually a bug in the program or just an error in operation or faulty configuration settings. Also read the documentation in `/usr/share/doc/packages` and `/usr/share/doc/howto`. The bug may have already been discovered. Check in the support database at `http://sdb.suse.de/sdb/en/html/`. Enter a keyword or work your way forward or backward via the History link. If it really is a bug, send a description of it by e-mail to `feedback@suse.de`.

21. **How can I install applications?**

    Applications included in the SUSE LINUX CDs are best installed with YaST.

    Another possibility is to start YaST from the command line with `yast -i package`. Replace the placeholder ⟨*package*⟩ with the file name of the RPM package (including the path). You can also specify multiple packages.

22. **I only have an application in source code. How can I install it?**

    Some know-how is required with some applications. Find more information in a good Linux book.

    Here a brief description: Decompress the archive with `tar xvzf name.tar.gz`, read the `INSTALL` or `README` files, and follow the instructions. Usually, the following command sequence needs to be executed: `./configure;make;make install`. No installation support is available for the compilation or self-compiled programs.

23. **Is my hardware supported?**

    It is best to refer to the component database at `http://hardwaredb.suse.de` or `http://cdb.suse.de`. `less /usr/share/doc/howto/en/Hardware-HOWTO.gz` can also provide some information.

24. **How can I defragment my hard disk?**

    Linux has an intelligent file system. This file system makes defragmentation superfluous, because it prevents fragments from occurring. Your partitions should not be more than ninety percent used. Use `df -h` to view information about used and available hard disk space.

25. **What is meant by partitioning?**

    Partitioning is dividing the hard disk into smaller sections. For the default configuration, SUSE LINUX requires at least two partitions (one for Linux itself and one swap partition for the virtual main memory).

26. **How much space do I need for Linux?**

    This depends on how many and which packages you want to install. A standard installation with office applications requires about 1 GB. 2 GB is recommended if you want space for your own data as well. To install just about everything, you need 3–6 GB, depending on the version.

27. **I need more space for Linux. How can I add another hard disk?**

    To make more space available, integrate a new hard disk or parts of it (partitions) into your Linux system at any time. For example, if it turns out that you need more space in `/opt`, mount an additional hard disk partition to this directory. To do so, follow this procedure:

    (a) Install your hard disk following the instructions of the manufacturer then start Linux.

    (b) Log in as the `root` user.

    (c) Partition the new hard disk with `fdisk`. For further information, refer to the manual page of fdisk with `man fdisk`.

    (d) Format the partition with `mke2fs /dev/hdb1`.

    (e) Enter the following commands:

    ```
    cd /opt
    mkdir /opt2
    mount /dev/hdb1 /opt2
    cp -axv . /opt2
    ```

Check thoroughly to see whether all the data has been copied. Afterwards, move the old directory and add a new one — an empty mount point:

```
mv /opt /opt.old
mkdir /opt
```

Use an editor to add the new partitions in `/etc/fstab`. This could resemble the line in File B.1.

Example B.1: *Sample Line in /etc/fstab for an Additional Partition*

```
/dev/hdb1        /opt      ext2        defaults   1   2
```

Now, shut down the computer and reboot.

(f) After rebooting, check that `/dev/hdb1` has actually been mounted to `/opt` using the command `mount`. If everything is working as desired, remove the old data from `/opt.old`:

```
cd /
rm -fr opt.old
```

28. **My computer crashed. Can I just press the reset button without risking anything?**

    If your computer no longer reacts to your mouse or keyboard, this does not necessarily mean that your entire system has crashed. Possibly one program is blocking the mouse or the keyboard, but all other programs are still running. If your machine can be accessed remotely (serial terminal, network), log in elsewhere and abort the respective program with `killall` ⟨*program name*⟩. If this does not work, try `killall -9` ⟨*program name*⟩.

    If this is not possible, try switching to another console using Ctrl-Alt-F2 to kill the faulty process from there. If the computer does not respond to any of the keys and network intervention is not possible, wait at least ten seconds before pressing reset to make sure there is no hard disk activity.

29. **How can I switch from a virtual text console to the graphical user interface?**

    By default, there are six virtual text consoles that can be accessed with Ctrl-Alt-F1 to F6. Press Alt-F7 to go to the graphical user interface.

Glossary

access permissions

The account is defined by the user name or login name and the password. The access permissions are generally set by the ☞*system administrator*. The access permissions define to which user group the new user is assigned and the resulting permissions.

account

See ☞*access permissions*.

ACL (Access Control List)

Extension of the conventional permission concept for files and directories.

ADSL (Asymmetric Digital Subscriber Line)

Transmission procedure that transmits data about one hundred times faster than ISDN in the telephone network.

AGP (Accelerated Graphics Port)

A high-speed slot for graphics cards based on PCI, but offering a larger ☞*bandwidth*. Furthermore, AGP graphics cards can revert directly (without routing around the processor) to the ☞*random access memory* and ☞*main memory*, in contrast to PCI models, to swap graphics data there.

ATAPI (Advanced Technology Attachment Packet Interface)

ATAPI is a type of CD-ROM drive that is connected to an (E)IDE controller. Apart from ATAPI drives, there are SCSI CD-ROM drives, handled by a SCSI controller, and proprietary CD-ROM drives that use their own controller or are connected to a sound card.

backup

A backup is a duplicate of data used to restore data that has been damaged or lost. Backups should be done regularly, especially the important files.

bandwidth

Maximum load capacity of a data channel.

BIOS

Small component responsible for the initialization of important hardware processes. This essential procedure is complete when the boot menu appears on the screen.

bookmark

A mostly personal collection of interesting web page or file references directly accessible in the browser.

booting

The sequence of computer operations from power-up until the system is ready for use.

browser

Program that searches and displays contents. Today it is mostly used for programs that graphically display contents of ☞*world wide web* pages.

cache

In relation to the ☞*main memory*, it is rather small, but still a fast memory buffer. For example, open files are saved to the cache to spare the hard disk next time the file is loaded.

client

Workstation in a computer network operated by a ☞*server*.

command line

Text-based mode of operating in which commands are entered at a prompt. A command line can be accessed from within a graphical environment as well as from virtual consoles.

console

Formerly synonymous with ☞*terminal*. In Linux, there are several *virtual consoles* that allos the screen to be used for several independent, parallel work sessions.

CPU (Central Processing Unit)

☞*processor*.

cursor

The cursor is normally a block character that marks the place for input on a computer screen. This term also often refers to the symbol representing the location of the mouse in graphical interfaces.

daemon

A daemon (disk and execution monitor) is a program that monitors in the background and comes into action when required. Daemons answer FTP or HTTP requests, for example, or control activity in the PCMCIA slots.

DDC (Direct Display Channel)

Communication standard between the monitor and the graphics card, which transmits various parameters, such as monitor name or resolution, to the graphics card.

directory

Directories make up the structure of a ☞*file system*. A directory lists file and directory names.

DNS (Domain Name System)

A system that converts name-based addresses to ☞*TCP/IP* addresses and vice versa.

driver

A program between the operating system and the hardware that translates the communication between these two layers.

e-mail (electronic mail)

The means of transporting mail electronically between registered users via a network. As with normal mail (often referred to as snail mail), the address must be entered. In e-mail, it is in the form sender@sender's-domain to recipient@recipient's-domain. E-mail not only lets you send text, but also sound files or pictures. It has many advantages: it is inexpensive and mail usually reaches its destination within minutes.

EIDE (Enhanced Integrated Drive Electronics)

Improved ☞*IDE* standard that allows hard disks with a size over 512 MB.

environment

A ☞*shell* usually provides an environment in which the user can perform temporary settings. These settings include path specifications for programs, the user name, the current path, and the appearance of prompts. The data is saved in an ☞*environment variable*. The assignment of the environment variables is possible, for example, by means of the configuration files of the shell.

environment variable

A position in the ☞*environment* of the ☞*shell*. Every environment variable has a name that is usually capitalized. The variables are assigned values, such as path names.

ethernet

Popular standard for less expansive computer networks.

EXT2 (Second Extended File System)

EXT2 is the default file system used by Linux.

FAQ (Frequently Asked Questions)

Widely-used acronym for documents providing answers to frequently-asked questions.

file system

A file system is a system for structuring files. There are many file systems available, which differ (sometimes quite extremely) in performance and power.

firewall

Protects a local network or host from unauthorized access from the Internet using various security measures.

free software

See ☞*GNU*.

FTP (file transfer protocol)

A ☞*protocol* based on ☞*TCP/IP* for transferring files.

GNOME (GNU Network Object Model Environment)

A user-friendly graphical desktop environment for Linux.

GNU (GNU is Not Unix)

GNU is a project of the Free Software Foundation (FSF)™. Closely linked to the GNU Project is the name of RICHARD STALLMAN (RMS). The aim of the GNU Project is to create a free Unix-compatible operating system free not so much in the sense of *free of cost*, but in the sense of *freedom*: having the right to obtain, modify, and change the software. To guarantee the freedom of the source code (the actual program code), every change of the original code must be free as well, so modifications of or additions to the original software cannot compromise this freedom in any way. The now classic GNU Manifesto (`http://www.gnu.org/gnu/manifesto.html`) explains many aspects of this thinking. In legal terms, GNU software is protected by the GNU General Public License, or GPL (`http://www.gnu.org/copyleft/gpl.html`), and by the GNU Lesser General Public License, or LGPL (`http://www.gnu.org/copyleft/lgpl.html`).In connection with the GNU Project, all Unix tools and utilities are being redeveloped and, in part, provided with more or enhanced functionalities. Even complex software systems, such as Emacs or glibc, are integral components of the project.The ☞*Linux* kernel, subject to the GPL, profits from this project (especially from the tools), but should not be seen as the same thing.

GPL (GNU GENERAL PUBLIC LICENSE)

See ☞*GNU*.

home directory

A private directory in the Linux system that belongs to a specific user (usually in `/home/<username>`). Except the superuser ☞*root*, only the user has full access rights in his home directory.

host name

Name of a machine in Linux, usually the name by which it can be reached on the network.

HTML (Hypertext Markup Language)

The most important language used in the ☞*World Wide Web* for designing the contents. The layout commands made available by HTML define how a document looks and how it is displayed in a ☞*browser*.

HTTP (Hypertext Transfer Protocol)

A protocol used between the ☞*browsers* and Internet servers to transmit ☞*HTML* pages over the ☞*World Wide Web*.

IDE (Integrated Drive Electronics)
A widely-used hard disk standard in low-grade and middle-grade PCs.

Internet
World-wide computer network based on ☞*TCP/IP*, which is used by a very large population.

IP address
A numerical 32-bit Internet address, appearing in four decimal series separated by periods (for example, 192.168.10.1), which is uniquely assigned to a machine connected to ☞*TCP/IP* networks.

IRQ (Interrupt Request)
A request to the ☞*operating system* carried out by a hardware component or a program to assign it processor capacity.

ISDN (Integrated Services Digital Network)
A popular digital standard for high-speed data transferral over the telephone network.

KDE (K Desktop Environment)
User-friendly graphical desktop environment for Linux.

kernel
The kernel is the central core of the Linux operating system. It manages memory, contains the drivers that enable communication with the hardware, and handles processes and tasks. Applications run on top of the kernel.

LAN (local area network)
A LAN is a local ☞*network* and is usually rather small.

LILO (Linux Loader)
Small program installed in the boot sector of the hard disk that not only can start Linux, but other operating systems as well.

link
A link is a pointer to a file, just as widely used in the Internet as in the Linux file system. In Linux, there is a distinction made between hard and symbolic links. While hard links refer to the exact position in the file system, the symbolic link only points to the respective name.

Linux

High performance UNIX-like operating system core distributed freely under the GPL (☞*GNU*). The name is an acronym (Linus' uniX) and refers to its creator, LINUS TORVALDS. Although the name, in a strict sense, only refers to the kernel itself, the popular understanding of the term Linux usually entails the entire system.

login

Authentication of a user by user name and password to gain access to a computer system or network.

logout

The procedure of closing down an interactive Linux session and getting back to the ☞*login* prompt where you enter your user name and password.

main memory

Physical memory of limited capacity that can be accessed rather quickly. This is often referred to as RAM, random access memory.

man pages

Traditional documentation for Unix systems, which can be read using the command `man`.

MBR (master boot record)

The first physical sector of the hard disk from which the content is loaded to the main memory and executed by the ☞*BIOS*. This code then loads either the operating system from a hard disk partition or a more sophisticated boot loader, such as ☞*LILO*.

MD5

Algorithm for generating check sums.

mounting

This describes the insertion of file systems into the directory tree of the system.

MP3

Very efficient compression procedure for audio files that reduces the size by a factor of ten in contrast to an uncompressed audio file.

multitasking

Operating systems that can invoke more than one program simultaneously are called multitasking systems.

multiuser

Enables more than one user to work simultaneously on the same system.

network

The interconnection of several computers, accomplished normally using ☞*servers* and ☞*clients*.

NFS (Network File System)

A ☞*protocol* for accessing a ☞*file system* shared over a network.

NIS (Network Information Service)

A centralized data administration system in networks. User names and passwords can be simultaneously managed network-wide by NIS.

operating system

Program that permanently runs in the background on a computer and enables basic system operations.

partition

Logically-independent section of a hard disk, each possibly containing different file systems. In Windows, also known as drives.

path

Unique description of a file's position in a file system.

plug and play

Automatic hardware component configuration technology. Resources, such as IRQ and DMA, are configured and managed separately from the system.

process

In Linux, started programs or executable files run as processes, often referred to as tasks. Processes can be controlled by commands like `top` entered in the ☞*shell*.

processor

The processor is the brain of every computer, working through and performing commands given by a user or a program in machine language. The processor has control over the entire system and is responsible for the actual performance of the computer.

prompt

See ☞*command line*.

protocol

Standard specifically defined for regulating communication for hardware, software, or networks. There is a multitude of these standards. The most common examples are ☞*HTTP* and ☞*FTP*.

proxy

Most commonly used cache implemented by Internet providers that stores frequently requested contents in a database to allow other machines requesting those pages to load them directly from it. This process not only reduces the time it takes to download this information, but also conserves the available bandwidth.

RAM (Random Access Memory)

See ☞*main memory*.

ReiserFS

A file system that logs its changes to a journal. Compared to Ext2, this features allows a file system to be restored very speedily. ReiserFS is optimized for small files.

root

The user undertaking the configuration and maintenance of a complex computer system, such as a network. This system administrator is usually the only person who has access to all parts of the system (root permissions).

root directory

The base directory of the ☞*file system* that does not have any parent directory (all other directories have a parent directory). In UNIX, the root directory is represented as a /.

SCSI (Small Computer Systems Interface)

Hard disk standard implemented in servers and other high-level machines because of its high-speed performance. See ☞*server*.

server

A server is usually a rather powerful computer that offers services, such as HTTP, DNS, and FTP, or data to other machines connected via a network. There are also programs called servers, like the ☞*X server*.

shell

An especially flexible command line often equipped with its own specific programming language. Examples of shells are Bash, sh, and tcsh.

SMTP (Simple Mail Transfer Protocol)

☞*Protocol* for transferring ☞*e-mails*.

SSL (Secure Socket Layer)

Encryption procedure for transferring ☞*HTTP* data.

superuser

See ☞*root*.

system administrator

See ☞*root*

task

See ☞*process*.

TCP/IP

Internet communication protocol finding increased use in local networks, known as intranets.

telnet

Telnet is the ☞*protocol* and command for communicating with other hosts. Normally, the user only sees telnet as a means for logging into a remote system.

terminal

Formerly, the designation of a keyboard and monitor combination connected to a central computer. On workstations, this term is also used for programs that emulate a real terminal.

Tux

Name of the Linux penguin (see `http://www.sjbaker.org/tux/`).

UNIX

UNIX is an operating system that is widely distributed, above all on workstations in networks. Since the beginning of the 1990s, there has been a freely available version for PCs: Linux.

URL (Uniform Resource Locator)

Unique Internet address that contains the type (e.g., `http://`) and the name of the host (e.g., `www.suse.de`).

user account

See ☞*access permissions*.

user directory

See ☞*home directory*.

VESA (Video Electronics Standard Association)

Industrial consortium that defines, among other things, important video standards.

wild card

A wild card stands for one (symbol: `?`) or more arbitrary characters (symbol: `*`).

wild cards

Placeholder for one (symbol: `?`) or more (symbol: `*`) unknown characters, most often used in commands (especially search commands).

window manager

A window manager is the layer that interacts between the ☞*X Window System* and the user. It is responsible, among other things, for your desktop display. There is a wide variety of window managers available, one of the more popular ones being kwm for ☞*KDE*.

WWW (World Wide Web)

Based on the ☞*HTTP* protocol, this is a hyperlinked collection of documents, files, and images that can be viewed with a web browser.

X Window System

The X Window System is the standard for graphical interfaces in Linux. It is simply the middle layer between the hardware and the ☞*window manager*, such as KDE or GNOME.

X11

See ☞*X Window System*.

YaST (Yet another Setup Tool)

The SUSE LINUX system assistant.

YP

See ☞*NIS*.

Index

D

L

U

V

W

X

Y